Humanistic Perspectives on Contemporary Counseling Issues

HUMANISTIC PERSPECTIVES ON CONTEMPORARY COUNSELING ISSUES

MARK B. SCHOLL, A. SCOTT MCGOWAN, AND JAMES T. HANSEN

Routledge
Taylor & Francis Group
New York London

Routledge
Taylor & Francis Group
711 Third Avenue
New York, NY 10017

Routledge
Taylor & Francis Group
27 Church Road
Hove, East Sussex BN3 2FA

Printed in the United States of America on acid-free paper
Version Date: 20110726

International Standard Book Number: 978-0-415-88595-9 (Hardback)

Library of Congress Cataloging-in-Publication Data

Scholl, Mark B.
    Humanistic perspectives on contemporary counseling issues / Mark B. Scholl,
Andrew Scott McGowan, and James T. Hansen.
        p. cm.
    Includes bibliographical references and index.
    ISBN 978-0-415-88595-9 (hardcover : alk. paper)
    1. Humanistic counseling. I. McGowan, Andrew Scott. II. Hansen, James T.
III. Title.

BF636.7.H86S36 2011
158'.3--dc22   2011015453

Visit the Taylor & Francis Web site at
http://www.taylorandfrancis.com

and the Routledge Web site at
http://www.routledgementalhealth.com

I want to dedicate this book to Kimberly and Wyatt, my loving wife and son. Throughout the development and completion of this book you have been continual sources of optimism, support, and encouragement. Thank you!

Mark B. Scholl

To my beloved family: my deceased parents, Andrew C. and Teresa McGowan, my beloved wife, Marian, my son, Andrew, his wife, Katie, and my granddaughters, Isabella and Ariela. All have been there for me always.

A. Scott McGowan

To my parents, Bill and Gail, my wonderful wife Mary, and my two extraordinary sons, Hayden and Hunter. Thank you for all of your love and support.

James T. Hansen

Contents

Foreword

Although you cannot tell a book by its cover, you can tell a book by its content. When this second and more important criterion is used, *Humanistic Perspectives on Contemporary Counseling Issues* is quite telling—in a most positive way. The 14 chapters of this text are written in exciting, informative, and interesting ways by professionals engaged in the practice of counseling from a number of humanistic perspectives. Within this volume are chapters on wellness, multiculturalism, creativity, substance abuse, couples work, school violence, at-risk youth, competitiveness, technology, college counseling, and counselor education and supervision. Indeed, almost all important contemporary topics in the counseling profession have been included in this excellently edited book of essays and research. Scholl, McGowan, and Hansen have collected significant writings and have arranged them in a way that is developmentally astute and openly enhancing for all who venture to read.

I applaud the fact that these editors and their authors have stressed the value and uniqueness of persons in this book over the mechanics of simply implementing change and that they have focused on the dignity and holistic nature of human beings. This collected work is about relationships and how they trump techniques. Throughout the chapters there is an emphasis on the subjective nature of experience and the meaning that events have in the lives of persons, especially those who may suffer from misguided direction, oppression, and mental distress.

In a day when there is so much emphasis on facts, it is refreshing to see a book that highlights people as individuals rather than as numbers or statistics. After all, information is limited, constantly changing, and of little value unless intimately linked to those from whom it originates. The constant in life for most people is the how and the now in their lives—how they are living in the now of their present reality. The intangibles in human society center on decisions related to growth, becoming, and finding meaning in the world through intimate encounters with others.

As you undertake reading this book, you will find it refreshing in its focus on wellness, purposefulness, and creativity. These are values that transcend time, place, and personalities. Within this volume are ideals and realities related to the ages, stages, and diversity of human life everywhere. It is through underscoring these principles that existence to its fullest is formed, reformed, and transformed. As contributors to this text point out, the myriad developmental and situational episodes that constitute the life span are a kaleidoscope. The beauty and wonder of the pieces come together harmoniously when seen from the hopeful and hope-filled perspective that lives can be more than they have ever been before individually and collectively.

So, read, reflect, and rejoice in the thoughts before you in these pages. The words will open you up to the humanity that is you and that is found in others too.

Samuel T. Gladding, PhD
Chair and Professor, Department of Counseling
Wake Forest University
Past President of the American Counseling Association

About the Editors

Mark B. Scholl, PhD, LMHC, NCC, is an assistant professor in the Department of Higher, Adult, and Counselor Education at East Carolina University in Greenville, North Carolina. He is an active member in both the American College Counseling Association (ACCA) and the Association for Humanistic Counseling (AHC). Dr. Scholl is a past editor of the *Journal of Humanistic Counseling, Education and Development* and the former chair of the ACA Council of Journal Editors. He has also received the Distinguished Journal Reviewer Award from AHC. Dr. Scholl's research interests include client preferences for counselor role, culturally responsive counseling, and constructivist career counseling.

A. Scott McGowan, PhD, NCC, ACS, an ACA fellow, holds the rank of distinguished university senior professor at Long Island University, C.W. Post. He is a past editor of the *Journal for the Professional Counselor* and the *Journal of Humanistic Counseling and Development* and served two terms as editor of the *Journal of Counseling & Development.* He is a past president of the Counseling Association for Humanistic Education and Development, and has received numerous professional awards, including ACA's Hitchcock Distinguished Professional Service Award. He is a licensed professional mental health counselor and a certified school counselor.

James T. Hansen is a professor at Oakland University in the Department of Counseling. His primary scholarly interests are philosophical and theoretical issues in counseling, critical examination of contemporary mental health culture, and professional identity issues. Dr. Hansen has published over 35 refereed articles in leading counseling journals. He has received honors for his scholarly contributions, including the Association for Humanistic Counseling Distinguished Journal Reviewer Award. Dr. Hansen has over 25 years of experience working in various capacities in the mental health realm. He has an active clinical consultation practice and serves as a clinical supervisor and consultant to various mental health agencies.

About the Contributors

Frank Brady, EdD, is the chair and a professor in the Department of Health, Physical Education, and Movement Science at Long Island University, C.W. Post. Dr. Brady has been actively involved in sports as a player, coach, and sports writer for many years. Dr. Brady's research and writings have focused principally on motor learning, the student-athlete, and issues in youth sports.

Jennifer Brown, MS, EdS, is an attorney and a doctoral student in the Department of Counseling and Educational Development at the University of North Carolina at Greensboro.

Tod Burke, PhD, is a professor of criminal justice and interim associate dean for the College of Humanities and Behavioral Sciences at Radford University in Virginia. Dr. Burke received his doctor of philosophy in criminal justice from the City University of New York (John Jay College of Criminal Justice). He has published over 100 peer-reviewed, professional articles and book chapters on various topics, including issues in policing, criminal investigation, forensic science, and victimology.

Denisha Champion, MS, NCC, is currently a doctoral student at the University of North Carolina at Greensboro completing her dissertation on the beliefs of college students in regard to their alcohol consumption behaviors. She is also a staff counselor at the Wake Forest University Counseling Center in Winston-Salem, North Carolina. Ms. Champion serves as a clinical supervisor for entry-level counseling students, and her professional roles include work in a chemical dependency intensive outpatient program and college counseling centers.

Philip Clarke, MEd, EdS, NCC, LPC (NC), is a nationally certified counselor, licensed professional counselor in North Carolina, and third-year doctoral student in counselor education at the University of North Carolina at Greensboro. Mr. Clarke has several years of experience providing mental health and co-occurring disorders counseling and also has given presentations and conducted research on incorporating wellness and developmental models in substance abuse counseling.

Michael D'Andrea, Ed D W, is the executive director of the National Institute for Multicultural Competence. His scholarly work includes the publication of six books and over 200 book chapters, journal articles, and research publications. While his scholarly contributions and professional awards are well respected, he is equally known for the strong stands he has taken and continues to take on a broad range of multicultural, social justice, and peace issues in the fields of psychology, counseling, and education. In this regard, Dr. D'Andrea's publications, presentations, and professional endeavors frequently focus on the important roles counselors can play in fostering positive transformative changes in our contemporary society.

Judy Daniels, EdD, is a professor at the University of Hawaii, where she has been a counselor educator for over 20 years. Currently she is the president of Counselors for Social Justice (CSJ). Dr. Daniels is a fellow with the American Counseling Association (ACA), received the prestigious ACA Wrenn award, and was honored with CSJ's anti-oppression award. She is a frequent presenter at national conventions, and has over 45 publications in the field of counseling.

Joseph A. Despres, EdD, is an adjunct associate professor in the Department of Counseling and Development at Long Island University, C.W. Post, in Greenvale, New York. He has spent years as a consultant and trainer in schools on career development issues, beginning with school-to-work, then with career academies together with a not-for-profit on Long Island, and most recently with college and career readiness models for high school graduates.

Colette T. Dollarhide, EdD, NCC, ACS, LPC-S (OH), LPC (Sc), is a senior lecturer at The Ohio State University, and has been a counselor and counselor educator for 20 years. For the past 10 years, her main teaching and research focus has been school counseling, leadership, professional identity development, and supervision. She has authored several books, presented at ACA, ACES, and ASCA conferences, and is the editor of the *Journal of Humanistic Counseling*.

Darcy Haag Granello, PhD, LPCC-S, is a professor of counselor education at The Ohio State University. She is the coauthor of three books, has published over 60 articles in peer-reviewed national journals, and has made over 100 national or international presentations. She has received over $1 million in funding for her work. Dr. Granello's research focuses on the cognitive development of counseling students and supervisees as well as suicide prevention, assessment, and intervention.

W. Bryce Hagedorn, PhD, LMHC, NCC, MAC, QCS (FL), holds a doctoral degree in counseling and counselor education; is a licensed mental health counselor, a nationally certified counselor, and a master addiction counselor; and currently works as the program director of counselor education at the University of Central Florida in Orlando. A nationally and internationally recognized speaker and author, Dr. Hagedorn's research has significantly contributed to the development of assessment and treatment strategies for working with addicted clients and their families.

Donna Henderson, NCC, ACS, LPC, is a professor in the Department of Counseling at Wake Forest University. She is a licensed school counselor in North Carolina. She has served in leadership positions in Chi Sigma Iota, Association for Counselor Education and Supervision (ACES), the North Carolina Counseling Association, and Southern Association for Counselor Education and Supervision (SACES). Ms. Henderson has over 20 years of experience as a professional counselor. Books she has coauthored include *Counseling Children* (8th ed.; Brooks/Cole, 2011)), *Developing an Effective and Accountable School Counseling Program* (2nd ed.; Merill, 2007), and *Counselor Preparation* (12th ed.; Taylor & Francis, 2008).

Emma L. Kendrick, MA, is a doctoral student in the counselor education program at the University of Central Florida. She holds a master's degree in mental health counseling and a certificate in career counseling. She is the current clinical supervisor at the University of Central Florida Community Counseling Clinic. Her clinical background includes working with children as a therapist in an inpatient setting and as a mental health specialist for the State of Florida Substance Abuse and Mental Health Program Office.

Linda L. Leech, PhD, is a professor at the University of South Carolina. She has developed a distance education program in rehabilitation counseling and has been teaching at a distance for over 10 years. She is a counselor educator, presenter, and curriculum developer with experience in training agency personnel and developing e-training courses. Dr. Leech is a former president of the Counseling Association of Humanistic Education and Development and a counselor in private practice.

Rolla E. Lewis, EdD, NCC, is an associate professor in educational psychology and school counseling coordinator at California State University–East Bay. His research and scholarly interests include developing an eco-humanistic model to guide school counseling education programs and practices, using structured narratives in counseling and supervision, and creating university–community collaborations that place counselors-in-training in service to high-need youth and families. He is the recipient of the Oregon Counseling Association's Leona Tyler Award for outstanding contributions to professional counseling.

Jane E. Myers, PhD, LPC, NCC, is a professor of counselor education at the University of North Carolina at Greensboro. A fellow of the American Counseling Association and the Chi Sigma Iota Academy of Leaders for Excellence, she is a past president of the American Counseling Association and two of its divisions and Chi Sigma Iota, International. Dr. Myers is a past chair of the Council for Accreditation of Counseling and Related Educational Programs (CACREP). She has written and edited numerous publications and has coauthored two wellness models and assessment instruments associated with those models.

Stephen S. Owen, PhD, is an associate professor of criminal justice at Radford University in Virginia. Dr. Owen's areas of research include interpersonal violence, institutional corrections, and criminal justice education. Dr. Owen regularly teaches courses on corrections, criminal justice policy, and security and crime prevention.

Paul R. Peluso, PhD, LMFT, LMHC, is an associate professor and doctoral program coordinator at Florida Atlantic University. He is the coauthor of several books and articles, most recently of *Principles of Counseling and Psychotherapy: Learning the Essential Domains and Nonlinear Thinking of Master Practitioners* (Routledge, 2009).

Alan M. "Woody" Schwitzer, PhD, is a licensed psychologist and professor of counseling at Old Dominion University. He has over 25 years of experience in college counseling, mental health, and psychological services at Virginia Commonwealth University, The University of Texas at Austin, Tulane University, and James Madison University. He has produced more than 40 publications examining college student counseling, health, and mental health and is a past editor of the *Journal of College Counseling.*

Robert Small, EdD, is the professor emeritus and former dean of the College of Education and Human Development at Radford University. Previously, Dr. Small was professor of education at Virginia Tech. Before completing his doctoral degree at the University of Virginia, he taught English at the middle and high school levels. Dr. Small has served in leadership positions on the National Council of Teachers of English, the Assembly on Literature for Adolescents, and the Virginia Association of Teachers of English.

Paula Helen Stanley, PhD, LPC, was a professor of counselor education and director of the Faculty Development Center at Radford University in Virginia. A licensed marriage and family therapist, she was a member of the Virginia New

River Valley Mental Health Association. Dr. Stanley was a dedicated advocate for invitational education, coauthoring two books on the subject. Dr. Stanley also served as the editor of the *Invitational Education Forum* and as associate editor of *the Journal for Humanistic Counseling, Education, and Development.*

Elizabeth Venart, MEd, NCC, LPC, has 20 years of experience as a counselor, educator, and clinical supervisor. She maintains a private practice and is the founder and director of The Resiliency Center LLC of Ambler, Pennsylvania, an innovative community of diverse health-care professionals collaborating to promote integral health. Ms. Venart provides training programs on trauma, resiliency, counselor wellness, and creating a vibrant clinical practice. Her work integrates humanism with cognitive therapy, mindfulness, eye movement desensitization and reprocessing (EMDR), and experiential modalities.

Steven R. Vensel, LCSW, has more than 25 years of experience working with children, families, and couples as a counselor and clinical supervisor. He is currently completing his doctorate in counseling at Florida Atlantic University. He is a visiting professor in the counseling psychology program at Palm Beach Atlantic University.

Michael Walsh, PhD, LPC, CRC, is an active clinician and counselor educator, specializing in delivering effective technology-assisted classes. He received his PhD in counselor education and supervision from the University of South Carolina, completing his doctoral research in the area of distance education and student satisfaction. Dr. Walsh is currently an assistant professor in the rehabilitation counseling program at the University of South Carolina School of Medicine.

Jane Webber, PhD, LPC, is an associate professor and coordinator of the counseling program at New Jersey City University. She is a certified disaster response crisis counselor and presents nationally on trauma, psychological first aid, and sandtray therapy. Dr. Webber has coedited books on disaster response and school counseling. She integrates multimodal and solution-focused approaches in her work with adolescents and families and consults with schools in their development of comprehensive K–12 counseling programs.

C. Dallas Wilkes, MS, is a doctoral student in the counselor education program at the University of Central Florida. He holds a master's degree in mental health counseling and currently serves as a clinic administrator for the University of Central Florida's Community Counseling Clinic. His clinical background includes working with adolescent males as well as couples and families. Mr. Wilkes also has a strong background in education and athletics.

I

INTRODUCTION

1

Introduction to Humanistic Perspectives on Contemporary Counseling Issues

MARK B. SCHOLL, A. SCOTT MCGOWAN, AND JAMES T. HANSEN

If you are one of the elders of the counseling or other helping professions, you may have some foggy recollections of a bygone era. During this strange, past age, practitioners held the therapeutic relationship in the highest regard and cared little about specific techniques. The "inner subjective experiences" (Hansen, 2005, p. 406) of clients were considered the most important element of the helping encounter. Odder still, counselors did not give their clients direct guidance or tell them how to live their lives. Clearly, we are now in a different age.

In contemporary mental health culture, practitioners generally care little about the subjective experiences of their clients. Instead of focusing on personal meaning systems, counselors spend their days implementing specific techniques designed to eradicate symptoms of mental disorders (APA, 2000). Conventional wisdom dictates that clients who are afflicted with a diagnosable mental health problem (not coincidentally all clients who use a third party to pay for treatment) are incapable of directing their own lives; their disease has hijacked their judgment. Operating under this medical ideology, counselors are obliged to provide direct guidance to these poor, sick beings. In short, subjectivity has been traded for symptoms, techniques have replaced the therapeutic relationship, and authentic encounters have been usurped by directive treatment models.

Not all emphasis on human meaning systems has been lost, though. The insights of the contemporary multicultural movement have helped practitioners appreciate individuals as bearers of a rich array of cultural traditions, rituals, and worldviews (Pedersen, 1990; Sue & Sue, 2008). Because of multiculturalism, counselors are now, thankfully, more accepting and appreciative of various cultural modes of being. In terms of meaning systems, then, the profession has generally replaced subjective individualism with cultural collectivism.

Given these changes in mental health culture, how should we regard the humanism that formerly dominated the profession? Perhaps we should wince with embarrassment when reminded of the sappy, relationship-oriented professionals we used to be, as if we had just seen a decades-old picture of ourselves wearing the now ridiculous-looking fashions that were in vogue at the time. Maybe humanism, like so many other bygone trends, should be placed on a shelf in the intellectual museum of the profession and occasionally dusted off and revisited as a shameful reminder of who we once were.

Completely contrary to the position that it should be abandoned, the authors of this book maintain that a strong infusion of humanism is precisely what contemporary mental health culture needs. Those of us who hold this view do not regard medicalization and multiculturalism (as useful as they can be) as advancements over subjectivity and individualism; we simply regard current perspectives as ideological trends, which, unfortunately, as trends tend to do, have eclipsed vital perspectives from past eras. Humanism is arguably the most important perspective that has been eclipsed. Indeed, some of us "displaced humanists" (Hansen, 2009, p. 65) argue that humanism is not a just a theory or treatment orientation but also a "moral imperative" (Hansen, 2006b, p. 115) that should form the basis of any helping encounter.

WHY HUMANISM?

Why, however, should humanism be held in such high regard? Multiple treatment orientations, as diverse as phrenology and primal scream therapy, have lain dormant for years. Why, out of all of those orientations, should humanism be selected as the one to revive? Moreover, are there particular reasons that humanism should be reintroduced at this particular point in mental health history? To understand why we selected humanism as the orientation to revive, it is helpful to first understand the philosophical assumptions, history, and basic elements of humanistic practices.

A Definition of Humanism and of the Humanistic Approach

Simply put by Gladding (2001, p. 59), humanism is "a philosophy that is primarily concerned with humanity (i.e., the worth of humans as individuals)." This is not to say that Gladding was implying that humanism is a simplistic concept. Indeed, humanism encompasses the richness of the human existential experience that emphasizes the crucial role of the here and now, of authenticity in our relationships with others, and the actual experience of "experiencing" ourselves and of our world. Gladding (p. 59) also defined the humanistic approach in counseling, to wit: "The collective *treatment* approaches in *counseling and psychotherapy* that distinguish humans from other animals.... Humanistic psychotherapy is sometimes called the *third force* (*psychoanalysis* is the first force and *behaviorism* the second force)." It may be the third force, but we believe that it is not third in terms of its effectiveness with working with individuals in a counseling situation. Gladding (2008) later further expanded his definition of humanism and of humanistic counseling approaches as focusing on "the potential of individuals to actively choose and purposefully decide about matters related to themselves and their environments. Professionals who embrace humanistic counseling approaches help people increase self-understanding through experiencing their feelings" (p. 207). Experiencing their feelings and not experiencing counseling techniques: That is kind of a shocker and kind of old-fashioned, is it not? It is not. The beauty of the humanistic approach is that its emphasis is on individuals as the decision makers and as the ones who control their growth and development. Those of us who espouse this approach also have the freedom to borrow "techniques" from other approaches if we find them helpful in working with our clients whom we assume are basically "good" and whom we assume can take ownership of their own lives (Gregoire & Jungers, 2007). This is not to say that other approaches are to be rejected. For example, we now know (Day, 2004) that certain conditions have components that are biologically and physiologically based and that people who suffer from, for example, schizophrenia, mood disorders, and attention deficit disorder (ADD) can benefit from biology-based interventions (e.g., Ritalin for ADD). Hence, physiological approaches and biological interventions, for example, have their place, but we contend that they should not hold a primary place. Because humanistic approaches such as person-centered counseling, existential counseling, or Gestalt therapy emphasize the role of persons in managing their lives, we hold that philosophically and practically they reflect most deeply what we all seek to achieve in counseling: responsible decision making and the development and growth of the wholeness and completeness of the human being.

Philosophical Foundations of Humanism

There are many diverse elements to humanism as a counseling orientation. The principle that unifies these elements, however, is the idea that *humans are irreducible to other phenomena* (Davidson, 2000). That is, humans can be understood only as whole beings and should never be thought of as by-products of other processes.

A brief historical perspective on humanism can help to make the principle of irreducibility clear. Renaissance humanism emerged as a reaction to the authoritarianism of the church, which understood humans as simply the subjects of God. Renaissance humanists insisted that humans were best understood on their own terms and not as pawns of God or scientific objects of study (Davidson, 2000).

During the mid-20th century, psychological humanism emerged as an important force in counseling. Just as the Renaissance humanists insisted that humans should not be reduced to God or science, the mid–20th century psychological humanists insisted that humans should not be reduced to stimulus–response contingencies (i.e., behaviorism) or psychic structures (i.e., psychoanalysis) (Davidson, 2000; Matson, 1971). Therefore, psychological humanism represented a holistic revolt against the dominant reductive theoretical orientations that were present in the mid-century (Hansen, 2006a).

Elements of Humanism

The other elements of humanism follow from this basic principle of irreducibility. Specifically, individualism, the focus on subjective experience, and the emphasis on the dignity of each person are all branches on the ideological tree of human irreducibility. Of relevance to all three branches is the importance of practices that are *people responsive.* This term applies to practices that highlight "relating to human beings in growth-producing ways" (Bohart, 2003, p. 107).

Along the same lines, individualism, respect for each person's dignity, and a focus on subjective experience are principles reflected in Ansbacher's list of humanistic principles, cited in Raskin, Rogers, and Witty (2008, p. 146):

1. Creativity is a powerful force in the lives of people.
2. A holistic approach is more effective than a reductionistic approach.
3. Counseling is essentially based on a good relationship.
4. Sense of purpose, rather than cause, is the primary influence on human behavior.
5. It is necessary for counselors to understand and value individuals' subjective experiences (e.g., feelings, opinions, values).

It follows logically that humanistic approaches to counseling, education, and leadership are consistent with the overarching principle of irreducibility and are people responsive. For example, Cain (2001, pp. 6–13) provided the following defining characteristics of humanistic approaches to counseling:

1. A positive view of the individual as self-actualizing
2. An emphasis on the critical role of empathy in enhancing the quality of the individual's experience
3. A belief that individuals have the capacity to actively and intentionally construct meaning in their lives
4. A belief that people have the freedom, right, and ability to choose their goals and how to achieve them
5. A belief in the dignity of every human being

A logical extension of the fourth and fifth characteristics is a belief in the importance of practices that promote tolerance and diversity and uphold human rights (Scholl, 2008).

Thus, humanism is unified by an overarching philosophy of human irreducibility. Accordingly, humans can be understood only as whole beings and should never be viewed as by-products of other processes. Individualism, respect for subjectivity, and respect for the dignity of each person are the three primary elements of human irreducibility. Humanistic principles and characteristics of humanistic approaches are consistent with a philosophical belief in human irreducibility and the three primary elements. In general, humanistic practices and approaches to counseling, education, and leadership may be understood as those that highlight relating to people in empathic, respectful, and growth-producing ways.

Empirical Evidence

Evidence supporting the contributions of humanistic principles to positive therapeutic outcomes is abundant. Two salient strands are research supporting the contributions of the counseling relationship and counselor empathy. There is strong empirical support dating back to the 1960s validating the beneficial effects of the therapeutic relationship (Rogers, Gendlin, Kiesler, & Truax, 1967). More recent research reports supporting the important role of the relationship include both qualitative (Gaston, 1990; Horvath, Gaston, & Luborsky, 1993) and quantitative reviews of the literature (Horvath & Symonds, 1991; Martin, Garske, & Davis, 2000). The positive influence of counselor empathy on therapeutic outcomes is one of the most robust findings in the professional counseling literature (Bohart, 2003).

This brings us back to the question originally posed: Why should humanism be selected as the one orientation to revive? We believe that humanism should be afforded a position of utmost regard because the extensive history, multiple philosophical influences, and consistent empirical support for effectiveness make humanism an extraordinarily compelling system of thought and practice.

WHY NOW?

This brings us to a second, equally important, question. Why is now the right time for exploring the potential of humanism for unifying diverse effective counseling approaches? For one reason, the tension between humanistic values and the prevailing medical model has been increasing over the past 20 years and has never been greater than it is today. Jensen (2006) cited several reasons for this tension; chief among them is the salient conflict between the values systems underpinning the two paradigms. In contrast to humanism's emphasis on the whole person and facilitating the development of human possibilities and potential, the medical model's reductionistic model focuses on deficits and pathology. In addition, Jensen noted that counselor educators are finding it increasingly difficult to teach counselors-in-training humanistic values while also preparing them for the realities of a world of work where symptom-focused treatments prevail.

However, a very real irony is evident in the fact that medical practitioners are also responsible for providing their patients with state-of-the-art empirically supported treatments. As previously noted, empirical support for the significant contribution of humanistic factors such as counselor empathy (Bohart, 2003), the quality of the working relationship, and counselor responsiveness to client preferences in counseling (Roth & Fonagy, 2005) is abundant. Further, humanistic counseling approaches are continually evolving (Scholl, 2008). One example of this evolution is the ongoing development of motivational interviewing (MI; Miller & Rollnick, 2002), an integrative approach to counseling individuals with addictive behaviors that is largely founded on Rogers's (1957) core conditions (i.e., genuineness, respect, and empathy). MI entails assessing the client's level of readiness for change and eliciting ideas for how change might be facilitated. Along the same lines, Cain (2001) noted that humanistic therapies are becoming increasingly "individualized" (p. 44) to meet the specific preferences and needs of the individual.

However, because the medical model is the dominant model in the helping professions, researchers are more likely to investigate counseling outcomes related to symptom removal than optimal functioning (Ballou, 2005). Outcomes such as the development of strengths, wellness, subjective sense of well-being, and sense of empowerment are less likely to be the focus of grant-funded research. Humanistic approaches that are more likely to be associated with these growth-oriented outcomes are marginalized in our contemporary symptom-focused climate. The present text makes a significant contribution to the literature by increasing professional awareness and understanding of humanistic approaches that might otherwise go unrecognized.

Roth and Fonagy (2005) stated that most models of counseling consider the quality of the relationship as an ingredient that is essential to all good counseling. Common factors research has supported the contention that the client's internal strengths and resources significantly contribute to positive therapeutic outcomes (Messer & Wampold, 2002). Humanism's underlying fundamental propositions subsume many other counseling theories and methods. A primary objective of the current text is to show that humanism has the potential for serving as a general theory of counseling for the helping professions.

Many contemporary movements are informed by humanism but do not give sufficient credit to the original humanistic foundation. One such movement is John Gottman's (1999) research-based method for practicing couples therapy. Gottman's method is so popular and widely respected that by 2006, 4,000 couples and 3,000 therapists had participated in at least one of Gottman's workshops

(Rogers, Minuchin, Satir, Bowen, & Gottman, 2007). Gottman's primary goals for couples include developing skills required for nonjudgmental active listening, enhancing partners' sense of liking for one another, and enhancing partners' understanding of each other's likes and dislikes—goals that clearly echo the Rogerian (1957) core conditions.

Another enormously popular movement informed by humanism is MI (Miller & Rollnick, 2002), which is a cutting-edge therapeutic approach originally developed for the treatment of substance abuse and other addictive behaviors. Results of a meta-analytic review indicated that MI was more efficacious than other treatments including skill-based counseling, directive-confrontational counseling, brief advice, and cognitive-behavioral therapy (Vasilaki, Hosier, & Cox, 2006). MI applications have recently been expanded to help individuals cope with anxiety, depression, posttraumatic stress disorder (PTSD), suicidal behavior, obsessive-compulsive disorder, eating disorders, gambling addictions, and schizophrenia (Arkowitz, Westra, Miller, & Rollnick, 2008).

Smith's (2006) strength-based model of counseling represents a recent paradigm shift away from approaches that emphasize client deficits toward those that emphasize client strengths. In Smith's model, individuals are affirmed as potentially possessing strengths including wisdom, character (e.g., integrity, courage), creativity, effective use of social support, nurturing skills, and intelligence, to name only a few. From this perspective, the counselor's role is to assist clients in recognizing, developing, and applying these strengths to their primary concerns (Kress & Hoffman, 2008). From a humanistic vantage point, counselors have a responsibility for recognizing the resources, assets, and virtues their clients possess and building upon these innate strengths. The recent shift to an emphasis on client strengths can be seen in a number of contemporary counseling models including resilience theory (Seccombe, 2002; West-Olatunji, Shure, Garrett, Conwill, & Torres Rivera, 2008), solution-focused therapy (de Shazer, 1988), narrative therapy (Freedman & Combs, 1996; White & Epston, 1990), and Ericksonian therapy (Erickson, 1989).

Finally, the wellness movement is yet another important historical trend closely allied with humanism and humanistic counseling. In the past decade, mental health practitioners, social workers, and medical personnel have become increasingly interested in promoting wellness in the clients and patients they serve (Constantine & Sue, 2006; Day-Vines & Holcomb-McCoy, 2007; Myers, 1992; Myers, Madathil, & Tingle, 2005; Prilleltensky & Prilleltensky, 2003). Recently, the American Counseling Association published a popular textbook titled *Counseling for Wellness: Theory, Research, and Practice* (Myers & Sweeney, 2005). In 2007, the *Journal of Humanistic Counseling, Education and Development* published a special issue titled *Toward a Culture of Counselor Wellness*. These publications reflect a shift in focus away from reductionism and symptoms and toward an emphasis on holism and actualization of human potential. Rather than the absence of disease, wellness represents the presence of highly adaptive functioning across the social, physical, and cognitive domains (Lawson, Venart, Hazler, & Kottler, 2007). The recent wellness movement may be viewed as a significant historical trend consistent with Davidson's (2000) humanistic principle of irreducibility and Raskin et al.'s (2008) assertion that a holistic approach is more effective than a reductionistic approach.

Contextualizing Practice Within a Humanistic Ideology

This book is intended to fulfill two primary objectives. First, it is intended to highlight humanistic principles inherent in current, effective counseling perspectives, approaches, and practices. Second, the book is intended to show the power of humanistic thinking to unite diverse elements of counseling practice.

Our text includes three primary content sections: Section II, Contemporary Trends and Applications to Counseling Practice; Section III, Applications in Educational Settings; and Section IV, Applications to Counselor Education and Training. Section II includes six chapters beginning with Chapter 2, "Wellness: Theory, Research, and Applications for Counselors." In this chapter, Jane Myers, Philip Clarke, Jennifer Brown, and Denisha Champion discuss the application of wellness to substance abuse—one of America's most serious social and mental health problems. In Chapter 3, "Humanism and Multiculturalism," Michael D'Andrea and Judy Daniels present a 10-factor model of multicultural counseling that is represented by an engaging heuristic, the acronym RESPECTFUL.

Today, many of us have become overly dependent on passive forms of entertainment and as a result have become less aware of personal creativity as a powerful inner resource. In a bygone era before the advent of entertainment centers, entertainment was more person centered. People were more inclined to entertain themselves through various modes of creative and artistic self-expression such as singing, storytelling, and playing musical instruments. In Chapter 4, "The Creative Arts in Counseling," Donna Henderson shares models for promoting client creativity and discusses approaches to incorporating the arts into the treatment of a wide range of counseling concerns.

In Chapter 5, "Humanism and Substance Abuse Counseling," Mark Scholl, Emma Kendrick, Dallas Wilkes, and Bryce Hagedorn observe that counseling approaches emphasizing harsh confrontation and the necessity of clients "hitting rock bottom" are giving way to humanistic approaches that are less confrontational, place more emphasis on the quality of the counseling relationship, and embrace a more individualized harm reduction model. The authors of Chapter 5 focus primarily on two widely respected approaches to treating substance abuse: MI (Miller & Rollnick, 2002) and 12-step facilitation. In Chapter 6, "Humanistic Couples Counseling," Paul Peluso and Steven Vensel address the relationship that for many of us is most central and salient in our lives. They describe the application of humanistic therapies to diverse couple concerns including loss of desire, needs for companionship and intimacy, and loss of trust as a result of infidelity. Of particular relevance are the authors' insightful recommendations for repairing relationships that have been strained or broken.

Humans living in modern times are vulnerable to a wide array of harms including abuse at the hands of other humans, terrorism, and natural disasters. Humanistic counselors are responsible for facilitating healing in clients who have been harmed by these all-too-common threats to our sense of safety and well-being. In Chapter 7, "Healing Trauma Through Humanistic Connection," Elizabeth Venart and Jane Webber assert that a humanistic framework is a necessity for promoting client healing as well as counselor wellness.

Section III begins with Chapter 8, "Humanistic Perspectives on Addressing School Violence." In this chapter, Paula Stanley, Robert Small, Stephen Owen, and Tod Burke apply an invitational theory (Purkey & Novak, 2008) framework to make recommendations for reducing and preventing school violence, one of contemporary society's most serious concerns.

One of the most profound examples of lost potential in our society occurs when a young person prematurely drops out of school and never returns. In Chapter 9, "Ecohumanism: Integrating Humanism and Resilience Theory," Rolla Lewis shares his humanistic insights including recommendations for integrating eco-humanism and resilience models to empower at-risk youth. Next, Scott McGowan, Frank Brady, and Joseph Despres discuss the potential positive benefits of participating in competitive sports in Chapter 10, "Competitive Sports for the Elementary and Middle School Child: A Developmental and Humanistic Perspective." In their holistic developmental treatment of the subject, they make timely recommendations for minimizing negative outcomes, maximizing positive outcomes, and reducing the high rate of attrition. The bottom line for them is that all children should be taught sports skills from a developmental point of view while also encouraging a lifelong love of sports. The emphasis is on the development of each child and not on "winning."

In Chapter 11, "Humanism in College and University Counseling," Woody Schwitzer discusses the extent to which humanism informs counseling practices in higher-education settings. Employing Drum and Lawler's (1988) tripartite model of counseling, which subdivides counseling services into preventive, intermediate, and psychotherapeutic, Schwitzer asserts that the preventive and intermediate categories are highly consistent with fundamental humanistic principles. Moreover, he deconstructs *Diagnostic and Statistical Manual of Mental Disorders,* fourth edition, text revised (*DSM-IV-TR*, APA, 2000) diagnosis, case conceptualization, and treatment planning to show that these psychotherapeutic processes, if conducted professionally and conscientiously, are in fact also consistent with humanistic principles.

Section IV begins with Chapter 12, "Humanistic Education and Technology in Counselor Education: Crossing the Streams." In this chapter, Michael Walsh and Linda Leech turn their attention to the intriguing question of whether humanism and technology can harmoniously coexist. They contend that the two, seemingly antithetical, paradigms can be blended to engender a powerful learning environment that is people responsive. Finally, in Chapter 13, "Humanistic Perspectives on Counselor Education and Supervision," Colette Dollarhide and Darcy Haag Granello employ humanistic theoretical perspectives (e.g., person centered, constructivist counseling) to make recommendations for counseling supervision practices that promote the holistic development and full actualization of supervisees.

In closing, it would be an unfair and unrealistic expectation for chapter authors to be dogmatically humanistic and not stray from any of the central tenets of humanism. Humanism may be viewed as a big ideological umbrella. In their chapters, the contributing authors explain how their practices fit under this umbrella. At times, the authors are candid regarding instances where there are potential limitations to a purely humanistic counseling approach. In our view, highlighting the effective application of humanistic principles across a diverse range of approaches is more valuable than sticking dogmatically to a humanistic practice orientation. Consequently, the primary contribution of this text is that it contextualizes the authors' various practice recommendations within a unifying humanistic ideology.

REFERENCES

American Psychiatric Association. (APA). (2000). *Diagnostic and statistical manual of mental disorders* (4th ed., text rev.). Washington, DC: Author.

Arkowitz, H., Westra, H. A., Miller, W. R., & Rollnick, S. (Eds.). (2008). *Motivational interviewing in the treatment of psychological problems.* New York: Guilford Press.

Ballou, M. (2005). Threats and challenges to feminist therapy. *Women and Therapy, 28,* 201–210.

Bohart, A. C. (2003). Person-centered psychotherapy and related experiential approaches. In A. S. Gurman & S. B. Messer (Eds.), *Essential psychotherapies: Theory and practice* (2nd. ed., pp. 107–148). New York: Guilford Press.

Cain, D. J. (2001). Defining characteristics, history, and evolution of humanistic psychotherapies. In D. J. Cain & J. Seeman (Eds.), *Humanistic psychotherapies: Handbook of research and practice* (pp. 3–54). Washington, DC: American Psychological Association.

Constantine, M., & Sue, D. W. (2006). Factors contributing to optimal human functioning in people of color in the United States. *Counseling Psychologist, 34,* 228–244.

Davidson, L. (2000). Philosophical foundations of humanistic psychology. *Humanistic Psychologist, 28,* 7–31.

Day, S. X. (2004). *Theory and design in counseling and psychotherapy.* Boston: Lahaska Press, Houghton Mifflin Company.

Day-Vines, N. L., & Holcomb-McCoy, C. (2007). Wellness among African American counselors. *Journal of Humanistic Counseling, Education and Development, 46,* 82–97.

de Shazer, S. (1988). *Clues: Investigating solutions in brief therapy.* New York: Norton.

Drum, D. J., & Lawler, A. C. (1988). *Developmental interventions: Theories, principles, and practice.* Columbus, OH: Merrill.

Erickson, M. H. (1989). *Healing in hypnosis: Volume 1.* New York: Irvington.

Freedman, J., & Combs, G. (1996). *Narrative therapy: The social construction of preferred realities.* New York: Norton.

Gaston, L. (1990). The concept of the alliance and its role in psychotherapy: Theoretical and empirical considerations. *Psychotherapy, 27,* 143–153.

Gladding, S. T. (2001). *The counseling dictionary: Concise definitions of frequently used terms.* Upper Saddle River, NJ: Merrill Prentice Hall.

Gladding, S. T. (2008). *Counseling: A comprehensive profession.* Upper Saddle River, NJ: Merrill Prentice Hall.

Gottman, J. M. (1999). *The marriage clinic: A scientifically based marital therapy.* New York: W.W. Norton & Company, Inc.

Gregoire, J., & Jungers, C. M. (2007). *The counselor's companion: What every beginning counselor needs to know.* Mahwah, NJ: Lawrence Erlbaum Associates.

Hansen, J. T. (2005). The devaluation of inner subjective experiences by the counseling profession: A plea to reclaim the essence of the profession. *Journal of Counseling & Development, 83,* 406–415.

Hansen, J. T. (2006a). Humanism as ideological rebellion: Deconstructing the dualisms of contemporary mental health culture. *Journal of Humanistic Counseling, Education and Development, 45*(1), 3–16.

Hansen, J. T. (2006b). Humanism as moral imperative: Comments on the role of knowing in the helping encounter. *Journal of Humanistic Counseling, Education and Development, 45*(2), 115–125.

Hansen, J. T. (2009). On displaced humanists: Counselor education and the meaning-reduction pendulum. *Journal of Humanistic Counseling, Education and Development, 48,* 65–76.

Horvath, A. O., Gaston, L., & Luborsky, L. (1993). The therapeutic alliance and its measures. In N. Miller, L. Luborsky, J. P. Barber, & J. P. Docherty (Eds.), *Psychodynamic treatment research: A handbook for clinical practice* (pp. 247–273). New York: Basic Books.

Horvath, A. O., & Symonds, B. D. (1991). Relation between working alliance and outcome in psychotherapy: A meta-analysis. *Journal of Counseling Psychology, 38,* 139–149.

Jensen, D. R. (2006). *Medical model influence in counseling and psychotherapy: Counseling psychology training directors' views.* Dissertation, Brigham Young University. Retrieved from http://contentdm.lib.byu.edu/ETD/image/etd/323.pdf on November 12, 2009.

Kress, V. E., & Hoffman, R. M. (2008). Empowering adolescent survivors of sexual abuse: Application of a solution-focused Ericksonian counseling group. *Journal of Humanistic Counseling, Education, and Development, 47,* 172–185.

Lawson, G., Venart, E., Hazler, R. J., & Kottler, J. A. (2007). Toward a culture of counselor wellness. *Journal of Humanistic Counseling, Education and Development, 46,* 5–19.

Martin, D. J., Garske, J. P., & Davis, M. K. (2000). Relation of the therapeutic alliance with outcome and other variables: A meta-analytic review. *Journal of Consulting and Clinical Psychology, 68*(3), 438–450.

Matson, F. (1971). Humanistic theory: The third revolution in psychology. *Humanist, 12,* 7–11.

Messer, S. B., & Wampold, B. E. (2002). Let's face facts: Common factors are more potent than specific therapy ingredients. *Clinical Psychology: Science and Practice, 9,* 21–25.

Miller, W. R., & Rollnick, S. (2002). *Motivational interviewing: Preparing people for change* (2nd ed.). New York: Guilford Press.

Myers, J. E. (1992). Wellness, prevention, development: The cornerstone of the profession. *Journal of Counseling & Development, 71*, 136–139.

Myers, J. E., Madathil, J., & Tingle, L. R. (2005). Marriage satisfaction and wellness in India and the United States: A preliminary comparison of arranged marriages and marriages of choice. *Journal of Counseling and Development, 83*, 183–190.

Myers, J. E., & Sweeney, T. J. (2005). *Counseling for wellness: Theory, research, and practice.* Alexandria, VA: American Counseling Association.

Pedersen, P. (1990). The multicultural perspective as a fourth force in counseling. *Journal of Mental Health Counseling, 12*, 93–95.

Prilleltensky, I., & Prilleltensky, O. (2003). Synergies for wellness and liberation in counseling psychology. *Counseling Psychologist, 31*, 273–281.

Purkey, W. W., & Novak, J. M. (2008). *Fundamentals of invitational education.* Kennesaw, GA: International Alliance for Invitational Education.

Raskin, N. J., Rogers, C. R., & Witty, M. C. (2008). Client-centered therapy. In R. J. Corsini & D. Wedding (Eds.), *Current psychotherapies* (8th ed., pp. 141–186). Belmont, CA: Thomson Brooks/Cole.

Rogers, C. (1957). The necessary and sufficient conditions of therapeutic personality change. *Journal of Consulting Psychology, 21*, 95–103.

Rogers, C., Gendlin, E. T., Kiesler, D. J., & Truax, C. B. (1967). The findings in brief. In C. Rogers (Ed.), *The therapeutic relationship and its impact: A study of psychotherapy and schizophrenics* (pp. 73–93). Madison: University of Wisconsin Press.

Rogers, C., Minuchin, S., Satir, V., Bowen, M., & Gottman, J. (2007, March–April). The most influential therapists of the past quarter century. *Psychotherapy Networker, 219*–239.

Roth, A., & Fonagy, P. (2005). The contributions of therapists and patients to outcome. In A. Roth & P. Fonagy (Eds.), What works for whom? A critical review of psychotherapy research (2nd ed., pp. 447–478). New York: Guilford Press.

Scholl, M. B. (2008). Preparing manuscripts with central and salient humanistic content. *Journal of Humanistic Counseling, Education and Development, 47*, 3–8.

Seccombe, K. (2002). "Beating the odds" versus "changing the odds": Poverty, resilience, and family policy. *Journal of Marriage and Family, 64*, 384–394.

Smith, E. J. (2006). The strength-based counseling model: A paradigm shift in psychology. *Counseling Psychologist, 34*, 134–144.

Sue, D. W., & Sue, D. (2008). *Counseling the culturally diverse: Theory and practice* (5th ed.). Hoboken, NJ: John Wiley & Sons.

Vasilaki, E. I., Hosier, S. G., & Cox, W. M. (2006). The efficacy of motivational interviewing as a brief intervention to excessive drinking: A meta-analytic review. *Alcohol and Alcoholism, 41*, 328–335.

West-Olatunji, C., Shure, L., Garrett, M. T., Conwill, W., & Torres Rivera, E. (2008). Rite of passage programs as effective tools for fostering resilience among low-income African American male adolescents. *Journal of Humanistic Counseling, Education and Development, 47*, 131–143.

White, M., & Epston, D. (1990). *Narrative means to therapeutic ends.* New York: Norton.

II

CONTEMPORARY TRENDS AND APPLICATIONS TO COUNSELING PRACTICE

2

Wellness
Theory, Research, and Applications for Counselors

Jane E. Myers, Philip Clarke, Jennifer B. Brown, and Denisha A. Champion

As mentioned in Chapter 1 of this text, wellness counseling is closely allied with humanism and humanistic counseling. Wellness—in addition to being a holistic approach to counseling that represents a shift from reductionistic approaches—consistent with the humanistic perspectives of Maslow and Rogers emphasizes the actualization of human potential. In this chapter, the history of wellness counseling is discussed, including definitions and a description of counseling-based models. An overview of research arising from these models is described. To facilitate evidence-based application of wellness concepts, two client populations are described, wellness risk factors are discussed, and intervention strategies are explored. College students were selected because of the size and diversity of this population: Nearly 50% of 18–24-year-old persons are enrolled in college, and more than one in three college students are of nontraditional age (i.e., over 24; National Center for Education Statistics, 2009). Substance abuse has been defined as "the nation's number one health problem" (Schneider Institute for Health Policy, 2001); hence, we chose substance abusers as a significant clinical population through which to describe the benefits of a wellness approach. Finally, we describe a case in which the wellness model is applied successfully to help a client choose to change in positive ways. Implications for practitioners are explored in the conclusion to the chapter.

WELLNESS COUNSELING: DEFINITIONS, MODELS, AND RESEARCH

Wellness was first identified as a philosophy of care over 2,000 years ago. Aesculapias, the Greek god of healing, had two daughters who espoused different views of health and illness. Panacea believed that healing meant treating people's existing health problems and illnesses. Hygeia believed that it was essential to teach people ways of living so they would not become sick. Panacea became the forerunner of modern medicine, while Hygeia is credited with initiating the wellness movement.

Definitions of Wellness

In 1947, the World Health Organization (WHO) defined health as "physical, mental, and social well-being, not merely the absence of disease" (WHO, 1958, p. 1). The WHO later provided a definition of optimal health as "a state of complete physical, mental, and social well-being and not merely the absence of disease or infirmity" (WHO, 1958, p. 1). Thus, wellness is not synonymous with health, a neutral state, and incorporates a positive sense of well-being and a movement in the direction of optimum functioning.

In the last half of the 20th century, medical researchers and clinicians began to adopt the WHO philosophy and question whether a "new" paradigm of medicine was needed. This paradigm would emphasize prevention of illness, personal responsibility for health outcomes, and empowerment of persons to be active determiners of their physical health needs and care. Dr. Halbert Dunn (1961, 1977), a physician who provided a weekly radio talk show to promote positive self-care, is widely credited with being the architect of the modern wellness movement. Dunn (1961) defined wellness as "an integrated method of functioning which is oriented toward maximizing the potential of which the individual is capable. It requires that the individual maintain a continuum of balance and purposeful direction within the environment where he is functioning" (p. 4). Dunn also defined movement along a continuum of wellness ending in a positive state defined in the title of his book *High Level Wellness*.

Dr. Bill Hettler, a public health physician, is often called the father of wellness as we now know it. Hettler established the National Wellness Institute (NWI) in the 1970s and through his writings and community service helped make *wellness* a household word throughout the United States. Hettler (1984) defined wellness as "an active process through which people become aware of, and make choices toward a more successful existence" (p. 13). Consistent with this definition, Archer, Probert, and Gage (1987), all psychologists, conducted an extensive literature review on wellness and concluded that wellness is "the process and state of a quest for maximum human functioning that involves the body, mind, and spirit" (p. 311).

Writing from a counseling perspective, Myers, Sweeney, and Witmer (2000), after reviewing literature from multiple disciplines, concluded that wellness is "a way of life oriented toward optimal health and well-being, in which body, mind, and spirit are integrated by the individual to live life more fully within the human and natural community. Ideally, it is the optimum state of health and well-being that each individual is capable of achieving" (p. 252). Wellness is thus both an outcome and a process, an overarching goal for living and a day-by-day, minute-by-minute way of being. The wellness concept is multifaceted and multidimensional, as reflected in the various models of wellness that have been developed.

All models of wellness, particularly those that originated in the counseling field, share common elements and a common philosophy. This philosophy is identical to what we find in the humanistic movement; thus, as stated so clearly by the authors in Chapter 1, the wellness movement is closely aligned with humanism. We might go further and say the two are inseparable. Notable among all wellness models are the following: (1) an emphasis on holism and the inability to separate parts of the individual in a reductionist manner; (2) a respect for individuals' ability to take responsibility for life choices and make choices that are in their best interest; and (3) a fundamental concern for individuals' subjective experiences and in-depth self-understanding as the basis of both medical and mental health interventions.

Again, as noted in Chapter 1, Ansbacher, who based his work in the theory and methods of Alfred Adler (Sweeney, 2009), emphasized the importance of the subjective experience and the inherent creativity of individuals. Adler defined his theory as *individual psychology* to underscore his core belief in the individual as the unit of concern, his respect for the value, worth, and dignity of the individual, and his belief in the ability of all individuals to uncover their private logic and goals and rewrite their lifestyle to live more satisfying and successful lives (Adler, 1954/1927). Humanists writing in the tradition of Adler, including Maslow and Rogers, emphasized the positive development of human potential and the goals of counseling in terms of facilitating optimal functioning rather than correcting pathology.

Adler's three key concepts—that human beings are socially embedded; goal oriented or purposive; and able to analyze their thoughts, feelings, and behaviors—were embedded in a theory in which humans were viewed as inherently good and able to change in positive ways when it became useful for them to do so. Not surprisingly, these concepts are the foundation of later wellness theories, which share a common foundation in humanistic principles and perspectives.

Models of Wellness

Early models of wellness were based in health sciences, particularly medicine and public health. In the early 1990s, the first counseling-based wellness model, the Wheel of Wellness (Sweeney & Witmer, 1991), was proposed. This model differed from earlier wellness models in its emphasis on spirituality as the core component of well-being and through the inclusion of multiple psychological constructs that emerged through multidisciplinary literature as correlates of better health, greater longevity, and enhanced quality of life.

Wheel of Wellness

Sweeney and Witmer (1991), Witmer and Sweeney (1992), and Myers, Sweeney, and Witmer (2000) proposed a holistic model of wellness and prevention over the life span based on cross-disciplinary literature, both theoretical and empirical, that "incorporates theoretical concepts from psychology, anthropology, sociology, religion, and education" (Witmer & Sweeney, 1992, p. 140). The results of research, as well as theoretical perspectives, from personality, social, clinical, health, and developmental psychology were foundations for this model as well as stress management, ecology, and contextualism.

The Wheel of Wellness model proposes five life tasks based in Adlerian individual psychology (Sweeney, 2009), depicted in a wheel (Figure 2.1), which are interrelated and interconnected. These five tasks, based in Adlerian individual psychology, include the following: spirituality, work, friendship, love, and self-direction.

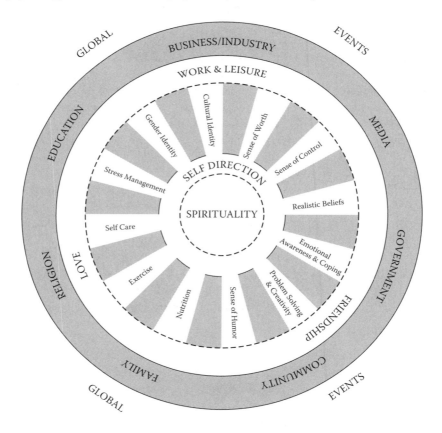

Figure 2.1   The wheel of wellness. (From Myers, J. E., & Sweeney, T. J., *Manual for the Five Factor Wellness Inventory*, Mindgarden, Inc., Palo Alto, 2005.)

The life task of self-direction is further subdivided into the following 12 tasks: (1) sense of worth; (2) sense of control; (3) realistic beliefs; (4) emotional responsiveness and management; (5) intellectual stimulation, problem solving, and creativity; (6) sense of humor; (7) exercise; (8) nutrition; (9) self-care; (10) gender identification; (11) cultural identification; and (12) stress management. These life tasks interact dynamically with a variety of life forces, including but not limited to one's family, community, religion, education, government, media, and business/industry. Global events, whether of natural (e.g., floods, famines) or human (e.g., wars) origin, also can have an impact on the life forces and life tasks depicted in the model. The model has been used successfully in both research and clinical practice.

The Indivisible Self

Myers and Sweeney (2005a) and Sweeney and Myers (2005b) developed the Indivisible Self (IS-WEL), a model of wellness based on more than a dozen years of research and clinical practice using the wheel of wellness and the Wellness Evaluation of Lifestyles Inventory (WEL). Statistical analyses of a large database developed from assessments of wellness revealed a lack of support for the hypothesized circumplex model with spirituality at the center. Through exploratory and confirmatory factor analyses, a structural model was identified to "explain" the relationship among the original wellness components included in the Wheel model.

Although the hypothesized interrelationships among the components of the wheel of wellness were not supported, the results of factor analyses did provide support for the 17 discrete components of the Wheel as third-order factors. Five clear second-order factors and one unidimensional higher-order factor, "wellness," were also identified. Relationships among the three levels of factors revealed a new, evidence-based wellness model called the IS-WEL (Figure 2.2; Sweeney & Myers, 2005b). In this model, the single, higher-order wellness factor reflects the Adlerian foundation of the original wellness model in terms of holism and indivisibility of the self.

In the IS-WEL model, five second-order factors comprise the indivisible self: creative, coping, social, essential, and physical. Seventeen third-order factors are grouped within these second-order factors. Four contexts are proposed that affect wellness of the individual. The factors in the IS-WEL model are briefly defined in Table 2.1. These factors comprise the basis of the Five Factor Wellness Inventory (5F-WEL; Myers & Sweeney, 2005a), which along with the Wellness Evaluation of Lifestyle Inventory (Myers, Sweeney, & Witmer, 1996) has been used in multiple studies to provide the evidence base for wellness counseling.

Wellness Research

Wellness factors have been examined in relation to diverse psychological constructs and demographic indices, and as outcome measures or dependent variables. They have also been used for program evaluation and as pretest–posttest

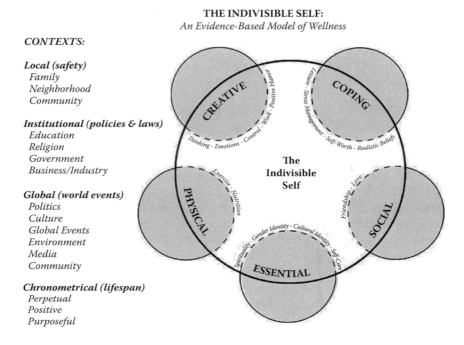

Figure 2.2   The indivisible self: An evidence-based model of wellness. (From Myers, J. E., & Sweeney, T. J., *Manual for the Five Factor Wellness Inventory*, Mindgarden, Inc., Palo Alto, 2005. With permission.)

measures for counseling outcome studies with individuals and groups. Much of this research is summarized in-depth by various authors in the edited text *Counseling for Wellness: Theory, Research, and Practice* (Myers & Sweeney, 2005a) and in a recent article by Myers and Sweeney (2008).

Studies of psychological correlates of wellness have established positive relationships between various wellness factors and a variety of other constructs. For example, both short-term state and long-term trait constructs of psychological well-being correlated positively with each of the major life tasks in the wheel of wellness model (Hermon & Hazler, 1999). A negative relationship between body shame and wellness and a positive relationship between appearance control beliefs and wellness have been found (Sinclair & Myers, 2004). There appear to be positive relationships between healthy love styles and the life tasks in the wheel of wellness (Shurts & Myers, 2006) and positive associations among job satisfaction, mattering, and the life tasks (Connolly & Myers, 2003). Perceived stress has been shown to be inversely correlated with wellness, especially with stress management (Gibson & Myers, 2006; Powers, Myers, Tingle, & Powers, 2004). For children and adults, self-esteem is highly correlated with most aspects of wellness (Myers & Sweeney, 2008).

Table 2.1   Abbreviated Definitions of Wellness Factors in the IS-WEL Model

Wellness Factor	Definition
Total wellness	The sum of all items on the 5F-WEL; a measure of one's general well-being or total wellness
Creative self	The combination of attributes that each of us forms to make a unique place among others in our social interactions and to positively interpret our world
Thinking	Being mentally active, open-minded; having the ability to be creative and experimental; having a sense of curiosity, a need to know and to learn; the ability to solve problems
Emotions	Being aware of or in touch with one's feelings; being able to experience and express one's feelings appropriately, both positive and negative
Control	Belief that you can usually achieve the goals you set out for yourself; having a sense of playfulness in life; being able to be assertive in expressing one's needs
Work	Being satisfied with one's work; having adequate financial security; feeling that one's skills are used appropriately; the ability to cope with workplace stress
Positive humor	Being able to laugh at one's own mistakes and the unexpected things that happen; the ability to use humor to accomplish even serious tasks
Coping self	The combination of elements that regulate our responses to life events and provide a means for transcending their negative effects
Leisure	Activities done in one's free time; satisfaction with one's leisure activities; having at least one activity in which "I lose myself and time stands still"
Stress management	General perception of one's own self-management or self-regulation; seeing change as an opportunity for growth; ongoing self-monitoring and assessment of one's coping resources
Self-worth	Accepting who and what one is, positive qualities along with imperfections; valuing oneself as a unique individual
Realistic beliefs	Understanding that perfection or being loved by everyone are impossible goals and having the courage to be imperfect
Social self	Social support through connections with others in our friendships and intimate relationships, including family ties
Friendship	Social relationships that involve a connection with others individually or in community but that do not have a marital, sexual, or familial commitment; having friends in whom one can trust and who can provide emotional, material, or informational support when needed
Love	The ability to be intimate, trusting, and self-disclosing with another person; having a family or family-like support system characterized by shared spiritual values, the ability to solve conflict in a mutually respectful way, healthy communication styles, and mutual appreciation
Essential self	Our essential meaning-making processes in relation to life, self, and others
Spirituality	Personal beliefs and behaviors that are practiced as part of the recognition that we are more than the material aspects of mind and body

(Continued)

Table 2.1 (continued)   Abbreviated Definitions of Wellness Factors in the IS-WEL Model

Wellness Factor	Definition
Gender identity	Satisfaction with one's gender; feeling supported in one's gender; transcendence of gender identity (i.e., ability to be androgynous)
Cultural identity	Satisfaction with one's cultural identity; feeling supported in one's cultural identity; transcendence of one's cultural identity
Self-care	Taking responsibility for one's wellness through self-care and safety habits that are preventive in nature; minimizing the harmful effects of pollution in your environment
Physical self	The biological and physiological processes that comprise the physical aspects of our development and functioning
Exercise	Engaging in sufficient physical activity to keep in good physical condition; maintaining flexibility through stretching
Nutrition	Eating a nutritionally balanced diet; maintaining a normal weight (i.e., within 15% of the ideal) and avoiding overeating
Contexts	
Local	Systems in which we live most often—families, neighborhoods, and communities—and our perceptions of safety in these systems
Institutional	Social and political systems that affect our daily functioning and serve to empower or limit our development in obvious and subtle ways, including education, religion, government, and the media
Global	Factors such as politics, culture, global events, and the environment that connect us to others around the world
Chronometrical	Growth, movement, and change in the time dimension that is perpetual, of necessity positive, and purposeful

Source: J. E. Myers and T. J. Sweeney, *Counseling for Wellness: Theory, Research, and Practice,* Alexandria, VA, American Counseling Association, 2005. With permission.

Wellness factors have been positively associated with aspects of acculturation and ethnic identity for adolescent (Chang & Myers, 2003; Garrett & Myers, 1996) and adult members of ethnic minority groups in the United States (Spurgeon & Myers, 2010). The wellness paradigm and assessment have been applied successfully in research with adult gay males (Dew, Myers, & Wightman, 2006) and midlife lesbian women (Degges-White & Myers, in press). For gay males, wellness is positively associated with healthy self-disclosure. For lesbian women, a variety of relationship factors, coping resources, and perceived age have been associated with greater wellness (Degges-White & Myers, in press).

Wellness factors have been used as pre- and postassessments for college student success courses for at-risk freshmen (Smith, Myers, & Hensley, 2002), elementary school students in classroom guidance (Villalba & Myers, 2006), and police officers receiving individual counseling (Tanigoshi, Kontos, & Remley, 2008). In all outcome studies, aspects of wellness have been enhanced through counseling interventions (Myers & Sweeney, 2008). Currently, over 40 doctoral dissertations and as many independent studies reported in the counseling literature lend support to the usefulness of wellness models for understanding and enhancing human functioning (Myers & Sweeney, 2008; see also http://www.uncg.edu/ced/jemyers). Counselors working with individuals from a wellness perspective are able to assess their clients, identify strengths, and choose interventions that build on strengths to help clients change their thoughts, feelings, and behaviors in positive ways (Myers & Sweeney, 2005). Strategies for strength-based interventions in college settings and with clinical populations are explored in the following sections.

WELLNESS IN COLLEGE STUDENTS

The definition of *college student* has expanded considerably from the conventional notion of the term. Thinking beyond the idea of traditional-aged students (age 18–21), there are nontraditional college students who are pursuing a first bachelor's degree after age 24, veterans pursuing an education after serving their country or being discharged from a branch of the armed services, and international students balancing college academics while possibly adjusting to a new language and culture. Today's college student may be returning to gain new knowledge, skills, or training due to unemployment after an economic downturn. The landscape of who we are talking about when we speak of college students is changing. Because of this, students are coming to campus at different levels of wellness as well as different levels of awareness about their own well-being.

In this section, research on college student wellness is briefly summarized, and wellness concerns among college students are described using the indivisible self model as an organizing framework. The benefits of using a wellness approach with college students are discussed, and strategies for working with students based on the IS-WEL model are provided.

Research on Undergraduate Wellness

Over the past 2 decades, the incidence, prevalence, and severity of mental health concerns on college campuses has increased. While this trend is an important one for college counselors to be aware of and respond to, the research on symptoms and severity of pathology is not analogous to research on undergraduate wellness. Osborn (2005) summarized the existing research on undergraduate students' wellness studies and noted the many discussions of physical and social aspects of wellness, yet multiple studies reveal that spirituality and coping behaviors are areas where undergraduates consistently experience lower wellness. Myers and Mobley's (2004) analysis of data for 1,567 students revealed that undergraduates experience lower wellness than nonstudent adults in most areas. Ethnic differences have also been identified, in that traditional students of color scored lower than Caucasian students on a majority of the wellness scales in this study. On the other hand, Spurgeon and Myers (2008) found differences in wellness of African American students based on type of college attended, with much higher social self wellness among students matriculating at historically Black colleges and universities (HBCUs).

Myers and Bechtel (2004) examined wellness among 179 first-year cadets at West Point in relation to age and gender. Younger cadets and males reported greater wellness on multiple factors. Gibson and Myers (2006), in a replication of this study with 234 cadets at the Citadel, found few differences between the two sets of cadets; however, in both studies cadets scored higher than available norm groups on a majority of wellness factors. These studies of cadets had markedly different outcomes from general studies of undergraduate student wellness, supporting the need to examine subgroups within the large population of students in various settings. Additional support for this need is found in studies of graduate student populations. For example, Myers, Mobley, and Booth (1993) found higher wellness among graduate students in counseling programs than undergraduates; however, there seemed to be a developmental progression in that doctoral student wellness was higher than that of master's level students. Wester, Trepal, and Myers (2009) also found that counselor educators' wellness exceeded that of both levels of students, again pointing out the need for wellness interventions with students regardless of age, level, or program of study.

Wellness Concerns and Problems Among College Students

Matriculation at colleges and universities each fall is a time of excitement and anxiety for new students. Normative developmental processes such as separation and individuation require adjustment for all students. In addition, increasing numbers of students each year are coming to college having already been diagnosed and treated for some mental health concern. For example, attention deficit disorder or mood disorders such as anxiety and depression are common on many college campuses.

The Center for the Study of Collegiate Mental Health released a pilot study in 2009 after collecting data from 66 institutions across the United States. They found that 19% of students had prior experience with counseling, 10% had been prescribed psychiatric medication before attending college, 11% reported seriously considering suicide before entering college, and 5% had made a suicide attempt. If students have not fully come to understand their diagnosis or mental health needs or if the added demands of college life upset the balance they have found, an even more pronounced dip in their overall wellness is likely to become evident. The following examples illustrate some behavioral manifestations of how a lower level of wellness might look in a college student based on the Indivisible Self Model of Wellness (Figure 2.2; Myers & Sweeney, 2005).

Creative Self

The creative self is a combination of attributes that individuals use to interpret the world around them (Myers & Sweeney, 2005). It includes a person's thinking and emotions. Students who struggle with test anxiety may have had negative experiences with receiving feedback or grades on an exam where they performed poorly due to anxiety. If our past experiences shape how we respond to future instances we perceive as similar, these students may be caught in a cycle of faulty thinking (negative self-talk about their ability to perform academically), which influences their emotional response (sadness, frustration). Students stuck in this cycle may score lower on the creative factor of wellness depending on how pervasive their negative perceptions are.

Cognitive-behavioral techniques or rational emotive behavioral therapy (REBT) might be used to address faulty thinking. Showing students the interrelationship between their thoughts and emotions can illuminate how improving one would serve to improve the other. Sense of control could be enhanced by focusing on environmental structuring and decision making to help students learn how small decisions allow them to feel empowered in their daily lives.

Coping Self

The elements of the coping self determine how one reacts to the stressors in life and include leisure and stress management. Students with low frustration tolerance and those with nonexistent or maladaptive methods of coping are likely to score lower on this second-order factor of wellness. Low frustration tolerance, or being easily perturbed by relatively small problems, can increase the level of stress students experience. Students without balance between their work and academic life and their leisure time may also score lower in this area because of the imbalance between stress and relaxation. This is often the case when counselors or student affairs professionals are puzzled by the student with the near-perfect grade-point average (GPA) who appears increasingly more and more frazzled and anxious as the semester unfolds. It is imperative to realize that a very high GPA is indicative of a student who is doing well academically, not necessarily one who is flourishing in all areas of wellness. A student may have the ability to perform to high standards but does not have the coping mechanisms in place to deal with the stress of midterms or final exams.

Students often present with a problem and are eager to learn better ways of coping. Counselors may want to increase students' self-efficacy by first inquiring what coping strategies have worked before and eliciting ideas that students can come up with on their own to enhance their coping ability. As a consequence, the counselor is not creating dependency by handing students the answers. However, there are times when a didactic approach is useful, such as when students are searching for solutions after having employed all known techniques. Motivational interviewing (MI) may be employed if students are using maladaptive coping methods (e.g., smoking marijuana to reduce stress and relax). Moving students toward change involving the use of more adaptive coping practices is called for when maladaptive coping styles are further endangering their overall wellness.

Social Self

In terms of better student outcomes and higher retention rates for the university, the social self may be the most important of all the areas of wellness in the college student population. The social self is composed of friendships and love relationships. Swartz-Kulstad & Martin (1999) studied the impact of psychosocial factors on college adjustment. Their report cited study results that nonacademic factors are better at predicting adjustment to college than ability variables (e.g., GPA, SAT scores) and that "social isolation was the single most important predictor of student drop out" (p.122). This provides great incentive for college and university administrators to provide outlets for social development and engaging students in these efforts. It is often thought that lifelong friendships are fostered during the college years. Students who enroll in college and are subsequently saddened by being away from family for the first time or students who take time from raising a family to pursue educational goals may be lacking in the social self arena. Homesickness is a common difficulty that new students face and is thus one that many residence hall assistants and housing staff are trained to notice and respond to. This may be worsened if students struggle with building new relationships and friendships. If students feel like they don't fit in at a particular university setting, they are more likely to transfer or drop out of school altogether. Social support from friends, family, and loved ones is absolutely essential in proper adjustment to college and retention rates among students.

The social needs of individuals vary greatly, and it is important for the counselor and student to work together to find the level of support the student needs and a mechanism by which those needs can be met. Cultivation of students' social self requires knowledge about the student population, clubs, and organizations when trying to help students find their niche. The counselor may inquire about students' goals and interests to gain an understanding of their individual personality to guide them toward outlets that suit them better. A freshman female may present with homesickness and the inability to make lasting friendships. The only social outlets that she knows of are sorority rush, and she may state that she is "not into the sorority, Greek life thing" but is interested in music and drama. Helping this student discover the performing arts center on campus or local players club can go a long way in helping her feel like there is a place on campus where she and others like her belong.

Essential Self

The essential self is composed of spiritual, gender, and cultural identity as well as self-care. College is a time of being placed in an environment where, sometimes for the first time in their lives, students are in close living and learning communities with a diverse group of individuals. College can also be a time when students feel more comfortable exploring their sexual and gender identity. The existential question of "Who am I really?" arises for the first time in traditional-aged students. Students returning to school after another career or first-time students who are older may grapple with personal identity questions as they seek to merge old and new concepts of themselves. Struggling with their understanding of their sexual or gender identity and being confused about religion or questioning beliefs about religious issues can cause existential concerns for students.

The use of narrative or feminist therapy techniques may be helpful in working with students facing questions about their gender or sexual identity. Often, they are contending not only with their own thoughts and feelings about who they are but also with negative perceptions or societal constructions of who they are. The narrative therapy approach allows students to write their story as it is happening to them and evokes a sense of control in the situation. Feminist therapy serves to address sociological influences on students' development.

Physical Self

Overindulgence in sedentary video games and remaining deskbound for long periods for studying, coupled with a diet of ramen noodles and fast food, can lead to low levels of physical wellness in college students. The physical self of wellness incorporates proper nutrition and exercise. Students struggling in hard economic times to keep up with rising costs of higher education often scrimp on spending when it comes to food and opt for cheaper and quicker choices to the detriment of a balanced diet. Personal values about the benefit of good nutrition and exercise play a role in whether students pay attention to this area of wellness.

The ease with which unhealthy eating and exercise habits are addressed is relative to students' motivation to engage in healthier habits. Most colleges and universities have mechanisms in place and included in most students' tuition costs that promote healthy behaviors, such as dining halls with organic and wholesome options and recreational centers for group and individual exercise pursuits. Most colleges and universities have organized sports programs from intramurals to Division I in which students can participate to develop better physical wellness. In cases where students' physical wellness is in jeopardy (e.g., with chronic illnesses, obesity, or malnutrition) it is necessary to refer them to the appropriate medical professionals. Students who are under the care of a physician or nutritionist or dietician in conjunction with a counselor can receive the services needed to restore health and move toward wellness.

Benefits of a Wellness Approach

There are many benefits of using a wellness approach with college students. As with any skill, early and comprehensive understanding of wellness practices can lay the foundation for a lifelong commitment to holistic wellness. By demonstrating the importance of wellness via investing time and funding into wellness centers, education, and programming, colleges and universities can communicate to students that their well-being is just as important as their academic instruction. Using a wellness approach with college students serves the purpose of moving beyond the symptom reduction of some therapy techniques to helping them work through presenting concerns, with the added benefit of moving them toward better wellness. In other words, wellness counseling seeks to help students progress beyond problem-focused counseling to learning how to nurture and maintain balance among the areas of wellness. By teaching students the interconnectedness of their wellness to all areas of their lives, we promote development of the whole self, not just the academic side that colleges and universities are expected to focus on. In addition, this holistic focus promotes consideration of the person–environment interaction and how this interaction affects individual well-being or lack thereof.

Contexts are an important component of the IS-WEL model. The contexts for wellness are the systems in which we operate on a daily basis that bolster or hinder our development (Myers & Sweeney, 2005). College counselors have the ability to advocate for students, particularly on the local and institutional levels. The climate of local systems such as family, residence halls, and neighborhoods can be discussed within the counseling dyad. Coconstruction of needed changes to these systems that would increase wellness for all students should be addressed. Institutional changes, such as the inception of a wellness center or wellness services that complement and supplement student health center and counseling services, need to be brought to the attention of university administration. By calling for institutional change, we can demonstrate the importance of college and university environments fostering the development of holistic wellness.

Infusing Wellness Into College Counseling

Because we recognize the increased mental health concerns and decreased levels of wellness students are exhibiting as they enter college, it is necessary to employ innovative methods of working with students. One approach would be for college counselors to find creative ways to increase awareness of wellness and teach students to foster diverse areas of themselves. A preventive approach could best serve students so that low levels of wellness are not exacerbated by the stresses of collegiate life. Because levels of wellness vary greatly among individuals, programming or treatment recommendations at the institutional levels need to be designed to address each area of wellness so that students struggling in different areas can benefit.

The most effective ways of promoting wellness among students would be on an individual level or by responding to trends and behaviors in the student population as a whole. Partnering with high school counselors in providing wellness education programs at the secondary school level will also plant the seeds of holistic wellness that can grow and flourish when students come to college. As student affairs professionals give students outlets for enhancing social and cultural aspects of themselves, faculty provide knowledge to cultivate students' academic selves, and counselors can offer insight into personal development.

One mission of every college and university should be to develop each student as a whole person by espousing the importance of continually assessing and nurturing each area of wellness. Failure to do so at best places all students potentially at risk in terms of adjustment to life circumstances and at worst allows students with significant needs to be overlooked or pathologized. An excellent example is seen with regard to substance abuse, which is discussed following in more detail. Traditional interventions for substance abuse range from punishment to use of strategies such as MI to encourage decisions to change. What the wellness perspective offers in addition is a nonpathologizing avenue to helping students not only choose to change but also *how, where,* and *what* in their lives to choose as a positive focus for that change.

SUBSTANCE ABUSE

Substance abuse continues to affect millions of people worldwide. It is estimated that 22.3 million people in the United States (9% of the population) meet diagnostic criteria for substance abuse and as many as 15.5 million people are dependent on alcohol alone (SAMHSA, 2009). The impact of substance abuse is arguably much greater than statistics reveal given the families, friends, and significant others who are affected directly or indirectly by a loved one's substance use.

The terms *substance abuse* and *addiction* are used here interchangeably to encompass both substance abuse and substance dependence. Substance abuse is differentiated diagnostically from dependence primarily on the criteria of tolerance and withdrawal symptoms experienced by the dependent person (APA, 2000). The psychological aspects of the substance use also distinguish the two in that dependent persons tend to feel a compulsion to use. Substance abuse is typically diagnosed when this has caused problems in various areas of their life but the physical and psychological symptoms of dependence are not prominent (APA, 2000).

Nearly 4 million people attended substance abuse treatment in 2007 (SAMHSA, 2009). Standard substance abuse treatments often involve cognitive, behavioral, cognitive-behavioral, and 12-step programs to address these issues. Newer treatments and frameworks include mindfulness, dialectical behavior therapy, and MI. Addictions treatment can be largely beneficial for its recipients. Of persons receiving treatment, approximately 40% remain abstinent from substances for 1 year, and 15% stay in remission, meaning they may have suffered a relapse but not a return to regular drug use (Fisher & Harrison, 2005).

Substance abuse treatment is not without its problems, however. Half of persons receiving treatment leave before completing 90 days, and 66% quit treatment after 6 months (Fisher & Harrison, 2009). Attrition in addictions treatment is particularly problematic given research suggesting that a minimum of 3 months of treatment is merited to effect substantive change with substance use disorders and that the longer individuals stay in treatment the better chance they have of a positive recovery (NIDA, 2009). The fact also remains that relapse is a common part of the recovery process and that persons often attend treatment several times before remission of their substance use disorder occurs (NIDA, 2009).

Treatment options need to be developed that engage clients and motivate them to stay in treatment longer. The National Institute on Drug Abuse (NIDA, 2009) reported that "to be effective, treatment must address the individual's drug use and any associated medical, psychological, social, vocational, and legal problems" (p. 2). Services thus must address issues of the mind, body, and spirit and not simply abstinence from the substance to better the quality of life of addicted persons. Additionally, interventions that have the potential to improve the long-term abstinence and overall well-being of persons who abuse substances should be used and studied.

Wellness counseling in conjunction with MI is a useful framework for client conceptualization and intervention from which cognitive-behavioral or other evidence-based techniques can be used. Wellness–MI interventions serve as an adjunct to best practices treatment and not a replacement for it. The application of wellness counseling with MI in substance abuse treatment will be described.

Wellness Counseling and Motivational Interviewing With Substance-Abusing Populations

While Wellness–MI counseling is not being presented here as a panacea for the field of substance abuse treatment, it holds potential to enhance current treatment and possibly improve quality of life outcomes in the short- and long-term for the recovering client. The indivisible self model (Myers & Sweeney, 2005c) is discussed as the focal point; however, the wheel of wellness (Witmer, Sweeney, & Myers, 1998) may also be used. The indivisible self model incorporates five components of wellness: coping self (stress management and self-worth); creative self (thinking and emotions); essential self (spiritual, cultural, gender identity); physical self (exercise and nutrition); and social self (friendship and love). These five dimensions are interrelated; hence, if one area of wellness improves, it is likely that additional wellness areas and overall wellness will increase.

Motivational interviewing is a counseling approach or framework developed by Miller and Rollnick (2002) that focuses on nurturing behavior change. Motivational Interviewing (MI) is most often used as a foundation from which other theories and techniques can be used. The four key principles that guide MI are express empathy, develop discrepancy, roll with resistance, and support self-efficacy (Miller & Rollnick, 2002). MI and wellness counseling both use Prochaska and DiClemente's (1984) transtheoretical model, which depicts change as a process rather than an event. Research supports the use of MI in effecting behavior change with substance abuse issues and many other present-ing concerns (Mason, 2009).

During the intake session, a counselor using the wellness–MI approach administers the 5F-WEL (Myers & Sweeney, 2005b) and substance abuse assess-ment questionnaires to clients seeking substance abuse counseling. It is helpful if the clients can complete the 5F-WEL prior to the intake session so that it can be scored and processed prior to the second session. The counselor can inform clients that he or she works from a holistic and wellness perspective, meaning the counselor and client will coconstruct goals that will benefit the mind, body, and spirit of the client. The counselor may introduce the assessments by stating, "I'm going to give you a questionnaire to assess your substance use and to assess your wellness. The substance-use inventory will ask questions about you and your use, and the wellness questionnaire will ask about your well-being in various aspects of your life."

During the first and second session, the assessments and treatment planning continue and are solidified. At this time the counselor provides some brief edu-cation about wellness. The counselor explains the five wellness factors, the sub-dimensions of the five factors, and overall wellness. The following definition of wellness can be presented and discussed: "...a means of living which is oriented toward optimal health and well-being; involves the integration of mind, body, and spirit; requires conscious choices to engage in healthful behaviors; and has a goal of helping you live your life more fully in all areas (social, personal, environ-mental)" (Myers & Sweeney, 2006, p. 3).

The counselor allows clients to ask any questions they might have about well-ness and can ask them to discuss personal examples of one or two of the five fac-tors to ensure they have a basic understanding of wellness. The clinician shows the client a visual copy of the indivisible self model and notes that each of the five factors is drawn equal in size despite the fact that in reality no one has equivalent wellness in all five areas. Clients are then instructed to draw their own "wellness pie" except that they should draw the pie pieces to scale for their corresponding level of wellness. For instance, if one perceives having a strong social self com-pared with other wellness areas, then this piece of the "wellness pie" should be drawn larger than weaker wellness areas.

An alternative to the "wellness pie" activity is having clients depict their per-ceived wellness levels using percentages that roughly add up to 100%. Stronger wellness yields higher percentages, and lower wellness yields lower percentages. Clients might write the following: 10% essential self; 30% coping self; 20% cre-ative self; 30% physical self; and 10% social self. These percentages reveal to client and counselor the comparative relationships among the five wellness factors as perceived by the client. Here, the essential and social selves are weakest, coping and physical selves are the strongest, and the creative self is moderately well.

The counselor then processes the scored 5F-WEL and compares and contrasts with clients' wellness pies. At this point the counselor encourages clients to talk at length about each area of wellness. Specifically, the counselor asks about how their substance use affects each area of wellness and how each wellness area might impact their substance use. This should be done with an MI spirit, using a sense of collaboration, exploration, and curiosity rather than confrontation. The counselor then processes with clients initial treatment goals centered on substance abuse–wellness areas that they would be agreeable to exploring or goal areas in which preparation or action changes will be made.

In one scenario, for example, a client identifies that his cocaine and alcohol use most greatly impacts his social self, which was his self-rated lowest wellness score and one of his lowest on the 5F-WEL. The client explains that most of his friends use substances and that he does not have a close relationship with them. He adds that his use has strained his marriage and his relationships with friends and other family members. If he wishes to focus on this wellness component, he may simply want to prioritize this area as a point of exploration but not wish to address specific changes to his substance use or social self. Incorporating MI, discrepancy can be developed between his value and desire for healthy relationships with family and friends and his drug use.

If the client is in a preparation or action stage, he and the counselor can create a change plan for the social self. The change plan might entail abstaining from drug use, repairing relationships with family and friends, involving family and friends in the counseling process, cutting ties with substance-using friends, and joining Narcotics Anonymous (NA) to obtain a nonusing social support network. The impact of the change plan can be processed. For example, the client notes how quitting drugs has caused changes in the quality of his relationships. He also notices a decrease in social self initially as he heals pieces of the social self damaged by drug use (specifically family and friend relationships or having to develop a new nonusing peer group). These thoughts and feelings can be validated and processed with the counselor by following the MI principle of expressing empathy.

If the client eventually notices improvements in social self, the counselor can inquire if these improvements in social self produced increases in other wellness areas. The client processes, for instance, that with duration of abstinence from cocaine and alcohol he is rebuilding trust with his wife and friends. The client shares that he and a nonusing friend have begun meeting weekly to work out at the gym. Consequently, his physical self has improved as well as his coping self, since getting physically active has increased his confidence and self-worth. Highlighting this "trickle-up" effect of wellness uses the MI principle of supporting self-efficacy and tends to further motivate clients in the change process. The 5F-WEL can be readministered in the future if the client seeks to examine progress, or he can simply redraw his wellness pie or percentages periodically to evaluate treatment progress.

The indivisible self model and MI principles also allow clients to process how levels of wellness impact on their substance use. For example, a marijuana-using client is mandated by her university for substance abuse counseling. The 5F-WEL and wellness pie reveal that her coping and creative selves have the lowest wellness levels. Through processing with the counselor, the client eventually identifies that one reason for her weaker coping self is that she has difficulty managing the stress of school at times and uses marijuana to blow off steam. The client processes how lower levels of coping self wellness have fueled her marijuana use and that if she wishes to abstain from use she will need to address this area. This is another example of the MI principle of developing discrepancy since the client experienced a dissonance between the goal of quitting marijuana and the necessity of strengthening her coping self. If the counselor can elicit client change talk that supports the goal of quitting marijuana, the client will then be motivated to improve her coping self to resolve the internal discrepancy. A change plan for the client's coping self might involve developing stress management skills. The client also processes reasons for a lower creative self and develops insight that she uses at times to cope with difficult emotions. Her change plan can involve exploring underlying issues resulting in these feelings and teaching coping skills using techniques such as cognitive-behavioral therapy.

It should be noted that wellness levels may be misleading because clients' substance use might enable them to perceive higher levels of wellness since substance use can serve as a coping mechanism that gives the illusion of wellness. The counselor can assess and explore this by asking questions such as, "How would your wellness levels be different if you were not using any substances?" or by stating, "Let's talk about what functions the substance serves for you (i.e., the benefits of substance use)." It is important to process the benefits of use to help clients understand any ambivalence about change, what motivates substance use, and benefits that pose barriers to change and to identify wellness areas that need to be addressed to fill the void left by discontinued substance use. The counselor might say to a client who is considering quitting drinking, "We've discussed how you used drinking to meet people (social self) and to expand your creativity while doing your artwork (coping self). If you were to begin exploring quitting alcohol, how might we build wellness in your social and coping selves?"

Benefits of a Wellness–Motivational Interviewing Framework

Wellness counseling with motivational interviewing offers several potential benefits regarding substance abuse treatment. A wellness framework provides a useful lens through which the clinician and client can conceptualize the interactive effects of wellness and substance use. Clients can process how their substance use affects different aspects of their well-being and how their level of wellness impacts their use. Wellness methods also demonstrate to clients that recovery is more than abstaining from a substance. Rather, it is a process of healing on multiple levels. Wellness offers a strength-based perspective in which clients are empowered to identify personal and social resources to support sobriety or harm reduction. This is critical since guilt and shame issues are common among those in recovery.

MI adds critical components to wellness counseling with substance-abusing clients. It serves as a guide for how to work with clients' wellness and recovery goals based on their stage of change. Expressing empathy, the first principle of MI, allows the counselor to validate clients' experiences and to build the counseling relationship so that change can occur. The principles of developing discrepancy and rolling with resistance provide ways for the counselor to work with clients who are ambivalent about addressing their wellness and substance use. Applying these two principles helps clients evaluate the costs and benefits of substance-use and wellness practices. Finally, supporting clients' self-efficacy (principle 4) helps them recognize previous and current successes in attending to their substance use and different areas of wellness. This will increase client confidence, readiness, and motivation for recovery and the wellness lifestyle needed to sustain it.

CASE STUDY: HELPING AN UNDERGRADUATE SUBSTANCE ABUSER THROUGH A WELLNESS APPROACH

We will use a hypothetical client, Adam, to illustrate the application of the wellness model. Adam is a 19-year-old biracial male college student. Adam has been sent to a counselor, as mandated by the dean of students, after being found in violation of the university drug and alcohol policy. Adam informs the counselor that he was caught smoking marijuana in his residence hall. When the counselor inquires about his typical use of marijuana, Adam tells the counselor that he smokes 2–3 days a week to stay "cool and relaxed." When asked about his use of other substances, Adam states that he is "not into anything hard like coke or meth" but that he occasionally goes out drinking alcohol with friends once or twice a month. Adam's description of these outings indicates that he engages in binge drinking (for men, more than five drinks in one sitting) when out with friends. He assures the counselor that "alcohol isn't really my thing" but that friends insist that Adam accompany them out and pressure him into taking shots with them. "After I get a few drinks in me, I feel much more confident and ready to party."

Further discussion with Adam in the intake session reveals that he has a prior diagnosis of attention deficit hyperactivity disorder (ADHD) and has been under the care of a psychiatrist and prescribed medication for the condition. Adam confides in the counselor that he quit taking his medication shortly after the second semester began because he felt the new friendships he had made with the guys on the hall would be in jeopardy if they noticed him taking medication and thought he was "unbalanced." Adam also feels that he had been living with ADHD long enough to deal with it without the medication, which makes him feel slow and devoid of energy. "Plus," Adam states, "it's a lot cooler to be able to chill out and calm down from the jitters with weed instead of a pill."

Traditional Treatment Approach

A traditional approach to Adam's case at an outpatient addictions counseling setting or college counseling center might include a formal assessment, treatment plan including a medication compliance regime, and a cognitive-behavioral therapy (CBT) technique. Depending on the counselor's theoretical orientation, a variation of CBT may be used. REBT, for instance, can be used when the counselor aims to focus on both the cognitions and emotions that are involved when an individual decides to engage in a behavior.

A formal assessment could include any one of several instruments for a specific demographic designed to ascertain problematic drinking or to differentiate between substance abuse and substance dependence, such as the adolescent form of the Substance Abuse Subtle Screening Inventory (SASSI-A2). In a traditional treatment setting, after the results from the assessment have been discussed with the client, the counselor and client may collaboratively decide on the need for treatment and the modality and pace of treatment. In some agencies a more directive approach of the counselor deciding the appropriateness of placing the client in an inpatient, intensive outpatient, or outpatient addictions counseling would be the next step. A treatment plan is set up with varying levels of client input, depending on the agency policies and counselor protocol.

Adam's treatment plan using traditional counseling approaches might include assignment of a diagnostic code/diagnosis, indications for individual or group sessions, and the emphasis or goals of treatment. Here the level of directiveness will again fall on a continuum from coconstruction between client and counselor to the counselor making decisions about how much decrease in substance use should be seen and by what intervals. The treatment plan will state the counselor's theoretical orientation in regards to the client and the presenting concern. A counselor using REBT may work with the client on the thoughts and emotions that lead to problematic drinking in an attempt to uncover faulty thinking patterns and address emotional concerns in an effort to remove stimuli for substance abuse. The counselor may intend to illuminate a pattern for the client so that the thought–emotion–drinking pattern can be broken. Let's take a look at the way a wellness approach would work with the same client.

Wellness–MI Approach With Adam

During the intake session, Adam appeared to be in a stage of contemplation or ambivalence about reducing or quitting his marijuana and alcohol use. Exploring

5F-WEL results allows for the client to explore the costs and benefits of use related to holistic wellness and often provides the opportunity for the counselor to develop discrepancy between the client's use and its effects on various areas of the client's life. Adam self-consciously informed his counselor that his ADHD had made focusing during the assessment challenging. Adam's counselor reassured him that he should not worry about whether he answered the questions correctly or incorrectly. At this point the IS-WEL model was presented, and the wellness factors and definitions were discussed. Emphasis was placed on the interactive nature of the factors and how change in any one area would influence and create changes in other areas—both positive and negative change being possible.

Adam and the counselor briefly reviewed each of the five wellness second-order factors and third-order factors as they came up during the session. Adam was encouraged to consider any factors that might invalidate his scores and to consider whether each score "fit" for him.

Discussion of 5F-WEL Scores

The counselor processed Adam's social self score and third-order factor scores (friendship and love). The counselor inquired if his scores on these dimensions fit with what Adam would rate himself. Adam commented he would have rated his social self as higher because he has many friends. The counselor asked how his substance use impacts his social self and how his social self impacts his substance use. Adam stated that his girlfriend also drinks heavily with him on weekends and that most of his friends drink and use marijuana often. Adam questioned how he would change or quit using substances when most of his friends and his girlfriend use regularly.

The counselor also asked Adam about the effects of his substance use on family relationships. Adam then talked about drinking when he was younger to "piss off my dad," a strict disciplinarian and workaholic who was not around much when Adam was growing up. He also stated that his younger sister is aware of his substance use and worries that it will cause problems for him. When talking about social life at college Adam mentioned that there is little else to do on or off campus besides "partying." Essential self scores were then reviewed. Adam remarked that he was not surprised that these scores were lower. The client asked about the meaning of cultural identity (a third-order factor of the essential self). Once explained by the counselor, Adam noted that he felt out of place at school at times. He commented, "I sometimes don't feel like I fit in. A lot of my friends don't even know that I am biracial. I'll hear them make racist comments, and it makes me feel awkward, but I never say anything." Adam added that drinking and marijuana use helped him relax more in these uncomfortable social situations.

Upon discussing Adam's coping self and relationships between this area and his substance use, he noted that marijuana use helps him manage his stress (stress management). He commented that at the same time his use has contributed to stress in his life such as being mandated for counseling, risk of being kicked out of the residence hall, the constant worry of being drug tested at work, and upsetting his younger sister with whom he has a close relationship.

Processing of the creative self revealed that Adam also enjoyed how marijuana and drinking "mellows him out." He described further that it reduced his anxiety about different stressors in his life and kept him in a better mood (emotions). Adam stated, however, that sometimes marijuana and drinking slowed or blurred his thinking. He noted that he had experienced blackouts from drinking and that sometimes his marijuana use made him "a step slower" when in class or feel as if he was "in a fog" (thinking).

Adam confirmed that his physical self was most neglected in his life. "I used to be a pretty good athlete in high school. It was nice to come to college and take a break from constant sports practices." He reported he had not engaged in any physical activity in several months (exercise) and that he ate fast food daily at the cafeteria (nutrition). Minimal physical activity, in addition to his substance use, had resulted in him often feeling sluggish and gaining 20 pounds since starting college.

Wellness–MI Interventions

At this point, the counselor elected to have the client list the pros and cons of his substance use based on their discussion from the 5F-WEL. Adam commented that he had not realized there were so many negative aspects to his substance use and acknowledged his use may have impacted his overall well-being. He then stated, "I enjoy using, and there are definitely benefits to it that I would have to give up if I quit partying." After brainstorming possible change goals with Adam, he decided that his marijuana use caused the most problems and that quitting for now would be best. He added that he also planned to cut down on the frequency and amount of his drinking but did not feel like he needed to quit drinking altogether.

Adam chose to make a change plan in the social self and physical self. He thought that finding a roommate who did not use marijuana would help him feel less isolated and would provide positive peer support for his new attitude toward drug use (i.e., social self supported with an environmental intervention). He noted he was most motivated to make changes in the physical self more than other areas and that this would help him not use marijuana. "If I start playing some basketball and tennis again and don't quit smoking pot, I won't be able to keep up with anybody because I know I'll be out of breath." The client set a goal to exercise a minimum of 3 days per week.

Adam was encouraged to connect his physical self goal to his social self by setting up times with some nonusing friends who played pick-up basketball each week. Adam chose to address his social self "because it will be most important in keeping me from smoking and probably will be affected the most when I quit." Adam decided to tell his girlfriend about his quitting goal and reported that she would be supportive of him. Adam commented, "She might cut down on her own drinking just to help me out." Adam mentioned he would also tell his sister, who would be supportive and excited about him quitting marijuana. Further, Adam's goals had perceived benefits regarding his parents: "Quitting will definitely get them off my back. Since getting in trouble, they interrogate me all the time."

Adam established plans to spend more time with nonusing friends and also to continue to spend some time with his using friends, although he planned to inform them that he was no longer using marijuana (social self). Adam processed that if he relapsed on marijuana or continued to binge drink with his friends he may need to further alter time spent with using friends.

Follow-Up Sessions

In later sessions, the counselor processed with Adam how other areas of his wellness had improved in addition to his goal areas of abstaining from marijuana, reducing drinking, and increasing his social self and physical self. The counselor reinforced Adam's progress by readministering the 5F-WEL, which revealed increases in social self, physical self, and several other second- and third-order factors. The counselor continued to discuss challenges to the aforementioned goals with Adam throughout the counseling process. Adam eventually sought to talk about other areas of wellness and to identify additional goal areas as they related to his substance-use goals and well-being.

Case Conclusion

Using a holistic wellness approach with a substance-abusing client offers an alternative to traditional interventions. Rather than operating from a deficit model, the wellness model allows clients to view their presenting problem from the perspective of how it contributes to or detracts from holistic health, thus avoiding pathologizing, criticizing, or blaming in regard to the behavior. Clients conceptualized and approached through this humanistic lens are empowered for self-change through understanding of the wellness model combined with MI to help them clarify the effects of their current behavior, anticipate the consequences of positive change, and make informed decisions to create and sustain positive lifestyle change.

REFERENCES

Adler, A. (1954/1927). *Understanding human nature.* New York: Fawcett.
American Counseling Association. (ACA). (2005). *Code of ethics and standards of practice.* Alexandria, VA: Author.
American Psychiatric Association. (APA). (2000). *Diagnostic and statistical manual of mental disorders* (4th ed., text rev.). Washington, DC: Author.

American School Counselor Association. (ASCA). (2003). *The ASCA national model: A framework for school counseling programs.* Alexandria, VA: Author.

Ansbacher, H. L., & Ansbacher, R. R. (Eds.). (1967). *The individual psychology of Alfred Adler.* New York: Harper & Row.

Archer, J., Probert, B. S., & Gage, L. (1987). College students' attitudes toward wellness. *Journal of College Student Personnel, 28,* 311–317.

Chandler, C. K., Holden, J., & Kolander, C. (1992). Counseling for spiritual wellness: Theory and practice. *Journal of Counseling and Development, 71,* 168–175.

Chang, C. Y., & Myers, J. E. (2003). Cultural adaptation of the Wellness Evaluation of Lifestyle (WEL): An assessment challenge. *Measurement and Evaluation in Counseling and Development, 35*(4), 239–250.

Choate, L. H., & Smith, S. L. (2003). Enhancing development in 1st-year college student success courses: A holistic approach. *Journal of Humanistic Counseling, Education, and Development, 42,* 178–193.

Connolly, K. M., & Myers, J. E. (2003). Wellness and mattering: The role of holistic factors in job satisfaction. *Journal of Employment Counseling, 40,* 152–160.

Degges-White, S, & Myers, J. E. (2006). Transitions, wellness, and life satisfaction: Implications for counseling midlife women. *Journal of Mental Health Counseling, 28* (2), 133–150.

Degges-White, S. E., & Myers, J. E. (in press). Midlife lesbians and bisexual women: Implications for mental health practitioners. *AGLBIC Journal.*

Degges-White, S. E., Myers, J. E., Adelman, J. U., & Pastoor, D. D. (2003). Examining counseling needs of headache patients: An exploratory study of wellness and perceived stress. *Journal of Mental Health Counseling, 25,* 271–290.

Derzon, J. (2006). How effective are school-based violence prevention programs in preventing and reducing violence and other antisocial behaviors? In S. R. Jimerson & M. Furlong (Eds.), *Handbook of school violence and school safety: From research to practice* (pp. 429–442). Mahwah, NJ: Lawrence Erlbaum Associates.

Dew, B. J., Myers, J. E., & Wightman, L. F. (2006). Wellness in adult gay males: Examining the impact of internalized homophobia, self-disclosure, and self-disclosure to parents. *Journal of LGBT Issues in Counseling, 1*(1), 23–40.

Dogan, T., Yıldırım, I., & Myers, J. E. Adaptation of the Wellness Evaluation of Lifestyle Scale to Turkish. Manuscript submitted for review.

Dunn, H. (1967). *High level wellness.* Bel Air, CA: R. W. Beatty.

Fisher, G. L., & Harrison, T. C. (2005). *Substance abuse: Information for school counselors, social workers, therapists, and counselors* (3rd ed.). Boston, MA: Pearson.

Fukuhara, M. (2006). Japanese adaptation of the 5F-Wel. Manuscript in progress.

Garrett, M. T., & Myers, J. E. (1996). The rule of opposites: A paradigm for counseling Native Americans. *Journal of Multicultural Counseling & Development, 24,* 89–104.

Gerstein, L. H. (2006). Counseling psychology's commitment to strengths: Rhetoric or reality? *Counseling Psychologist, 34*(2), 276–292.

Gibson, D., & Myers, J. E. (2006). Perceived stress, wellness, and mattering: A profile of first-year Citadel cadets. *Journal of College Student Development, 47,* 647–660.

Gill, C., Moorhead, H. H., & Myers, J. E. The impact of forgiveness on the wellness of counseling students. Manuscript in progress.

Ginter, E. J. (2005). Wellness research: An agenda for the future. In J. E. Myers & T. J. Sweeney (Eds.), *Counseling for wellness: Theory, research, and practice* (pp. 151–165). Alexandria, VA: American Counseling Association.

Gustainiene, L., & Pranckeviciene, A.. (2006). Adaptation of the Five Factor Wellness Inventory in Lithuanian. Manuscript in progress.

Hermon, D. A., & Hazler, R. J. (1999). Adherence to a wellness model and perceptions of psychological well-being. *Journal of Counseling & Development, 77,* 339–343.

Hettler, W. (1984). Wellness: Encouraging a lifetime pursuit of excellence. *Health Values: Achieving High Level Wellness, 8,* 13–17.

Hill, N. R. (2004). The challenges experienced by pretenured faculty members in counselor education: A wellness perspective. *Counselor Education and Supervision, 44,* 135–146.

Holcomb-McCoy, C. (2005). Wellness and children: Research implications. In J. E. Myers & T. J. Sweeney (Eds.), *Counseling for wellness: Theory, research, and practice* (pp. 59–66). Alexandria, VA: American Counseling Association.

Hong, C. Y. (2006). Korean adaptation of the 5F-WEL. Manuscript in progress.

Ivers, N., & Myers, J. E. (2006). Spanish adaptation of the Five Factor Wellness Inventory, Elementary School Version. Manuscript in progress.

Jones, A. J. (1934). *Principles of guidance* (2nd ed.). New York: McGraw-Hill.

Korkut, F., & Myers, J. E. (2006). Wellness of middle school students in Turkey: Cultural adaptation of the 5f-WEL-K. Manuscript in progress.

Larson, J. S. (1999). The conceptualization of health. *Medical Care Research and Review, 56,* 123–136.

Lau, P., Yuen, M., Chan, M., & Myers, J. E. (2006). Adaptation of the Five Factor Wellness Inventory in Chinese. Manuscript in progress.

Lee, C. C. (2005). Ethnicity and wellness. In J. E. Myers & T. J. Sweeney (Eds.), *Counseling for wellness: Theory, research, and* practice (pp. 105–115). Alexandria, VA: American Counseling Association.

Mahoney, M. J. (1997). Psychotherapists' personal problems and self-care patterns. *Professional Psychology: Research and Practice, 28*(1), 14–16.

Makinson, L., & Myers, J. E. (2003). Wellness: An alternative paradigm for violence prevention. *Journal of Humanistic Counseling, Education and Development, 42,* 165–177.

Mason, M. J. (2009). Rogers redux: Relevance and outcomes of Motivational Interviewing across behavioral problems. *Journal of Counseling and Development, 87*(3), 357–362.

Miller, W. R., & Rollnick, S. (2002). *Motivational interviewing: Preparing people for change* (2nd ed.). New York: Guilford Press.

Moorhead, H. H., Green, J., McQuistian, R., & Ozimek, B. (2006). Asperger's in a new light: A case-study in conceptualizing Asperger's within a wellness paradigm. Manuscript submitted for review.

Myers, J. E. (1992). Wellness, prevention, development: The cornerstone of the profession. *Journal of Counseling and Development, 71*(2), 136–139.

Myers, J. E., & Bechtel, A. (2004). Stress, wellness, and mattering among cadets at West Point: Factors affecting a fit and healthy force. *Military Medicine, 169*(6), 475–483.

Myers, J. E., Cervera, V., Wilse, J., & Henson, R. (2006). Wellness in the Philippines and the U.S.: A cross-cultural comparison. Manuscript in progress.

Myers, J. E., & Degges-White, S. E. (2006). Aging well in an upscale retirement community: The relationships among perceived stress, mattering, and wellness. Manuscript submitted for review.

Myers, J. E., Madathil, J., & Tingle, L. R. (2005). Marriage satisfaction and wellness in India and the United States: A preliminary comparison of arranged marriages and marriages of choice. *Journal of Counseling & Development, 83*(2), 183–190.

Myers, J. E., & Mobley, K. A. (2004). Wellness of undergraduates: Comparisons of traditional and nontraditional students. *Journal of College Counseling, 7,* 40–49.

Myers, J. E., Mobley, K., & Booth, C. S. (2003). Wellness of counseling students: Practicing what we preach. *Counselor Education & Supervision, 42*(4), 264–274.

Myers, J. E., & Sweeney, T. J. (2005a). *Counseling for wellness: Theory, research, and practice.* Alexandria, VA: American Counseling Association.

Myers, J. E., & Sweeney, T. J. (2005b). The indivisible self: An evidence-based model of wellness. *Journal of Individual Psychology, 61*(3), 234–245.

Myers, J. E., & Sweeney, T. J. (2005c). *Manual for the five factor wellness inventory, elementary.* Palo Alto, CA: Mindgarden, Inc.

Myers, J. E., & Sweeney, T. J. (2005d). *The five factor wellness inventory, adult (5F-WEL-A).* Palo Alto, CA: Mindgarden, Inc.

Myers, J. E., & Sweeney, T. J. (2005e). *The five factor wellness inventory, elementary (5F-WEL-E).* Palo Alto, CA: Mindgarden, Inc.

Myers, J. E., & Sweeney, T. J. (2005f). *The five factor wellness inventory, middle school (5F-WEL-T).* Palo Alto, CA: Mindgarden, Inc.

Myers, J. E., & Sweeney, T. J. (2008). Wellness counseling: The evidence base for practice. *Journal of Counseling & Development, 86,* 482–493.

Myers, J. E., Sweeney, T. J., & Witmer, J. M. (1998). *The wellness evaluation of lifestyle.* Palo Alto, CA: Mindgarden, Inc.

Myers, J. E., Sweeney, T. J., & Witmer, J. M. (2000). The wheel of wellness counseling for wellness: A holistic model for treatment planning. *Journal of Counseling and Development, 78*(3), 251–266.

National Center for Education Statistics. (2009). Retrieved April 5, 2011 from http://nces.ed.gov/

National Institute on Drug Abuse (2009). *Principles of effective treatment: A research based guide* (2nd ed.). Retrieved from http://www.drugabuse.gov/PDF/PODAT/PODAT.pdf

Osborn, C. O. (2005). Research on college student wellness. In J. E. Myers & T. J. Sweeney (Eds.), *Counseling for wellness: Theory, research, and practice* (pp. 77–88). Alexandria, VA: American Counseling Association.

Powers, A., Myers, J. E., Tingle, L., & Powers, J. (2004). Wellness, perceived stress, mattering, and marital satisfaction among medical residents and their spouses: Implications for education and counseling. *Family Journal, 12,* 26–36.

Prochaska, J. O., & DiClemente, C. C. (1984). *The transtheoretical approach: Towards a systematic eclectic framework.* Homewood, IL: Dow Jones Irwin.

Rayle, A. D. (2006). Spanish adaptation of the 5F-Wel. Manuscript in progress.

Schneider Institute for Health Policy. (2001). Retrieved April 5, 2011 from http://sihp.brandeis.edu

Sexton, T. (2001). Evidence-based counseling intervention programs: Practicing "best practices." In D. C. Locke, J. E. Myers, & E. H. Herr (Eds.), *The handbook of counseling* (pp. 499–512). Thousand Oaks, CA: Sage Publications.

Shurts, W. M., & Myers, J. E. (2006). The relationships among liking, love, and wellness: Implications for college student romances. Manuscript submitted for publication.

Sinclair, S. L., & Myers, J. E. (2004). The relationship between objectified body consciousness and wellness in a group of college women. *Journal of College Counseling, 7,* 150–161.

Smith, S. L., Myers, J. E., & Hensley, L. G. (2002). Putting more life into life career courses: The benefits of a holistic wellness model. *Journal of College Counseling, 5,* 90–95.

Spurgeon, S. L., & Myers, J. E. (2010). African American males: Relationships among racial identity, college type, and wellness. *Journal of Black Studies, 40*(2), 527–543.

Substance Abuse and Mental Health Services Administration. (2009). Results from the 2008 National Survey on Drug Use and Health: National Findings (Office of Applied Studies, NSDUH Series H-36, HHS Publication No. SMA 09-4434). Rockville, MD.

Swartz-Kulstad, J. L., & Martin, W. E. (1999). The impact of culture and context on psychosocial adaptation: The cultural and contextual guide process. *Journal of Counseling and Development, 77*(3), 281–293.

Sweeney, T. J. (1995). Accreditation, credentialing, professionalization: The role of specialties. *Journal of Counseling and Development, 74,* 117–125.

Sweeney, T. J. (1998). *Adlerian counseling: A practitioners approach* (4th ed.). Philadelphia, PA: Taylor & Francis.

Sweeney, T. J. (2001). Counseling: Historical origins and philosophical roots. In D. C. Locke, J. E. Myers, & E. L. Herr (Eds.), *The handbook of counseling* (pp. 3–26). Thousand Oaks, CA: Sage.

Sweeney, T. J., & Witmer, J. M. (1991). Beyond social interest: Striving toward optimum health and wellness. *Individual Psychology, 47,* 527–540.

Tanigoshi, H., Kontos, A. P., & Remley Jr., T. P. (2008). The effectiveness of individual wellness counseling on the wellness of law enforcement officers. *Journal of Counseling & Development, 86,* 64–74.

Tatar, M., & Myers, J. E. (2010). Wellness of children in Israel and the United States: A preliminary examination of culture and well-being. *Counseling Psychology Quarterly, 23*(1), 17–33.

Travis, J. W., & Ryan, R. (1988). *The wellness workbook* (2d ed.). Berkeley, CA: Ten Speed Press.

Villalba, J., & Myers, J. E. (2006). The effectiveness of wellness-based classroom guidance in elementary school settings. Manuscript submitted for review.

Witmer, J. M., Sweeney, T. J., & Myers, J. E. (1998). *The wheel of wellness.* Greensboro, NC: Authors.

Witmer, J. M., & Sweeney, T. J. (1992). A holistic model for wellness and prevention over the lifespan. *Journal of Counseling and Development, 71,* 140–148.

Wester, K., Trepal, H., & Myers, J. E. (2006). Wellness of counselor educators: Do we practice what we preach? Manuscript submitted for review.

World Health Organization. (WHO). (1958). *Constitution of the World Health Organization, Annex.* Geneva, Switzerland: Author.

World Health Organization. (1958). *Constitution of the World Health Organization, Annex.* Geneva, Switzerland: Author. (change from 1964 to this citation)

3

Humanism and Multiculturalism

Michael D'Andrea and Judy Daniels

Humanism and multiculturalism represent two complementary theoretical forces that have profoundly impacted the counseling profession over the past several decades. Despite the tremendous impact these theoretical forces have had on the counseling profession, it is surprising to note the dearth of publications that describe how the complementary aspects of these important perspectives have impacted the field. Consequently, when the editors of this book invited us to write a chapter that focuses on issues related to humanism and multiculturalism, we quickly accepted the opportunity to do so.

Our enthusiasm was largely based on the recognition that writing such a chapter represented an opportunity to expand the limited knowledge base related to the complementary nature of humanism and multiculturalism. From a more practical perspective, we were also excited to have a chance to describe some of the practical ways that counselor educators and practitioners can use information presented in this chapter to foster their personal and professional development. Thus, the two goals of this chapter are to expand counselors' understanding of (1) how humanism and multicultural counseling principles complement one another and (2) how counselors can concretely use humanistic principles to foster their own personal and professional development.

To achieve these chapter goals, we first describe some of the specific theoretical principles shared by humanistic and multicultural counseling perspectives. Particular attention is directed to five humanistic principles that are shared with the multicultural counseling theoretical perspective: (1) integrity; (2) self-actualization; (3) holism; (4) nonreductionism; and (5) irreducibility. We direct particular attention to the principles of nonreduction and irreducibility discussed in Chapter 1. Our purpose in doing so is to provide a foundation to elaborate on the importance of counselors more fully understanding these principles as they relate to the multidimensional nature of human development.

To extend counselors' understanding in these areas, we discuss a relatively new counseling theory that illuminates a number of factors counselors are encouraged to keep in mind when implementing humanistic and multicultural counseling approaches anchored in the concepts of holism and irreducibility. Also, in an effort to move the discussion in this chapter from theoretical concepts to practical action, we present a short case study that reflects some of the ways that humanistic and multicultural counseling concepts were used to address the concerns of a 70-year-old African American client from a holistic perspective.

Finally, an activity is presented at the end of the chapter to assist the reader in acquiring new skills that are useful when implementing the humanistic and multicultural concepts in counseling practice. Like the case study, this activity is designed to help counselors move beyond just thinking about theoretical concepts to learning how the information related to the multidimensional, holistic, and irreducible nature of human development can be used in practical terms to stimulate one's personal and professional development.

THEORETICAL PRINCIPLES SHARED BY HUMANISTIC AND MULTICULTURAL COUNSELING PERSPECTIVES

Humanistic and multicultural counseling advocates agree with and strive to implement several fundamental theoretical principles in their work. The following section describes a number of these shared and complementary principles. This includes a discussion of the concepts of integrity, self-actualization, irreducibility, and holism from both humanistic and multicultural perspectives of counseling.

The Principle of Integrity

The principle of integrity has special meaning within a humanistic counseling and psychology perspective. This concept underscores the importance of reflecting critically on (1) how one's own belief system, worldview, and needs impact the work that a person does in the field and (2) the values underlying mainstream counseling and psychotherapy interventions and their impact on clients from culturally diverse groups and backgrounds (Association for Humanistic Psychology, 1009).

From its onset, the multicultural counseling movement has strongly complemented the humanistic principle of integrity in two fundamental ways. First, multicultural theorists have consistently emphasized that it is vital for counselors to reflect critically on the potential impact that their own cultural worldviews, preferences, values, and biases have in counseling situations (Duran, 2006; Sue & Sue, 2008). In doing so, multicultural advocates have been particularly assertive in discussing the ineffective and even harmful outcomes that may ensue when counselors operate from a set of personal preferences, beliefs, values, needs, and biases that conflict with the worldviews held by persons in cultural groups that are different from their group-referenced identity (Parham, 2002; Sue & Sue, 2008).

Second, multicultural counseling advocates have and continue to articulate the ways that traditional counseling theories are embedded within Western perspectives of mental health and help-seeking behaviors and how these culturally biased perspectives differ from the way many clients in different cultural, ethnic, and racial groups construct meaning of such concepts (Ivey, D'Andrea, Ivey, & Simek-Morgan, 2007). By serving as critical purveyors of mainstream counseling theories in these complementary ways, humanistic and multicultural counselors serve as the conscience of the counseling profession.

The Self-Actualization Principle

The need for self-actualization is one of the best known principles of humanistic counseling. Abraham Maslow (1970) not only is responsible for increasing mental health practitioners' understanding of the important role this need plays in healthy human development but also helped to popularize this concept among the general public. Essentially, the self-actualization principle is grounded in the belief that everyone is born with an innate evolutionary propensity to develop as a result of realizing one's unique and untapped human potentials (D'Andrea, 1988). Humanistic counselors intentionally strive to establish the sort of supportive, accepting, and empathic helping relationship that nurtures clients' motivation to realize new aspects of their human potential in the counseling process.

From a humanistic perspective, it is believed that all people in all cultures are born with an innate propensity to actualize new aspects of their human potential. While this inborn need for self-actualization is a universal characteristic of all humanity, the manner in which individuals strive to actualize their potentials and the types of potentials realized differ depending on their cultural contexts.

Prior to the emergence of the multicultural counseling movement in the late 1960s, counselor educators and practitioners directed little attention to the impact cultural factors have on human development in general and self-actualization processes in particular. However, the onset of the multicultural counseling movement has done much to extend the humanistic perspective by increasing counselors' knowledge of the impact that cultural and related factors have on people's actualizing behaviors.

Culturally competent counselors recognize that individuals' actualizing behaviors are significantly affected by the worldview, values, beliefs, and constructions of appropriate behavior that characterize the culture within which people are situated and identify. For instance, individuals whose personal identity is strongly impacted by collectivistic cultural values will predictably manifest actualizing behaviors that differ from persons who are raised in and identify with a highly individualistic culture (Parham & Parham, 2002). The concepts of holism and irreducibility are closely related to self-actualization and complementary of the multicultural theoretical perspective of counseling.

The Principles of Holism and Irreducibility

The term *holism* comes from the Greek root *holos,* which means the "whole." As used in the humanistic tradition, the concept of *holism* refers to the importance of viewing individuals as "whole" beings operating as a gestalt of physical–biological, psychological–mental, and social–emotional factors and reactions to life experiences. By placing the principles of self-actualization and holism at its core, the humanistic counseling movement gained tremendous popularity with many persons in both the professional and general publics during the 1950s and 1960s. This perspective provided a particularly welcomed alternative to another theoretical force, behaviorism, which was gaining much popularity in the fields of counseling and psychology at the time. Advocates of humanism not only relied on the concept of holism when criticizing behaviorists for focusing on a single aspect of their clients' lives (e.g., clients' behavioral responses to environmental reinforcements) but also popularized the concept of irreducibility in the process.

As noted earlier in this book, the principle of irreducibility is grounded in the belief that a person is more than any one of the three previously mentioned components (i.e., physical–biological, psychological–mental, and social–emotional). Consequently, the humanistic perspective of counseling emphasizes that counselors need to avoid viewing clients' problems through the lens of any one of the aforementioned components alone and intentionally work to maintain a more complex and holistic view of the human beings with whom they are working. This perspective helps to ground counselors in an awareness of three key aspects of humanism: (1) the multidimensional nature of human development; (2) the intimate interconnections that exist in people's physical–biological, psychological–mental, and social–emotional reactions to life experiences; and (3) the irreducibility of these three dimensions of clients' lives and experiences.

Multiculturalism not only complements these concepts but also has helped many counselors to make a quantum leap in their thinking about the principles of holism and irreducibility over the past 40 years. This leap has been facilitated by the scholarly contributions of multicultural theorists and researchers who have discussed issues related to the irreducible and holistic nature of human development. Such contributions extended the traditional way counselors were trained to think about the irreducible and holistic nature of human development by describing how clients' group referenced identities and contexts from which they operate relate to the aforementioned humanistic principles.

A case study is presented to illuminate the importance of using a humanistic-multicultural counseling approach that is driven by the principles of self-actualization, integrity, and holism. After you have read this case study and the brief discussion that accompanies it, you will be asked to identify how the counselor's comments and the client's responses help to generate information related to the physical–biological, psychological–mental, and social–emotional aspects of this 70-year-old African American client's depression and anger following the unexpected death of his wife, Sarah.

CASE STUDY

Roy is a 70-year-old African American retired male, who was referred to counseling by his grown son and daughter. According to his son and daughter, Roy has changed significantly as a result of the unexpected death of his wife of 49 years. Since the death of his wife, Roy has reportedly shifted from manifesting serious depression (by spontaneously crying around the house where he was temporarily living with his grown son and his family) to unpredictable outbursts of heightened anger. As reported by Roy's son and daughter, this anger was expressed with "loud yelling and cursing over the littlest things, which is just not like our father at all."

Roy was very resistant to participate in counseling. However, based on his comments in the first therapy session, he "knew that I was not right and needed to do something about it." His grief over the unexpected loss of his wife was evident in the first meeting he had with the therapist as he shifted from openly weeping to expressing anger at the responses the counselor had to his comments.

Roy continued in counseling for 10 sessions. Although his grief over the loss of his wife continues, his spontaneous outbursts of crying were greatly reduced. Roy's son and daughter also reported that his uncontrollable outbursts of anger had almost completely subsided. As Roy's daughter noted, "My dad is more like his old self. Although he will continue to be sad about losing Mom, I am much more hopeful that he will lead a more satisfying and balanced life than before he came to therapy."

In his last meeting with his therapist, Roy stated, "I know I will always be grieving over Sarah's death, but I have a different outlook on that now. I have gained some acceptance of this situation that, quite frankly, I did not think I could feel. I also know that I have things and people to live for and am glad I understand that more clearly now than when I first came to counseling."

DISCUSSION

Multicultural counseling theorists have noted that many African American clients prefer more directive counseling interventions than a completely nondirective, person-centered approach to helping (Ivey et al., 2007). Consequently, while the counselor intentionally worked to build a positive relationship with this client by communicating genuine empathy early in the helping setting, the practitioner used a more directive approach associated with the Motivational Interviewing (MI) theory (Miller & Rollnick, 2002) later in the helping process. The following interactions demonstrate how the counselor communicated his empathic understanding of Roy's situation.

Roy: I am so lost without my wife. I know I have to go on with my life, but it is so hard to even get out of bed in the morning. Most days I just want to stay there and not bother with things. Then when I do get up, I am frustrated by many little things that happen around me. I want to continue leading a life that is worth living, but it is so hard without her. I just don't know if I can adjust to having her gone. It feels hopeless a lot of the time.

Therapist: I can feel how hard that is for you. Your wife was such an important part of your life for so long that you feel lost without her. You know that it is important to find ways to go on with your life, but it often feels like you are in a hopeless situation without her.

Roy: Yes, that's it. I do want to go on with my life, but it does really seem hopeless a lot of the time. I frequently want to just do nothing but sit around and think of her, and when I do I get stuck not doing other things that would be good for me to do.

DISCUSSION

The effective manner in which the counselor communicated an empathic understanding of Roy's feelings encouraged Roy to talk more about his reactions to the unexpected loss of his wife. This resulted in Roy providing additional information that helped the humanistic-multicultural practitioner more fully understand the impact of the unexpected death of this client's wife on various aspects of his physical–biological, psychological–mental, and social–emotional life.

The counselor uses a more directive approach later in the helping process with Roy, which is consistent with multicultural counseling theorists who discuss how existential-humanistic theories can be used effectively with African American clients (Ivey et al., 2007; Vontress, Johnson, & Epp, 1999).

Therapist: I understand you are torn between feeling as if you really do not want to do anything and figuring out what changes you can make to improve the way you are feeling and how you get along with other people.

Roy: Yeah, that's right. Most of the time I find myself not wanting to do anything because without Sarah it all seems so pointless.

Therapist: When you think of things you could do to feel better about yourself and others, what ideas do you come up with.

Roy: Well, I often think about going to some of the activities our church sponsors. Sarah and I were very involved in our church community, and I just can't muster the energy to get back with them since she died. And I do like the tutoring work I did at the elementary school that is close to my son's house. But I just don't know....

Therapist: What sort of church activities do you enjoy the most?

Roy: Well, I really like working with the Church Planning Committee. This committee can really set an agenda for projects the church will get involved with in the community. I also like to help teach children in our Sunday school classes. When I started working with the Sunday School Education Program I didn't do much. But the regular teacher thought I could be helpful in planning lessons and helping her coteach the course with the younger children in our church community. To be honest with you, I think it is partly because she thinks I can be more patient with the kids than she is.

Therapist: It sounds like you give to your church in a number of ways. What do you get out of participating in your church in these ways?

Roy: Well, I feel like I am a contributor when I help in planning community events, and I feel good about working with the kids.

Therapist: Feel good? Why does that make you feel good?

Roy: Because I am doing something worthwhile that helps other people and makes our church community stronger. Those are things I value.

Therapist: And in addition to things you have done with your church community, what other things could you do that would be helpful in dealing with your thoughts and feelings about losing Sarah?

Roy: I don't think anything could replace Sarah. And I am not sure I want to do much of anything.

Therapist: I didn't mean ideas you might have to "replace" Sarah. No one or no activity could replace her. I do want to learn more about other things you think would be helpful in dealing with your thoughts and feelings about losing Sarah. After we have taken time to look at new ways of dealing with your situation, you may decide that there is nothing you are going to do to make changes in the way you lead your life presently. I respect the fact that you are in charge of whatever decision you eventually make. In addition to respecting your decision, my job is to help you look at new ideas to deal with your life challenges at this point in time and see what if any idea is something you might decide to try out to cope with the loss of Sarah in different ways.

Roy: I wish I knew what would be helpful. What kinds of things are helpful for someone in my situation?

Therapist: Well, we are learning a great deal about the types of things that help people find new satisfaction in life after experiencing a serious loss that leads a person to feel depressed and frustrated with life in general like yourself. Many people in the field agree that it is important to take a holistic approach in these situations. This includes helping clients learn about the benefits of making sure their daily diets support psychological wellness, learning new stress management and relaxation techniques, talking about new physical activities and exercises you could do that would stimulate positive changes in how your brain functions, and exploring positive activities you may be willing to get involved in, much like we were doing when we were talking about your interest in your church community and the tutoring program at the elementary school that is near your son's house. It is clear that people benefit the most from doing a combination of these four strategies instead of agreeing to do just one of them.

Roy: All of those things sound very practical and things I could do. Tell me more about this holistic approach you mentioned.

Discussion

This brief counselor–client interaction demonstrates ways that counselors can address issues related to the humanistic principles of self-actualization, integrity, irreducibility, and holism in multicultural helping settings. In these interactions, one can see how the counselor works in an empathic manner to help Roy explore possible interests that underlie his ability for self-actualization during a very difficult time in his life. The counselor also uses a directive approach by confirming his respect for whatever decision Roy makes in terms of dealing with the intense grief over the death of his wife.

As recommended by numerous multicultural counseling theorists (Ivey et al., 2007; Parham, 2002), the counselor proceeds to use an educational strategy by discussing what it means to use a holistic approach in counseling. Using this strategy in ways that are culturally congruent with Roy, the counselor is able to pique his interest in exploring new ways that he might be able to more effectively cope with his situation.

To more fully understand how this case study complements issues related to a humanistic-multicultural approach to helping, we encourage you to review the counselor–client interactions with the following two questions in mind:

1. How did the counselor's approach in the counseling session with Roy help the humanistic-multicultural practitioner to more fully understand the impact of the unexpected death of his wife on various aspects of Roy's physical/biological, psychological/mental, and social/emotional life?
2. In what ways did the counselor's approach increase Roy's interest in and possible motivation to explore new coping strategies that would be helpful in having this client realize new dimensions of his potential for self-actualization?

EXPANDING THE SCOPE OF UNDERSTANDING PEOPLE'S HOLISTIC AND IRREDUCIBLE NATURE

The genesis of the multicultural counseling movement primarily focused on the important ways that clients' and counselors' racial-ethnic backgrounds, experiences, and identities affect their personal lives and professional practices. Later, in the 1980s and 1990s, multicultural advocates helped the counseling profession explore new factors that multicultural advocates view as important cultural and related considerations that complement and extend traditional thinking about the holistic and irreducible nature of human development and counseling. These efforts resulted in increasing advocacy for the inclusion of issues related to clients' gender, affectional orientation, and religious and spiritual identities when conceptualizing the counseling process and particularly clients' strengths, needs, and problem-solving strategies. Presently, the multicultural counseling movement is directing increasing attention to the ways that all of these factors and other relevant variables interface with one another to shape people's lives in general and the content, process, and outcomes of counseling in particular (Pope-Davis, & Coleman, 2001; D'Andrea, Daniels, & Noonan, 2003).

In our own work we have developed and field tested a new model of counseling that builds on the principles of humanism and multiculturalism discussed in this chapter. The name of this model is RESPECTFUL counseling. The following description of this model is provided as a kind of theoretical roadmap for counselors interested in learning more about the specific factors that multiculturalists have indicated are important to keep in mind when implementing counseling interventions grounded in humanistic principles including but not limited to holism and irreducibility.

The RESPECTFUL Counseling Model

The RESPECTFUL counseling framework (Cartwright & D'Andrea, 2004; D'Andrea & Daniels, 2001) stresses the importance of incorporating a holistic model of human diversity into the work of counselor educators and practitioners. This theoretical framework:

1. Is comprised of 10 factors that represent vital considerations to keep in mind when working with persons from a humanistic-multicultural counseling perspective
2. Emphasizes the importance of incorporating these factors into counseling interventions that are grounded in the humanistic principles of holism
3. Stresses the need for counselors to exhibit a high level of respect with their clients by implementing the principle of irreducibility and thereby not reducing their conceptualization of their clients' situations to one or even a few of the factors that comprise the RESPECTFUL counseling model. Rather, counselors are urged to keep in mind three points:
   a. Assessing how all of the factors in the RESPECTFUL model impact their clients' development, strengths, and challenges
   b. Reflecting on how all of the factors in this model affect the counselor's development, strengths, and limitations in multicultural counseling situations
   c. How all of these factors may influence the counseling process with clients from diverse groups and backgrounds

It is important to point out that the components contained in the RESPECTFUL counseling model do not represent an exhaustive listing of all the factors that impact human development from a humanistic-multicultural perspective. Rather, the factors that comprise this framework constitute a detailed list of variables multicultural and humanistic counseling theorists and researchers have noted as being important considerations when implementing helping strategies that are anchored in the principles of holism and irreducibility. These variables include a person's:

R—Religious and spiritual identity
E—Economic class background
S—Sexual identity
P—Psychological maturity
E—Ethnic-racial identity
C—Chronological challenges and identity
T—Traumatic experiences and other threats to one's well-being
F—Family identity and history
U—Unique physical characteristics
L—Language preference and location of residence

Each of these factors not only influences the manner that people learn to view themselves and others but also frequently affects the way clients and counselors construct meaning of the different strengths, challenges, and problems individuals present in counseling. It is important to point out that the variables included in the RESPECTFUL counseling do not operate in isolation from one another but rather represent an irreducible and holistic set of variables that impact clients' and counselors' development, beliefs, and perceptions in many ways. By briefly describing these factors below, we hope to (1) increase your awareness of the ways that these variables might influence your clients' and your own development and (2) underscore the importance for counselors to think in comprehensive and holistic terms when working with clients from diverse groups.

Religious and Spiritual Identity

The first component in the RESPECTFUL model focuses on the manner in which individuals personally identify with established religions or hold beliefs about extraordinary experiences that go beyond the boundaries of what is thought to be the strictly objective, empirically perceived world that characterizes Western, modern, psychological thought (D'Andrea & Daniels, 2001). Kelly (1995) notes that the terms *religion* and *spirituality* are grounded in an affirmation of transcendental experiences typically manifested in religious forms extending beyond the boundaries of ordinary and tangible life experience. As used in the RESPECTFUL counseling framework, religion and spirituality refer to a person's belief in a reality that transcends physical nature and provides individuals with an extraordinary meaning of life in general and human existence in particular.

Because clients' religious and spiritual identities may play a vital role in the way they construct meaning in life experiences, it is important that counselors take time to assess the degree to which this factor impacts their psychological development early in the helping process. It is equally important that mental health practitioners take time to consider how their own religious and spiritual identities and beliefs may positively or negatively impact the work they do with clients who embrace perspectives different from their own in this cultural domain.

Economic Class Background

Numerous researchers have explained how a person's attitudes, values, worldview, and behaviors are all affected by one's economic class standing, background, and identity (Liu, 2001). Given the influence that this aspect of clients' multidimensionality has on their psychological development, practitioners would do well to be attentive to the ways this cultural consideration contributes to their clients' identified strengths and expressed problems from a holistic counseling perspective.

It is also suggested that many counselors may develop inaccurate and negative views and prejudices about persons from economic backgrounds that are different from their own. For this reason, it is important that counselors evaluate their own class-based assumptions, biases, and stereotypes when working with individuals from diverse economic class backgrounds.

It is particularly important for counselors to examine how economic factors impact the psychological health and personal well-being of poor clients. This assertion is made knowing that traditional counseling theories have largely been developed by middle-class individuals who did not direct much attention to the ways that poverty and related economic stressors impact people's psychological development and sense of personal well-being.

Sexual Identity

One of the most complex, though often understudied, aspects of human development involves the sexual identity development of clients from diverse groups and backgrounds. As used in the RESPECTFUL counseling model, the term *sexual identity* relates to a person's gender identity, gender roles, and sexual orientation.

Gender identity relates to an individual's subjective sense of what it means to be male or female. A person's gender identity is clearly affected by the different roles men and women are expected to play within different cultural, ethnic, and racial contexts. A person's sexual identity is also influenced by one's *sexual orientation*. There are a number of ways to conceptualize this dimension of human development. Generally speaking, sexual orientation includes such concepts as bisexuality, heterosexuality, and homosexuality.

Bisexuality refers to individuals who demonstrate a sexual interest in both males and females. *Heterosexuality,* in contrast, refers to individuals whose sexual interests are directed toward persons of the opposite sex. A third way of viewing this dimension of one's sexual orientation involves the concept of *homosexuality,* which is a term that has been used to identify individuals whose sexual orientation involves persons of the same sex. In light of the negative stereotypes that have historically been associated with the term *homosexuality,* terms such as *gay males* and *lesbians* are considered more acceptable and respectful in describing this dimension of a person's sexual orientation (D'Andrea & Daniels, 2001).

Psychological Maturity

Counselors often work with clients who share common demographic characteristics (e.g., age, gender, socioeconomic identity) and cultural and racial background but appear to be very different psychologically. In these situations, counselors might refer to one client as being "more or less psychologically mature" than another person who is the same age, identifies with the same cultural and racial reference group, and shares a similar sexual identity.

Some descriptors that are commonly used to describe "immature" clients include statements such as, "He demonstrates limited impulse control in social interactions," or, "She has a low capacity for self-awareness." When describing "more mature" clients, we may say, "He is able to discuss his problems with much insight," "She is highly self-aware," and, "She has developed a much broader range of interpersonal and perspective-taking skills than many of my other clients."

Cognitive-developmental theories view psychological development as a process in which individuals move from simple to more complex ways of thinking about themselves and their life experiences. This movement can be traced along a set of invariant, hierarchical stages that reflect qualitatively different ways of thinking, feeling, and acting in the world (Sprinthall, Peace, & Kennington, 2001).

By assessing clients' levels of psychological maturity, counselors are better positioned to design more effective interventions that respectfully meet their clients' unique psychological strengths and needs. It is also important that counselors take time to reflect on their own level of psychological development, as the therapeutic process can easily be undermined when practitioners are matched with persons who are functioning at a higher level of psychological development than they are themselves.

Ethnic-Racial Identity

Clearly, tremendous psychological differences exist among persons who come from the same ethnic-racial groups in our society. This variation is commonly referred to as *within-group differences*. Given the within-group variation that is manifested among persons from the same ethnic-racial groups, it is important that counselors develop the knowledge and skills necessary to accurately assess these important differences from a holistic perspective and respond to them in effective and respectful ways in counseling. It is also imperative that counselors understand how their own ethnic-racial experiences have affected their psychological development, the way they construct meaning of the world, and the types of biases counselors may have acquired toward others in the process.

Chronological Developmental Challenges

The RESPECTFUL counseling model refers to age-related developmental changes as *chronological challenges*. Counselors are familiar with many of these challenges as they represent characteristics normally associated with infancy, childhood, adolescence, and adulthood. The normal age-related developmental changes that people predictably manifest from infancy through adulthood include physical growth (e.g., bodily changes and the sequencing of motor skills), the emergence of different cognitive competencies (e.g., the development of perceptual, language, learning, memory, and thinking skills), and the manifestation of a variety of psychosocial skills (e.g., the ability to manage one's emotions and demonstrate more effective interpersonal competencies over time).

Human development researchers have made substantial contributions that help counselors refine their thinking about the unique challenges clients face at different points across the life span. Practically speaking, this knowledge enables practitioners to work more effectively with persons who face difficult chronological challenges by implementing age-appropriate intervention strategies in counseling.

These considerations also allow practitioners to be mindful of the unique challenges they are likely to encounter when significant chronological differences exist between themselves and their clients. We have suggested that many young practitioners are likely to encounter major challenges in gaining a high level of trust, respect, and professional legitimacy when working with some clients who are much older than themselves (D'Andrea & Daniels, 2001).

Trauma and Other Threats to One's Well-Being

Trauma and threats to one's well-being are included in the RESPECTFUL counseling model to emphasize the complex ways that stressful situations put people at risk of psychological harm. Such harm typically occurs when the stressors individuals experience exceed their ability to cope with them in constructive and effective ways. An individual's personal resources (e.g., coping skills, self-esteem, social support, the personal power derived from one's cultural group) may be overtaxed when one is subjected to ongoing environmental stressors. Persons who experience stressors for extended periods of time are commonly referred to as vulnerable or at risk for future mental health problems (Lewis et al., 2003).

Counselors are frequently called on to work with persons in various vulnerable at-risk groups including poor, homeless, and unemployed people; adults and children in families undergoing divorce; pregnant teenagers; traumatized war veterans; individuals with HIV or AIDS; persons with cancer; and individuals who are victimized by various forms of ageism, racism, sexism, and cultural oppression. Heightened, prolonged, and historical stressors often result in more severe and adverse psychological outcomes for many persons from oppressed cultural, ethnic, and racial groups in our contemporary society.

To be effective in their work, counselors need to be able to (1) accurately and holistically assess the different ways that environmental and historic stressors contribute to the onset and perpetuation of various forms of psychological and spiritual trauma in the lives of clients who come from diverse cultural and racial groups and (2) develop intervention strategies intentionally aimed at effectively ameliorating these problems.

It is equally important that counselors become knowledgeable of the ways that intergenerational trauma may contribute to the adverse psychological problems many persons from diverse cultural and racial groups experience in their lives. Duran (2006) writes extensively about the adverse impact of this sort of trauma, referring to it as an intergenerational "soul wound" that significantly contributes to the complex psychological and spiritual problems many Native American Indians experience today. The negative effect of the "soul wound" is also thought to adversely impact the lives of other individuals in our nation including many persons of African descent as well as women, children, and gay, lesbian, and bisexual persons who have been subjected to various forms of abuse and violence in their lives (Lewis et al., 2003).

With this knowledge in mind, mental health professionals are better able to develop and implement helping strategies that are deliberately aimed at addressing the negative psychological and spiritual ramifications of such complex forms of trauma. It is also important for mental health practitioners to consider how various life stressors and traumatic events may have a lasting impact on their own psychological development as such experiences can influence the way mental health professionals work with their clients.

Family Background and History

The rapid cultural diversification of the United States includes an increasing number of families that are very different from the traditional notion of *family* many counselors have historically used as a standard for determining normal family life and healthy family functioning. The different types of families (e.g., single-female-headed families, blended families, extended families, families headed by gay and lesbian parents) that counselors increasingly encounter in their work challenge practitioners to reassess the traditional concept of the nuclear family that has been used as a standard against which all types of other families have been compared.

As a result of these changes in our society, counselors will be increasingly pressed to (1) understand the unique strengths clients derive from these different family systems and (2) implement counseling strategies that effectively foster the healthy development of these diverse familial units. In addition to learning about the personal strengths individuals derive from such diverse family systems, mental health practitioners are encouraged to assess the biases and assumptions they may have developed about family life as a result of their own familial history and experiences. If left unexamined, these biases and assumptions may adversely impact the counseling relationship mental health practitioners have with clients who come from families that are very different from their own.

Unique Physical Characteristics

The RESPECTFUL counseling framework emphasizes the importance of being sensitive to the ways that society's idealized images of physical beauty negatively impact the psychological development of many persons whose physical nature does not fit the narrow view of beauty that is fostered by our contemporary culture. When working with clients whose unique physical characteristics may be a source of stress and dissatisfaction, it is important for counselors to reflect on the ways that the idealized myth of physical beauty may have led such clients to internalize negative views and stereotypes about persons who do not fit this culturally biased perspective.

Also, when working with women and men whose psychological development has been negatively affected by some aspect of their unique physical nature, practitioners need to be able to assist them in understanding the ways being socialized into a society that adheres to myopic views of beauty contribute to irrational thinking about some clients' sense of self-worth (Worrell & Remer, 2003).

Counselors need to also be sensitive to and knowledgeable of issues related to various physical disabilities when working with persons who experience these personal challenges. To respectfully assist these clients, practitioners are encouraged to help them identify and build on the unique personal strengths they bring to counseling (Cartwright & D'Andrea, 2004).

Location of Residence and Language Differences

The location of one's residence refers to the geographic region and setting where one resides. D'Andrea and Daniels (2001) identify six major geographic areas in the United States: the northeastern, southeastern, midwestern, southwestern, northwestern, and far western regions. These geographical areas are distinguished by the types of persons who reside there. They also differ in terms of climate patterns, geological terrain, and the types of occupations and industry commonly available to workers who reside in these locations.

When mental health practitioners work with persons from geographical regions or residential settings that are different from their own, it is important to reflect on the possible stereotypes and biases they may have developed about such individuals and regions. This is particularly important when working with persons who use a different dialect or language in interpersonal interactions. As is the case with the other components of the RESPECTFUL counseling model, this self-assessment is very important because stereotypes and biases counselors may have developed about persons whose residential background and language dialect is different from their own may lead to inaccurate assumptions and clinical interpretations within the helping setting.

As has been repeatedly emphasized in this discussion, it is important that counselors take time to holistically assess the ways that each component of the RESPECTFUL counseling framework impacts their clients' as well as their own personal and psychological development prior to and during the counseling process. The *RESPECTFUL Counseling Self-Assessment Activity Form* is provided to assist counselors in formally conducting this sort of holistic self-assessment. More specifically, this activity is designed to help counselors gain (1) new insights into some of their own cultural-contextual preferences, biases, and values; (2) a greater understanding of the complex, holistic, and irreducible nature of their own personal and professional development; and (3) greater clarity about the types of clients they are likely to be more or less effective working with in the future based on this self-knowledge.

THE RESPECTFUL COUNSELING SELF-ASSESSMENT ACTIVITY FORM

Instructions: We are all "multidimensional" beings who are affected by the various factors that make up the RESPECTFUL counseling model. As repeatedly stated in the materials you have read that describe the RESPECTFUL counseling model, it is vital for counselors to become aware of any assumptions, stereotypes, and biases they may have about clients who are different from themselves in terms of their religious and spiritual identity, economic class background, sexual identity, ethnicity-race, and the other dimensions of the RESPECTFUL framework. As you think about the clients you are working with or are likely to work with in the future, it is useful to reflect on the RESPECTFUL model and consider the impact diversity issues may have in the here and now of every interview you have with your clients as well as understanding how these issues impact your own view of the clients you serve.

Now that you have had an opportunity to learn about the RESPECTFUL counseling model, please take a few minutes to reflect on the ways each factor that comprises this theoretical framework impacts your own life and worldview. In doing so it is helpful to write a short description of yourself as it relates to each component of this model. Then briefly state how your understanding of these components and their impact on your development may affect the work you do with clients from different groups and backgrounds you may work with in the future:

Religious and spiritual identity
Economic class background and identity
Sexual identity
Psychological maturity
Ethnic-racial developmental identity
Chronological challenges and identity
Trauma and threats to well-being
Family history and experiences
Unique physical characteristics
Location of residence and language preference

Source: D'Andrea, M., and Daniels, J., University of Hawaii, Department of Counselor Education, Honolulu, 2005. With permission.

CONCLUSIONS

This chapter is designed to explore the relationship between the humanistic and multicultural perspectives of counseling. In addressing this task we have discussed several principles associated with the humanistic perspective and described how they are complemented and extended by the multicultural counseling movement. Particular attention was directed to the similarities shared by both the humanistic and multicultural counseling perspectives in terms of the principles of self-actualization, holism, and irreducibility. The RESPECTFUL counseling model was presented to extend counselors' thinking about traditional humanistic concepts of holism and irreducibility from a multicultural perspective. Last, an activity was presented to assist counselors in acquiring the skills necessary to develop a more expansive and holistic understanding of the ways that the 10 factors comprising the RESPECTFUL counseling model impact their own development, their clients' development, and interactions that occur in multicultural counseling situations. It is hoped that the information included in this chapter and the activity presented foster a greater appreciation of the complementary nature of humanism and multiculturalism and ultimately in the advancement of professional practices that more effectively promote the dignity and development of the persons counselors serve.

REFERENCES

Association for Humanistic Psychology. (2009). *Principles of humanism.* Washington, DC: American Psychological Association.

Cartwright, B., & D'Andrea, M. (2004). Counseling for diversity. In T. F. Riggar & D. R. Maki (Eds.), *Handbook of rehabilitation counseling* (pp. 171–187). New York: Springer.

D'Andrea, M. (1988). The counselor as pacer: A model for revitalization of the counseling profession. In R. Hayes & R. Aubrey (Eds.), *New directions for counseling and human development* (pp. 22–44). Denver, CO: Love Publishing.

D'Andrea, M., & Daniels, J. (2001). RESPECTFUL counseling: An integrative multidimensional model for counselors. In D. Pope-Davis & H. Coleman (Eds.), *The intersection of race, class and gender in multicultural counseling* (pp. 417–466). Thousand Oaks, CA: Sage.

D'Andrea, M., & Daniels, J. (2005). *The RESPECTFUL counseling activity form.* University of Hawaii, Department of Counselor Education, Honolulu.

Duran, E. (2006). *Healing the soul wound: Counseling with American Indians and other native peoples.* New York: Teachers College Press.

Ivey, A. E., D'Andrea, M., Ivey, M. B., & Simek-Morgan, L. (2007). *Theories of counseling and psychotherapy: A multicultural perspective* (5th ed.). Needham Heights, MA: Allyn and Bacon.

Kelly, E. W. (1995). *Spirituality and religion in counseling and psychotherapy: Diversity in theory and practice.* Alexandria, VA: American Counseling Association.

Lewis, J. A., Lewis, M. D., Daniels, J. A., & D'Andrea, M. J. (2003). *Community counseling: Empowerment strategies for a diverse society* (3rd ed.). Pacific Grove, CA: Brooks/Cole-Thomson Learning.

Liu, W. M. (2001). Expanding our understanding of multiculturalism: Developing a social class worldview model. In D. B. Pope-Davis & H. L. K. Coleman (Eds.), *The intersection of race, class and gender in multicultural counseling* (pp. 127–170). Thousand Oaks, CA: Sage.

Maslow, A. H. (1970). Holistic emphasis. *Journal of Individual Psychology, 26,* 39.

Miller, W. R., & Rollnick, S. (2002). *Motivational interviewing: Preparing people for change* (2nd ed.). New York: Guilford Press.

Parham, T. (Ed.). (2002). *Counseling persons of African descent: Raising the bar of practitioner competence* (pp. 52–74). Thousand Oaks, CA: Sage.

Parham, T. A., & Parham, W. D. (2002). Understanding African American mental health. In T. A. Parham (Ed.), *Counseling persons of African descent* (pp. 25–37). Thousand Oaks, CA: Sage.

Pedersen, P. B., Draguns, J. G., Lonner, W. J., & Trimble, J. E. (Eds.). (2008). *Counseling across cultures* (6th ed.). Thousand Oaks, CA: Sage.

Pope-Davis, D., & Coleman, H. (Eds.). (2001). *The intersection of race, class and gender in multicultural counseling.* Thousand Oaks, CA: Sage.

Pope-Davis, D. B., Coleman, H. L. K., Liu, W. M., & Toporek, R. L. (Eds.). (2003). *Handbook of multicultural competencies in counseling and psychology* (pp. 154–168). Thousand Oaks, CA: Sage.

Sprinthall, N. A., Peace, S. D., & Kennington, P. A. D. (2001). Cognitive-developmental stage theories for counseling. In D. C. Locke, J. E. Myers, & E. L. Herr (Eds.), *The handbook of counseling* (pp. 109–130). Thousand Oaks, CA: Sage.

Sue, D. W., & Sue, D. R. (2008). *Counseling the culturally diverse: Theory and practice* (5th ed.). New York: Wiley.

Vontress, C. E., Johnson, J. A., & Epp, L. R. (1999). *Cross-cultural counseling: A casebook.* Alexandria, VA: American Counseling Association.

Worrell, J., & Remer, P. (2003). *Feminist perspectives in therapy: Empowering diverse women* (2nd ed.). Hoboken, NJ: Wiley.

4

The Creative Arts in Counseling

DONNA A. HENDERSON

INTRODUCTION

Earlier you read that humanism embraces the richness of the human experience. Creative arts embody that magnificence of life. Furthermore, people's creative power constitutes a critical, positive force in their lives (Ansbacher, 1977; Maslow, 1968; Matson, 1969). Humanistic philosophy and creative activity emphasize the importance of the present—right here and right now. Humanism also honors the authenticity of relationships, the value of being who we are as we interact and engage others in our world. Creativity allows a forum for demonstrating that communication and meaningfulness to others. Furthermore, humanism encompasses the ideal of deep participation or "experiencing" ourselves and our world. Creativity strengthens that engagement with the optimal experience and flow, a state of deep concentration and purpose (Csikszentmihalyi, 1990). Thus, the creative arts capture these connections of being present, authentic, and participatory. Johann Wolfgang Goethe captured the importance of arts in life most eloquently:

> One should hear a little music, read a little poetry, and see a fine picture every day of his life, in order that worldly cares may not obliterate the sense of the beautiful implanted in the human soul.

SIGNIFICANCE OF THE CREATIVE ARTS IN COUNSELING

Arons and Richards (2001) outline the historical focus of creativity and humanism as well as the current impact on health and healing. Their overview highlights the inherent connections of humanism referring to the fullest realization and actualization of self and creativity relating to originality and meaningfulness. Their synopsis provides a theoretical rationale for the coupling. Our discussion will focus on the advantages of creative activities in the counseling encounter, a practice approach.

An empathic understanding of the person's internal frame of reference is critical to humanistic counseling. The counselor demonstrates an interest and appreciation of the world of the client, creating a process to deepen the counseling relationship as well as get closer to the client's meanings and feelings (Raskin, Rogers, & Witty, 2008).

Zimring (1995) expands an explanation of how empathic understanding relates to the therapeutic process. He asserts that a person's self should be understood as a perspective that takes shape and disintegrates constantly in each minute of every situation. Self is dynamic rather than static and emerges from the interaction of the person and the situation. According to Zimring we build a subjective, reflexive inner world as well as an objective, everyday world. People exist with varying awareness and access to their internal representations of their context. Counselors validate the person's subjective context through empathic understanding. That support strengthens the client's internal frame of reference and has far-reaching consequences that allow individuals to grow.

Creative arts provide an expressive capacity beyond talk. Creative arts introduce the counselor to that subjective, reflexive inner world of the client and may help individuals communicate relevant concerns in a way talk therapy cannot (Malchiodi, 2005). This is what Don Jones calls "drawing from within," the inner experience of knowing oneself through art or other creative media (Malchiodi, 2007, p. 4). Indubitably, the counselor's empathic understanding would likewise be enhanced. Creative arts sensitize people to untapped aspects of themselves (Gladding, 2005) and provide the therapeutic alliance with not only self-exploration but also enhanced self-expression as the sense of stories and memories unfold through the expressive media. Creative arts help us communicate feelings and ideas that words cannot, help us understand ourselves, and enhance lives through self-expression (Malchiodi, 2007). Humanistic counselors who want to offer empathic understanding will find creative arts a unique way to explore the inner world of the client.

FOUNDATIONAL LITERATURE

Humanism focuses on a person's potential rather than on deficits. Smith (2006) expresses that in her strength-based model of counseling in which people are affirmed. According to Smith individuals have wisdom, character, creativity, social support, intelligence, and other assets. The counselor's role is to help them recognize, develop, and apply those strengths to their concerns. Again, creative arts provide a bridge to the expression of those positive aspects. Indeed, Garai (2001) explains how the process of making art provides a way to grow through self-expression and self-transcendence. Creativity is a force in the path to wellness.

Rogers (1954) believed creativity was motivated by people's self-actualizing drive toward their potential. Humanistic approaches that include creative arts focus on changing troubling emotions, behaviors, and experiences by encouraging the individual's authentic expression of those concerns (Malchiodi, 2005), the counselor's understanding and accepting of those issues, and the individual's innate movement toward health.

Natalie Rogers (1999), the daughter of Carl Rogers, discussed creative arts as allowing the counselor an opportunity to "see" what the person is explaining by paying careful attention to what the person is communicating. The counselor helps the person explore by reflecting what has been expressed and by asking for more clarification. Creative arts expression adds a way to enhance the person's ability to communicate and also serves as a nonverbal way to understanding. The focus is on acknowledging the complexity of the client as a person and helping him or her achieve meaning and fulfillment in a variety of circumstances.

For Carl Rogers, "The mainspring of creativity appears to be the same tendency which we discover so clearly as the creative force in psychotherapy—man's tendency to actualize himself, to become his potentialities.... The individual creates primarily because it is satisfying ... because this behavior is felt to be self-actualization" (Rogers, 1995, pp. 351–352). Gladding (2005) expanded this quotation by stating that creativity encourages playfulness, divergent thinking, flexibility, humor, risk taking, independence, and openness, qualities associated with a healthy personality. Creek (2002) said that as a vehicle of self-expression creative activities aid in expressing feelings, increasing self-awareness, and insight. For all these reasons humanistic counselors will be well advised to incorporate creative arts in their practice to enhance the therapeutic experience for the client and to increase empathic understanding for the counselor.

LITERATURE REVIEW

The National Coalition of Creative Arts Therapies Association (NCCATA) was founded in 1979. It is an alliance of professional associations dedicated to the advancement of the arts as therapeutic modalities. That group identifies the creative arts therapies as art therapy, dance/movement therapy, drama therapy, music therapy, poetry therapy, and psychodrama. The therapies use the arts and creative processes intentionally to foster health, communication, and expression; to promote the integration of physical, emotional, cognitive, and social functioning; to enhance self-awareness; and to facilitate change (www.nccata.org/index.htm). The following sections define some of those modalities and provide activities that can be used in counseling. Next I discuss a review of some current studies of creative arts and therapy.

Two research studies explore the use of creative activities with those who have mental health problems and are in occupational therapy. Reynolds (2000) studied the experience of 39 women managing depression through needlecraft. She found effects of relaxation such as relief from worrying thoughts, building self-esteem, social support, and energizing thoughts among the group members. Griffiths (2008) explored the clinical utility of creative activities with five occupational therapists and eight of their clients. She used grounded theory in her study, which included observing and interviewing. She concluded that creative activities provide opportunities for relaxing, refreshing, and peaceful engagement. She noted the potential health gains from using creative activities as clients gained a sense of achievement, growth in self-confidence, and some control over negative thoughts and stress.

Stewart and Schneider (2000) used improvisational music in a neonatal intensive care unit with the goal of influencing the sound environment. The researchers interviewed the staff who perceived the environment as being noisy with a negative effect on the babies and the staff. For a 5-week period the music therapist took a humanistic approach and played a dulcimer in a central area matching the music to the various machines and integrating the environmental sounds into the music. After the intervention the researchers again interviewed the staff members and found that for 24 of the 25 people the music was perceived as beneficial. The staff reported a lowered level of noise perception, a decrease in tension and stress, more awareness of how they related to each other, and an overall mood lift.

Smeijsters and Cleven (2006) used creative arts therapies in forensic psychiatry in the Netherlands. Among other conclusions, their results indicated that dance/movement therapy provides options for expression and control of anger through movement. Milliken (2008) held a dance/movement therapy group to help individuals move from the anger or shame of their addiction into a more healthy and positive sense of responsibility for themselves and their actions. Her description of integrating movement experiences includes group members releasing their toxic feelings and developing a sense of themselves as creative, functional members of society.

An application of creative arts work with chemically dependent people was outlined by Feen-Calligan, Washington, and Moxley (2008). They used art reproductions to help 17 minority women identify feelings evoked by the art and to reconnect to their emotions dampened by the addictions. As the women learned to talk about their feelings and reflect on their circumstances through their interpretative interactions with the visual art, they gained insight into their own emotions as well as the issues they faced in their recovery. Their self-expression allowed them to confront the pain and sorrow they experienced as an addict, to address their recovery challenges, and to begin to develop hope for a new life.

Creative arts bring power and possibility to the therapeutic encounter even with those who have little hope. A striking summary of that can be found in

Camilleri's (2007) overview of work with inner-city children using creative arts therapies. Her stories of hope and growth uncovered through dance, art, and other media will inspire other counselors to incorporate the arts in their practice. Gladding (2005) also wrote an engaging and informative volume about using the arts in counseling. In the following section I discuss ways to integrate arts into the counseling process.

THE CREATIVE ARTS AND THE HUMANISTIC PERSPECTIVE

Using the creative arts in counseling allows for opportunities to celebrate connectedness, deep feeling, intuition, integration, purpose, and the human experience (Atkins et al., 2003). Malchiodi (2005) encouraged creative forms of communication as a way to explore life, to facilitate discovery of personal meaning, and to participate fully in counseling. Counselors may create an environment for creative expressions in many ways. I will begin by looking at two models for provoking creative thinking and then look at using the modalities of art, music, drama, and the written word as ways to help a person discover a new sense of self.

Teaching a person to move beyond traditional ways of seeing a situation may boost a range of possibilities and solutions. Edward De Bono (1990, 1999) and Robert Eberle (1971) developed models to enhance creative thinking. Their ideas are summarized in the next section.

Creative Thinking

De Bono (1990) proposed a model of lateral thinking, or solving problems through indirect and creative approaches. His book *Lateral Thinking* outlines a process to practice moving from a logical step-by-step process to a more creative, generative way of thinking. A particular development of lateral thinking processes, *parallel thinking* focuses on explorations—looking for what can be rather than for what is by unscrambling the thinking process. He explains that when we think we get confused because we try to incorporate too much at one time—emotions, facts, logic, hope, and creativity crowd our minds. He likens this to trying to juggle too many balls. His system allows a thinker to do one thing at a time, thus separating all the important parts of thought into six ways of approaching anything.

According to De Bono (1990) the brain operates in some distinct ways, but people are befuddled when they mix all the ways together. He suggests that those methods of thinking can be defined and planned to develop strategies about considering an issue. He uses the metaphor of colored hats to symbolize the states of thinking and encourages people to put on the "hats" to think deeper about problems and solutions. The assigned color of each hat is related to a distinct brain state:

- Questions (white hat)—neutral and objective focus on information and facts
- Emotions (red hat)—the emotional view and reaction
- Judgment (black hat)—somber and serious, cautious, logic applied to finding flaws or barriers
- Benefits (yellow hat)—sunny and positive, optimistic and hopeful, seeks harmony
- Creativity (green hat)—new ideas, investigations and seeing where an idea goes
- Thinking (blue hat)—concerned with control, organizing the thinking process, and using other hats

Case Illustration

De Bono's (1990) ideas have been used by governments, businesses, and schools to lead people through meetings and decision making in a more systematic way than a brainstorming model. Likewise, counselors can help their clients move from hat to hat to look at a situation in many ways. An example of a counseling situation with fuller explanations of the hats illustrates the possibilities of improving the quality of decision making. The counselor helps a woman who is considering a divorce through these processes.

Counselor: Vidia, we have talked about what a difficult time you are having deciding on your future. If you'd like today we can try to organize your ideas differently. We can use the idea of "thinking hats" to work through different styles of thinking and see what we uncover. Okay?

Vidia: Yes let's try.

Counselor: Okay, with the white hat we can concentrate on the information and facts. First review what we know and then maybe what else we need to know.

Vidia: Well, what I know is that the lawyer told me you have to be separated a year before the divorce is final in this state. I know that our assets would be divided equally and that since we do not have children we would not have to decide on custody. I know we can request a court-appointed mediator, and I know how much my attorney charges for consulting and for the paperwork. We'll have to figure out what to do with all the things we own, I know. I'm not sure of anything else I need to know that's just factual.

Counselor: We will come back to that white hat and add if something else occurs to you. But now let's try the red hat and look at the decision using intuition and emotion. Also try to think how other people will react emotionally, and try to understand the responses of people who do not fully know your reasoning.

Vidia: It is so draining to even be thinking about divorce. I cry and cry whenever I look at the papers my lawyer gave me. But it also feels like a big relief. We have been fighting for so long, and now he doesn't even pay attention to me at all. And really I just don't have any feelings left for him. I'm just done with trying to make this empty relationship more than it is. But it's like giving up my childhood dream of a home and family and happily ever after—I think that's what makes me so sad. And other people? Oh my. His parents will be delighted, and mine will understand—they always support me. Most of my friends expect this, so that won't be difficult. I just wish I could stop crying and make the decision.

Counselor: Sounds like you are sad about the split but optimistic about other people's reactions. Let's turn to the black hat and really look at things pessimistically, cautiously, and defensively. Try to see why the changes related to the divorce might not work. That way we can highlight the weak points in a plan and either eliminate them, do something else, or develop some plans to counter problems that arise.

Vidia: This will be easy! This is exactly the way I think. I'll have less money, and I will lose a great deal of status—being married to a doctor brings you a social network that I won't have anymore. I've never lived by myself, and that scares me. We were married right after college, and even though I've handled all the household things I'm not sure how I will do without someone to help me take care of things like the car and bigger financial things. He may never talk to me again, and we have known each other for a long time. Even if things are bad between us right now, I cannot imagine him not being in my life at all. There are probably lots more I could say with my black hat on, but I'm getting so discouraged that I don't want to think like this.

Counselor: Of course we can change hats. Black hat thinking helps you plan for problems before you take action so you may be better prepared for problems. But let's try the yellow hat and think positively. This hat is the optimistic view in which you can see all the benefits of the decision, the value in it, and maybe even the opportunities that arise from it. Yellow hat thinking helps you to keep going when everything looks gloomy and difficult.

Vidia: Hmmm. That is a switch. Definitely one benefit would be exactly what I said was scary. I would be on my own and have a chance to be a person rather than just the doctor's wife. I would really like to take some art classes and get back to my photography. When I was in school several professors urged me to pursue a career in either drawing or photography, and I just gave that up when we got married. I have a decent job with enough money to get along too, so I don't have to worry about starving. I would also like to stop fighting and to stop feeling invisible. I just don't like the conflict and really want to have more peace in my life. I'd also like to learn to enjoy myself without feeling like I was letting him down. I think it would be good for me to depend on my family and friends to get me through the emotional ups and downs instead of trying to do it all on my own. Everyone I love keeps asking me, and I keep bottling things up. Wow, I hadn't even considered these possibilities—I could even go on, but I'd like to see what's next.

Counselor: We just have two more hats. The green hat is for creativity and a free-wheeling way of thinking. What are some outlandish ideas you've had about this divorce decision? Do you have a picture that you see or a song that you hear?

Vidia: I've got it. That perfect song [is] "I can't make you love me if you don't," and I don't even care anymore. Wow, that's the first time I've been able to say that aloud. And just like that song says, I've been walking around on eggshells, and he's been patronizing me and treating me like some fragile flower that needs correcting and corralling to grow—not the life I want. And a picture—maybe you remember that old, old film *The Way We Were*? You can find some clips on YouTube, and I was putting myself in that story. It was sad and disappointing, but things turned out okay—better than them staying together and destroying each other. That gave me hope and a different ending. What's next?

Counselor: The blue hat is the last one, and it's about managing the process of thinking this way. If you think you have enough ideas now, maybe you could talk about which of these different ways of thinking is most helpful to you right now and what you think is important.

Vidia: Everything—I can tell that I have the information I need, and I recognize the mixed emotions that I have not been able to discuss. The barriers and the possibilities are much clearer to me, and I keep going back to that movie that seemed to capture my distress in a way that leads to a better future. I want to think more, but I would like to come back next week and talk more about what's next for me.

This shortened version of a possible use of the six hats thinking in counseling illustrates ways to help people see something from a variety of views in a systematic rather than scrambled way. Another author provides a process to stimulate creative ideas.

Eberle (1971) explained a model of creativity called SCAMPER as way to develop the imagination. It is an acronym for a list of words to help you think differently. The purpose of this framework is to provide strategies for becoming more creative. The letters provide a mnemonic for activities that may allow a more productive self-sufficiency. Gladding (2005) suggested that the SCAMPER model also helps counselors provide a checklist of suggestions to stimulate ideas for counseling and for clients. Specifically the letters, their meanings, and definitions are as follows:

Letter	Word	Definition/Thought	Thought	Example Response for a Stagnant Friendship
S	Substitute	To replace a person or thing with another	"Instead of … I can …."	"Instead of pouting I can call my mom."
C	Combine	To bring things together, to unite	"I can bring together … and …to…."	"I can bring together my optimism and my love of movies to get past some disappointment."
A	Adapt	To adjust in order to meet a situation or purpose	"I can adapt…this way… to…."	"I can adapt my expectations and not expect her to call."
M	Modify	To change the form or quality, to alter	"I can change this…in this way…to…."	"I can find my other friends that I've been missing."
	Magnify	To enhance, to make larger in form or quality		
	Minify	To make lesser, lighter, slower, less significant		
P	Put to other uses	To apply for purposes other than original uses	"I can re-use …in this way…by…."	N/A
E	Eliminate	To remove or omit a quality, part or whole	"I can eliminate… by…."	"I can eliminate my sadness by accepting what we have."
R	Reverse	To turn around	"I can rearrange…in this way….so that…."	"I can rearrange my schedule to free time for a personal trainer so that I can learn yoga."
	Rearrange	To change the order, to make a different plan		

Both of these formulas for creative thinking, different hat thinking, and SCAMPER may generate ideas that had not previously been considered. Likewise, incorporating creative arts themselves into counseling will add spice to the process.

CREATIVE ARTS THERAPIES

The domains of creative arts therapies contain sets of approaches. In this section the professional organizations associated with each are presented as well as the history of the approach for art therapy, music therapy, and drama therapy. I also look at bibliotherapy. After some specifics about the practice of each particular therapy, a discussion is offered of how some of the media could be incorporated into counseling, not as the focus of the process but as an additive component to humanistic counseling.

Art Therapy

According to the American Art Therapy Association (2004), art therapy involves art media, images, and process:

> Art therapy is an area of specialization in the mental health profession that uses the creative process of art making to improve and enhance the physical, mental and emotional well-being of individuals of all ages. It is based on the belief that the creative process involved in artistic self-expression helps people to resolve conflicts and problems, develop interpersonal skills, manage behavior, reduce stress, increase self-esteem and self-awareness, and achieve insight.

The patient/client responses to the created products are respected as reflections of development, abilities, personality, interests, concerns, and conflicts. Art therapy is considered a way of reconciling emotional conflicts, increasing self-awareness and social skills, managing behavior, solving problems, easing anxiety, helping with an orientation to reality, and enhancing self-esteem (American Art Therapy Association, 2004).

Using visual arts in counseling has been built on the ideas of Margaret Naumburg, Edith Kramer, Hanna Kwiatkowska, Janie Rhyne, and Elinor Ulman. Naumburg (1966) stressed art as a distinctive form of therapy and saw art as a window to the unconscious. She emphasized the importance of asking clients to explain their art images and considered the images a form of symbolic speech (Malchiodi, 2007). Kramer (1971) considered art a way to control and integrate destructive impulses and conflicting feelings. She viewed art as a place where new feelings and attitudes can be expressed and tested. Kwiatkowska (1978) worked at the National Institute of Mental Health and connected her work in psychiatric settings with helping families through art. Rhyne used art expression to help individuals achieve self-awareness and self-actualization. She emphasized the person's interpretation and the person-centered approach to counseling

(Malchiodi). Ulman created the first professional journal of art therapy and published a seminal collection of essays (Ulman & Dachinger, 1996) that served as a text for many years.

Gladding (2005) outlined the benefits of using visual arts in counseling and notes that through visual arts people recognize the range of emotions that occurs within them. Visual arts symbolize feelings in ways that are unique, tangible, and powerful. Malchiodi (2007) suggested that art helps people grow, rehabilitate, and heal. Furthermore, the visual arts allow individuals to become more aware of the growth edges of their personalities and can help someone reveal problems that are difficult to discuss. For example, visual art may offer a unique opportunity to express trauma, expressing what words cannot (Malchiodi). Gladding concluded that visual arts can be easily combined with other creative arts such as movement, writing, and imagery. That flexibility allows the artistic expression to move from being static to dynamic.

Visual arts can include drawing, painting, clay, sculpture, photography, collage, and other media. In *The Art Therapy Sourcebook* Malchiodi (2007) provided guidelines for using art in therapy. She noted that for humanistic art therapy the techniques are the counselor's attitudes of empathy, caring, respect, acceptance, and reflection. Counselors have their choice of art making. Central to the therapy process is empowerment through art and exploring one's creative potential as a key to transformation.

Counselors will need some basic art supplies. Drawing paper, pencils and eraser, felt markers, oil and chalk pastels, scissors, glue or rubber cement, masking tape, a box with collage materials, watercolors, tempera or acrylic paints, watercolor paper, palettes on which to mix paint, a large jar or can for water, brushes, and clay would outfit a counselor's tool box for visual arts.

Visual arts can be used during any part of the counseling process in a variety of ways. Clients might be asked to draw their life, to make a collage of the past 2 years, to show their anger in clay, or to paint their dream. Counselors may suggest keeping a visual journal between sessions. Malchiodi (2007) recommended asking a client to scribble with closed eyes or the nondominant hand and then title the "work." Creating a mandala or totem may provide a way for clients to discover the symbols significant in their lives. The AIDS Memorial Quilt demonstrates people's expression of loss and grief through the images in the panels. Clients may also create a self-soothing image book to help them when they are depressed, anxious, or in a crisis. Feeling maps represent six emotions: anger, joy, sadness, fear, love of others, and love of self. Colors represent feelings, and people choose the size and shape of the emotions. Discussion about connections of feelings and reactions to the map help individuals identify their predominant response and the interrelatedness of their emotions after a trauma. Clients can identify movies that portray their emotions. They may also be asked to react to art reproductions as mentioned earlier in this chapter regarding a study of minority women coping with chemical dependence (i.e., Feen-Calligan et al., 2008). Perhaps the healing powers of art and self-expression are best captured with this directive from Shaun McNiff (1994, as cited in Malchiodi, 2007, p. 162):

> Just paint. Begin to move with the brush in different ways. Watch what comes. If you paint, it will come. Nothing will happen unless you begin to paint, in your own way. Start painting as though you are dancing with your whole body, and not just using your fingers and your wrist. Use your arms with the force of the body behind them. Look at the shapes that appear, and think about what you can do with them.

Obviously, art therapy has a wealth of possibilities for the humanistic counselor. Likewise, the use of musical interventions in therapy creates multiple options.

Music Therapy

Music therapy uses music to produce change in the psychological, physical, cognitive, or social functioning of people with problems (American Music Therapy Association, 2005). This form of therapy uses clinical- and evidence-based music interventions to accomplish individualized goals within a therapeutic relationship by a credentialed professional who has completed an approved music therapy program (American Music Therapy Association, 2005). Interventions can be designed to:

- Promote wellness
- Manage stress
- Alleviate pain
- Express feelings
- Enhance memory
- Improve communication
- Promote physical rehabilitation

Music therapists look at a person's emotional well-being, physical health, social functioning, communication abilities, and cognitive skills through musical responses. They design music sessions for individuals and groups based on client needs using music improvisation, receptive music listening, song writing, lyric discussion, music and imagery, music performance, and learning through music. Therapists also participate in interdisciplinary treatment planning, ongoing evaluation, and follow-up (American Music Therapy Association, 2005).

The idea of music as a healing influence that could affect health and behavior is at least as old as the writings of Aristotle and Plato and has been used to communicate and express feeling across time (Gfeller, 2002). According to the American Music Therapy Association (2005), the 20th-century discipline of music therapy began after World War I and World War II when community musicians of all types played at VA hospitals around the country to thousands of veterans suffering both physical and emotional trauma from the wars. The patients' physical and emotional responses to music led the medical professionals to ask for the hospitals to hire musicians. It became evident that the hospital musicians needed some prior training before entering the facility, so the demand grew for a college curriculum. The first music therapy degree program in the world was founded at Michigan State University in 1944, and the American Music Therapy Association was founded in 1998 as a union of the National Association for Music Therapy and the American Association for Music Therapy. According to Voices: A World Forum for Music Therapy (n.d.), a world forum, today music therapy is taught and practiced in Europe, Asia, South America, Australia, and Russia.

The process of music therapy begins with the practitioner assessing the strengths and needs of each client. The qualified music therapist then delivers the indicated treatment that might include creating, singing, moving to, or listening to music. Through the musical involvement in therapy, clients' abilities are strengthened and transferred to other areas of their lives. Music therapy also provides avenues for communication that can be helpful to those who find it difficult to express themselves in words. Research in music therapy supports its effectiveness in many areas such as overall physical rehabilitation and facilitating movement, increasing people's motivation to become engaged in their treatment, providing emotional support for clients and their families, and providing an outlet for expression of feelings (American Music Therapy Association, 2005). That process outlines the use of music therapy.

According to Forinash (2005), humanistic music therapy emphasizes helping individuals find self-actualization and personal meaning. This therapy can occur in numerous settings including medical hospitals, psychiatric hospitals, and schools, to name only a few. Therapists recognize the person as a complex individual and work to help the client find meaning and fulfillment in life. Nordoff and Robbins (1977) outlined this process in a technique they called clinical improvisation. Those authors worked with children who have severe disabilities. They used music to create a musical portrait of the child, a musical reflection of the child's world. The music therapists worked with the visual cues like rocking and also the therapist's intuition and sense of the child as the improvisation was created. Once the child connected to the music the therapist brought the child into the musical relationship.

Music can also be used during counseling in a less encompassing and direct manner than music therapy (Gladding, 2005). Counselors could incorporate activities like listening, singing or performing, improvising, and composing to benefit clients. Listening to music allows someone to relax, thus reducing anxiety and diverting attention from stress. Music may also enliven a person's mood and encourage smiles and action through the tempo or lyrics. Clients may select songs to express what they are feeling or what their world is like. Counselors can also provide music and ask the client to respond by drawing, moving, or imagining. In these and other ways the music serves as a catalyst.

Counselors could incorporate music performance into therapy by asking clients to introduce themselves via a song or an instrumental sound. The counselor could have a variety of musical devices such as a harmonica, a keyboard, simple drums, a flute, and some kind of horn. Singing a song may allow a client to calm down or to explain something with the lyrics. Clients may choose a tune as a self-soothing aid. For clients who have musical backgrounds, they may improvise or do variations on a musical theme, making it faster, slower, or deeper. Finally, those with the abilities may be asked to compose something that represents their lives. Gladding (2005) explained that composing music puts someone in close touch with feelings, empowers, and enhances perseverance and discipline. Clients may accomplish their composition without using instruments by tapping, stomping, snapping, clicking, humming, or other ways of making noise. They can also write lyrics to be put to a tune they know. The incorporation of music into counseling provides a forum of expression that enriches the counseling alliance.

Drama Therapy

Drama therapy is the intentional use of drama or theater processes to reach therapeutic goals. It is active and experiential. Drama therapy provides a way for participants to tell their stories, set goals and solve problems, express feelings, or achieve catharsis. By using drama, a person's inner experience can be actively explored, and interpersonal relationship skills can be built. Participants can enhance their repertoire of dramatic roles to find that their own life roles have been strengthened. The goals of behavior change, skill building, emotional and physical integration, and personal growth can be achieved through drama therapy in prevention, intervention, and treatment settings (National Association for Drama Therapy, 2004).

Spiritual healers have used drama, dance, and chant throughout time. Sophocles, Aeschylus, and Euripides wrote Greek drama to engage the audience and provide opportunities for developing insight. Aeschylus realized that some themes are common to all humanity and that humans are fundamentally alike and wrote plays that focused on the issues most basic to man (Dayton, 1990). Much later, Jacob Moreno (1945; 1993) developed a system of psychodrama, a system of dramatic enactment. The client plays the protagonist and would replay distressing experiences in front of an audience who served to aid in dramatizing the scene and to release the repressed emotions stimulated by the play. After the enactment the audience supports the client and shares their own feelings stimulated by the drama. Drama therapy was pioneered by several individuals and has several different approaches. An anthology by Lewis and Johnson (2000) incorporates the many ways drama therapy is delivered.

Landy (2005) explains that the human ability to dramatize is innate. Throughout life people have an inner life through thoughts and their social life through behavior. Both of these are dramatic to the extent that a separation exists between the I and me or the part that thinks or acts and the part that is thought about or acted upon. Therefore, taking on and playing out roles are a natural and common means of expression. Another connection to drama and counseling has been identified. The goals of being sensitive to roles and being sensitive to those with whom you interact are parallels to the counseling process. According to Gladding (2011) both those who practice drama and those who practice counseling are deeply involved in all parts of life and experience their existence with rich understanding.

Drama therapy methods integrate role play, stories, improvisation, and other techniques taken from the theater with the theories and methods of therapy. The result is an active, experiential process that draws on the capacity for imagination, a means of accessing and expressing feelings, gaining insight, and practicing successful approaches to difficult situations. Sometimes the stories drama therapists listen to are real; sometimes they are fantasy. Sometimes stories are told by people who are in role, sometimes not. Stories may be played through objects, such as puppets, dolls, or other toys, using one's body, or one's voice. Dramatic techniques can help clarify, communicate, and define a person's feelings.

The reason for using drama in counseling would be to help a person express life difficulties in a dramatic way. By playing different roles people will become more aware of a range of emotions and may integrate parts of themselves they had previously ignored. Additionally, by witnessing movies, role plays, stories, and other productions, clients may gain some insight into themselves by recognizing emotions that have been expressed by others. Those viewings may help them change their patterns of interactions and enhance their relationships (Gladding, 2011). The National Association for Drama Therapy (2004) emphasizes that drama may also help in reducing feelings of isolation, developing new coping skills and patterns, broadening the range of expression of feelings, experiencing improved self-esteem and self-worth, increasing sense of play and spontaneity, and developing relationships.

Using drama in counseling may include watching movies or clips of movies or shows that the counselor has chosen or that the client has identified. For example, Vidia had viewed a film that captured many of the emotions she was feeling. Gladding (2011) pointed out that films have a more lasting effect than other forms of communication. Dollarhide (2003) told counselors to choose videos that are relevant, positive, appropriate, consistent, and engaging. Hesley and Hesley (2001) compiled a helpful book for using cinema in therapy.

Other dramatic activities that may be incorporated into counseling may be things like acting out a fairy tale and playing all the parts. Puppets could interview each other. People can use only their bodies to show an emotion. Counselors can engage their clients by saying, "Let's pretend." Clients could also be asked to act out their latest triumph or most stressful situation. They could be asked to act out a commercial "selling" themselves. Group experiences that incorporate dramatic exercises are also beneficial. The options are boundless. Two valuable resources have been compiled by Ruby and Ruby (2009) and Wiener (1994). Wiener's rehearsals for growth are tied to the goals of therapy and provide multiple options for incorporating drama into counseling.

Bibliotherapy

Bibliotherapy is the intentional use of books, poetry, and other forms of written materials for healing and growth. In other words bibliotherapy is the use of literature to promote mental health (National Association for Poetry Therapy, n.d). The poetry therapist is trained in both psychology and literature as well as group dynamics.

Bibliotherapy can be used for the following therapy goals:

- To develop an accurate understanding in perceptions of self and others
- To develop creativity, self-expression, and greater self-esteem
- To strengthen interpersonal skills and communication skills
- To express overpowering emotions and release tension
- To find new meaning through new ideas, insights, and information
- To promote change and increase coping skills and healthy functioning

Gorelick (2005) traced the history of healing with words. He began by noting shamanic incantation, picture language engraved on clay tablets, and the recorded events of the pharoahs' lives engraved in their tombs. He also noted that in Egypt magic words were written on papyrus and eaten by patients to cure disease. Chinese ideograms were created which combined two or more images and invented an alphabet that was visual poetry. Compilations of stories across the world as well as the influential Greek tragedies are also other early influences of the written word. The field of poetry therapy was originated by Jack Leedy who began a poetry therapy clinic in a Brooklyn hospital. Other founders of the field included Arthur Lerner, Arleen Hynes, and Sherry Reiter (Gorelick). In accordance with the principles of humanism, counselors using bibliotherapy evoke their clients' expression of subjective feelings and creativity. In addition, consistent with Rogers's (1957) recommendations, these counselors need to be genuine, spontaneous, and imaginative to be optimally effective in facilitating their clients' growth and change.

Gladding (2011) explained the rationale for bibliotherapy. First, counselors who use written materials can help people discover things about themselves and others, highlighting the positive aspects of life. Another rationale is the belief that a greater understanding of the world will emerge from the reading. People may realize that others have similar problems and may learn a connectedness across time, culture, and circumstances. Including literature in counseling leads to more constructive, positive thinking as well as more creative problem solving. All those reasons support using literature in counseling.

Bibliotherapy involves three components: the writing, the counselor, and the client. The writing is selected to serve as a stimulus and to evoke emotional responses for discussion. The focus is on the client's reaction to the literature with the primary objective being the psychological health and well-being of the client (National Coalition of Creative Arts Therapies Associations, 2005).

To use literature the counselor provides a safe, nonthreatening environment in which the clients are invited to share their feelings. The literature is chosen for its therapeutic potential. The process of bibliotherapy involves the participants recognizing and identifying with the selection (recognition). Next the participants explore specific details of the selected material (examination). Then the process involves exploring the comparisons and contrasts of the experience portrayed (juxtaposition), and finally the client makes the connection among the individual, the literature, and the application of the knowledge (application to self). This process has been captured by Borders and Naylor (1993) in their work on helping children talk about books. After the book is read the facilitators pose these statements:

- Talk about what you notice in the story.
- Talk about how the story made you feel.
- Talk about what the story reminds you of in your life.

Those statements could be used to probe for reactions to art, music, or drama as well and are invaluable guides for humanistic counselors.

As with other creative arts media, materials to include for bibliotherapy must be chosen carefully and must be discussed with particular sensitivity to the client's reactions and meaning-making process. The counselor will want to build a collection of books, poems and other written resources to have on hand as they incorporate bibliotherapy in their work. Joshua and DiMenna (2000) have a helpful volume. Also Borders and Naylor's (1993) book is written for children, but the themes and activities are ageless.

APPLICATIONS AND IMPLICATIONS FOR PRACTITIONERS

Richards (2007) compiled a guide to everyday creativity that identifies 12 beneficial features or characteristics of functioning more creatively. She acknowledged that creativity may be used for destructive, antisocial means but at best can improve psychological health and integration by breaking down barriers. Creativity can build connections with others, advance caring and empathy, and move us all toward more peaceful and collaborative ways of being together. Her premise is that everyday creativity helps us live better and move toward broader life possibilities, meaning, and joy.

The specific benefits Richards (2007) and the other contributors to the volume identify read like a manual for humanistic counselors. In responding to the stimulus "when I am creative, I am…" these qualities emerge: dynamic, conscious, healthy, nondefensive, open, integrating, observing actively, caring, collaborative, androgynous, developing, and brave. Descriptors follow.

The first six benefits of living more creatively involve a lifestyle. *Dynamic* refers to knowing oneself as emerging and as a part of a larger system. *Conscious* can be defined as being aware of and attentive to all aspects of the present experience. *Healthy* signifies following a lifestyle that is wholesome and sustains active participation with life. *Nondefensive* suggests being alert to forces that restrict self-awareness and limiting their barriers. *Open* represents a stance that is welcoming new experiences, being aware, intuitive, sensitive, and avoiding preconceptions. The sixth benefit is *integrating*, a position that enjoys complexity and functions across many modalities but integrates toward healing simplicity.

The next six benefits refer to actions a creative person engenders. *Observing actively* means active mental participation. *Caring* represents being guided by values and concerns that are based in love, compassion, and larger realms of meaning. *Collaborative* denotes the actions of working with others toward greater goals, resolving conflicts while honoring uniqueness. *Androgynous* implies bridging false dichotomies and being open to as-yet-unknown possibilities. *Developing* indicates the awareness of personal development that continues and will persist across many generations. Finally, *brave* denotes the acceptance of risks in exploring the unknown, trusting the process and the greater good, as well as embracing the mystery of life.

Richards's (2007) summary of the benefits of being creative supports the imperative for humanistic counselors to enhance that capacity for themselves. So take some time to draw a picture of your idea for that next client, read some poetry and ask yourself what stands out for you in the words, listen to that rumba beat and consider how it fits your life. Open your imagination and reap the benefits.

SUMMARY

The creative arts allow opportunities for experimenting with new ways of communication and with experiences that involve pretending. People are asked to invest energy in something different and hopefully discover new ways to understand their story, to reflect, and to explore their feelings. Doing, making, and creating bring energy into an encounter. Creativity can be a healing agent that opens the pathway to self-actualization, the penultimate humanistic goal.

REFERENCES

American Art Therapy Association. (2004). *Definition*. Downloaded May 2, 2010 from http://www.arttherapy.org/aata-aboutus.html

American Music Therapy Association. (2005). *Definition*. Downloaded May 3, 2010 from http://www.musictherapy.org/

Ansbacher, H. L. (1977). Individual psychology. In R. J. Corsini (Ed.), *Current psychotherapies*. Itasca, IL: F.E. Peacock.

Arons, M. F., & Richards, R. (2001). Two noble insurgencies: Creativity and humanistic psychology. In J. K. Schneider, J. F. T. Bugental, & J. F. Pierson (Eds.), *The handbook of humanistic psychology: Leading edges in theory, research and practice* (pp. 127–142). Thousand Oaks, CA: Sage.

Atkins, S., Adams, M., McKinney, C., McKinney, H., Rose, L. Wentworth, J., et al. (2003). *Expressive arts therapy*. Boone, NC: Parkway.

Borders, S. G., & Naylor, A. P. (1993). *Children talking about books*. Phoenix, AZ: Oryx Press.

Camilleri, V. A. (2007). *Healing the inner city child: Creative arts therapies with at-risk youth*. London: Jessica Kingsley Publishers.

Creek, J. (2002). *Occupational therapy and mental health* (3rd ed.). Edinburgh: Churchill Livingstone.

Csikszentmihalyi, M. (1990). *Flow: The psychology of optimal experience*. New York: Harper.

Dayton, T. (1990). *Drama games: Techniques for self-development*. New York: Innerlook, Inc.

De Bono, E. (1990). *Lateral thinking: Creativity step by step*. New York: Harper & Row.

De Bono, E. (1999). *Six thinking hats*. New York: Little Brown and Company.

Dollarhide, C. T. (2003). Cinematherapy: Making media work for you. *School Counselor, 42*(6), 16–17.

Eberle, R. F. (1971). *SCAMPER: Games for imagination development*. Buffalo, NY: DOK.

Feen-Calligan, H., Washington, O., & Moxley, D. (2008). Use of artwork as a visual processing modality in group treatment of chemically dependent minority women. *Arts in Psychotherapy, 35*(4), 287–295.

Forinash, M. (2005). Music therapy. In C. Malchiodi (Ed.), *Expressive therapies* (pp. 46–67). New York: Guilford.

Garai, J. (2001). A humanistic approach to art therapy. In J. Rubin (Ed.), *Approaches to art therapy* (pp. 188–207). New York: Brunner-Routledge.

Gfeller, K. E. (2002). Music as therapeutic agent: Historical and sociocultural perspectives. In R. F. Unkefer & M. H. Thaut (Eds.), *Music therapy in the treatment of adults with mental disorders: Theoretical bases and clinical interventions* (2nd ed., pp. 60–67). St. Louis, MO: MMB Music.

Gladding, S. T. (2011). *The creative arts in counseling* (4th ed.) Alexandria, VA: American Counseling Association.

Goethe, J. W. (1917). Wilhelm Meister's apprenticeship. In W. A. Neilson (Ed.), *The Harvard Classics Shelf of Fiction*, vol. 14, selected by C. W. Eliot (paraphrased from p. 288). New York: P. F. Collier.

Gorelick, K. (2005). Poetry therapy. In C. Malchiodi (Ed.), *Expressive therapies* (pp. 117–140). New York: Guilford.

Griffiths, S. (2008). The experience of creative activity as a treatment medium. *Journal of Mental Health, 17*(1), 49–63.

Hesley, J. W., & Hesley, J. G. (2001). *Rent two films and let's talk in the morning: Using popular movies in psychotherapy* (2nd ed.). New York: Wiley.

Joshua, J. M., & DiMenna, D. (2000). *Read two books and let's talk next week*. New York: Wiley.

Kramer, E. (1971). *Art as therapy with children*. New York: Schocken.

Kwiatkowska, H. Y. (1978). *Family therapy and evaluation through art.* Springfield, IL: Charles C. Thomas.

Landy, R. J. (2005). Drama therapy and psychodrama. In C. Malchiodi (Ed.), *Expressive therapies* (pp. 90–116). New York: Guilford.

Lewis, P., & Johnson, D. R. (Eds.). (2000). *Current approaches in drama therapy.* Springfield, IL: Thomas.

Malchiodi, C. A. (2005). Expressive therapies: History, theory, and practice. In C. Malchiodi (Ed.), *Expressive therapies* (pp. 1–16). New York: Guilford Press.

Malchiodi, C. A. (2007). *Art therapy sourcebook.* New York: McGraw-Hill.

Maslow, A. H. (1968). *Toward a psychology of being* (2nd ed.). Princeton, NJ: Van Nostrand.

Matson, F. W. (1969). Whatever became of the Third Force? *American Association of Humanistic Psychology Newsletter, 6*(1), 14–15.

McNiff, S. (1994). *Art as medicine.* Boston: Shambhala.

Milliken, R. (2008). Intervening in the cycle of addiction, violence, and shame: A dance/movement therapy group approach in a jail addictions program. *Journal of Groups in Addiction & Recovery, 3*(1–2), 5–22.

Moreno, J. L. (1945). *Group psychotherapy: A symposium.* New York: Beacon House.

Moreno, J. L. (1993). *Who shall survive? Foundations of sociometry, group psychotherapy, and sociodrama.* Roanoke, VA: Royal. (Original work published 1934.)

National Association for Drama Therapy. (2004). *Definition and frequently asked questions.* Downloaded June 21, 2010 from http://www.nadt.org/faqs.htm

National Association for Poetry Therapy. (n.d.). *Definition.* Downloaded June 20, 2010 from http://www.poetrytherapy.org/

National Coalition of Creative Arts Therapies Associations. (2005). *Overview.* Downloaded June 10, 2010 from http://www.nccata.org/

Naumburg, M. (1966). *Dynamically oriented art therapy.* New York: Grune & Stratton.

Nordoff, P., & Robbins, C. (1977). *Creative music therapy.* New York: John Day.

Raskin, N. J., Rogers, C. R., & Witty, M. C. (2008). Client-centered therapy. In R. J. Corsini & D. Wedding (Eds.), *Current psychotherapies* (8th ed., pp. 141–186). Belmont, CA: Thomson.

Reynolds, F. (2000). Managing depression through needlecraft creative activities: A qualitative study. *Arts in Psychotherapy. 27,* 107–114.

Richards, R. (2007). Twelve potential benefits of living more creatively. In R. Richards (Ed.), *Everyday creativity and new views of human nature: Psychological, social, and spiritual perspectives* (pp. 289–320). Washington, DC: American Psychological Association.

Rogers, C. R. (1954). Toward a theory of creativity. *ETC: A Review of General Semantics, 11,* 249–260.

Rogers, C. R. (1957). The necessary and sufficient conditions of therapeutic personality change. *Journal of Consulting Psychology, 21,* 95–103.

Rogers, C. R. (1995). *On becoming a person: A therapist's view of psychotherapy.* Boston: Houghton Mifflin. (Original work published 1961.)

Rogers, N. (1999). *The creative connection: Expressive arts as healing.* Palo Alto, CA: Science and Behavior Books.

Ruby, J. R., & Ruby, N. C. (2009). Improvisational acting exercises: Their potential use in family counseling. *Journal of Creativity in Mental Health, 4*(2), 152–160.

Smeijsters, H., & Cleven, G. (2006). The treatment of aggression using arts therapies in forensic psychiatry: Results of a qualitative inquiry. *Arts in Psychotherapy, 33*(1), 37–58.

Smith, E. J. (2006). The strength-based counseling model. *Counseling Psychologist, 34*(1), 13–79.

Stewart, K., & Schneider, S. (2000). The effects of music therapy on the sound environment in the NICU: A pilot study. In J. V. Loewy (Ed.), *Music therapy in the neonatal intensive care unit* (pp. 85–100). St. Louis, MO: MMB Music.

Ulman, E., & Dachinger, P. (1996). *Art therapy in theory and practice.* New York: Schocken. (Original work published 1975.)

Voices: A World Forum for Music Therapy. (n.d.). *Overview.* Downloaded on June 6, 2010 from www.voices.no

Wiener, D. (1994). *Rehearsals for growth: Theater improvisations for psychotherapists.* New York: W.W. Norton.

Zimring, F. M. (1995). A new explanation for the beneficial results of client-centered therapy: The possibility of a new paradigm. *Person-Centered Journal, 2*(2), 36–48.

5

Humanism and Substance Abuse Counseling

MARK B. SCHOLL, EMMA KENDRICK, DALLAS WILKES, AND W. BRYCE HAGEDORN

Of all the contemporary mental health problems addressed by the chapters of the current text, none has a more pervasive and pernicious influence upon the growth, development, and potential of America's youth than substance abuse. Tobacco, alcohol, and illicit drug use are leading causes of disease and mortality both during adolescence and later in life (Substance Abuse and Mental Health Services Administration, 2009). The National Institute on Drug Abuse (NIDA) funded the 2009 Monitoring the Future Study, which indicated that by the end of twelfth grade 72% of students have consumed at least one drink, and 37% of eighth graders have done so. Further, 57% of twelfth graders and 17% of eighth graders reported having been drunk at least once. Results of the same study indicated that as early as eighth grade, 7% (1 in 15) of all students have become current habitual smokers, (i.e., has been smoking daily for at least several weeks). Perhaps the most alarming finding from the survey was that the prevalence of marijuana use (at least once over the previous 30-day period), which had gradually declined over a preceding decade (1997–2007), significantly increased from 12% to 14% (2007–2009) for an aggregate sample of 8th-, 10th-, and 12th-grade students.

In models of adolescent development (e.g., Erikson, 1959; Jessor, 1991), adolescence is described as a sensitive period for exploration and experimentation. Unfortunately, adolescence is also frequently a period for experimentation with drugs. Because this time period is also a sensitive one for the development of abilities including managing emotions, critical thinking, social skills, and capacity for intimacy, drug use can lead to a lack of development in one or more of these areas. Drug use has been linked to underdeveloped social and vocational skills, dropping out of school, unemployment, and lack of an adequate social network (Ferdinandi & Li, 2007). For these reasons, and because research indicates that early legal and illegal drug use is a significant predictor of subsequent legal substance abuse (Boreham & Shaw, 2001; Measham, Aldridge, & Parker, 2001; Ramsey & Partridge, 1999; Sutherland & Willner, 1998) and psychosocial difficulties (Anthony & Petronis, 1995; Fergusson & Horwood, 2000) later in life, it is vitally important for mental health practitioners to be aware of the history, trends, and the most current empirical evidence with regard to efficacious treatment methods. Accordingly, this chapter focuses on two widely respected and empirically validated approaches to substance abuse counseling: (1) motivational interviewing (MI); and (2) 12-step facilitation. In presenting these two approaches, we explain how humanistic principles are integral to both as well as how they play a critical role in their effectiveness.

TRENDS IN THE HISTORY OF SUBSTANCE ABUSE COUNSELING

Two highly significant trends in the evolution of substance abuse counseling treatments both entail changes that involved the incorporation of humanistic elements into counseling approaches for working with individuals addicted to drugs and alcohol. The first of these two trends was the advent of the Minnesota model (Anderson, McGovern, & Dupont, 1999), and the second was changes in the uses of confrontation in substance abuse counseling eventually leading to the development of motivational interviewing (Miller, 1983; Miller & Rollnick, 2002).

The Minnesota model began as a result of the efforts of Daniel McGovern and associates in the early to mid-1950s. While working at Wilmar State Hospital in Chicago they were appalled at the treatment that alcoholics received at the time. In their words, "Everyone looked down on them … even our mentally ill patients" (Anderson et al., 1999, p. 110). Further, McGovern observed that clinicians and staff viewed the alcoholics as the lowest functioning and the most hopeless of all the patients at Wilmar. Consequently, they sought to provide more effective and humane services for these patients. They created a highly structured program that they described as "patient-centered in a social learning environment" (p. 112). Of particular relevance to humanism, McGovern asserted that the most important characteristic of the program was that it was founded on respect for the individual as unique. In addition, they were committed to the belief that it was possible to recover with the help of a higher power and the fellowship of an Alcoholics Anonymous (AA) support group. The program was first known as the Wilmar model in the early 1950s, then as the Hazelden model in the 1960s, and most recently, as it gained popular acceptance, as the Minnesota model.

Second, changes in the use of confrontation in substance abuse counseling represent a trend that is particularly relevant to a discussion of humanistic counseling practice. From a humanistic perspective, clients are considered to be the greatest authority regarding their inner subjective experiences including sense of well-being, personally meaningful goals, and life satisfaction (Rogers, 1957). In effective confrontation, the counselor describes client inconsistencies among clients' thoughts, feelings, and actions, or between their behaviors and goals. Considerable care should be taken to communicate respect for clients and to ensure that the confrontation contributes to their growth and welfare.

In the mid–20th century, "fairly aggressive confrontational strategies" became prevalent in individual, group, and family substance abuse counseling in the United States as a result of a number of cultural factors (White & Miller, 2007, p. 13). Between the 1920s and 1950s theories of addiction shifted from those emphasizing biological causal models to those emphasizing flawed character as the source. Proponents of confrontational strategies believed that an aggressive approach was required to penetrate the defense mechanisms and flawed character armor that was believed to accompany substance abuse disorders. The communications used in confrontational approaches to the treatment of alcoholism included "profanity-laden indictments, screamed denunciations of character, challenges and ultimatums, intense argumentation, ridicule, and purposeful humiliation" (White & Miller, 2007, p. 13). Such harsh forms of confrontation reflected the prevalent "tear 'em down to build 'em up" philosophy.

The late 1970s saw a significant shift in the use of confrontation approaches resulting from reevaluation of methods at Hazelden where the use of the "hot seat" in women's units became viewed as disrespectful. The treatment of men was altered to include an assessment of character assets. Overall, the use of aggressive confrontation was replaced with a novel concept—*compassionate confrontation* (White & Miller, 2007), which, consistent with humanism, is grounded in the counselor's empathic concern for the client's welfare.

Research has failed to support the efficacy of confrontational approaches, whereas a number of studies provide evidence of the harmful effects of such approaches (Boardman, Catley, Grobe, Little, & Ahluwalia, 2006). In addition, studies indicate that more effective substance abuse counselors employ an empathic, supportive style (Boardman et al., 2006; White & Miller, 2007). There are now a number of evidence-based alternatives to confrontational substance abuse counseling, including motivational interviewing (Miller & Rollnick, 2002).

CLIENT-CENTERED SUBSTANCE ABUSE COUNSELING: FOCUS ON MOTIVATIONAL INTERVIEWING

Brooks and McHenry (2009) emphasized the importance of the quality of the therapeutic relationship for effectively helping drug- and alcohol-addicted clients. In support of client-centered counseling, they view Rogers's (1957) facilitative conditions (i.e., genuineness, respect, empathy) to also be the core counselor characteristics essential to effectively counseling clients coping with painful feelings such as fear, shame, and embarrassment, which are commonly experienced by addicted clients. Brooks and McHenry asserted that a "genuine, truthful, and in-the-moment relationship allows clients to know, without question, that they are understood and cared for during their emotional pain and time of crisis" (p. 2). Also consistent with Rogers's client-centered philosophy is their belief in the importance of the counselor's self in the therapeutic relationship and the importance of counselor characteristics including genuineness, creativity, and spontaneity. Perhaps the importance of these characteristics is reflected in the finding of a recent meta-analytic study that demonstrated that effect sizes for MI were larger when practice was not manual guided (Hettema, Steele, & Miller, 2005).

First described in an article written by William R. Miller in 1983, motivational interviewing's evidence base began growing rapidly and shows no signs of slowing. A group of researchers, including the originator, recently described MI as a "client-centered, directive therapeutic style to enhance readiness for change" and "an evolution of Rogers's person-centered counseling approach" (Hettema et al., 2005, p. 91).

MOTIVATIONAL INTERVIEWING: GENERAL DESCRIPTION

MI (Miller & Rollnick, 2002) is an integrative approach combining elements of client-centered and cognitive-behavioral therapies (CBT). Similar to Carl Rogers's (1957) identification of core conditions in counseling, Miller and Rollnick advocated the use of humanistic counselor characteristics: empathy, unconditional positive regard, nonpossessive warmth, and counselor authenticity. From the CBT model, MI employs active influence techniques including eliciting change statements, and summaries highlighting the client's desire for change. Consistent with humanism, these active techniques support the client's internal locus of control and decision making.

Additional features of MI convey respect for clients' internal subjective experience and respect for the client as an individual. These features respectively include assessing the clients' ambivalence about, and readiness for, changing their behaviors. Rather than being viewed as a sign of resistance, ambivalence is openly reflected and normalized by the counselor.

With regard to level of readiness, an integral component of MI is the transtheoretical model (TTM) of intentional human behavior change (DiClemente & Prochaska, 1998; Prochaska & DiClemente, 1984), which includes the stages-of-change model (Prochaska, DiClemente, & Norcross, 1992). The stages-of-change model has been used to assess clients' readiness to facilitate a host of behaviors including cessation of smoking, alcohol and drug abuse, gambling, and eating habits (Carney & Kivlahan, 1995; DiClemente & Hughes, 1990; DiClemente & Prochaska, 1998; DiClemente, Story, & Murray, 2000; Glanz et al., 1994; Grimley, Riley, Bellis, & Prochaska, 1993; Isenhart, 1994; Marcus, Rossi, Selby, Niaura, & Abrams, 1992; Weinstein, Rothman, & Sutton, 1998; Werch & DiClemente, 1994; Willoughby & Edens, 1996). In TTM as incorporated in MI, changes in substance use behaviors are viewed as progressing from the first *precontemplative stage* (individual is not considering change or aware of need to change) to the *contemplative stage* (individual considers but usually experiences feelings of ambivalence regarding change) to the *planning stage* (individual becomes committed to a change plan) to making a behavior change in the *action stage* to finally striving to maintain the change in the *maintenance stage* (DiClemente & Velasquez, 2002). Motivation is essential as it provides the impetus, focus, and energy required to progress through the five stages of change (DiClemente, 1999). In keeping with the fundamental humanistic belief that individuals possess an innate self-righting tendency, these stages are applicable to behavior change whether it occurs with or without the assistance of a therapist.

MI is perhaps best applied to developing the motivation necessary for individuals to change behaviors (i.e., in the precontemplation and contemplation stages) but is also a useful adjunct to therapy in the latter stages of change (i.e., planning, action, and maintenance). Although more action-oriented approaches to substance abuse counseling are recommended during the latter three stages (also known as phase 2 of MI; Miller & Rollnick, 2002), clients are still more responsive when the counselor continues to employ the basic strategies and counselor attitudes (e.g., empathic, nonjudgmental, supportive of self-efficacy) are continued (DiClemente & Velasquez, 2002).

Four primary strategies guide counselors' MI work with clients: (1) expressing empathy; (2) developing discrepancies (e.g., between what clients are doing and their personal goals); (3) rolling with resistance (i.e., avoid confronting or arguing with clients and make every attempt to understand their perspective); and (4) supporting clients' self-efficacy (Miller & Rollnick, 2002). Scaling is commonly employed in the form of readiness or confidence rulers (see the following case illustration), and a high priority is placed on intentionally eliciting and reflecting clients' self-motivational statements (also referred to as *change talk*) rather than giving advice. Counselor use of eliciting statements has been demonstrated to be positively associated with client self-motivational statements (Vader, Walters, Prabhu, Houck, & Field, 2010). The four primary strategies have been referred to as the technical aspects or structural elements of MI (Markland, Ryan, Tobin, & Rollnick, 2005) and these structural elements have been found to contribute to greater reductions in drinking behavior than psychoeducation alone (Sellman, Sullivan, Dore, Adamson, & MacEwan, 2001).

With regard to the importance of rolling with resistance and avoiding confrontation, it is important to remember that individuals in the precontemplation and contemplation stages are resistant to forceful confrontation on the part of significant others and counselors. For this reason, a confrontation response should be expressed in a caring manner and should not take place without sufficient motivation for change on the part of the client. Ideally, the confrontation should emphasize the discrepancy between clients' behavior and their self-expressed goals or desire for change. MI's collaborative approach to eliciting change statements rather than employing feedback that confronts or labels has been praised as "an important improvement over past feedback delivery approaches" (Burke, Dunn, Atkins, & Phelps, 2004, p. 313).

Self-Determination Theory

Markland et al. (2005) proposed that self-determination theory (SDT; Ryan & Deci, 2000) may be a potentially useful framework for understanding clients' developmental process in the context of effectively applying the MI approach. SDT is a theory of identity development and self-motivated behavior change. In SDT, Ryan and Deci asserted that individuals, consistent with humanism, have an innate tendency to move toward growth, to increase integration of self, and to resolve psychological inconsistencies. Furthermore, all human behaviors are believed to fall somewhere along a continuum that ranges from externally regulated to internally regulated. Correspondingly, individuals' behaviors are expected to be intrinsically motivating and internally regulated to the extent that behaviors are integrated with their identity and are consistent with their self-concepts, values, and goals. Therefore, by supporting clients' autonomy, a counselor increases the likelihood that clients will acquire more adaptive, and more internally regulated, behaviors. Counselors who provide more autonomy-supportive conditions are also likely to increase client involvement and persistence toward achieving personally meaningful goals (Markland et al., 2005; Moyers, Miller, & Hendrickson, 2005).

In their SDT, Ryan and Deci (2000) posit that three basic needs must be met for clients to become optimally engaged and persist in counseling: a need for competence; a need to feel autonomous; and a need to feel connected to others. In keeping with recommendations made by Rogers (1957), counselors employing MI should enact an interpersonal role that supports these primary needs in their clients (Miller & Rollnick, 2002; Moyers & Rollnick, 2002). Rather than relying primarily on techniques, it is important for counselors to primarily emphasize adopting the *spirit of MI* with regard to their interpersonal style. More specifically, the spirit of MI entails providing empathy and nonjudgmental acceptance and facilitating a collaborative and egalitarian relationship with the client. Without provision of the appropriate interpersonal style, there is a real danger that MI techniques can be used in a manner that is manipulative, cynical, and potentially harmful to the client (Moyers & Rollnick).

Research Findings

There is encouraging evidence of the effectiveness of MI, originally developed as an adult intervention, as a brief approach for addressing smoking and substance use among adolescents, young adults, and adults. An advantage of MI is that its nonconfrontational and individualized approach is potentially attractive to autonomy-oriented adolescents and young adults (Lawendowski, 1998; Scholl & Schmitt, 2009; Tober, 1991). Outcome research has supported the effectiveness of brief MI interventions for addressing teenage client cigarette smoking (Colby et al., 1998), alcohol consumption (Monti et al., 1999), and cannabis use (Stephens, Roffman, & Curtin, 2000). Finally, a more recent study (McCambridge & Strang, 2004) indicated that a single session of MI was effective in reducing cigarette, alcohol, and cannabis use in a sample of 200 young people (age range 16–20 years) who were multiple-drug users.

Additional studies have supported the effectiveness of MI for reducing heavy drinking for college student clients (Baer, Kivlahan, Blume, McKnight, & Marlatt, 2001; Borsari & Carey, 2000, 2005; LaBrie, Pederson, Lamb, & Quinlan, 2007; Michael, Curtin, Kirkley, Jones, & Harris, 2006; Roberts, Neal, Kivlahan, Baer, & Marlatt, 2000). Support for MI's effectiveness in reducing drinking for adult clientele has come from a number of meta-analytic studies (Burke et al., 2003, 2004; Dunn, Deroo, & Rivara, 2001; Hettema, Steele, & Miller, 2005; Vasilaki, Hosier, & Cox, 2006). Research has not supported the effectiveness of MI for addressing nicotine addiction in young adults and adult clients (Burke, Arkowitz, & Menchola, 2003).

The results of a limited number of studies indicate that MI shows promise as a means of enhancing intrinsic motivation, and reducing drinking, in dually diagnosed clients with substance abuse disorders and a severe mental illness (DiClemente, Nidecker, & Bellack, 2008; Graeber, Moyers, Griffith, Guajardo, & Tonigan, 2003; Martino, Carroll, Kostas, Perkins, & Rounsaville, 2002). Martino et al. reason that MI appears to be well suited for use with clients suffering from severe symptoms that have frequently contributed to feelings of discouragement and reduced intrinsic motivation for changing drinking behaviors. Graeber et al. (2003) found that use of MI with clients presenting with comorbid schizophrenia resulted in a significant reduction in drinking and an increase in abstinence rates relative to clients receiving an educational treatment. Particularly intriguing are Martino et al.'s descriptions of modifications to "primary MI skill sets (e.g., simplifying open-ended questions)" (p. 297). In effect the authors recommend dual diagnosis motivational interviewing (DDMI) modifications to better accommodate clients' impairments, symptoms, and psychiatric issues. For example, because individuals with a severe mental illness may have difficulty organizing responses to compound open-ended questions, practitioners are advised to employ simple open questions. Other recommended DDMI modifications include use of repetition to accommodate cognitive impairments and added emphasis on affirming clients to counteract the social stigma of mental illness.

Few studies have examined whether MI works better for some types of clients than others (Scholl & Schmitt, 2009). However, the National Institute on Alcohol Abuse and Alcoholism oversaw a series of empirical investigations—Matching Alcoholism Treatments to Client Heterogeneity (Project MATCH)—conducted to analyze the effectiveness of competing approaches for treating different types of clients (Project MATCH Research Group, 1997, 1998a, 1998b). Because MI is frequently used in combination with other treatment approaches, the Project MATCH researchers studied the relative effectiveness of adaptations of motivational interviewing (AMI), defined as approaches in which MI principles are the core treatment. Few significant client-by-treatment matches were found. Two of the more robust findings indicated that AMI outperformed 12-step facilitation (TSF) and CBT for clients who scored high on an anger measure, whereas TSF and CBT outperformed AMI for clients scoring low on the anger measure (Miller & Rollnick, 2002). A possible interpretation of these findings is that MI's nonconfrontational approach is more effective with clients who are mandated or have high levels of anger.

Operationalizing the spirit of MI for purposes of empirical investigation represents a complex challenge. This may partly explain why research supporting the effectiveness of MI has primarily provided evidence for the effectiveness of the four technical elements or strategies (Roth & Fonagy, 2005). However, limited evidence does indicate the counselor's interpersonal style contributes to the effectiveness of MI. In one study, Moyers et al. (2005) demonstrated that the counselors' interpersonal skills were positively associated with clients' levels of engagement in MI sessions. Further, as previously mentioned, the results of a meta-analytic review revealed greater effect sizes when MI was used in a manner that was not manual guided (Hettema et al., 2005). Borsari and Carey (2005) found that MI counselors who outperformed alcohol education counselors were also rated as more collaborative than their alcohol education counterparts. Finally, Boardman et al. (2006) found that counselor characteristics consistent with the spirit of MI (i.e., egalitarian, empathic, collaborative) were positively associated with the quality of the therapeutic alliance and client engagement. Counselor confrontation was negatively associated with the alliance. Additional research is needed to determine the relative contributions to therapeutic outcomes made by the counseling style and each of the four technical elements.

CASE ILLUSTRATION

The counselor in this case illustration is an experienced college counseling professional and associate director at the counseling center at a midsized private university in a large northern U.S. city. The counselor uses MI extensively with all judicially mandated and self-referred clients who have alcohol use concerns. To maintain anonymity, individuals in this case illustration will be referred to by pseudonyms.

Description of the Client

Nick is a 21-year-old junior majoring in business with a grade point average (GPA) of approximately 2.5. He was born in the United States but spent some of his childhood with members of his extended family in a South American country. His parents are divorced. His mother is remarried, and he has no contact with his father. He has one brother and one half-brother. His initial presenting problem in counseling was to deal with the stress of going to school and taking a full-time 15-credit class load and with balancing school and a full-time, 38-hour-per-week job. He works to pay tuition and living expenses.

As Nick became more comfortable with the counseling process, he revealed to his counselor, Lisa, that he uses alcohol as a means of stress reduction. He disclosed that he would like to stop drinking, if only because he does not have the money to spend on it. Lisa used MI to facilitate exploring and resolving Nick's ambivalence regarding his drinking behaviors. The counselor and client were able to collaboratively identify alternative behaviors that could be adopted to counteract this overreliance on drinking.

Session Transcript

Consistent with humanism's emphasis upon the individual's internal subjective experience, one of Lisa's primary goals in the first session was assessing Nick's own level of concern about his drinking behavior. Another goal was to use relatively nonconfrontational MI techniques (e.g., reflecting change talk, double-sided reflections) to motivate Nick to think seriously about the need to change his drinking behavior. Early in the session, Lisa provided responses that supported his needs for a quality relationship, autonomy, and sense of competence. Regarding the need for a quality relationship, Lisa joined with Nick by communicating her understanding of his view of the situation. This included a double-sided reflection of the fact that he enjoys drinking but would like to cut down to save money. In support of his need for autonomy, Lisa emphasized his freedom of personal choice in deciding whether to change and in deciding whether he needs to quit drinking or, alternatively, to cut down the amount he drinks. In both of these instances, she also supported Nick's need to feel competent by indicating that she believed him to be intelligent and rational enough to make these decisions on his own. His interest in spending less money was also viewed as relevant to his need to feel competent.

Nick: I think I am drinking too much, and I realize I am spending way too much money on drinking every weekend.
Lisa: You're looking at the amount of drinking you are doing and how much it is costing you.
Nick: I spend $40 to $50 every weekend.
Lisa: Your hard-earned money.
Nick: Yes, and I really can't afford it.
Lisa: It sounds like you are looking at what you are doing and are thinking about making some changes.
Nick: I like to drink, though. It makes me forget my problems.
Lisa: You enjoy drinking but realize the amount you are drinking is costly.
Nick: True, I don't have that kind of money and when I drink, I like to drink a lot.
Lisa: It's enjoyable for you to drink large amounts.
Nick: Well, when you put it that way, it's not like it's that bad.
Lisa: Money not being a factor, the amount is not so bad.
Nick: I guess not. Do you think it is too much?
Lisa: More importantly, it's what you think. It sounds like you are questioning whether you are drinking too much and that is what we have on the table here.
Nick: I am. Like I said, it's costing me a lot of money.

Lisa: It's hard-earned money that you don't have a lot of and you realize how much of it is going toward alcohol.

Nick: I really need to cut down or stop.

Lisa: Which do you think you are ready to do?

Nick: I guess I just need to cut down.

Later in the Session

Lisa provided a number of responses that supported Nick's need for a collaborative counselor–client relationship. For example, she used humor, and this aided their rapport. She also empathized with Nick's concerns related to enjoying quality time with his friends, and they began to explore together the options for drinking less while maintaining these relationships. Her openness to his self-directed decision to reduce his drinking is consistent with humanism and a harm reduction approach that more flexibly accommodates Nick's identity development needs.

Toward the end of this session, Lisa provided Nick with a summary that highlighted his desire for change and the nature of his ambivalence. In support of his autonomy, she then asked him whether her summary seemed accurate.

Nick: There are many things that I'd like to change. Cutting down drinking is definitely one of them.

Lisa: Well, looking at things one at a time is helpful, so as not to get too overwhelmed.

Nick: True. I guess cutting down drinking is what I should really concentrate on.

Lisa: What might be good or not so good about cutting down on drinking?

Nick: Good and not so good…. Hmmm. Well, I know a good part will be having more money in my pocket. Like I've been saying, I spend way too much money on drinking. The not so good is what would I do on the weekends. If I don't go out to clubs drinking with my friends, what will I do?

Lisa: Well, let's look at some alternative to drinking or clubbing on the weekends. What might be some other things that you can do?

Nick: Nothing seems to be as fun as drinking.

Lisa: Drinking really is the only fun thing to do. There is nothing else.

Nick: (laughs) Well, not really, but it is hard to think of other things when all my friends go to clubs.

Lisa: How much of the fun is drinking versus the fun in being with your friends?

Nick: Well, I enjoy both, but it is really important to be with my friends. It's not like I would go out to the clubs by myself. Maybe I can go to the clubs with them and not drink so much.

Lisa: I just want to go over what we've been looking at. There are changes that you want to make, and cutting down or stopping your drinking is one of them. In fact, you've identified it as the one thing you want to focus on right now. You are seeing that there are good and bad—positive and negative—results from this decision. The money you save is one of the positive results that is important to you; however, a negative is your concern as to what you will do on the weekends. Does this sound accurate?

Nick: Yup. That's it right there.

Lisa: I think it will be helpful if we explore more options for you to do in your free time, so that drinking with your friends is not the only option you can think of doing on weekends.

At the End of the Session

At the end of the session, Lisa used scaling techniques. Although the use of scaling in the form of readiness and confidence rulers is quite structured, in Lisa's experience scaling is also a particularly effective means for facilitating a collaborative relationship with the client. The readiness and confidence rulers (Sciacca, 2003) have 11 points, beginning with 0, which is labeled *Not at all important* or *Not at all confident,* and ending with 10, which is labeled *Extremely important* or *Extremely confident.* The rulers do not include any intermediate labels. The dialogue from the session's end illustrates the way a counselor implicitly communicates to the client that their work together is a collaborative relationship, even when using the scaling technique. In addition, she asks Nick to think about what it would take to increase his levels of readiness and confidence. Consistent with a humanistic client-centered approach, Lisa is expressing confidence in his competence and supporting his need for autonomy.

Lisa: [Gives Nick a copy of the readiness ruler] How important would you say it is for you to cut down your drinking? On a scale of 0 to 10, with 0 being not at all important and 10 being extremely important, where would you say you are?

Nick: I would have to say a 4.

Lisa: [Gives Nick a copy of a confidence ruler] And how confident would you say you are that if you decide to cut down your drinking you could do it? Again, using a scale of 0 to 10, with 0 being not at all confident and 10 being extremely confident, where would you say you are?

Nick: Probably a 6.

Lisa: OK. My homework assignment for you to do this week is to think about what you need to do to move from a 4 to a 5 in readiness and from a 6 to a 7 in confidence. What would it take for this to happen? How can you envision this happening? Can you think about that?

Nick: I can do that. Thanks, and I'll see you next week.

Counseling Outcome and Discussion

The use of MI with Nick led to an increase in his recognition of the discrepancy between his drinking behavior and his stated goal of saving money. Discrepancies between client-identified behaviors and goals, when amplified and explored by the client and counselor, are critical in helping the client move toward change. Consistent with humanism, this type of exploration enhanced the client's intrinsic motivation for behavior change.

In support of Nick's psychosocial needs for relatedness, autonomy, and competence, Lisa provided empathy, encouragement, and structure (Markland et al., 2005). Her use of empathy helped her to remain nonjudgmental and to meet him where he was developmentally. She understood that abstaining from alcohol entirely might threaten his need for peer relationships. Nick went on to successfully cut down on his drinking, reporting to Lisa in later sessions that he was enjoying going to movies and other campus events with friends. She encouraged Nick concerning his goal of cutting down to save money. In this way, she supported his autonomy and probably distinguished herself from other authority figures in his life. Lisa's use of the structure of MI contributed to Nick's progress in a number of ways. In addition to giving him tangible evidence of change, using the readiness and confidence rulers enhanced the collaborative nature of the counselor–client relationship and underscored Nick's responsibility for coming up with his own solutions. The readiness and confidence rulers supported his need for competence through facilitating his accomplishment of goals of his own choosing.

Reprinted from "Using Motivational Interviewing to Address College Client Alcohol Abuse," by M. B. Scholl and D. M. Schmitt, 2009, *Journal of College Counseling, 12,* pp. 62–65. The American Counseling Association. Reprinted with permission.

Implications and Recommendations for Use With Clients

We recommend an approach to substance abuse counseling that incorporates as much of the client's whole identity into the process as possible (Scholl & Schmitt, 2009). As self-determination theory suggests, it is important to support the client's sense of competence, developing autonomy, and need for relationships. We believe counselors should not only be proficient in the delivery of the technical aspects of MI (e.g., developing discrepancy, rolling with resistance) but also should adhere to the fundamental intention or spirit of MI by providing the core conditions of empathy, positive regard, and authenticity described by Rogers (1957).

RELIGION AND SPIRITUAL VALUES IN SUBSTANCE ABUSE COUNSELING: FOCUS ON 12-STEP FACILITATION

Having explored the foundations of humanistic counseling and its applications to addiction counseling, with a special emphasis on motivational interviewing, we now turn to the impact of client belief systems on the successful resolution of addictive disorders. The inclusion of religion and spiritual values in the practice of addiction counseling is particularly relevant given the research that supports its inclusion in the recovery process (Johnson, 2002; Worthington & Sandage, 2002). For example, a study by George, Larson, Koenig, and McCullough (2000) used multivariate studies from 12-step programs (and similar, spiritually based models) to examine the substance abuse treatment outcomes of two groups of patients. The first group, identified as having "low-level" religious involvement, was compared with a second group who were identified by their "stronger" religious involvement. Research findings suggested that individuals with higher levels of religious involvement were more likely to be successful in their recovery and that their overall recovery from addiction would occur at a quicker pace compared with those individuals identified as not having high degrees of religious involvement. The degree to which these elements are included in the counseling process is of course dependent upon the client, the counselor providing the therapeutic services, and the nature of the relationship. In this portion of the chapter, we begin with establishing the rationale for including clients' religious and spiritual (R/S) beliefs as a part of a humanistic approach to addiction counseling, during which we will differentiate between religion and spirituality. Then we turn to the relevance of working within clients' beliefs and value systems as they enter into the recovery process. We conclude with an experiential exercise and accompanying case study where a client is led to explore the utility of his past and current R/S practices on the maintenance of his recovery.

As it has been established, humanistic or person-centered counseling approaches are driven by the exploration of clients' subjective life experiences and the meaning they have derived from their existence. When discussing the relevance of R/S values to humanistic counseling, it is important to first identify that "religion" and "spirituality" are not synonymous with one another. Whereas it is beyond the scope of this chapter to spend a significant amount of time differentiating the two (for a more thorough discussion, see Cashwell and Young, 2005), there are significant differences in the two terms, and these differences are important when considering their relevance to the therapeutic process. Oftentimes *spirituality* encompasses a broad perspective, unique to each individual and defined by one's beliefs about the world, the meaning making that occurs as a result of personal experiences, and the practices connected to these beliefs. The term *religion* differs in that it is most often defined by the practice of such beliefs and practices within particular world religions (e.g., Christianity, Judaism, and Hinduism) or denominations (e.g., Catholic, Baptist, and Seventh-Day Adventist). Whereas religion is similar to spirituality in that it is rooted in a person's beliefs about the meaning of life, it typically includes a form of corporate worship (or other practices) with a set of rites and rituals, such as prayer or meditation (McCullough & Willoughby, 2009). Some view the two as inextricably linked, while others distinguish the two separately (M. M. Carroll, 1998).

Having established some important definitions, we next need to explore the importance of including clients' R/S beliefs as a part of a humanistic approach to addiction counseling. When using a humanistic orientation, the competent counselor should ensure that each domain of clients are assessed and used according to their wishes, especially given human irreducibility (discussed in Chapters 1 and 3). To fully understand our clients, we must see them as whole beings rather than a sum of parts. This holistic view is particularly important to working with clients from a bio-psycho-social-spiritual model. Failing to understand and acknowledge the interactions between the biological–physical, psychological–emotional, social–relational, and spiritual–religious components of the client prevents the counselor from seeing the larger picture. By assessing each of these domains, the counselor is able to identify which areas might be of greatest concern for the client and how these areas influence the other areas.

Clients' R/S beliefs or practices are typically first assessed during the intake process, most notably through a thorough psychosocial assessment (or what we like to call the bio-psycho-social-spiritual assessment). The degree to which this information is used during the therapeutic process varies greatly, however, and is often dependent upon clients' wishes ("I would like to use/avoid my R/S beliefs in the pursuit of my recovery goals") or counselors' competency/comfort levels (Graham, Furr, Flowers, & Burke, 2001). From a humanistic perspective, it is important to understand and, when beneficial, to accommodate the preferences of clients. Studies have produced evidence that identifies spirituality as a significant personal strength that many clients turn to as a form of support during the therapeutic process (Hodge, 2002). It is reasonable to expect that client engagement and satisfaction with the counseling process would be enhanced when counselors endeavor to accommodate and incorporate R/S values into the counseling process.

As noted earlier, the basic tenets of humanism are (1) individualism, (2) valuing inner subjective experience, and (3) an emphasis on the dignity of each person (Davidson, 2000). Keeping these perspectives in mind throughout humanistic-based counseling helps to guide the practitioner and client through the goal-setting and treatment processes. Studies have produced evidence that identifies spirituality as a significant personal strength that many clients turn to as a form of support during the therapeutic process (Hodge, 2002). It is reasonable to expect that client engagement and satisfaction with the counseling process would be enhanced when counselors endeavor to accommodate and incorporate R/S values into the counseling process.

Worthington and Sandage (2002) noted the importance of understanding the values of clients who place a large emphasis on their religious beliefs (e.g., practicing Jews, Mormons, Roman Catholics, and Protestants) and how these values influence the counseling process. Such clients tend to prefer counselors with similar religious backgrounds (Worthington et al., 1996) and tend to expect more explicit integrations of religious interventions into the counseling process (e.g., prayer or reference to scripture) (Wyatt & Johnson, 1990). These clients may anticipate negative experiences in counseling with secular or nonreligious counselors (Worthington & Scott, 1983; Ripley, Worthington, & Berry, 2001) and therefore it is important for counselors to be culturally responsive and to respond intentionally to the R/S beliefs of the clients they serve (Sue & Sue, 2008; Wade, Worthington, & Vogel, 2007). By responding to the client's specific needs and beliefs, the counselor shows that they value the beliefs of the client. These ideas are in line with a humanistic perspective.

Twelve-Step Facilitation: General Description

As discussed in the previous section, counselors working from a humanistic theoretical orientation will benefit from understanding what place R/S beliefs have in their clients' lives and how these values can be incorporated to assist in the therapeutic process. Researchers Gallup and Castelli (1989) found that approximately 60% of people viewed their faith as a key resource in addressing the problems they experience in life. In response, both the American Psychological

Association (APA) and the American Counseling Association (ACA) created professional divisions specifically focused on promoting the inclusion of spirituality and religion in therapeutic practice. In the counseling profession, the ACA's Association for Spiritual, Ethical, and Religious Values in Counseling (ASERVIC) has become widely known as the leading organization for the development of spiritually based counseling professionals (Miller, 2003).

When counseling clients with specific issues, such as addictive disorders, research supports treatment models that infuse the major tenets (e.g., the 12 steps) of such groups as AA, where spirituality plays a central role in supporting the behavioral interventions guiding the recovery process (George et al., 2000). Based upon the original 12 steps as articulated by Alcoholics Anonymous, a spiritual awakening is a foundational process that occurs as a result of following 12 specific steps (Hshieh, 1997). Following AA's success, many additional support groups have been formulated to address a multitude of addictive disorders, from gambling to sexuality to mental disorders (Room & Greenfield, 1993). The variety of 12-step support groups are regarded by their members as a "spiritual fellowship," which since AA's creation by Bill W. and Dr. Bob in 1935 has helped thousands of people attain a form of spiritual awakening that led to their recovery (Galanter, 2006). These support groups, in and of themselves, are not therapy; they are not facilitated by trained counselors, they do not involve any form of informed consent, and they do not have treatment plans. Rather, the success of 12-step groups is based on the principle of one addict helping another (Straussner & Byrne, 2009). Given their success over the years, it is no wonder that they have been incorporated into most treatment programs: In fact, many inpatient and intensive outpatient addiction treatment programs have their own in-house AA or Narcotics Anonymous (NA) meetings (Kelly, Dow, Yeterian, & Kahler, 2010). It is important to note the evidence that suggests that participation in 12-step programs is most successful when used in conjunction with ongoing addiction counseling by a trained counselor. For example, better treatment outcomes and higher rates of abstinence have been demonstrated (Fiorentine & Hillhouse, 2000; Knack, 2009). Studies indicate that the integration of individual psychotherapy and the 12-step program works well because 12-step programs and related counseling services work toward similar goals of being aware of the uniqueness of the client and working toward overcoming the addiction.

A counselor's sensitivity to the individual differences in a client's R/S beliefs is a vital component to the success of providing a person-centered therapeutic approach to addiction counseling, particularly when helping clients navigate the spiritual components of the 12 steps. Working with clients to identify their personal belief systems, whether they are rooted in clients' R/S values, will help the counselor understand the framework from which their clients interpret the wording of the steps and their utility for recovery.

Out of the 12 actual steps associated with this recovery approach, 7 have spiritual elements: steps 2, 3, 5, 6, 7, 11, and 12. A brief description of each of these seven steps, and the process whereby a humanistic counselor would help clients integrate their belief system into the step, is offered herein. We believe this is an important process for all clients to follow, regardless of their R/S background (or lack thereof). The initial stage of the 12-step process allows for the counselor to identify clients' definition of a higher power (i.e., God, Goddess, Allah, the 12-step group, Buddha, Nature). Once the higher power is identified, it should be used as clients' reference point throughout the remainder of exploring how they navigate the 12 steps. At the same time, the humanistic counselor should be cognizant that clients' definition of a higher power may change as they develop in recovery. Therefore, sensitivity to a variety of R/S practices is necessitated. All 12 steps of AA (AA, 2001) are listed as follows. We italicize the steps that have an explicit spiritual component and then offer various humanistic-based questions and interventions to help clients explore the meaning they attach to each of these steps.

Step 1: We admitted we were powerless over alcohol—that our lives had become unmanageable.

Step 2: Came to believe that a Power greater than ourselves could restore us to sanity.

Describe how your belief in a higher power has assisted your recovery thus far. What does a *restoration by your higher power* mean to you?

Spiritual Life Map: The spiritual life map (Hodge, 2005) allows the counselor and client to track the client's spiritual development and to articulate ways in which the client's higher power has helped restore them.

Step 3: Made a decision to turn our will and our lives over to the care of God as we understood Him.

How do you currently *understand* God (or whatever term the client chooses)?

What sort of meaning does *turning your life over* to the care of God have for you?

Does *surrender* and *giving up* mean the same thing to you?

How has your spiritual journey allowed you to turn your life over to the care of God?

Step 4: Made a searching and fearless moral inventory of ourselves.

Step 5: Admitted to God, to ourselves, and to another human being the exact nature of our wrongs.

What does *admitting to God* look like for you? How will you go about doing this?

What feelings occurred for you when you admitted the nature of your wrongs?

How was this experience significant to you?

Step 6: Were entirely ready to have God remove all these defects of character.

What will you need in order to be ready to surrender these *defects of character*?

What does opening yourself to change look like for you?

How has your belief in God facilitated this change in you?

Step 7: Humbly asked Him to remove our shortcomings.

How do you go about asking God to *remove your shortcomings*?

What was this process like?

Step 8: Made a list of all persons we had harmed, and became willing to make amends to them all.

Step 9: Made direct amends to such people wherever possible, except when to do so would injure them or others.

Step 10: Continued to take personal inventory and when we were wrong promptly admitted it.

Step 11: Sought through prayer and meditation to improve our conscious contact with God, as we understood Him, praying only for knowledge of His will for us and the power to carry that out.

What does it look like for you to *connect with God*? How have you used prayer or meditation in the past (what was effective, what was not)?

What tools do you need to help you to *improve your conscious contact with God*?

During what times do you find yourself seeking this connection? How does this change the meaning of your actions and decisions?

Step 12: Having had a spiritual awakening as the result of these Steps, we tried to carry this message to other addicts, and to practice these principles in all our affairs.

What does *carrying this message* look like?

How do you continue to find meaning in this step?

Throughout the therapeutic process, a person-centered approach can be used to explore the beliefs associated with these steps. This discussion can also be used to explore the options for those clients who are agnostic or atheist or who may just be uncomfortable with the spiritual orientation of the 12-step model. By having these clients define what a higher power means to them, the counselor is able to adapt the 12-step model to each client's current life position. The idea of meeting clients where they are falls in line with the humanistic or client-centered approach. Addiction recovery and mutual aid groups include those that are explicitly religious (e.g., Celebrate Recovery) as well as those that use a secular approach that avoids a spiritual component (SMART Recovery, Rational Recovery) (Brooks & McHenry, 2009; White, 2008). Therefore, clients can be intentionally matched to programs to accommodate their R/S worldview and values (or lack thereof). The aim of the humanistic approach should naturally facilitate discussions that will help the counselor determine the best types of programs that are available to support their clients through the recovery process. By meeting clients where they are and developing a treatment plan in which the interventions and direction are tailored to match the needs of each client, the humanistic approach fosters a sense of ownership for the client.

Research Findings

As an example of the empirical support for meeting clients where they are, Project MATCH has been regarded as the largest patient–treatment matching study conducted to date. This extensive research was intended to evaluate and identify interaction effects between patients and treatment rather than treatment main effects (K. M. Carroll, 1998). Findings from Project MATCH included significant client ratings of the benefit of AA meeting attendance, while the practice of prescribed behaviors common to 12-step programs (e.g., having a sponsor) were positively related with R/S connectedness (Tonigan, Miller, & Connors, 2000). Counselors need to be aware that one of the most significant findings indicated that clients' success in incorporating a support network (such as a 12-step model) into their treatment was reliant upon the initiation of such attendance during the therapeutic process. That is, the counselor's sensitivity to this need and fostering clients' exploration of support groups was instrumental in their staying connected after therapy was concluded (Babor & Del Boca, 2003).

To support the findings of Project MATCH, we propose that to match clients with an appropriate support network addiction counselors will need to have adequate knowledge of the available 12-step (and other support groups) programs to assess the individual for appropriate referral for supportive service. TSF is a well-known approach used to introduce and incorporate the 12-step model as a supportive element of an individual's addiction counseling work. Hayes et al. (2004) described TSF as a "structured, manualized psychosocial intervention designed to both parallel and facilitate a 12-step perspective" (p. 668). TSF places significant emphasis on clients' acceptance of responsibility for the addiction. It is believed that this process leads to the clients "surrendering" of control by actively engaging in the 12-step process and committing to a lifestyle in recovery (Hayes et al.).

A recent article (Hook et al., 2010) provided an overview of empirically supported R/S therapies. Among the therapies covered was TSF, which encourages clients to view addiction as a spiritual and medical disease. The authors concluded that relative to behavioral coping skills therapy and motivational interviewing, TSF was as efficacious at addressing client levels of drinking frequency and severity (Project MATCH Research Group, 1997, 1998a, 1998b). Further, TSF clients demonstrated higher levels of abstinence at 3-month follow-up relative to the behavioral coping skills and MI treatment groups. Hook et al. concluded that whereas there is a relative paucity of research validating R/S treatment approaches for substance abuse, TSF should be regarded as an efficacious treatment for alcoholism.

Another advantage of 12-step support groups is the availability of these groups. Miller and McCrady (1993) estimated that 1 in 10 Americans have participated in an AA meeting with 1 in 8 Americans having attended any 12-step program at some point in their lives. With the popularity of 12-step groups, there is usually one in almost every town or at least a nearby city. Professionals providing addiction counseling services need to be aware of the limitations to the 12-step model to appropriately refer clients to the correct support network and incorporate such participation into the counseling process.

In regard to such limitations, Steigerwald and Stone (1999) reported that additional empirical research needs to be conducted to determine what, if any, correlation exists between clients' recovery from addiction and the collaboration between attendance at 12-step programs and counseling professionals providing supportive services. Although there is support for 12-step programs, criticisms are also present. A common criticism of the 12-step model is that it is too religiously based and that it alienates individuals who do not want to base a significant portion of their recovery support in a spiritually oriented model. Hshieh and Srebalus (1997) also noted that the model's "emphasis on spiritual development takes recovery outside the range of empirical analysis, leaving the researcher with subjective reports of epiphenomenon" (p. 64). Even though some researchers believe that the spiritual world serves only as a derivative of the physical change involved in the 12-step process, the use of clients' spiritual beliefs can serve as a strong foundation that the therapist can use to facilitate change. For example, a spiritual life map (Hodge, 2005) can be used to gain a better understanding of clients' journeys and how spirituality has been used to overcome various trials.

Case Illustration: Using the Spiritual Life Map

One way to intentionally employ a humanistic-based intervention that matches clients' R/S values and worldviews is to use an exercise called the spiritual life map (Hodge, 2005). This is particularly important given that Hodge attributed the following qualities to the spiritual life map, which overlap considerably with client-centered counseling: (1) clients' creativity is encouraged—spiritual life maps "provide a creative forum in which clients can express themselves" (Hodge, 2005, p. 353); (2) collaboration between the client and counselor is fostered during the interpretation and discussion of the life map, with an emphasis placed on the quality of the therapeutic relationship; (3) spiritual life maps are client directed; (4) spiritual life maps implicitly communicate by placing a client-constructed medium at the center of the therapeutic process, which highlights the fact that "the client is a competent, proactive, self-directed, fully engaged participant in the therapeutic process" (p. 353); and (5) life maps promote counselor empathy and accurate understanding by empowering clients to educate their counselors on their spiritual worldviews, increasing counselors' spiritual competence.

Client Description

David is a 29-year-old man of Irish descent who has been in recovery from drugs and alcohol for 1 year. Recently married and the father of one child from a prior relationship, David has been experiencing some "puzzling temptations" to return to old addictive patterns, temptations that he felt "marriage should have cured." David began this period of counseling in the hopes of regaining a hold on his life to reconnect with his wife and child (with whom he has joint custody). This is David's first time in individual counseling, though he went through a 28-day treatment program 1 year prior. During one of his sessions, David discussed his spiritual journey with the hopes of using some of his recovery tools to help address his current concerns. The counselor suggested that he create a spiritual life map (Figure 5.1) as a way to explore these areas.

Session Transcript

The discussion of David's life map is as follows:

Counselor: David, when we left last week we had decided that you would work on your life map for this week. It looks like you really spent some time working on that.

David: I did. I used to enjoy drawing when I was younger. This is the first time that I have done anything like this.

Counselor: Before we discuss the specific elements of your life map, I am wondering if there was anything that was particularly difficult for you in this process.

David: Yeah, there were a couple of things that I kind of struggled with. Once I started drawing all the things on my map I was able to see just how far off track that I had gotten.

Counselor: Could you expand on what you mean by "off track"?

David: I don't know, I guess you have this idea of where you want to be at certain points of your life. You know, like having a good job, being able to provide for your family, being a good dad and husband, that kind of stuff. It just happened so slowly for me that I didn't realize it until it was too late.

Counselor: Do you believe that it's too late to get back on track?

David: Yeah, I do. I've screwed up so much in the past few years that I don't think there is much that I can do to fix it.

Counselor: David, can you recall the reason why you decided to come to counseling?

David: Yes. I wanted to get better so that I could get back in my kid's life.

Counselor: That sounds like hope to me.

David: I guess you're right.

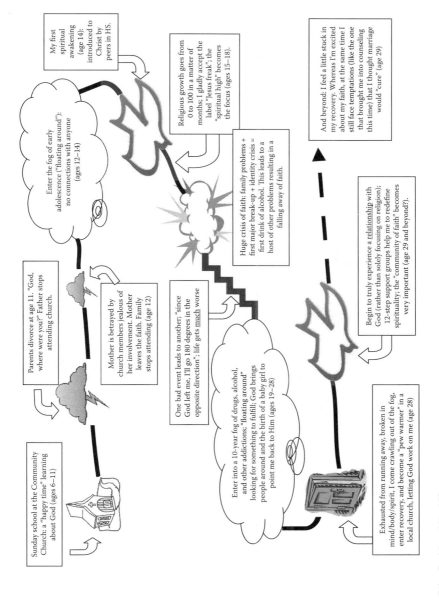

My first spiritual awakening (age 14): introduced to Christ by peers in HS.

Enter the fog of early adolescence ("floating around"): no connections with anyone (ages 12–14)

Religious growth goes from 0 to 100 in a matter of months; I gladly accept the label "Jesus freak"; the "spiritual high" becomes the focus (ages 15–18).

And beyond: I feel a little stuck in my recovery. Whereas I'm excited about my faith, at the same time I still face temptations (like the one that brought me into counseling this time) that I thought marriage would "cure" (age 29)

Parents divorce at age 11. "God, where were you?" Father stops attending church.

Mother is betrayed by church members jealous of her involvement. Mother leaves the faith. Family stops attending (age 12)

Sunday school at the Community Church: a "happy time" learning about God (ages 6–11)

One bad event leads to another; "since God left me, I'll go 180 degrees in the opposite direction"; life gets much worse

Huge crisis of faith: family problems + first major break-up + identity crisis = first drink of alcohol. This leads to a host of other problems resulting in a falling away of faith.

Begin to truly experience a relationship with God (rather than solely focusing on religion); 12-step support groups help me to redefine spirituality; the "community of faith" becomes very important (age 29 and beyond?).

Enter into a 10-year fog of drugs, alcohol, and other addictions; "floating around" looking for something to fulfill; God brings people around and the birth of a baby girl to point me back to Him (ages 19–28)

Exhausted from running away, broken in mind/body/spirit, I come crawling out of the fog, enter into recovery, and become a "pew warmer" in a local church, letting God work on me (age 28)

Figure 5.1   David's spiritual life map.

Counselor: And the great thing about our life map is this is not where it has to end; you have the ability to change where you go from here and it sounds like you are already taking steps to change your course.

David: It's just going to be really hard to do.

Counselor: It may be difficult, but from what you've shared so far in our time together, it sounds like you are headed in the right direction. Are you ready to discuss your life map?

David: Sure, let's hit it.

Counselor: Great. I'm going to ask you a series of questions and will ask that you take some time to explore the answers with me. First, could you discuss some of the symbols that you drew and what they may mean to you?

David: Ok. The first symbol I drew was the church where I grew up; this was a safe and secure time in my life. But when my parents split up when I was 11 and with my dad leaving the church, followed by my mother getting slammed by the people of the church, my ideas of church and religion were pretty smashed. That's what the lightning clouds are all about.

Counselor: What things do you think about when you think about a church?

David: Well, it was supposed to be like a family being together and supporting one another, learning about God...

Counselor: And you felt like you lost that when they divorced?

David: Yeah, because the people in the church really hurt my family. I think that I held onto that for a long time and even blamed God for abandoning us. That's when I entered the fog or smoke of my early teen years.

Counselor: What is the next symbol, the dove, all about?

David: The dove was when I met Steve, a guy I went to high school with. He's the one who showed me what it meant to be saved. I was a "Jesus freak" all through high school.

Counselor: This next symbol looks pretty scary.

David: Yeah, it was a rough time. It was the first time that a girl broke my heart. I never saw it coming, and my parents drug me into all of their fighting, and I was a new kid in college. I just wanted to fit in and forget about everything else. That was the first time that I ever took a drink of alcohol. Things just went downhill from there.

Counselor: Is that what the stairs represent?

David: Yeah, but I don't know if stairs are the best representation to that time of my life. It seemed like everything spiraled out of control so fast that I just woke up one day and was in the dark. I had no clue how I got there.

Counselor: And you stayed in that place for a while?

David: It must have been close to 10 years where I was just trying to find whatever I could find to help me forget about my problems. I moved past the alcohol and started getting into other drugs and sleeping with whoever was around.

Counselor: Your next symbol is a cracked door. Tell me about that.

David: It shows me coming out of the darkness.

Counselor: What happened during that time that brought you out of the darkness?

David: I don't think there was something that happened. I mean I had a little girl during that time, and it didn't even wake me up. I think I just finally hit rock bottom and gave up.

Counselor: What did walking through the door look like for you?

David: It was more like crawling through the door, but I'm not real sure how it happened. I ended up running into Steve one night. I was out looking for another fix and when I saw him it was as if God was using him to help me. He didn't even have to say anything. He recognized me, and all that I said was, "I need some help." I was in rehab the next day.

Counselor: How did you get from rehab to the dove?

David: While I was in there I had to go to AA meetings and I found myself slowly but surely walking through the 12 steps. I was just taking it one day at a time. I also found myself having to depend on God to get me through each day. I finally started to understand what a relationship with God was. Those that were helping me grow closer to him became really important to me.

Counselor: It sounds like you have regained your strength and are standing pretty firm at the moment.

David: I thought I was, but I am trying to reconnect with my daughter and it seems like all those old feelings and temptations are creeping back in. I thought I was over that stuff. I don't know what to do.

Counselor: Does your wife know about your feelings?

David: No, I can't tell her I'm still struggling with those feelings. I thought that once I got married they would all go away, but they are still there and so tough to deal with.

Counselor: I wonder how she would respond if you did tell her?

David: She says that she will be there for me if I ever face those struggles again, but I just can't tell her about these feelings. That's too much for her to have to deal with. She didn't sign up for the recovering addict; she signed up for the guy who was seeking the Lord and had things together.

Counselor: You have the chance to write your next symbol on your life map, and it sounds like you have someone who wants to be there with you for that.

David: I guess I do. I'm just scared that I won't live up to who she wants me to be and that I'll lose her too.

Counselor: David, I can tell that your fear of disappointing and potentially losing your wife is a very serious concern, but unfortunately we are about out of time. But I'd love to pick up with your feelings about your relationship with your wife next week if that's OK with you.

David: That's fine.

Counselor: Thank you for sharing your life map with me, David.

Counseling Outcome and Discussion

From the preceding transcript it is evident that the client-constructed life map encouraged and validated his active meaning-making process. The client-constructed life map was a primary focus of the session. Consistent with a client-centered approach, the life map empowered David to effectively communicate his spiritual worldview with the counselor. David's spiritual life map enhanced his counselor's empathy and understanding regarding his life events and feelings of worry, insecurity, and fear. David was fully engaged in the counseling process, which was highly collaborative as a result of David using the life map to actively educate the counselor. In future sessions, with the help of the counselor, David explored his relationship with his wife and developed the ability to confide in his wife and to use his marital relationship as an adaptive coping resource.

Implications and Recommendations for Use With Clients

Although the spiritual life map is designed to be an activity in which clients have the freedom to explore their own experiences, Hodge (2005) noted the importance of prompting clients to include both those experiences that were viewed as trials or difficulties as well as the spiritual tools that they may have used to overcome those various trials. The counselor is also encouraged to include an array of resources for clients to use (e.g., markers, colored paper, stencils, large paper to draw on). The spiritual life map is limited in regards to clients' stage of change, in that they need to be at a place in which they are ready to divulge and discuss the various trials that will be presented during the life map exercise. Such a humanistic and experiential intervention might not be suitable for certain clients with specific concerns (e.g., personality disorders, psychosis). Clients' method of communication should also be considered. If they are not responsive to drawing, other mediums could be used (e.g., music or movement). These limitations aside, we have found experiential exercises like the spiritual life map to be instrumental to helping our clients to explore the R/S questions and strengths and how they can bring these to bear on their successful recovery.

CONCLUSION

In this chapter we began by discussing two critical trends in the treatment of alcoholism and substance abuse counseling: (1) the development of the Minnesota model; and (2) changes in the use of confrontation in substance abuse counseling leading to the recent advent of motivational interviewing (Miller, 1983; Miller & Rollnick, 2002). As we noted, these developments are noteworthy examples of ways substance abuse treatments have progressively become increasingly aligned with humanistic principles and values. In addition, this chapter focused on two widely respected and empirically validated approaches to substance abuse counseling: MI and TSF. Recommendations and case illustrations were presented to explain the humanistic principles underlying the effectiveness of these two approaches. With regard to the practice of MI, we recommended enacting the spirit of MI emphasizing the establishment of a relationship based on trust, empathy, and respect for clients' autonomy needs. With regard to the practice of TSF, we recommended respecting the individuality of clients with regard to incorporating their R/S identity into the counseling process; we introduced an approach called spiritual life maps (Hodge, 2005) as a means toward this end. The spiritual life map is a client-constructed medium that facilitates a collaborative client–counseling relationship and a client-centered approach to addressing substance abuse–related issues.

It may be argued that the evolution of the treatment of substance abuse in contemporary society is following a definitively humanistic developmental trajectory. Importantly, additional contemporary substance abuse counseling approaches such as Stephanie Brown's (2004, 2006) developmental approach might have been included but were outside of the scope of the current chapter. Brown's approach entails the construction of a nonalcoholic identity for the client. Her approach is clearly client centered and supports the capacity of the client to create meaning that represents in her words "radical transformation" on the part of clients. It is also consistent with the recommendation that counselors enlist as much of a client's identity as possible in the treatment process (Scholl & Schmitt, 2009). We believe that by continuing to explore and describe the humanistic principles inherent in effective and cutting-edge counseling approaches we can foster the ongoing evolution of increasingly effective therapeutic approaches.

REFERENCES

Alcoholics Anonymous (AA). (2001). *Alcoholics anonymous.* (4th ed.). New York: AA World Services.

Anderson, D. J., McGovern, J. P., & Dupont, R. L. (1999). The origins of the Minnesota model of addiction treatment—A first person account. *Journal of Addictive Diseases, 18,* 107–114.

Anthony, J. C., & Petronis, K. R. (1995). Early-onset drug use and risk of later drug problems. *Drug and Alcohol Dependence, 40,* 9–15.

Babor, T. F., & Del Boca, F. K. (2003). *Treatment matching in alcoholism.* New York: Cambridge University Press.

Baer, J. S., Kivlahan, D. R., Blume, A. W., McKnight, P., & Marlatt, A. G. (2001). Brief intervention for heavy-drinking college students: 4-year follow-up and natural history. *American Journal of Public Health, 91,* 1310–1316.

Boardman, T., Catley, D., Grobe, J. E., Little, T. D., & Ahluwalia, J. S. (2006). Using motivational interviewing with smokers: Do therapist behaviors relate to engagement and therapeutic alliance? *Journal of Substance Abuse Treatment, 31,* 329–339.

Bohart, A. C. (2003). Person-centered psychotherapy and related experiential approaches. In A. S. Gurman & S. B. Messer (Eds.), *Essential psychotherapies: Theory and practice* (2nd ed., pp. 107–148). New York: Guilford Press.

Boreham, R., & Shaw, A. (2001). *Smoking, drinking and drug use among young people in England in 2000.* London: Office of National Statistics.

Borsari, B., & Carey, K. B. (2000). Effects of a brief motivational intervention with college student drinkers. *Journal of Consulting and Clinical Psychology, 68,* 728–733.

Borsari, B., & Carey, K. B. (2005). Two brief alcohol interventions for mandated college students. *Psychology of Addictive Behaviors, 19,* 206–302.

Brooks, F., & McHenry, B. (2009). *A contemporary approach to substance abuse and addiction counseling: A counselor's guide to application and understanding.* Alexandria, VA: American Counseling Association.

Brown, S. (2004). *A place called self: Women, sobriety, and radical transformation.* Center City, MN: Hazelden.

Brown, S. (2006). *Treating the alcoholic: A developmental model of recovery.* New York: Wiley.

Burke, B. L., Arkowitz, H., & Menchola, M. (2003). The efficacy of motivational interviewing: A meta–analysis of controlled clinical trials. *Journal of Consulting and Clinical Psychology, 71,* 843–861.

Burke, B. L., Dunn, C. W., Atkins, D. C., & Phelps, J. S. (2004). The emerging evidence base for motivational interviewing: A meta-analytic and qualitative inquiry. *Journal of Cognitive Psychotherapy, 18,* 309–322.

Cain, D. J. (2001). Defining characteristics, history, and evolution of humanistic psychotherapies. In D. J. Cain & J. Seeman (Eds.), *Humanistic psychotherapies: Handbook of research and practice* (pp. 3–54). Washington, DC: American Psychological Association.

Carney, M. M., & Kivlahan, D. R. (1995). Motivational subtypes among veterans seeking substance abuse treatment: Profiles based on stages of change. *Psychology of Addictive Behaviors, 9,* 135–142.

Carroll, K. M. (1998). Internal validity of Project MATCH treatments: Discriminability and integrity. *Journal of Consulting and Clinical Psychology, 66*(2), 290–303.

Carroll, M. M. (1998). Social work's conceptualization of spirituality. *Social Thought, 18*(2), 1–13.

Cashwell, C. S., & Young, J. S. (2005). *Integrating spirituality and religion into counseling: A guide to competent practice.* Alexandria, VA: American Counseling Association.

Christodoulou, G. N. (Ed.). (1987). *Psychosomatic medicine.* New York: Plenum.

Colby, S. M., Monti, P. M., Barnett, N. P., Rohsenow, D. J., Weissman, K., Spirito, A., et al. (1998). Brief motivational interviewing in a hospital setting for adolescent smoking. *Journal of Consulting and Clinical Psychology, 66,* 574–578.

Davidson, L. (2000). Philosophical foundations of humanistic psychology. *Humanistic Psychologist, 28,* 7–31.

DiClemente, C. C. (1999). Prevention and harm reduction for chemical dependency: A process perspective. *Clinical Psychology Review* [Special issue: Prevention of children's behavioral and mental health problems: New horizons for psychology], *19*(4), 473–486.

DiClemente, C. C., & Hughes, S. O. (1990). Stages of change profiles in outpatient alcoholism treatment. *Journal of Substance Abuse, 2,* 217–235.

DiClemente, C. C., Nidecker, M., & Bellack, A. S. (2008). Motivation and the stages of change among individuals with severe mental illness and substance abuse disorders. *Journal of Substance Abuse Treatment, 34*(1), 25–35.

DiClemente, C. C., & Prochaska, J. O. (1998). Toward a comprehensive, transtheoretical model of change: Stages of change and addictive behaviors. In W. R. Miller & N. Heather (Eds.), *Treating addictive behaviors* (2nd ed., pp. 3–24). New York: Plenum Press.

DiClemente, C. C., Story, M., & Murray, K. (2000). On a roll: The process of initiation and cessation of problem gambling among adolescents. *Journal of Gambling Studies, 16*(2–3), 289–313.

DiClemente, C. C., & Velasquez, M. M. (2002). Motivational interviewing and the stages of change. In W. R. Miller & S. Rollnick, *Motivational interviewing: Preparing people for change* (2nd ed., pp. 201–216). New York: Guilford Press.

Dunn, C., Deroo, L., & Rivara, F. (2001). The use of brief interventions adapted from motivational interviewing across behavioral domains: A systematic review. *Addiction, 96*(12), 1725–1742.

Erikson, E. (1959). Identity and the life cycle. *Psychological Issues Monograph, 1,* 1–171.

Ferdinandi, A. D., & Li, M. H. (2007). Counseling persons with comorbid disorders: A quantitative comparison of counselor active rehabilitation service and standard rehabilitation counseling approaches. *Journal of Humanistic Counseling, Education and Development, 46,* 228–241.

Fergusson, D. M., & Horwood, L. J. (2000). Does cannabis use encourage other forms of illicit drug use? *Addiction, 95,* 505–520.

Fiorentine, R., & Hillhouse, M. P. (2000). Drug treatment and 12-step program participation: The additive effects of integrated recovery activities. *Journal of Substance Abuse Treatment, 18,* 65–74.

Galanter, M. (2006) Spirituality in Alcoholics Anonymous: A valuable adjunct to psychiatric services. *Psychiatric Services Online, 57*(3), 307–309.

Gallup, G. J., & Castelli, J. (1989). *The people's religion: American faith in the 90s.* New York: Macmillan Publishing.

George, L. K., Larson, D. B., Koenig, H. G., & McCullough, M. E. (2000). Spirituality and health: What we know, what we need to know. *Journal of Social and Clinical Psychology, 19,* 102–116.

Glanz, K., Patterson, R. E., Kristal, A. R., DiClemente, C. C., Heimendinger, J., Linnan, L., et al. (1994). Stages of change in adopting healthy diets: Fat, fiber, and correlates of nutrient intake. *Health Education Quarterly, 21*(4), 499–519.

Graeber, D. A., Moyers, T. B., Griffith, G., Guajardo, E., & Tonigan, S. (2003). A pilot study comparing motivational interviewing and an educational intervention in patients with schizophrenia and alcohol use disorders. *Community Mental Health Journal, 39*(3), 189–202.

Graham, S., Furr, S., Flowers, C., & Burke, M. T. (2001). Religion and spirituality in coping with stress. *Counseling & Values, 46,* 2–13.

Grimley, D. M., Riley, G. E., Bellis, J. M., & Prochaska, J. O. (1993). Assessing the stages of change and decision-making for contraceptive use for the prevention of pregnancy, sexually transmitted diseases, and acquired immunodeficiency syndrome. *Health Education Quarterly, 20*(4), 455–470.

Hansen, J. T. (2000). Psychoanalysis and humanism: A review and critical examination of integrationist efforts with some proposed resolutions. *Journal of Counseling and Development, 78,* 21–28.

Hayes, S. C., Wilson, K. G., Gifford, E., Bissett, R., Batten, S., Piasecki, M., et al. (2004). A preliminary trial of twelve-step facilitation and acceptance and commitment therapy with polysubstance-abusing methadone-maintained opiate addicts. *Behavior Therapy, 35,* 667–688.

Hettema, J., Steele, J., & Miller, W. R. (2005). Motivational interviewing. *Annual Review of Clinical Psychology, 1,* 91–111.

Hodge, D. R. (2002). Equipping social workers to address spirituality in practice settings: A model curriculum. *Advances in Social Work, 3*(2), 85–103.

Hodge, D. R. (2005). Spiritual assessment in marital and family therapy: A methodological framework for selecting from among six qualitative assessment tools. *Journal of Marital and Family Therapy, 31,* 341–356.

Hook, J. N., Worthington Jr., E. L., Davis, D. E., Jennings II, D. J., Gartner, A. L., & Hook, J. P. (2010). Empirically supported religious and spiritual therapies. *Journal of Clinical Psychology, 66,* 46–72.

Hshieh, T. M. (1997). Incorporating spiritual identity into the treatment of alcoholism. *Alcoholism Treatment Quarterly, 15*(4), 23–42.

Hshieh, S. Y., & Srebalus, D. J. (1997). Alcohol treatment issues: Professional differences. *Alcoholism Treatment Quarterly, 15*(4), 63–73.

Isenhart, C. E. (1994). Motivational subtypes in an inpatient sample of substance abusers. *Addictive Behaviors, 19,* 463–475.

Jessor, R. (1991). Risk behavior in adolescence: A psychosocial framework for understanding and action. *Journal of Adolescent Health, 12,* 597–605.

Johnson, B. R. (2002). *Objective hope: Assessing the effectiveness of faith-based organizations: A review of the literature.* Philadelphia: University of Pennsylvania, Center for Research on Religion and Urban Civil Society.

Kelly, J. F., Dow, S. J., Yeterian, J. D., & Kahler, C. W. (2010). Can 12-step group participation strengthen and extend the benefits of adolescent addiction treatment? A prospective analysis. *Drug and Alcohol Dependence, 110,* 117–125.

Knack, W. A. (2009). Psychotherapy and Alcoholics Anonymous: An integrated approach. *Journal of Psychotherapy Integration, 19,* 86–109.

LaBrie, J. W., Pederson, E. R., Lamb, T. F., & Quinlan, T. (2007). A campus-based motivational enhancement group intervention reduces problematic drinking in freshmen male college students. *Addictive Behaviors, 32,* 889–901.

Lawendowski, L. A. (1998). A motivational intervention for adolescent smokers. *Preventive Medicine, 27,* A39–A46.

Marcus, B. H., Rossi, J. S., Selby, V. C., Niaura, R. S., & Abrams, D. B. (1992). The stages and processes of exercise adoption and maintenance in a worksite sample. *Health Psychology, 11*(6), 386–395.

Markland, D., Ryan, R. M., Tobin, V. J., & Rollnick, S. (2005). Motivational interviewing and self-determination theory. *Journal of Social and Clinical Psychology, 24,* 811–831.

Martino, S., Carroll, K., Kostas, D., Perkins, J., & Rounsaville, B. (2002). Dual diagnosis motivational interviewing: A modification of motivational interviewing for substance-abusing patients with psychotic disorders. *Journal of Substance Abuse Treatment, 23*(4), 297–308.

McCambridge, J., & Strang, J. (2004). The efficacy of single–session motivational interviewing in reducing drug consumption and perceptions of drug–related risk and harm among young people: Results from a multi–site cluster randomized trial. *Addiction, 99,* 39–52.

McCullough, M. E., & Willoughby, B. L. B. (2009). Religion, self-regulation, and self-control: Associations, explanations, and implications. *Psychological Bulletin, 135,* 69–93.

Measham, F., Aldridge, J., & Parker, H. (2001). *Dancing on drugs: Risk, health and hedonism in the British club scene.* London: Free Association.

Mezzich, J. E. (2007). Psychiatry for the person: Articulating medicine's science and humanism. *World Psychiatry, 6,* 65–67.

Michael, K. D., Curtin, L., Kirkley, D. E., Jones, D. L., & Harris Jr., R. (2006). Group-based motivational interviewing for alcohol use among college students: An exploratory study. *Professional Psychology: Research & Practice, 37*, 629–634.

Miller, G. (2003). *Incorporating spirituality in counseling and psychotherapy: Theory and technique.* New York: Wiley.

Miller, W. R. (1983). Motivational interviewing with problem drinkers. *Behavioural Psychotherapy, 11*, 147–172.

Miller, W. R., & McCrady, B. S. (1993). The importance of research on Alcoholics Anonymous. *Research on Alcoholics Anonymous 5*, 3–11.

Miller, W. R., & Rollnick, S. (2002). *Motivational interviewing: Preparing people for change* (2nd ed.). New York: Guilford Press.

Monti, P. M., Colby, S. M., Barnett, N. P., Spirito, A., Rohsenow, D. J., Myers, M., et al. (1999). Brief intervention for harm reduction with alcohol-positive older adolescents in a hospital emergency department. *Journal of Consulting and Clinical Psychology, 67*, 989–994.

Moyers, T. B., Miller, W. R., & Hendrickson, S. M. L. (2005). How does motivational interviewing work? Therapist interpersonal skill predicts client involvement within motivational interviewing sessions. *Journal of Consulting and Clinical Psychology, 73*, 590–598.

Moyers, T. B., & Rollnick, S. (2002). A motivational interviewing perspective on resistance in psychotherapy. *JCLP/In Session: Psychotherapy in Practice, 58*(2), 185–193.

Perepiczka, M., & Scholl, M. B. (in press). C-AHEAD: The heart and conscience of the counseling profession. *Journal of Humanistic Counseling, Education and Development.*

Prochaska, J. O., & DiClemente, C. C. (1984). *The transtheoretical approach: Crossing traditional boundaries of therapy.* Malabar, FL: Krieger.

Prochaska, J. O., DiClemente, C. C., & Norcross, J. (1992). In search of how people change: Applications to addictive behaviors. *American Psychologist, 47*, 1102–1114.

Project MATCH Research Group. (1997). Matching alcoholism treatments to client heterogeneity: Project MATCH posttreatment drinking outcomes. *Journal of Studies on Alcohol, 58*, 7–29.

Project MATCH Research Group. (1998a). Matching alcoholism treatments to client heterogeneity: Project MATCH three-year drinking outcomes. *Alcoholism: Clinical and Experimental Research, 22*, 1300–1311.

Project MATCH Research Group. (1998b). Matching alcoholism treatments to client heterogeneity: Treatment main effects and matching effects during treatment. *Journal of Studies on Alcohol, 59*, 631–639.

Ramsey, M., & Partridge, S. (1999). *Drug misuse declared in 1998: Results from the British crime survey.* Home Office Research Study no. 197. London: Home Office.

Ripley, J. S., Worthington Jr., E. L., & Berry, J. W. (2001). The effects of religiosity on preferences and expectations for marital therapy among married Christians. *American Journal of Family Therapy, 29*, 39–58.

Roberts, L. J., Neal, D. J., Kivlahan, D. R., Baer, J. S., & Marlatt, A. G. (2000). Individual drinking changes following a brief intervention among college students: Clinical significance in an indicated preventive context. *Journal of Consulting and Clinical Psychology, 68*, 500–505.

Rogers, C. R. (1957). The necessary and sufficient conditions of therapeutic personality change. *Journal of Consulting Psychology, 21*, 95–103.

Room, R., & Greenfield, T. (1993). Alcoholics Anonymous, other 12-step movements and psychotherapy in the US population, 1990. *Addiction, 88*, 556–562.

Roth, A., & Fonagy, P. (2005). Substance abuse: Alcohol, cocaine, and opiate dependence and abuse. In A. Roth & P. Fonagy (Eds.), *What works for whom? A critical review of psychotherapy research,* (2nd ed., pp. 320–362). New York: Guilford Press.

Ryan, R. M., & Deci, E. L. (2000). Self-determination theory and the facilitation of intrinsic motivation, social development, and well-being. *American Psychologist, 55,* 68–78.

Scholl, M. B., & Schmitt, D. M. (2009). Using motivational interviewing to address college client alcohol abuse. *Journal of College Counseling, 12,* 57–70.

Sciacca, K. (2003, March). *Motivational interviewing: Preparing people for behavior change: A theory and skill building seminar.* Seminar sponsored by Sciacca Comprehensive Service Development for Mental Illness, Drug Addiction, and Alcoholism, New York.

Sellman, J. D., Sullivan, P. F., Dore, G. M., Adamson, S. J., & MacEwan, I. (2001). A randomized controlled trial of motivational enhancement therapy (MET) for mild to moderate alcohol dependence. *Journal of Studies on Alcohol, 62*(3), 389–396.

Steigerwald, F., & Stone, D. (1999). Cognitive restructuring and the 12-step program of Alcoholics Anonymous. *Journal of Substance Abuse Treatment, 16,* 321–327.

Stephens, R. S., Roffman, R. A., & Curtin, L. (2000). Comparison of extended versus brief treatments for marijuana use. *Journal of Consulting and Clinical Psychology, 68,* 898–908.

Straussner, S. L. A., & Byrne, H. (2009). Alcoholics Anonymous: Key research findings from 2002–2007. *Alcoholism Treatment Quarterly, 27,* 349–367.

Substance Abuse and Mental Health Services Administration. (2009). *Monitoring the future: Results from the 2009 National Survey on Adolescent Drug Use.* Retrieved July 28, 2010 from http://www.monitoringthefuture.org/pubs/monographs/overview2009.pdf

Sue, D. W., & Sue, D. R. (2008). *Counseling the culturally diverse: Theory and practice* (5th ed.). New York: Wiley.

Sutherland, I., & Willner, P. (1998). Patterns of alcohol, cigarette, and illicit drug use in English adolescents. *Addiction, 93,* 1199–1208.

Tober, G. (1991). Motivational interviewing with young people. In Miller, W. R., & Rollnick, S., (Eds.), *Motivational interviewing: Preparing people to change addictive behavior,* (pp. 248–259). New York: Guilford Press.

Tonigan, J. S., Miller, W. R., & Connors, G. J. (2000). Project MATCH client impressions about Alcoholics Anonymous: Measurement issues and relationship to treatment outcome. *Alcoholism Treatment Quarterly, 18*(1), 25–41.

Vader, A. M., Walters, S. T., Prabhu, G. C., Houck, J. M., & Field, C. A. (2010). The language of motivational interviewing and feedback: Counselor language, client language, and client drinking outcomes. *Psychology of Addictive Behaviors, 24,* 190–197.

Vasilaki, E. I., Hosier, S. G., & Cox, W. M. (2006). The efficacy of motivational interviewing as a brief intervention for excessive drinking: A meta-analytic review. *Alcohol and Alcoholism, 41,* 328–335.

Wade, N. G., Worthington Jr., E. L., & Vogel, D. L. (2007). Effectiveness of religiously tailored interventions in Christian therapy. *Psychotherapy Research, 17,* 91–105.

Weinstein, N. D., Rothman, A. J., & Sutton, S. R. (1998). Stage theories of health behavior: Conceptual and methodological issues. *Health Psychology, 17*(3), 290–299.

Werch, C. E., & DiClemente, C. C. (1994). A multi-component stage model for matching drug prevention strategies and messages to youth stage of use. *Health Education Research: Theory and Practice, 9*(1), 37–46.

White, W. (2008). Toward a philosophy of choice: A new era of addiction treatment. *Counselor, 9*(1), 38–43.

White, W., & Miller, W. (2007). The use of confrontation in addiction treatment: History, science and time for change. *Counselor, 8*(4), 12–30.

Willoughby, F. W., & Edens, J. F. (1996). Construct validity and predictive utility of the stages of change scale for alcoholics. *Journal of Substance Abuse, 8*(3), 275–291.

Worthington Jr., E. L., Kurusu, T. A., McCollough, M. E., & Sandage, S. J. (1996). Empirical research on religion and psychotherapeutic processes and outcomes: A 10-year review and research prospectus. *Psychological Bulletin, 119,* 448–487.

Worthington Jr., E. L., & Sandage, S. J. (2002). Religion and spirituality. In J. C. Norcross (Ed.), *Psychotherapy relationships that work: Therapist contributions and responsiveness to patients* (pp. 383–400). New York: Oxford University Press.

Worthington Jr., E. L., & Scott, G. G. (1983). Goal selection for counseling with potentially religious clients by professional and student counselors in explicitly Christian or secular settings. *Journal of Psychology and Theology, 11,* 318–329.

Wyatt, S. C., & Johnson, R. W. (1990). The influence of counselors' religious values on clients' perceptions of the counselor. *Journal of Psychology and Theology, 18,* 158–165.

6

Humanistic Couples Counseling

PAUL R. PELUSO AND STEVEN VENSEL

Perhaps one of the most complex and dynamic human relationships is the romantic pair-bonding couples relationship. It requires two people to negotiate through the intricate emotional issues of desire, security, companionship, attraction, and intimacy. This couple relationship is unique to human beings and combines elements of both resiliency and fragility. As a result, while it may provide individuals with a lifelong partnership and deep emotional satisfaction, it can also be tumultuous, chaotic, and fleeting. When these relationships are strained or broken, it is often left to couples counselors to help pick up the pieces and either repair the relationship or begin again. As such, couples counseling can be simultaneously one of the most rewarding and most taxing forms of counseling.

While no clearly defined humanistic couples counseling approach currently exists, we will argue that much of what has emerged as traditional couples counseling, and even some of the more modern approaches, reflects the humanistic philosophy (defined in Chapter 1) that characterizes humanistic counseling. In this chapter, several issues will be presented to give an overview of couples counseling. In addition, the chapter will demonstrate how many of its traditional systems-oriented forms are rooted in humanistic philosophy (including Adlerian and symbolic-experiential couples counseling) and how many of the more modern approaches and practitioners (emotion-focused couples counseling, Gottman's couples approach) are also reflective of the humanistic perspective. In addition, issues related to the processes of emotions, their impact on couples' relationships, and their unique role in the treatment of couples will also be addressed. This is an especially important topic as it is a central human element in couples that has been (until recently) relatively overlooked in the counseling field. An approach based on the newest research, grounded in humanistic principles for couples counseling, and involving each of the fundamentals described in the chapter will be discussed.

TRADITIONAL COUPLES THERAPY APPROACHES
AND HUMANISTIC COUNSELING

In a 2000 special issue of *Family Process,* noted couples therapists Richard C. Schwartz and Susan M. Johnson authored the lead article titled "Does Couple and Family Therapy Have Emotional Intelligence?" In it, they challenged some of the theories of couples therapy (most notably solution-focused couples therapy) as being indifferent to emotions:

> Family therapy has never been terribly comfortable with emotions. The models that dominated its early development (structural and strategic) were primarily aimed at changing behavior patterns, and, through reframing, the cognitions that maintained them. Virginia Satir's empathic style and focus on getting family members to express their emotions clearly to one another was disdained as "touchy/feely" by the systemic thinkers of the day who, over the years, have introduced a variety of intellectual philosophers to buttress their nonemotional preferences (from Bateson to Maturana to Foucault); and de Shazer's version of solution-focused therapy continues that legacy of marginalizing emotion within the field. (p. 29)

Indeed, the issue of the role of emotion has been a debate within schools of therapy from the time of Sigmund Freud, Jean-Martin Charcot, and Pierre Janet. The main problems have been (1) how to understand it and (2) what to do with it. Initially, it was thought that catharsis and abreaction (venting of repressed feelings) were important avenues to a "cure," and various versions of that (most notably primal-scream therapy from the 1960s and 1970s and its heir, rebirthing techniques) have endured though they have never proven to be effective. In fact, many researchers found that merely venting or ruminating over negative affect without placing it in some meaningful framework can in fact be damaging to a client (Nolen-Hoeksema, McBride, & Larson, 1997). This strengthened the argument of theorists from behaviorally and cognitively oriented schools of therapy that emotion is a quagmire that only can suck in a therapist and for which no therapeutically meaningful work can be done (Schwartz & Johnson, 2000).

In fact, humanism, and the humanistic counseling perspective may shed some light here and may provide a bridge between the mistaken notions of human emotion in the past and overcorrection toward the overly cognitive and behavioral approaches that ensued. Chapter 1 of this volume suggests that "humanism encompasses the richness of the human existential experience that emphasizes the crucial role of the here and now, of authenticity in our relationships with others, and the actual experience of 'experiencing' ourselves and of our world." Along these same lines, Schwartz and Johnson (2000) found that many of the modern approaches of couples therapy have embraced this same movement and "have developed approaches that center on inner and outer conversations about vulnerable emotions.... It seems that the field is slowly catching up with that 'touchy/feely' visionary Virginia Satir, and shaking off its no-emotion legacy" (p. 29). Thus, we argue that the heart of couples therapy today is coming closer to its original roots and that these roots have an unacknowledged shared history with the humanistic perspective.

Couples Therapy Based on Systems Theory

Although there may be a sense that humanistic ideals have slipped into the foggy past of a bygone era, we contend that humanistic principles are so universally accepted that they have become embedded within the very structure of our thinking. Because they are such a part of our thinking, humanistic principles are inherent in the structure of our techniques, models, and theories. This embeddedness, if you will, is deeply entrenched, and we've substituted new terminology for many of the traditional humanistic phrases. But the principles of humanism are quite apparent. According to Sperry, Carlson, and Peluso (2006):

> The therapist takes responsibility for observing the patterns of behavior and changing the interaction through either direct or indirect interventions. The couple is viewed as a constantly changing and evolving system. Problems arise when the old procedures for handling issues do not fit current situations. The therapist's role is to help the couple develop a new way for handling the problem by creating an environment in which new information is introduced and change occurs spontaneously. (p. 146)

Within the structure of a systemic approach to couples counseling, we find several key elements that are rooted in the humanistic perspective. Theories, models, and techniques are all connected by the underlying principles of humanistic philosophies. As indicated in Chapter 1 of this volume, "humanism is unified by an overarching philosophy of human irreducibility. Accordingly, humans can be understood only as whole beings and should never be viewed as by-products of other processes."

One of the hallmarks of irreducibility is the view of people as creative, purpose seeking, and able to construct meaning in their lives (Cain, 2001). Systems theory is quite humanistic in this regard as it capitalizes on clients' subjective experiences and perceptions to make creative changes in their relationship. Sperry et al. (2006) contended that relationships in systemic therapies are organized and conceptualized in terms of wholeness, boundaries, and hierarchy, which are all reflective of humanistic values. Wholeness refers to the understanding and perception of the patterns of couples' interactional choices of movement, role, and response. Boundaries and hierarchical structures can be changed within couples' relationships as the therapist seeks to assist them in making creative changes. A positive view of individuals as self-actualizing, possessing dignity, able to intentionally construct meaning in their lives, and having the freedom, right, and ability to choose and achieve their goals are all examples of humanistic values embedded within a systems approach to helping.

The underlying principles of a humanistic perspective can be found throughout a variety of helping therapies. For example, looking at three "traditional" systemic couples therapies—Bowenian systemic therapy, symbolic-emotional family therapy, and the communication approach pioneered by Virginia Satir—the connection to humanistic principles will become obvious.

Bowen Systems Theory (Murray Bowen)

Bowen systems couples therapy is an extension of the family systems theory approach as developed by Murray Bowen. Central to his approach is the idea of differentiation of the self—or individuals' ability to remain nonreactive in the face of their own anxieties or someone else's (Bowen, 1978; Papero, 2000). Individuals who are well differentiated are not as likely to get overwhelmed cognitively or emotionally when under stress. Bowen believed that this was a natural, developmental force, which exerts pressure on each person. At the same time, an opposite force, fusion (or the togetherness force), pressures individuals to be connected to another person or (family) group. A proper balance between the two is the mark of good health in a relationship and is considered to be the basis for wellness. Again, the key is growth and self-determinism. These opposing forces of differentiation and fusion are responsive in nature and are related to individuals' ability to negotiate connections with their partners (Sperry et al., 2006). It is important to notice here that this process is inherently humanistic in that each couple is constructing individual meaning and actively choosing behaviors that express that meaning. The humanistic values of choice, self-actualizing, dignity, and purpose are all imbedded within this approach. Because it takes into account, and respects, myriad influences impacting the individuals (e.g., family of origin), it is holistic in nature, another quality of a humanistic approach. Although not explicitly articulated in the theory, one can easily see how a humanistic orientation is part of the overarching framework of the approach.

Relationship difficulties, from a Bowen systems perspective, are the result of a mixture of the level of differentiation of self plus the level of anxiety within the relationship. As anxiety increases in the relationship, pressure is exerted on each person to conform to the expectations that the other person has. The level of differentiation of each individual can either mediate or amplify the pressure on the relationship. As anxiety mounts in current relationships, individuals bring the basic sensitivities and reactivity from their own family of origin and other relationship experiences and act on them (Kerr & Bowen, 1988). A pattern of couples behavior begins to emerge and takes on one of four qualities: distance, conflict, reciprocal shifts in functioning (via negotiation), or projection of tension on a third party (triangling). The present relationship develops over time its own reactive patterns based on past and present experience (Papero, 2000). If the tension is not resolved satisfactorily and a destructive pattern is established, eventually resentment builds and instability can result (Sperry et al., 2006).

Bowen referred to this dynamic or situation as *triangles*. Triangles are a way for couples to decrease their anxiety and tension by projecting their attention away from each other and onto a third person (often a child), who becomes emotionally entangled. This temporarily stabilizes the couple but does not resolve the underlying issues (Kerr & Bowen, 1988; Papero, 2000; Roberto-Forman, 2002). This is often a trap that many couples therapists fall into as well by taking one person's side over the other.

Clinically, Bowenian couples therapists operate from the belief that if there was a third person who remained emotionally neutral and would refuse to take sides, tension between two people could be resolved, thus allowing the couple to balance their reactivity to one another as the systemic anxiety decreases. Thus, for a couples therapist operating from a Bowen systems perspective, in addition to remaining neutral in the therapy there are two main tasks to accomplish: (1) increase differentiation of each partner to decrease reactivity to one another; and (2) decrease level of anxiety within the relationship (Papero, 2000). In terms of humanistic principles the role of the therapist is that of an assistant as the couple is guided toward greater levels of freedom and choice. If a couple's subjective experiences are stuck in patternistic responses, not only are their choices limited, but their ability to construct meaning within the context of their relationship is also diminished. In a very real way, the therapist is a broker of humanistic ideals that not only enhances the dignity of each partner but also assists them in developing greater dimensions of self-expression and meaning. If these tasks can be accomplished, according to Bowen (1978), the couple should negotiate a balanced, reciprocal shift in functioning on their own without resorting to triangles or other dysfunctional patterns of interaction (Roberto-Forman, 2002).

Symbolic-Experiential Relationship Therapy

Perhaps no other "classic" systemic approach to couples therapy is more closely aligned with humanism than the symbolic-emotional family (or relationship) therapy (S-EFT) pioneered by Carl Whitaker and Gus Napier. According to Napier (1999), the symbolic-experiential approach is very difficult to describe definitively, partly due to the power of the character and personality of its progenitor, Carl Whitaker, and partly because it borrows or shares many different elements with other theories (Keith, 1998). As Whitaker (2000) put it, "I'm a lumper, not a shredder" (p. 7).

From an S-EFT perspective, when couples get together it is often with the unexpressed desire for a *reparenting* process whereby the other partner completes them in the ways that they feel inadequate or deficient. When the partner either fails to do this or refuses to continue acting in this role (as with some long-term relationships), the partners feel as if they are reliving their experiences from their families of origin (in a symbolic way). This produces feelings of dependence, isolation, and defensiveness and can provoke childish acting-out behaviors (e.g., affairs, withholding affection, and excessive arguments) as a type of self-protection (Napier, 1999; Napier & Whitaker, 1978; Sperry et al., 2006; Whitaker & Keith, 1981).

An S-EFT therapist understands that when couples come to therapy they bring in these unmet emotional needs and expect the therapist not only to fix their problems as a couple but also to complete the uncompleted parenting (Napier, 1999). Napier (1999) expanded this sentiment thusly:

> We S-EFT practitioners share many of the concerns of structural therapists regarding the desirability of within-generation coalitions, and of firm between-generation boundaries. When couples find it difficult to make their primary investment in their own marriage, we work intensively on current family-of-origin issues that are often blocking this commitment. We also target historical issues in the family of origin, such as childhood disruption in bonding that may have produced fearfulness about intimacy. (p. 305)

As a result, the therapeutic alliance with the couple takes on additional significance (Keith, 1998). In terms of the structure of the therapy team, S-EFT employs a cotherapy team approach and whenever possible a male–female pair (Napier, 1988). In a metaphorical sense, the couple's (or family's) relationship to the therapist is likened to a foster home where the couple temporarily comes in and receives the care that they need until the difficult time in the relationship has passed. This configuration "reactivates for the patient couple the symbolism of the two-parent family; it also provides them with a visible model for intimacy, fairness, openness, and peer negotiation" (Napier, 1999, p. 303). However, for S-EFT to be effective, the pair must be aware and honest about their own countertransference issues and must be emotionally mature enough in their own right to delve into the "emotional currents of the family" (Keith, 1998, p. 180).

In this regard S-EFT is all about the couple's responsiveness to interventions that rely on the subjective meaning they have constructed within the context of their relationships with each other, their children, and their parents. This "whole being" perspective is deeply rooted in humanistic thought. One of the unique humanistic qualities of this approach is the extent to which the therapist goes to assure responsiveness and growth.

In terms of the therapy itself, S-EFT begins with an extended assessment that can last several hours or go on for several initial sessions. During this time, the couple provide information related to their histories, complaints, and wishes for the future. The therapists listen for reoccurring themes or patterns (i.e., dominance–submission; pursuit–distance; self–other focus), strength of the relational bond, as well as outside influences from the social context (e.g., family-of-origin loyalties, job pressures, physical stressors). Demonstrated by this extensive assessment phase, in which as many of the couple's subjective experiences as realistically possible are ascertained, is a holistic understanding of the individuals' construction of meaning (Sperry et al., 2006). Indeed, the very term symbolic denotes meaning that is subjectively constructed and individually valued. Humanistically, S-EFT relies on the clients' dignity, freedom, as well as their right and ability to construct meaning, choose goals, and make changes.

S-EFT therapists have several beliefs about therapy that are not negotiable. First, if there are children, at some point they will be incorporated into the therapy. According to Napier (1999), "this is done in order to see directly how relationships are organized, and how the couple's interactional dynamics are truly played out (rather then relying on the couple's report)" (p. 303). Like Bowenian and other systems theory approaches, S-EFT couples therapy involves understanding patterns that extend across three generations. This includes the couple, their children, and their parents, all of whom will (at some point) be invited to participate in treatment. The timing of involving the clients' parents in the couples therapy is usually dependent on the issues that are presented or the extent of the parents' involvement (e.g., emotional, financial) in the couple's lives and how that involvement impedes their independence and differentiation. Napier (1988) referred to this as the "battle for structure" that must be "won" by the therapist (e.g., who attends or does not attend, whether the couple is late).

S-EFT therapists believe that these are ways for the couple to present the least anxiety-producing face of the family, which sabotage treatment effectiveness (Sperry et al., 2006; Whitaker & Keith, 1981). The goals of S-EFT include increasing anxiety and ambiguity, understanding the symbolic relationships between and among family members, and freeing up a person's ability to be an emotionally differentiated, whole individual for their partner (Keith, 1998). For Whitaker (2000), "mobilizing the family by inducing anxiety brings a better morale and increases its power to neutralize the family infighting and actuate an operational readiness for change in the family system" (p. 12).

In spite of this seemingly deterministic role of the therapist, the intentionality toward increasing client choices, as well as a deep respect for the client's ability and capacity to change, must be noted. Connell, Mitten, and Bumberry (1998) noted, "Symbolic-experiential therapy focuses on unique family symbols that deter growth. Merely arriving at our office does not guarantee change. The journey is theirs, traveled by their footsteps. They pay the price and exert the effort. This is intentional, for the gains and losses are theirs, not ours. Anything we do to obscure this fundamental fact is countertherapeutic" (p. 1). Length of treatment is not as much of a concern for S-EFT therapists, as they endorse a more long-term approach to relational and individual functioning (though it can take less time to have a positive impact). This type of experience in therapy produces a change (growth and maturity) in a couple that encompasses the emotional, cognitive, and behavioral. In this way, the ultimate goal of psychotherapy is for clients to be able to have as much access to the self as possible within the context of a deeply intimate relationship. Again, this is highly reflective of a humanistic perspective and philosophy. Indeed, according to Keith (1998), "Marriage is one of the best ways of getting a Ph.D. in being a person" (p. 180).

Satir's Communications Approach

Virginia Satir was one of the most visible and influential (as well as one of the only female) marketers of couples and family therapy to both professionals and lay audiences alike from the 1960s until her death in 1988. Her trainings and video demonstrations have inspired thousands of couples therapists (Gurman & Fraenkel, 2002). Although remembered primarily as a family therapist, she focused on the dyadic and relational level, making her work applicable to couples therapy (Banmen, 2002). Her focus on the affective and the personhood of clients makes her approach deeply congruent with a humanistic approach.

This humanistic philosophy is reflected in her belief that when two individuals form a couple, they form a couple system that is composed of three parts: (1) each person's perceptions of themselves and the other; (2) how each person thinks and feels; and (3) each person's reaction to the other (Satir, 1964). Psychological health, for the individual and the couple, would be the result of several factors, including awareness of one's own needs and feelings, accepting oneself and others, accepting disagreements and others' points of view, and the ability to communicate clearly (Gurman & Fraenkel, 2002; Haber, 2002). According to Sperry et al. (2006), for Satir, "the overarching goal of couples therapy was to foster greater self-actualization and self-esteem, which, in turn, would make each partner more congruent in his or her communication with the other person" (p. 151). According to Satir (1964), her goal was "not to maintain the relationship nor to separate the pair but to help each other to take charge of himself" (p. 125).

As a clinician, Satir often worked with the body and affect. She believed that these nonrational (or not cognitive) pathways were a more direct path to reach an individual's core issue. Satir believed that these methods were natural survival mechanisms for handling emotional threats when individuals have no other method for coping (i.e., fight-or-flight responses). As a result, her famous sculpturing technique would create opportunities for couples to explore these long-held beliefs and feelings that had shaped their views of each other and the relationship (Sperry et al., 2006). Even though they might seem dysfunctional and warped to the outside observer, Satir was generally respectful of these behaviors, since they represented individuals' best attempts to cope with a threat. This is why Satir was often quoted as saying, "The problem is not the problem, coping is the problem" (Haber, 2002, p. 24). Virginia Satir was very much ahead of her time. Indeed, her influence is still felt in such modern-day approaches as emotionally focused couples therapy and solution-focused couples therapy (Sperry et al., 2006). However, she also reflected a core emphasis of the humanistic approach, as illustrated in Chapter 1: "the person in managing his or her own life, … responsible decision making and the development and growth of the wholeness and completeness of the human being."

HUMANISTIC PERSPECTIVE ON CONTEMPORARY COUPLES COUNSELING APPROACHES

Adlerian Theory and Couples Therapy

There is a direct link between the individual psychology approach of Alfred Adler (1870–1937) and humanistic counseling. For approximately 10 years prior to Adler's death, Abraham Maslow was affiliated with Adler and his approach and frequently consulted with Adler himself (Hoffman, 1994). This directly influenced his eventual creation of what is called "humanistic counseling" today and can be seen in the central tenets of both approaches, particularly the irreducibility of the person, the valuing of individual decision making, and the primacy of the subjective over the objective. Adler (1956) believed that individuals actively participate in the creation of the main personality factor in individual psychology, the style of life. This subjective creation of reality is shaped from a very early age as a result of interactions within the family unit. According to Adler, it is from this subjective view of life (which he called the "schema of apperception") that individuals construct a "private logic"—which is the collection of attitudes and reactions individuals have about life and their place in it. This process takes place by about the age of 6 with some variability due to individual and cultural differences. At this stage of development, children make decisions about their place in the world, what behaviors or strategies they will need to use to belong, and how this belonging to a social group will help them get their basic physical and emotional needs met. The social feeling (*Gemeinschaftsgefül*) that individuals innately have, and the extent to which it gets expressed, is tied into the overall family atmosphere and the conclusions the individuals draw from it. Hence, the family, as the prototypical social group for the child, plays a crucial role related to the development of this "private logic" and eventual style of life. According to Adler (1956), this style of life becomes the response set for life and is the common thread that weaves together individuals' thoughts, feelings, and actions into a coherent pattern. In addition, once it is set in place, the style of life remains relatively stable through adulthood (Peluso, Peluso, Buckner, Kern, & Curlette, 2004). While the style of life is stable, it does not mean that it is unchanging. In fact, Adlerians believe that individuals can learn how to make their particular style of life work better for them through either life experiences or psychotherapy (Adler, 1956; Peluso, 2006). It is clear how Adlerian principles have been influenced by the humanistic perspective and have influenced the development of humanistic counseling as an approach.

Of course, the purpose of individual psychology is to provide a framework for understanding human behavior and development to help those individuals who are either suffering from serious mental illnesses or having difficulty mastering the basic tasks of life. As such, the style of life is probably the most crucial element in Adlerian psychotherapy. The style of life results from clients' perceptions and experiences of the world (especially in the family of origin) and is shown in their behavior, or movement in the world. It is also revealed in the clients' relations with others in terms of the quality and quantity of relationships (Peluso, 2006; Peluso & Macintosh, 2007).

In terms of mate selection and couples treatment, from an individual psychology perspective, "*partners are chosen based on the compatibility of styles of life, goals, and belief systems.* The couple comes together and forms a relational dyad that is influenced by each partner and creates a system whereby the individual choices of each partner have a unique bearing on the functioning of the system. The thoughts, feelings, and attitudes all influence the behavior of either person as well as the direction of the couple system" (Peluso & Macintosh, 2007, p. 249). Dreikurs (1946) believed that when there is stress or discord those elements in one's partner that attracted us become the same behaviors that create problems. This is why, according to Adlerian theorists, the choices that a couple makes are not accidental and are (ideally) directed toward the goal of communication and respect as equals (Carlson & Dinkmeyer, 1999). However, this goal is not always realized. Individual private logic, goals, and style-of-life dynamics can uniquely guide the system into either function or dysfunction. So even if the behavior that is exhibited by a couple is destructive (on the surface), it may actually represent a creative attempt at negotiating a balance between each partner's needs. Again, this is reflective of the conceptualization of the humanistic approach presented in Chapter 1.

Stages of Couples Treatment

Almost all Adlerian therapy uses some variation of the four-stage model outlined by Dreikurs (1967): (1) relationship building; (2) investigation; (3) interpretation; and (4) reorientation. In the first stage of *relationship building*, the therapist must create a solid therapeutic alliance with the couple, deal with both partners fairly, and provide a secure base from which to work. In the next phase, *assessment*, a style-of-life analysis is conducted for each person, which includes an examination of family-of-origin dynamics (psychological birth order, family atmosphere) and early recollections. From this analysis, the couple's private logic and goals can be determined. *Interpretation* allows the therapist to place the styles of life of both partners side by side and reflect how the dynamics and behavioral choices of each partner are contributing to the disruption in the marital system. The insight into the couple's relationship allows the therapist to intervene and help the couple to make some new choices in relating to one another. In the *reorientation* phase, the couple, under the guidance and encouragement of the therapist, create an action plan based on the result of the style of life assessment and in light of the presenting problem. The couple make specific changes in their interactions with each other and evaluate the effect on the relationship. Once the main goals of therapy have been accomplished, termination usually occurs based upon mutual agreement between client and therapist (Peluso & Macintosh, 2007; Sperry et al., 2006).

Adlerian couples therapy is not deterministic or fatalistic about the potential for change. Instead, at any time, either partner can effect change in the relationship by making different choices and thus impacting the system (Peluso & Macintosh, 2007). In Adlerian therapy, each member of the couple must take responsibility for his or her own behavior. Once a person knows how mistaken goals or style-of-life dynamics create problems in the relationship, then that person can make the effort to change behavior toward the other person. The Adlerian therapist looks for the creativity in the solution and attempts to harness the same resources toward a more constructive and equitable solution (Carlson & Dinkmeyer, 1999). The ability to make changes within a system, however, requires insight, courage, and a sense of humor about one's self and life. Thus, the therapist must act as encourager, detective, and sometimes a humorist (Sperry et al., 2006). During couples treatment, Adlerian therapists may use several interventions (e.g., "the question," paradoxical intention, "spitting in the client's soup," catching one's self, and assigning homework) to help uncover these underlying goals and ultimately give the clients the courage to be able to change their behavior on their own. In addition, because Adlerian theory relates to many different systems of psychotherapy, Adlerian psychotherapists are able to use new techniques without necessarily abandoning their own theoretical framework. Many times the technique that is "borrowed" is actually a revisitation of an original Adlerian technique (e.g., the miracle question, the push-button technique). However, several Adlerian theorists have begun to incorporate new modalities of treatment (e.g., attachment theory) and integrate them well within an Adlerian context (Peluso et al., 2004; Peluso & Macintosh, 2007; Peluso, Peluso, Buckner, Kern, & Curlette, 2009).

Emotion-Focused Couples Therapy

Emotion-focused couples therapy (EFT) was developed in the 1980s by Leslie Greenberg and Susan Johnson in response to an absence of standardized and validated nonbehavioral clinical approaches to couple distress. Primarily, the field up to that point had focused on behavioral and cognitive change while leaving the role of emotion largely unexplored both in theory and practice. EFT is a form of couples therapy that integrates experiential and systemic approaches in the process of therapeutic change (Peluso & Macintosh, 2007). EFT is compatible with family systems theory, but it also represents an extension of it. Systems theory–based therapies have the tendency to focus on the development and maintenance of a couple's patterns of interaction, while EFT focuses on the couple's experience of the emotions of security, separation, and loss in the relationship. In general, systems theory offers basic principles for understanding any system, while attachment theory gives more information about the intimate relationship (Johnson, 2003; Johnson & Whiffen, 1999). According to Johnson and Best (2003), "the name, emotionally focused, was given to this model of intervention to stress the primary significance of emotion and emotional communication in the organization of the reciprocally determining system of responses that constitute an attachment relationship" (p. 165).

EFT has been empirically validated and presently is recognized as one of only two empirically validated extant couple interventions (Baucom, Shoham, Mueser, Daiuto, & Stickle, 1998; Alexander, Holtzworth-Munroe, & Jameson, 1994). EFT has been investigated extensively and has been found to be effective with diverse populations including depressed women (Dessaulles, 1991; Johnson, 1998) and families experiencing chronic stress or coping with a chronically ill child (Gordon Walker, Manion, & Clothier, 1998). Case studies have been presented on the use of EFT with couples coping with one partner who has survived severe trauma and has symptoms of posttraumatic stress disorder (PTSD).

The Process of Change

Johnson (2002) argued that when no secure base is available to a partner in a relationship, attachment behaviors such as protesting and clinging, avoidance, or withdrawal would be provoked and exaggerated. She further argued that this process would evolve until neither partner would be able to be responsive or accessible to the other. This unresponsiveness would then continue to provoke increased insecurity until both partners became unable to sustain emotional engagement, and couples would then become emotionally misattuned with each other.

Johnson expanded upon the concept of attunement in parent–child dyads by suggesting that in adult relationships attunement is the sensitive moment-to-moment being with partners as they experience and express an emotion. This attunement is demonstrated through the exhibition of behaviors that suggest the ability to empathize and share partners' emotional experience. In conclusion, Johnson argued that as insecure attachment styles become rigid, and polarize, the insecurity would manifest itself in the inability for individuals to be open and trusting with their partners, whom she argued represent the foundation of the secure bond with others. This insecurity would then result in avoidance from engagement with each other, which would then make modification of attachment styles difficult until eventually both partners withdraw, and the relationship is in jeopardy (Peluso & Macintosh, 2007).

EFT emphasizes the role of affect in therapeutic change. Additionally, the role of communication and rigid interactional cycles in maintaining dysfunctional interactions are emphasized. Critical elements in relationship distress are hypothesized to be the absorbing states of negative affect such as anger or fear (Johnson & Whiffen, 1999). EFT melds experiential (intrapsychic), systemic (interpersonal), and humanistic theoretical approaches. By uncovering the shrouded emotional needs and identifying negative cycles that maintain each partner's interactional stance, these interactional patterns can begin to change (Johnson, 1998). Not only is the expression of needs facilitated, but also new responses on the part of the partner can be created. Johnson (1998) suggested that communication and emotional expression are primary forms of self-regulation that enable individuals to identify what is important to the partner, allowing couples to more adequately meet each other's emotional needs (Peluso & Macintosh, 2007).

The process of change in EFT is illustrated by three stages and nine treatment steps:

> Stage 1, Deescalation: This stage is composed of four steps, each of which has foundations in the humanistic principles of nonreduction and holism (see Chapter 1 in this volume):
>
> Step 1 delineates the conflict and includes an assessment of the core issues and conflict using an attachment perspective. The therapeutic alliance is developed and the unveiling process is begun.
>
> Step 2 involves identifying the negative interaction cycles such as pursue–withdraw or attack–defend. Both individuals' presenting concerns are made relational through the identification of these cycles.
>
> Step 3 involves delving into the unacknowledged emotions underlying these self-reinforcing interactional patterns. The therapist begins to identify and validate the primary emotional responses.
>
> Step 4 reframes the problems in terms of the cycle, the underlying emotions, and attachment needs (Peluso & Macintosh, 2007).
>
> Stage 2, Reengagement/Softening: This stage has three steps. During this stage, key interventions support the couples in expressing vulnerability with the result of the emergence of new relational cycles which create a large shift in the relationship positions (Peluso & Macintosh, 2007). Again, there is an emphasis on holism, self-determinism, and the development of client potential, derived from a humanistic perspective:
>
> Step 5 promotes identification with disavowed needs and facets of the self that have been withheld and integration of the elements into the relationship.

Step 6 involves the promotion of acceptance of the partner's new ways of being and responding in the relationship.

Step 7 is the facilitation of the expression of specific needs and wants and creating emotional engagement.

Stage 3, Consolidation/Integration: This stage has two steps:

Step 8 develops new solutions to old problem relationship issues.

Step 9 involves consolidating new positions and new cycles of attachment behavior (Johnson, 1996).

EFT focuses on reshaping the structured, repetitive interactional patterns and the emotional responses that evoke these patterns and fostering the development of a secure emotional bond (Johnson & Whiffen, 1999). EFT provides couples with a safe corrective experience of trying new responses, in highly emotionally charged attachment situations, instead of old default attachment models that automatically arise. However, attachment models that are closely guarded, defensive, rigid, or undifferentiated may be difficult to access and revise. As a result, these couples are more likely to be reactive and distressed. Therapy can be slower with these couples, but it is not hopeless, though it will require more traditional family-systems work (Johnson & Whiffen).

Emotionally focused couples therapy is distinctively humanistic. The inclusion of affective and emotional states in the helping process provides an expansion to the more traditional systemic approaches, which essentially minimizes emotional systems and attempts to work around emotionally charged states. In a sense, EFT offers a deeper, whole-person experience by facilitating expression of emotional need, encouraging vulnerability as well as empathic support, and promoting affective discovery in the change process. EFT also relies heavily on the helping relationship to facilitate growth. Using the therapeutic relationship, a collaborative alliance is made that respectfully offers the couple the security they need to explore the relationship. In addition, the therapist takes a nonpathologizing stance toward the couple by validating attachment needs and processes as adaptive instead of pathological. Taken all together this approach is highly reflective of humanistic values. The following case study illustrates how emotion-focused couples therapy facilitates emotional expression and uses here-and-now vulnerabilities in promoting change in a couple's relationship.

Case Study

Jane and Ed came to therapy following Jane's discovery of Ed's online "cyber affair." Married only 2 years, Jane was in considerable pain, which was primarily expressed through control and anger. For the past 2 months Ed's use of the computer was closely monitored and restricted. In addition, Jane also closely monitored Ed's cell phone call history and text messages. Ed maintained that he understood why his wife was upset and had no problem submitting to his wife's controlling behavior and occasional angry outbursts. Ed believed the cyber relationship was meaningless, was not an extramarital affair as no sex was involved, and was surprised that it hadn't "blown over" yet. Both Jane and Ed were seeking help as their previously close relationship had deteriorated to a point of mutual concern.

After providing a history of the dating and marital relationship, the conflict, and how the partners responded to the conflict, was explored. It was evident that the primary emotion expressed by Jane was anger, with Ed acquiescing to her demands. Therapy began with a simple question directed to promote expression of vulnerability and need through metaphor.

Therapist: Jane, what was it like for you when you discovered Ed's cyber relationship?
Jane: It makes me angry.
Therapist: Yes, it makes you angry, but what was it like?
Jane: It just makes me mad.
Therapist: Yes, it makes you mad and angry, but what was it like for you?

Jane is silent as she struggles to find words to describe what the experience was like for her. She begins to softly cry then whispers:

Jane: Small and alone.
Therapist: Small and alone. Small and alone like what?

Jane takes more time and continues to softly cry.

Jane: Like a kitten.
Therapist: Like a kitten. And what is happening to that kitten?

Jane is silent as she struggles with her vulnerability. She begins to cry in earnest.

Jane: Like a kitten locked out of the house on a rainy night.
Therapist: And what does a kitten locked out on a rainy night feel?

Jane takes more time; Ed puts his hand on her knee.

Jane: So scared and helpless and afraid. It's all alone and doesn't understand; it just wants to be held and safe and comforted.

Jane is sobbing at this point, and Ed takes her hand.

Ed: I had no idea, I'm so sorry.

Ed is teary eyed and whispering. He repeats this several times as Jane cries and then begins to recover herself.

This deep expression of affect and vulnerability, in the here and now, facilitated Ed's understanding of the meaning of his cyber affair and how it impacted his wife. This sequence of affective exploration and expression ("What is … like for you?") was then used as a model in helping this couple develop new pathways of communication and intimacy in their relationship. In subsequent sessions, Ed was able to explore and express how Jane's anger and controlling responses to conflict and what it was like for him had resulted in him becoming emotionally guarded and distant from his wife. When viewed from this emotional vulnerability perspective the meaning of the cyber affair was revealed as an expression of the couple's marital relationship. Both Jane and Ed realized how they had become less vulnerable with each other and subsequently less emotionally intimate.

Gottman's Approach

The work of John Gottman and his laboratory support many assertions about successful healthy marriages and unhealthy ones. Gottman and his associates (Driver, Tabares, Shapiro, Nahm, & Gottman, 2003; Gottman, 1994, 1999; Gottman & Levenson, 2002) are singular in their empirical observation and verification of these relational qualities and in providing therapists with powerful information about relationships and their processes. Gottman's method is so popular and widely respected that by 2006, 4,000 couples and 3,000 therapists had participated in at least one of Gottman's workshops (Rogers, Minuchin, Satir, Bowen, & Gottman, 2007). As noted in Chapter 1 of this volume, "Gottman's primary goals for couples include developing skills required for nonjudgmental active listening, enhancing partners' sense of liking for one another, and enhancing partners' understanding of each other's likes and dislikes—goals that clearly echo the Rogerian (1957) core conditions." Gottman and his associates found that "success or failure of a marriage depends not on whether there is conflict, but rather how conflict is handled when it does occur" (Driver et al., 2003, p. 493). Couples who successfully handle conflicts can be grouped into one of three typical styles: validators, volatiles, and avoiders (Driver et al., 2003; Gottman, 1994, 1999):

1. Validator couples: Have a tendency to talk out problems; be supportive of each other and emphasize the couple ("we-ness"); validate the other's position, feelings, and opinions; have a strong sense of mutual respect; and resolve conflict through compromise.
2. Volatile couples: Have a tendency to have explosive conflicts with heated arguments that do not become ugly or personal but are energetic and passionate; are high energy and passionate; express affection and warmth with equal passion; and view each other as equals and attempt to persuade by argument.

3. Avoider couples: Have a tendency to ignore or downplay the negative interactions; choose to emphasize the positive qualities of the relationship; will often "agree to disagree" and move forward.

An additional hallmark of these healthy relationship conflict styles is the 5:1 ratio of five positive statements or behaviors to one negative statement or behavior. Even in the midst of a disagreement, these successful couples keep to this ratio, which communicates respect and affection for the other person (Gottman, 1994; Gottman & Levenson, 2002).

The "Four Horsemen of the Apocalypse"

One of the methods by which Gottman and his colleagues have been able to quantify the qualities and interactions of unhealthy couples is through their destructive communication styles (Driver et al., 2003; Gottman, 1994, 1999). When these couples get into conflict, they often exhibit one of the "Four Horsemen of the Apocalypse," which, according to Gottman, is indicative of problem relationships (Gottman, 1994, 1999). The Four Horsemen are criticism, contempt, defensiveness, and stonewalling (Gottman, 1999):

1. Criticism: A broad and sweeping character attack that seems unfair to the other person and usually includes the words always and never.
2. Contempt: Characterized by corrosiveness, hostility, and disrespect. It can be conveyed with nonverbal behavior (i.e., eye rolls, scowls, looks of disgust) or directly by verbal behavior (i.e., mockery, insults, sarcasm). It usually provokes defensive responses or retaliation and cuts off any attempt for immediate reconciliation or deescalation.
3. Defensiveness: The hallmark of a stalemate in the relationship, where each person is protecting themselves against the other's contemptuous attacks. Defensiveness always leads to more retaliation and escalation and can provide an excuse to place blame on the other person for the negative cycle (which provokes further attack).
4. Stonewalling: When one member simply withdraws completely from almost all interactions with the other partner. Usually a signal that one or both partners is feeling overwhelmed or emotionally flooded and must shut the other out (even if they are not being negative) for self-protection.

Criticism is different from complaints, which exist in every relationship and are limited to a specific incident (e.g., "I'm upset that you forgot our anniversary") while maintaining respect for the other person. Criticism is a more broad and sweeping character attack and usually includes the words *always* and *never* (e.g., "You are so selfish, you never think about anyone other than yourself").

Contempt is the next horseman and is even more corrosive since it adds a sense of hostility and disrespect to the criticism. An example of contempt might be, "Oh, I can see that your diet is really melting the pounds off. How much have you lost, 2 maybe 3 pounds in the last 4 months?" Since these contemptuous behaviors usually provoke defensive responses or retaliation, they short-circuit any attempt by the other person to try to reconcile or scale back from the conflict (Driver et al., 2003; Gottman, 1994, 1999). According to Gottman, the presence of contempt is a very negative marker for relationships.

In defensiveness, the third horseman, contempt is prevalent, but it is now being employed by both participants (rather than just one): "Congratulations, because of your drinking you've lost another job." "Oh yeah? Well if you weren't so lazy and spent so much money, I wouldn't *have* to drink so much!"

The final horseman, stonewalling, sends the message, "I don't want to have *anything* to do with you." This usually increases the polarization between the two partners. There is no communication at any level and very little hope of the couple deescalating without outside help (i.e., couples therapy).

Gottman's (1999) research highlights the effect of negative emotions and highly structured interaction patterns to predict the future of a relationship. Those relationships high in negative emotional discourse and very rigidly structured interactions (particularly with regard to gender roles) seemed to do more poorly in the long run than those that were more positive, reciprocal, and soothing in their exchanges (Johnson & Lebow, 2000). EFT also echoes and reinforces Gottman's research on negative affect and how it impacts couples. In fact, according to Johnson and Best (2003):

> Negative attachment-related events, particularly abandonments and betrayals, often then cause seemingly irreparable damage to close relationships.... These incidents, usually occurring in the context of life transitions, loss, physical danger, or uncertainty, can be considered relationship traumas and, if unresolved, tend to block the creation of trust and undermine relationship repair.... When the other partner then fails to respond in a reparative, reassuring manner or when the injured spouse cannot accept such reassurance, the injury is aggravated. (p. 177)

The results of Gottman and his associates' work have been so profound that they claim they can predict, with approximately 91–94% accuracy, which couples are likely to get divorced based on the observation of 15 minutes of conversation between partners (Carrere, Buehlman, Coan, Gottman, & Ruckstuhl, 2000; Gottman, 1994; Gottman & Levenson, 2002). Other factors such as the presence of emotional disengagement and negative reciprocity in the couple's interactions also add to the negative atmosphere of relationships in trouble (Driver et al., 2003; Gottman, 1994).

What Makes Marriages Succeed: The "Sound Marital House"
and Bids for Connection

Not only did Gottman's research yield important information about distressed couples, but it also produced a framework for understanding sound, healthy marriages. He solidified his finding around seven factors he calls the sound marital house theory (Gottman, 1999), amongst them are: (1) turning toward versus turning away from one another; (2) positive sentiment override (vs. negative sentiment); (3) dialoguing about perpetual problems and effectively solving problems together; and (4) making dreams and aspirations come true for each person in the couple. Gottman found that when these behaviors (and others) were present in relationships, they tended to be more successful than those relationships that did not have them present.

So, how do you do this? A simple way that Gottman (1999) found was that successful couples (what he calls "masters of marriage") would have successful bids for connection:

> A bid [for connection] can be a question, a gesture, a look, a touch—any single expression that says, "I want to feel connected to you." A response to a bid is just that—a positive or negative answer to somebody's request for emotional connection. (p. 4)

Indeed, they found that the price of failed bids for connection was high for troubled couples. In their research, Gottman and his associates found that husbands headed for divorce dismissed their wives' bids for connection 82% of the time, while husbands in stable relationships disregard their wives' bids just 19% of the time. For their part, wives headed for divorce ignored their husbands bid for their attention 50% of the time, while happily married wives ignored their husbands' bids just 14% of the time (p. 4). For example, in a typical dinner conversation, happily married couples engaged with each other over 100 times in a 10-minute period, while couples headed for divorce engaged with each other only 65 times. These positive interactions also allowed for greater access to humor and other positive emotions during conflict, which helped to deescalate arguments and constructively solve problems.

In many ways, Gottman's approach is a celebration of these humanistic ideals, and the popularity of the approach is a testament to the power of humanistically oriented methods. Gottman expresses an inherent respect for the dignity of individuals and couples in the chosen terminology of the method. In his descriptions of healthy couples, the use of the terms validator couple, volatile couple, and avoider couple are descriptors of interaction and response, not descriptors of individual causality. In other words, the terminology is an indication of how individuals and couples are viewed as *in* process, *in* relationship, and *in* response to each other and not as being *in* a diagnosable medical condition that determines the dysfunctional pattern. Additionally, the descriptions contained in the Four Horsemen of the Apocalypse also demonstrate the same level of respect for individual dignity and irreducibility.

In this regard, the humanistic qualities of Gottman's approach are unmistakable and distinctive. The way Gottman incorporates the whole of the person's experience in the therapy process is worthy of special note. First, notice how the approach is committed to clearly understanding the couple's experience through observation and verification. This duality in the assessment process, observation and verification, reveals the inherent respect for the clients' subjective construction of meaning. It also is an indication that clients are viewed as irreducible to other phenomena in that there is no linking of observations to diagnosis or psychopathology. Another duality that is holistic in nature is how Gottman's method is grounded in observations of both healthy and unhealthy couples. This is significant in that comparisons are made based on real-life observations of healthy couple interaction, not on reducing partners to individual pathology based on the medical model or some other reductionistic concepts.

CONCLUSION—TOWARD A UNIFIED HUMANISTIC APPROACH TO COUPLES THERAPY

Humanistic ideals are grounded in the conviction that human beings are a hopeful species with the capacity to be self-determining, intentional, creative, and possessing of dignity. Any humanistic-oriented therapy can be readily identified by how these characteristics of irreducibility are expressed and revealed in their approach to helping. Additionally, humanistic therapeutic approaches will be oriented toward expanding client choices, increasing opportunities for empathic relating, and enhancing personal and prosocial competencies. Interpersonal skill development, development of nonjudgmental active listening, enhancement of understanding, and increasing ability to resolve conflicts are all expressive of a commitment toward strengthening critical empathic capacities while helping couples relate to each other in growth-producing ways.

One of the primary intentions of this book is to highlight humanistic principles inherent in approaches to helping. As the editors note in Chapter 1, humanism encompasses the richness of the human experience, and while it is true that a well-defined humanistic couples counseling approach does not currently exist it is clear that humanistic ideals are quite representative in the existing methods of helping couples. The belief that humans are irreducible to other phenomena and the inclusion of the whole person into a coherent and integrative system of helping is at the core of the call for a humanistic milieu of care. Understanding humans as whole beings that are able to make individual choices, make meaning within their own subjective experiences, and have an inherent dignity are the big three of humanistic values. These values are clearly articulated within many of the models and approaches, past and present, to helping couples.

Another intention laid out by the editors is to show the power of humanistic thinking to unite diverse elements of counseling practice. The fact that so many humanistic systems of care already exist and that they are inherently respectful of the dignity of each client, are holistic in nature, rely upon the client's innate ability to construct meaning from their experiences, and provide a meaningful relationship that assists them in finding creative solutions is a testament to the uniting power of the humanistic perspective. As we have demonstrated, Bowen's systems theory, Adlerian theory, symbolic-experiential relationship theory, EFT, Satir's approach, and Gottman's approach all reveal a strong and profound infusion of humanistic ideals.

A unified systematic humanistic approach to helping may be what is most needed to impact the barrage of designer drugs and cosmetic medications hocked by the pharmaceutical companies and used so pervasively, especially in the "treatment" of children. This growing medical monster represents a very real threat not only to individual dignity but also to the very foundation of individual, family, and marital well-being. Communicating to parents and children that something is wrong with them that only chemicals can correct is an outright assault to humanistic values. Perhaps what humanism has needed for a reemergence of importance is to have a battle that goes deeper than philosophical ideologies that are too easily viewed, at least by nonacademics, as semantics.

From a marital perspective the potential of humanistic ideals in helping couples lies not so much in the specifications of a singular model of humanistic care. Rather, as we have shown, the power lies in a philosophy of regard for people's right, freedom, and ability to construct purpose and meaning from their experiences and relationships. Effective humanistic approaches cultivate dignity, nurture creativity, and till the grounds of human potential. We look forward to seeing what the future holds in helping couples from this important perspective.

REFERENCES

Adler, A. (1956). The individual psychology of Alfred Adler. In H. L. Ansbacher & R. R. Ansbacher (Eds.), *The individual psychology of Alfred Adler*. New York: Harper & Row.

Alexander, J. F., Holtzworth-Munroe, A., & Jameson, P. (1994). The process and outcome of marital and family therapy: Research review and evaluation. In A. E. Bergin & S. L. Garfield (Eds.), *Handbook of psychotherapy and behaviour change* (4th ed., pp. 595–612). New York: Wiley.

Banmen, J. (2002). The Satir model: Yesterday and today. *Contemporary Family Therapy, 24*(1), 7–22.

Baucom, D. H., Shoham, V., Mueser, K. T., Daiuto, A. D., & Stickle, T. R. (1998). Empirically supported couple and family interventions for marital distress and adult mental health problems. *Journal of Consulting and Clinical Psychology, 66*(1), 53–88.

Bowen, M. (1978). *Family therapy in clinical practice.* New York: Jason Aaronson.

Cain, D. J. (2001). Defining characteristics, history, and evolution of humanistic psychotherapies. In D. J. Cain & J. Seeman (Eds.), *Humanistic psychotherapies: Handbook of research and practice* (pp. 3–54). Washington, DC: American Psychological Association.

Carlson, J., & Dinkmeyer, D. (1999). Couple therapy. In R. E. Watts & J. Carlson (Eds.), *Interventions and strategies in counseling and psychotherapy* (pp. 87–100). Philadelphia: Accelerated Development.

Carrere, S., Buehlman, K. T., Coan, J., Gottman, J. M., & Ruckstuhl, L. (2000). Predicting marital stability and divorce in newlywed couples. *Journal of Family Psychology, 14*(1), 42–58.

Connell, G., Mitten, T., & Bumberry, W. (1998). *Reshaping family relationships: The symbolic therapy of Carl Whitaker.* Philadelphia: Brunner/Mazel.

Dessaulles, A. (1991). *The treatment of clinical depression in the context of marital distress.* Unpublished doctoral dissertation, Clinical Psychology, University of Ottawa.

Dreikurs, R. (1946). *The challenge of marriage.* New York: Hawthorne.

Dreikurs, R. (1967). *Psychodynamics, psychotherapy, and counseling.* Chicago: Alfred Adler Institute.

Driver, J., Tabares, A., Shapiro, A., Nahm, E. Y., & Gottman, J. M. (2003). Interactional patterns in marital success and failure: Gottman laboratory studies. In F. Walsh (Ed.), *Normal family processes* (3rd ed., pp. 493–513). New York: Guilford Press.

Gordon Walker, J., Johnson, S. M., Manion, I., & Clothier, P. (1996). Emotionally focused marital interventions for couples with chronically ill children. *Journal of Consulting and Clinical Psychology, 64,* 1029–1036.

Gordon Walker, J., Manion, I., & Clothier, P. (1998). A follow-up on an emotionally focused intervention for couples with chronically ill children. *Journal of Marital and Family Therapy, 28,* 391–399.

Gottman, J. M. (1994). *What predicts divorce? The relationship between marital processes and marital outcomes.* Hillsdale, NJ: Lawrence Erlbaum.

Gottman, J. M. (1999). *The marriage clinic.* New York: W. W. Norton & Company, Inc.

Gottman, J. M., & Levenson, R. W. (2002). A two-factor model for predicting when a couple will divorce: Exploratory analyses using 14-year longitudinal data. *Family Process, 41*(1), 83–96.

Gurman, A. S., & Fraenkel, P. (2002). The history of couple therapy: A millennial review. *Family Process, 41*(2), 199–260.

Haber, R. (2002). Virginia Satir: An integrated, humanistic approach. *Contemporary Family Therapy, 24*(1), 23–34.

Hoffman, E. (1994). *The drive for self: Alfred Adler and the founding of individual psychology.* Reading, MA: Addison-Wesley Publishing Company, Inc.

Johnson, S. M. (1996). *The practice of emotionally focused marital therapy: Creating connection.* New York: Brunner-Routledge.

Johnson, S. M. (1998). Emotionally focused couple therapy: Straight to the heart. In J. Donovan (Ed.), *Short-term couple therapy* (pp. 13–42). New York: Guilford.

Johnson, S. M. (2002). *Emotionally focused couple therapy with trauma survivors: Strengthening attachment bonds.* New York: Guilford Press.

Johnson, S. M. (2003). Couples therapy research: Status and directions. In G. P. Sholevar (Ed.), *Textbook of family and couples therapy* (pp. 797–814). Alexandria, VA: American Psychiatric Publishing.

Johnson, S. M., & Best, M. (2003). A systematic approach to restructuring adult attachment: The EFT model of couples therapy. In P. Erdman & T. Caffery (Eds.), *Attachment and family systems: Conceptual, empirical, and therapeutic relatedness* (pp. 165–189). New York: Brunner-Routledge.

Johnson, S. M., & Lebow, J. (2000). The "coming of age" of couple therapy: A decade review. *Journal of Marital and Family Therapy, 26*(1), 23–38.

Johnson, S. M., & Whiffen, V. E. (1999). Made to measure: Adapting emotionally focused couple therapy to partners' attachment styles. *Clinical Psychology: Science & Practice, 6*, 366–381.

Keith, D. V. (1998). Symbolic-experiential family therapy for chemical imbalance. In F. M. Dattilio (Ed.), *Case studies in couple and family therapy* (pp. 179–202). New York: Guilford Press.

Kerr, M. E., & Bowen, M. (1988). *Family evaluation: An approach based on Bowen theory.* New York: Norton.

Napier, A. Y. (1988). *The fragile bond.* New York: Harper/Collins.

Napier, A. Y. (1999). Experiential approaches to creating the intimate marriage. In J. Carlson & L. Sperry (Eds.), *The intimate couple* (pp. 298–327). Philadelphia: Brunner/Mazel.

Napier, A. Y., & Whitaker, C. (1978). *The family crucible.* New York: Harper/Collins.

Nolen-Hoeksema, S., McBride, A., & Larson, J. (1997). Rumination and psychological distress among bereaved partners. *Journal of Personality and Social Psychology, 72*(4), 855–862.

Papero, D. V. (2000). Bowen systems theory. In F. M. Dattilio & L. J. Bevilacqua (Eds.), *Comparative treatments for relationship dysfunction* (pp. 58–78). New York: Springer.

Peluso, P. R. (2006). The style of life. In S. Slavik & J. Carlson (Eds.), *Readings in the theory of individual psychology* (pp. 294–304). New York: Routledge.

Peluso, P. R., & Macintosh, H. (2007). Emotion-focused couples therapy and individual psychology: A dialogue across theories. *Journal of Individual Psychology, 63*(3), 247–269.

Peluso, P. R., Peluso, J. P., Buckner, J. P., Kern, R. M., & Curlette, W. L. (2004). An analysis of the reliability of the BASIS-A inventory using a northeastern and southeastern U.S. sample. *Journal of Individual Psychology, 60*(3), 294–307.

Peluso, P. R., Peluso, J. P., Buckner, J. P., Kern, R. M., & Curlette, W. L. (2009). Measuring lifestyle and attachment: An empirical investigation linking individual psychology and attachment theory. *Journal of Counseling and Development, 87*, 394–403.

Roberto-Forman, L. (2002). Transgenerational marital therapy. In A. S. Gurman & N. S. Jacobson (Eds.), *Clinical handbook of couple therapy* (3rd ed., pp. 118–150). New York: Guilford.

Rogers, C. (1957). The necessary and sufficient conditions of therapeutic personality change. *Journal of Consulting Psychology, 21*, 95–103.

Rogers, C., Minuchin, S., Satir, V., Bowen, M., & Gottman, J. (2007, March–April). The most influential therapists of the past quarter century. *Psychotherapy Networker, 219*–239.

Satir, V. (1964). *Conjoint family therapy.* Palo Alto, CA: Science and Behavior Books.

Schwartz, R. C., & Johnson, S. M. (2000). Does couple and family therapy have emotional intelligence? *Family Process, 39*, 29–33.

Sperry, L., Carlson, J., & Peluso, P. R. (2006). *Couples therapy: Integrating theory and technique* (2nd ed.). Denver, CO: Love Publishers.

Whitaker, C. A. (2000). Hypnosis and family depth therapy. *Family Journal: Counseling and Therapy for Couples and Families, 8*(1), 7–13.

Whitaker, C. A., & Keith, D. V. (1981). Symbolic-experiential family therapy. In A. Gurman & D. P. Kniskern (Eds.), *Handbook of family therapy* (pp. 187–224). New York: Brunner/Mazel.

7

Healing Trauma Through Humanistic Connection

ELIZABETH VENART AND JANE WEBBER

There is a growing awareness in the world about the prevalence of trauma. The news is inundated with the tragedies of people who suffer at the hands of one another and from the unpredictable natural world. The recent earthquakes in Haiti and Chile left thousands dead and more homeless, injured, and psychologically wounded. In 2009, suicide among the military rose to its highest rate; two thirds of army suicides were committed by deployed soldiers, and those soldiers suffering with posttraumatic stress disorder (PTSD) were six times more likely to commit suicide (Thompson, 2009). Traumatic events are pervasive, including school violence, terrorist bombings, hurricanes, fires, and the interpersonal tragedies of child abuse and rape. In response, the literature is filled with new theories and treatment protocols for trauma, PTSD, and disaster mental health (Baranowsky, Gentry, & Schultz, 2010; Briere & Scott, 2006; Brymer et al., 2006; Chu, 1998; Courtois & Ford, 2009; Foa, Keane, & Friedman, 2000; Levine, 1997; Rothschild, 2000; Shapiro, 2001; Solomon & Siegel, 2003). This chapter provides an overview of humanistic perspectives of trauma and examples of approaches that illustrate how humanism frames all effective trauma counseling.

"From a humanistic perspective, a traumatic event is a disruption so serious that it threatens our existence, shaking the foundation of who we are and who we once were" (Serlin & Cannon, 2004, p. 314). Trauma is a subjective experience following an event in which individuals' internal capacities are overwhelmed (Briere & Scott, 2006). Humanistic trauma and disaster mental health counselors see traumatized responses as understandable and adaptive reactions to extreme stress—normal responses to abnormal situations. Given the context of trauma and its power to shatter survivors' assumptions of safety and trust, reactions of hypervigilance and retreat into isolation make sense. Similarly, the fluctuation between distressing intrusive thoughts and the desire to avoid them is seen as a normal process to "reintegrate self with experience" (Joseph, 2004, p. 112).

Traumatic experiences change a survivor's frame of reference, often resulting in a view of the world as unsafe and others as untrustworthy (Herman, 1997; Pearlman & Saakvitne, 1995). Trauma also may erode survivors' sense of competency and control, leaving them feeling powerless, disconnected from others, and mistrusting of self. Those who have experienced trauma often develop self-protective, defensive behaviors to keep distance between themselves and others (Pearlman & Saakvitne, 1995). When therapists conceptualize trauma as a disorder, those who experience trauma may feel pathologized, marginalized, or blamed.

Humanistic theory provides the foundation for trauma counseling as a process of discovering resources and facilitating natural growth tendencies. Humanistic counselors view the symptoms of trauma as adaptations that make sense within the context of the experience of trauma and individuals' attempts to recover from the resulting distress (Briere & Scott, 2006; Pearlman & Saakvitne, 1995). This humanistic framing of the trauma experience reflects client-centered therapy: "The clue to understanding their behavior is that they are striving, in the only ways that they perceive as available to them, to move toward growth, toward becoming" (Rogers, 1980, p. 119).

Rogers' (1951) core conditions are critical in healing trauma. Although there is little reference in the literature on PTSD to humanistic and person-centered therapy (Joseph, 2004), many trauma theorists concur that empathic attunement is central in healing trauma (Briere & Scott, 2006; Chu, 1998; Fosha, 2000; Gil, 2006; Paivio & Pascual-Leone, 2010; Siegel, 2003). Humanists' ability to believe in the inner resources of the traumatized person and to convey hope through these conditions is critical to the effectiveness of trauma counseling. Neuroscience research confirms the centrality of empathy in promoting growth and traumatic resolution (Siegel, 2003). Changes that occur are seen "more as self-healing, self-righting and actualization than as 'repair'" (Bohart, 2007, p. 59). Without establishing a feeling of safety at the beginning of trauma counseling and paying attention to safety issues throughout the process, clients are likely to withhold aspects of their trauma story and reactions (out of fear of judgment or being misunderstood), to experience the therapy process itself as retraumatizing, and to leave therapy prematurely (Fosha, Paivio, Gleiser, & Ford, 2009; Webber, Mascari, & Runte, 2010). Safety is created as the therapist demonstrates patience, caring, and the willingness to engage interpersonally (Chu, 1998).

Trusting every trauma survivor's innate potential, humanistic counselors embody hope by mirroring back to clients their implicit strengths. Therapists' empathic attunement, mindfulness, and optimism require continual monitoring by the therapist to nurture personal wellness and resiliency. Humanistic theory can inform all trauma counselors, regardless of orientation. Integrating humanism with the strengths of diverse cognitive, affective, mindfulness, body-focused, spiritual, and neurobiological approaches can effectively meet the unique needs of individuals in trauma therapy.

HUMANISTIC TRAUMA COUNSELING

Humanism respects clients as experts of their own lives and focuses on inner sub-jective experiences and personal meaning systems (see Chapter 1 in this volume) that provide the foundations for trauma survivors to begin to tell their story and move toward healing. Research confirms Rogers' (1951) early assertion that it is the nature of the therapeutic relationship that promotes change (Bratton & Ray, 2002; Kirschenbaum, 2004; Norcross, 2002; Wampold, 2001). In fact, a strong working alliance is more powerful and efficacious than any specific interven-tion or theory (Gurman & Messer, 2003; Wampold, 2001). While most trauma theories emphasize the centrality of safety in treatment, the authors found mini-mal mention of the contributions of humanistic theory and its focus on the core conditions necessary to create safety. This chapter strives to reawaken an under-standing of the humanistic principles inherent in effective trauma counseling and to demonstrate how humanism supports counselors in creating sustained, empathic alliances with clients who have been traumatized.

A Person-Centered Framework for Trauma

Rogers' (1961) theory of incongruence provides a solid framework for under-standing trauma treatment. Joseph (2004) argued that Rogers' experience work-ing with war veterans influenced his conceptualization of the "disorganization of the self-structure" (p. 105) as the root of psychopathology. Traumatic experience can deliver a profound blow to individuals' sense of meaning and psychological safety, resulting in distortion or fragmentation of previous understandings of self and the world in which they live (Herman, 1997; Pearlman & Saakvitne, 1995). In trauma resolution, individuals construct more adaptive meanings to aid them in trusting self and others again and venturing into the world with a more secure, newly integrated framework (Herman, 1997).

Joseph (2004) demonstrated the applicability of person-centered counseling to the treatment of trauma, highlighting how conditions of worth or internalized messages from others can impede individuals' actualizing tendency and lead to distortions and denial. Traumatic events challenge innate beliefs (e.g., trusting that life is fair and under our control), leading to the intense distress associ-ated with trauma. When faced with the disorganizing reality of a breakdown in self-structure, individuals often deny aspects of their experience that contradict previous assumptions—a pattern reflective of the reexperiencing and avoidance that occurs with PTSD (Joseph, 2004). Whether an event leads to breakdown depends on one's *perception* of "incongruence between self and experience" (Joseph, 2004, p. 107). Thus, some people will experience traumatic events as debilitating, whereas others will heal naturally within a relatively short period of time (Bowman, 1997; Briere & Scott, 2006).

Resilient survivors use natural connections in the community to manage the emotional impact of trauma, cope with their losses, and create personal meaning about their traumatic experience so they can move forward with their lives (Echterling, Presbury, & McKee, 2005; Echterling & Stewart, 2010; Webber & Mascari, 2010). Humanistic trauma counselors believe that individuals can move *beyond* previous levels of functioning toward posttraumatic growth (Tedeschi & Calhoun, 1995). In fact, most survivors experience positive psychological changes after trauma. These changes include recognition of one's strength, expanded view of possibilities, increased intimacy and compassion for others, greater appreciation for life, greater sense of purpose and meaning, and a deeper sense of spirituality (Calhoun & Tedeschi, 2006). Person-centered counseling is based on a core hypothesis about human growth and personality change that presupposes that "…the client has within himself the capacity, latent if not evident, to understand those aspects of his life and of himself which are causing him pain, and the capacity and the tendency to reorganize himself and his relationships to life in the direction of self-actualization" (Kirschenbaum, 2004, p. 118).

Joseph (2004) concluded that explaining and anticipating growth following trauma may be person-centered counseling's most important contribution. While various trauma therapies may resolve symptoms, approaches designed to support the congruent integration of "self and experience" will also result in posttraumatic growth (PTG) (Joseph, 2004, p. 110).

Research and the Process of Change in the Humanistic Treatment of Trauma

Several authors examined the effects of person-centered counseling with traumatized individuals. Edwards and Lambie (2009) highlighted the difficulties women with a history of child sexual abuse have with trust, safety, feelings of control, and relationships with others. They stressed the compatibility of a person-centered counseling approach with its emphasis on clients as active leaders in their own healing process. This approach reduces the anxiety and resistance trauma survivors may experience with directive therapies in which they perceive little control over the process. The core conditions of person-centered counseling "provide a way to tap into, strengthen, or restart a client's naturally occurring positive growth potential" (p. 25).

Payne, Liebling-Kalifani, and Joseph (2007) examined the effectiveness of person-centered group therapy with survivors of interpersonal trauma. They found that members who perceived the core conditions to be present experienced benefits from the group, including a decrease in PTSD symptoms and negativity as well as an increase in positive affect and outlook. Goodman, Morgan, Juriga, and Brown (2004) explored the benefits of person-centered therapy with children whose fathers worked for the New York City Fire and Police Departments and died in the terrorist attacks on the World Trade Center. Engaging families through a nondirective, empathic counseling approach allowed clients to guide the process and "let the story unfold" (p. 210) in their own time. Sharing insights gained from work with one specific family, Goodman et al. explained:

> To be in the presence of another who will not turn away under such circumstances inescapably has the effect of strengthening one's sense of trust. It is the exposure to the relationship, as much as belief in one's power to cope, that leads to the subsiding of symptoms and to engagement in new relationships. (p. 209)

Humanistic interventions in acute trauma focus on facilitating the natural resiliency of individuals by connecting them with relational support and resources in their families and communities (Briere & Scott, 2006). Defensiveness may be the largest barrier in the actualizing process because it inhibits individuals' ability to perceive and integrate more adaptive information (Bohart, 2007). The humanistic approach facilitates clients becoming less afraid of their emotions as they begin to trust themselves more deeply (Rogers, 1961). Through empathic witnessing, counselors validate and normalize trauma survivors' experiences and provide a safe haven in which all aspects of the trauma can be explored without judgment.

Humanistic trauma counseling facilitates client empowerment by allowing clients to set the pace for therapy, to identify meaningful goals, and to give feedback to counselors about their collaboration (accuracy of reflective statements, attunement or distraction, client expectations vs. progress). While the therapist remains responsible for adherence to the frame of the therapeutic model, the frame is coconstructed to respect the needs of both client and counselor (Courtois, Ford, & Cloitre, 2009). Before any memory processing work begins, trust, mutual respect, and collaboration within the therapeutic relationship are essential. Clients must feel comfortable expressing what they experience in the session so counseling is productive rather than retraumatizing (Briere & Scott, 2006). For clients with interpersonal trauma who may fear both intimacy and judgment, the experience of receiving support creates safety and is healing in itself.

Because trauma impacts affect regulation, many theories focus on direct skill building in the early stages of healing (Kinsler, Courtois, & Frankel, 2009). Steele and van der Hart (2009) recommend that therapists model skills to provide relational regulation, to maintain high levels of reflective awareness, and to monitor their own self-regulation continuously throughout intense emotional interactions. Clients can learn to break the avoidance pattern in trauma by building self-soothing skills that will equip them to tolerate reexperiencing trauma (Kinsler et al., 2009). Briere and Scott (2006) advise that effective therapy requires staying within the *therapeutic window*, so that work is neither too emotionally charged (which would trigger defenses and elicit dissociation, flight, or fight) nor so removed from affect as to be ineffective. Only when clients have sufficient distance from "sensory imprints and trauma-related emotions" can they productively "observe and analyze" their experiences (van der Kolk, 2003, p. 187). Van der Kolk (2009) highlighted the importance of techniques beyond "figuring out" and concluded that "talking about traumatic events does not necessarily allow mind and brain to integrate the dissociated images and sensations into a coherent whole" (p. 463). Understanding that words alone are often inadequate to capture the depth of pain experienced in trauma, counselors may encourage expression through nonverbal modalities including play, movement, sandplay, somatic exercises, and the creative arts.

Humanistic Approaches to Trauma Treatment

Person-centered counseling's emphasis on congruence, unconditional positive regard, and empathy as cornerstones for therapeutic change provides the foundation for trauma counseling. We identified elements that are present across many current trauma approaches, concluding that a humanistic model for trauma healing includes the following key components: (1) the therapist's mindful presence and empathic attunement; (2) instillation of hope through a focus on the client's self-actualizing capacities; (3) genuineness of the therapist; (4) safety within the therapeutic relationship; (5) remembrance, telling, and resolution of the trauma story; (6) mindful experiencing and acceptance of the client's whole self (e.g., affective, somatic, and cognitive dimensions of awareness); (7) freedom to create new, more adaptive meanings and connections; and (8) movement toward posttraumatic growth (Briere & Scott, 2006; Calhoun & Tedeschi, 2006; Chu, 1998; Echterling et al., 2005; Fosha, 2000; Gil, 2006; Herman, 1997; Joseph, 2004; Paivio & Pascual-Leone, 2010; Siegel, 2003). To explore these key components in practice, we describe four trauma models with strong humanistic foundations: (1) psychological first aid (Brymer et al., 2006); (2) emotion-focused trauma therapy (EFTT; Paivio & Pascual-Leone, 2010); (3) accelerated experiential-dynamic psychotherapy (AEDP; Fosha, 2000); and (4) an integrative treatment model for sexually abused children (Gil, 2006). While these models may not self-identify as humanistic, their approaches to healing trauma clearly reflect humanistic principles.

Psychological First Aid

In the immediate aftermath of a mass disaster or tragedy, survivors need safety, comfort, and relational support. Although the majority of people exposed to traumatic events will return to their normal routine quickly and without intervention (Echterling et al., 2005), the initial hours or days can be extremely distressing and terrifying. In the midst of overwhelming chaos surrounding survivors, disaster mental health (DMH) counselors use a humanistic approach that affirms and validates the experience of each individual. Survivors' responses are not viewed as pathological; rather, the immediate distress after disaster is a normal response to abnormal events that require genuine human connection. This approach honors survivors' experiences and taps their capacity and resources to adapt, thereby restoring emotional control and promoting recovery.

The manual *Psychological First Aid: Field Operations Guide* (Brymer et al., 2006) provides an empirically supported, person-centered model for trauma response grounded in humanistic assumptions and practices.

Among the psychological first aid objectives that incorporate humanistic principles are (Brymer et al., 2006, p. 2):

- Establish a human connection in a nonintrusive, compassionate manner.
- Enhance immediate and ongoing safety, and provide physical and emotional comfort.
- Calm and orient emotionally overwhelmed or distraught survivors.
- Support active coping, acknowledge coping efforts and strengths, and empower survivors; encourage adults, children, and families to take an active role in their recovery.

Although DMH interactions with survivors are often brief, empathy and respect remain central to every connection. Counselors provide a nonintrusive, empathic presence, promoting the natural ability of survivors to become actively involved in their own healing.

Emotion-Focused Trauma Therapy

An evidence-based approach for counseling adults with complex trauma, this model is grounded in humanistic principles that promote the natural human ability for growth and interpersonal relatedness in spite of unspeakable physical, sexual, and emotional trauma and neglect in childhood. This approach is an application of emotion-focused therapy (Greenberg, 2002) designed specifically to address the deep interpersonal wounding of complex traumatic stress disorders. Complex psychological trauma is defined as "involving traumatic stressors that (1) are repetitive or prolonged; (2) involve direct harm or neglect and abandonment by caregivers or ostensibly responsible adults; (3) occur at developmentally vulnerable times in the victim's life, such as early childhood; and (4) have great potential to compromise severely a child's development" (Courtois & Ford, 2009, p. 1). The foundation of EFTT builds on the innate capacity of survivors to express distressing feelings about their trauma and to actively create meaning from their experiences within a secure therapeutic relationship. The slow, attuned process of empathic exploration and empathic response is central to the model (Paivio & Pascual-Leone, 2010). While the treatment procedures guide counselors and clients through multiple levels of interventions, therapy is driven by *moment-by-moment processes* (Paivio & Pascual-Leone, 2010) with counselors observing clients' somatic and emotional experiences and using these observations to guide responses. The relationship between therapist and client is deeply humanistic, as therapists provide a secure attachment bond, emotion coaching, and empathic validation of clients' trauma stories.

Phase one in EFTT cultivates this alliance through attuned exploratory questions, careful tracking, and empathic responses that encourage deepening awareness. This process assures a safe collaborative relationship, reflecting Rogers' (1951) core conditions. Paivio and Nieuwenhuis (2001) view the therapeutic relationship as "directly curative in disconfirming negative relational experiences" (p. 117). Phase two focuses on developing awareness of clients' internal experiences by exploring previously avoided, painful emotions of fear and anxiety. Expressing primary emotions and unmet needs through empathic exploration and imaginal confrontation is an intense experience for both client and therapist, facilitating change in clients' perceptions of self and others. Phase three achieves trauma resolution through the healthy expression of adaptive anger, sadness, and grief. The EFTT therapist directly intervenes in the moment-to-moment experience of the session to help clients become empowered to express new and adaptive emotions to promote self-development.

> Finally letting go and allowing the self to fully feel the pain of traumatic experiences typically is followed by a sense of relief, an increased sense of agency or control, and an implicit challenging of beliefs that perpetuated avoidance (e.g., "I *can* handle it. It won't destroy me"). (Fosha et al., 2009, p. 308)

Survivors of complex trauma may not have experienced healthy attachments at developmentally sensitive times; thus, strengthening the working alliance through emotion coaching is essential. Although new adult figures may offer intimacy and trust, trauma survivors meet them with feelings of anxiety, suspicion, shame, and fear of betrayal. Therapists encounter startling emotional shifts when the victims of "violations of human connection" (Herman, 1997, p. 54) are overwhelmed with secondary emotions, fearing more abuse and even death if they become genuinely angry with the perpetrator. Until survivors feel the differences in interpersonal relatedness between the "other" (perpetrator) and the unwavering validation by the EFTT therapist, they will struggle with emotional dysregulation. Paivio and Pascual-Leone (2010) emphasized that "...therapist empathic attunement and responding strengthens the bond for both parties.... As clients feel understood and cared for, therapists feel closer to their clients as well, which in turn facilitates deeper understanding and connection" (p. 111). This meaning is processed through deeper levels of emotions until clients are comfortable with expressing primary emotions toward the perpetrator of the trauma (Fosha et al., 2009; Paivio & Pascual-Leone, 2010).

Complex trauma is characterized by emotional, intrapersonal, and interpersonal dysregulation; clients' disrupted affective processes work against trust, change, and the expression of congruent affective experience (Paivio & Pascual-Leone, 2010). The therapist directly affirms clients' feelings of vulnerability and fear, validating the client's norm that no one including the therapist is to be trusted:

> I am interested in you as a whole person. You are in the driver's seat.... My job is to ensure your safety and, at the same time, to support and promote your growth. Of course that will mean helping you get in touch with painful stuff so you can work it through, here, in this safe environment, and at a pace you can handle. (Paivio & Pascual-Leone, 2010, p. 108)

Through empathic responding and deepening the experience, the EFTT therapist helps clients attend to bodily felt experiences and find the right emotional words to restore the core self. These powerful changes in both emotional and relational regulation lead to self-awareness, positive growth, and healthy attachments. This process is humanistic, nonpathological, compassionate, and self-validating.

Accelerated Experiential-Dynamic Psychotherapy

The philosophical foundation of AEDP is rooted in a "metatherapeutic paradigm" (Fosha et al., 2009, p. 288) that strongly resonates with the core principles of person-centered counseling, including an emphasis on relational, experiential, and affective domains. AEDP is grounded in the assumption that individuals possess biological and innate healing resources, and secure attachments activate this potential, promoting resolution to trauma and growth (Fosha et al., 2009). AEDP fosters a secure therapeutic relationship through humanistic conditions of presence, "the therapist's active and explicit empathic, caring, emotionally engaged, affirming stance" (Fosha et al., 2009, p. 289), and mindful attention to the moment-to-moment experiencing of self and client within the relationship. The transformative process in AEDP parallels the healing journey described in person-centered counseling: "This acceptance of each fluctuating aspect of this other person makes it for him a relationship of warmth and safety" (Rogers, 1961, p. 34). When counselors can stay unconditionally present with intense emotions and defenses as well as efforts to avoid the intimacy of the relationship, clients internalize this acceptance and begin to trust that it is okay to experience whatever feelings and somatic sensations may emerge (Fosha, 2003). The therapeutic bond provides the safety necessary for the deep emotions of trauma to be "experientially accessed, processed, and worked through, so that they can eventually be integrated within the individual's autobiographical narrative" (Fosha, 2003, p. 232).

Healing occurs as a result of close attention to the process of attunement, disruption, and repair throughout the therapeutic process. While ruptures in attunement will invariably occur in therapy (as counselors are human and can become tired, distracted, or emotionally overloaded), Siegel (2003) stressed the importance of "repair" (p. 39) in facilitating a secure therapeutic attachment and identified key elements of repair as *contingent communication, reflective dialogue,* and *emotional connection* (pp. 38–39). In AEDP, counselors facilitate repair through transparency, communication of unconditional positive regard, and a return to empathic attunement (Fosha et al., 2009). Therapists help regulate affect through nonverbal empathic attunement (eye contact, tone and rhythm of speech, use of touch) and facilitate the exploration of emotions that arise within the therapeutic relationship (Fosha et al., 2009). The interpersonal learning that occurs in the therapeutic relationship is an essential part of the process and the dialogue. Therapists make this learning explicit with clients, emphasizing how the therapeutic relationship creates a foundation for the development of positive emotions and healthy attachments outside of therapy as well (Fosha et al., 2009).

Fully expressing previously inhibited emotions is stressed because these emotions, while painful and overwhelming, are "healthy resources that aid in self-development and adaptive interpersonal functioning" (Fosha et al., 2009, p. 309). Using experiential techniques reflective of Gestalt therapy, AEDP facilitates trauma resolution by bringing the emotional and bodily pain of the past into the present moment (Fosha, 2000; Fosha et al., 2009). Whereas clients originally suffered trauma in isolation, they now join this experience with the reparative witnessing, empathy, and coregulation of the therapeutic alliance (Fosha, 2003; Fosha et al., 2009). The process of healing in AEDP involves clients moving from a state of distress and defensive avoidance to a state of *core affect* "where adaptive emotions are accessed, deepened, and processed through to completion" to a *core state* of calm, confidence, wisdom, and clarity (Fosha et al., 2009, p. 290). *Core state* strongly parallels Rogers' (1961) description of the "fully functioning person" (p. 191) who has openness to experience, creativity, the ability to be spontaneously present in the current moment, and increased trust in and empathy for self. Through the secure therapeutic relationship and the empathic reflection process, clients express emotions, learn to regulate affect, gain somatic awareness, and experience transformations in affect and meaning (Fosha, 2003). The primary goal in AEDP is powerfully humanistic: the creation of a safe therapeutic environment in which the vast inner resources of clients can manifest.

Gil's Integrative Approach

Gil's (2006) trauma therapy for sexually abused children is an integrative model grounded in the core elements of humanism that promote a "child-friendly therapeutic environment" and "construct a genuine, respectful, trust-filled earnest relationship with each child client and his or her family" (pp. 60–61). Children are affirmed as whole persons, who know themselves best and have the innate ability to grow, express their feelings, solve problems, and create meaning of their experiences (Axline, 1974; Gil, 2006).

Building a trusting relationship can be a slow process with a child or adolescent "who has learned that adults can be dangerous, and that emotional attachment is a recipe for potential abandonment" (Gil, 2006, viii). A totally safe and accepting relationship is necessary in working with children who have experienced sexual abuse. Because abused children may be hesitant to trust a new adult, Gil facilitates healing through the child's natural developmental process of play. As children play freely in a safe space, they experience the unconditional acceptance and attention of the therapist and begin to trust their new feelings. Kalff (2003) stressed the importance of this unique empowering process:

> This free space occurs in the therapeutic setting when the therapist is fully able to accept the child fully, so that the therapist, as a person, is as much a part of everything going on in the room as is the child himself. When a child feels he is not alone, not only in his distress but also in his happiness, he then feels free and protected in all his expressions. (p. 7)

As a gentle and collaborative witness, the therapist is attuned to every moment of children's verbal and nonverbal play and mirrors their experience and feelings. "We actually become part of the world building process.... We enter the experience" (DeDomenico, 2002, p. 47). The therapist unconditionally accepts children's ways of communicating and mastering traumatic events and does not direct or pressure them. Thus, children's subjective experiences are affirmed and honored as real and genuine (Bratton, Ceballos, & Ferebee, 2009; Bratton & Ray, 2009; Gil, 2006).

Complex trauma in childhood leads to neurological changes in children's brains where fragments of traumatic memories are separated from the words that give them meaning (Gil, 2006; Terr, 1990; van der Kolk, 2009). For children, these terrifying visual images, sounds, or touch act like instant replay or "a VCR stuck on pause" (Baggerly, 2010, p. 131). Fundamental to trauma processing with children is the integration of multisensory art, play, and sandtray tools to encourage their natural expression. Play helps children to externalize their feelings and experiences at their own pace, so they can access and integrate fragments of the trauma experience (Gil, 2006; Webber, Mascari, & Runte, 2010). Protected from emotional and physical harm, traumatized children transition from a world of chaos and danger to one of predictability and safety, mastery and control. "When a child's story unfolds in the course of therapeutic play and is responded to with empathy, genuine warmth, and acceptance by the therapist, the child begins to gain empathy and acceptance of self and subsequently for others" (Green, Crenshaw, & Kolos, 2010, p. 100). Children are able to integrate their trauma story, feel whole, and gain a new sense of control in the presence of a caring adult who mirrors their experience.

HUMANISTIC TRAUMA COUNSELING: CASE ILLUSTRATIONS

When counselors stay unconditionally and authentically present, tremendous potential for posttraumatic growth is evident. We present four cases with key components of humanistic approaches to trauma counseling listed earlier in this chapter. The case of Justin was chronicled briefly in VISTAS in 2008 (Webber & Mascari, 2008). The cases integrate elements of various trauma models and are cited here to illustrate how broad humanistic principles and approaches are integrated into effective trauma counseling.

Valerie

Valerie, a 31-year-old client, experienced repeated, pervasive emotional abuse and invalidation during childhood. Her parents' strict adherence to conservative religious teachings and pattern of overprotective and invasive behaviors were coupled with a failure to listen empathically or try to understand their daughter's needs, goals, or perspective. In her present life, Valerie found it difficult to trust herself or others. She was initially reluctant to believe in her therapist's authenticity and unconditional support. Early in their work together, she questioned her therapist's reflections of empathy, doubting the possibility she could be understood well. During this time, she also responded defensively and was quick to assume negative judgment from the counselor and to judge herself. Through the therapist's patient attunement, trust in Valerie's self-actualizing capacities, and willingness to have her set the pace and direction for their counseling work, Valerie slowly grew to trust the therapeutic relationship, herself, and her experiencing more fully.

Over the years, Valerie had self-protectively created distance in her relationship with both parents, learning to keep her projects and passions to herself. In one session, shortly after an experience where her mother attempted to take over a project the client was confidently pursuing, Valerie shared a beautiful metaphor describing her relationship with her mother, a metaphor that also aptly captured the process of her growth in counseling:

> Butterflies need their own challenges if they are to grow strong enough to emerge from the cocoon. People think they are helping but really they inhibit the butterfly's growth when they try to intervene and do the work of emerging for the butterfly. It is in the process of fighting so hard to emerge from the cocoon that the butterfly gains the strength to fly and succeed on its own. I know the hardest thing

for her to do is to not *do* anything. But that is what *I* need. And it is through this struggle that I have grown.

Valerie's ability to share this insight with her therapist reflected evidence of profound growth in her ability to trust herself and to trust her therapist to listen and respect her wisdom. In the aftermath of trauma, humanistic counselors accompany people on a journey of healing that involves such a metamorphosis. Rogers (1961) identified each person's innate drive toward growth as "the tendency upon which all psychotherapy depends" (p. 35).

Carlos

Carlos, a successful 37-year-old college counselor, was the first in his family to graduate from high school. He recently completed both his bachelor's and master's degrees while working full time and moved from his family home in New Orleans to New York City for a better position and a fresh start. While he felt settled with his wife and two young children, he missed his parents, grandmother, and extended family from whom he had received nurturance and support.

When the levees broke after Hurricane Katrina, Carlos could not reach his parents in the 9th Ward. He watched the devastation of New Orleans on TV and left New York in a hurry to find them in New Orleans. Blocked at several checkpoints, he frantically searched shelters for his family. Carlos had always been there to help them and felt guilty for having moved away. Eventually he was able to enter his old neighborhood, which he found destroyed and underwater. He helped survivors—neighbors and strangers—wherever he could, often risking his own safety. He had a strong need to help his community and felt connected to the spirit of resiliency growing there in spite of the losses experienced by so many. Carlos finally located his parents and his grandmother, who had attempted to evacuate but never left the city. His ailing grandmother died a few days after their reunion. He felt guilty and heartbroken leaving his family again to return to work.

Several months later back in New York, Carlos began having flashbacks and often woke up terrified and shaking. Despite the pleas of his wife, he would not talk about his experiences. At work, he had difficulty focusing on his clients, with his thoughts continually returning to his parents. His supervisor convinced him to work with a trauma therapist, and, although he felt very comfortable with the therapist, he resisted initially. This was a huge role shift for him to be the client, and he struggled to allow himself to trust the counselor fully with the honest expression of his feelings. Facing these fears and processing them aloud helped Carlos and his counselor engage more deeply. Although he could not tell his father that he cried "like a baby," Carlos allowed himself to cry freely with his therapist. He began to explore his contradictory feelings about his hard life growing up that he had "stuffed inside myself and never let anyone know about." Letting go and expressing his authentic feelings marked a dramatic turning point for Carlos. Through empathic connection and the emotionally focused work of humanistic trauma counseling, he learned to recognize and express his feelings, to be more open to present experiences, and to strengthen his connections with both his family and his clients.

Justin

Justin returned to high school a few weeks after the funeral of his two closest friends who were killed in a car accident in which Justin had been seriously injured. When Justin was extricated from the wreck, he was still conscious, wedged between the front and back seats next to his best friend's severed body parts. He did not resemble the outgoing 17-year-old student athlete his teachers and friends knew before the tragedy. Justin wished that he had died with his friends, saying, "If only I insisted on driving, they wouldn't be gone."

Justin resented the first therapist he saw, and their sessions became a power struggle. He refused to continue, explaining that "therapy was being done to me." Justin engaged in risk-taking behaviors endangering his life and terrifying his friends and family. He often cut class and wandered in the woods behind the school. One day his school counselor found Justin sitting on the edge of the building's roof.

Calling himself a "walking ghost," Justin retreated to two safe places when he felt emotionally out of control: art class and his school counselor's office. Both the art teacher and counselor were caring, patient adults who gave Justin space without pressuring him to get over the trauma as his friends had advised. He found his voice through drawing and sandplay. These multisensory experiences promoted a sense of safety, mastery, and control (Gil, 2001, 2006; Webber & Mascari, 2008).

Justin first selected ghost figures, each with the name of a living or deceased friend. Later, he created dangerous battles, destroying and burying the soldiers in the sand. Justin began recreating scenes of the accident, retelling his story, and revising the ending, depicting himself at times as a spectator, victim, hero, and friend. Although Justin was silent through most of the process, his counselor was an attentive observer and nonintrusive partner. They photographed each tray, and he sketched the scenes in great detail. Paging through his booklet of illustrations and photographs calmed him without words.

Justin began dividing the tray into two worlds: before the accident with his two deceased friends at soccer games and parties; and after the accident with his family, current friends, and new life. Between the two worlds, he created a gorge filled with water separating them. Later, Justin's trays depicted only his current life, with his deceased friends watching from a corner of the tray. As the sandtray process helped to access fragments of his experience, he was able to integrate them with the words of his story. Justin's intrusive symptoms lessened, providing emotional and physical relief (Gil, 2006; Webber & Mascari, 2008). As therapy progressed, his sandtray scenes became more emotionally integrated, reflecting his personal growth, acceptance of the permanence of the deaths, and positive memories of his friends (Herman, 1997). By respecting Justin's wisdom about what he needed to do, this counselor created a collaborative relationship in which Justin could promote his own healing.

John

John was a 61-year-old retired mathematics professor who had been hospitalized twice for major depression following experiences of heightened suicidal ideation and hopelessness. When he first met his counselor, he expressed the belief that he was "permanently damaged" and had little to no hope of his life improving. He described witnessing terrifying incidents of violence inflicted by his alcoholic father toward his mother and younger brother throughout his childhood and how he had attempted to prevent his father's attacks of rage by being hypervigilant, quiet, and as "perfect" as possible. At the final counseling session, 6 months after he began, he reflected on his progress: the absence of the anxiety that had permeated his life previously, his desire to re-engage life, and his optimistic view that he was looking forward to the adventure of writing the next chapters in the book of his life. When asked by his counselor what he found most helpful about their work together, he sat silently for a moment and then shared, "I can't quote you," reflecting on his insight that what helped did not come from words spoken by the counselor so much as her unconditional presence. The simple act of asking questions and encouraging him to find his own answers was transformative. He said, "You raise ideas through the questions you ask, not by telling." When asked how he might describe her participation in their work together, he offered this: "Nurturing. Terribly sincere. There is no looking at your watch. You are real, a real person." He described the sense of safety he felt in the office and in the relationship as a "sanctuary."

> I was maybe afraid the first week or two or maybe three until I knew who you were. But there was this sense of understanding and identification like you had been there before. And all of this is unspoken and felt and understood.

It was the counselor's ability to trust his inner knowing and stay empathically present that had made the difference in his healing process.

IMPLICATIONS FOR PRACTICE: CHALLENGES IN SUSTAINING HUMANISTIC CONNECTION

> The more I am open to the realities in me and in the other person, the less do I find myself wishing to rush in to "fix things." (Rogers, 1961, p. 21)

Being fully present within the humanistic relationship is perhaps never more challenging than when empathically connecting with people in intense pain from their trauma. "To study psychological trauma is to come face to face both with human vulnerability in the natural world and with the capacity for evil in human nature. To study psychological trauma means bearing witness to horrible events" (Herman, 1997, p. 7). The same psychological defenses that contribute to denial and dissociation in the victim may also manifest in the counselor. When counselors believe they must have all the answers, the stress and pressure they feel may intensify with the vulnerability, anger, and despair of the wounded person before them. Humanistic counseling challenges us as counselors to shift from therapy as a *set of skills* we learn through training to a *way of being* we continually practice. Rogers (1961) acknowledged how difficult it can be to establish and maintain the core conditions: "I am by no means always able to achieve this kind of relationship with another, and sometimes, even when I feel I have achieved it in myself, he may be too frightened to perceive what is being offered to him" (pp. 34–35).

Counselor Wellness

Our greatest tool is our person; it is essential that we nurture our own personhood with the same care and compassion that we nurture others. Counselors have a responsibility to continually monitor and assess their wellness, using instruments such as the Professional Quality of Life Scale (Stamm, 2009) and the Five-Factor Wellness Inventory (Myers & Sweeney, 1999). Key components of counselor wellness include (1) attending to physical health and well-being, (2) tuning into and expressing emotions, (3) challenging cognitive distortions, (4) identifying the rewards of the work, and (5) nurturing a range of meaningful interpersonal relationships (Venart, Vassos, & Pitcher-Heft, 2007). Spirituality is another key aspect of counselor wellness, as trauma counselors repeatedly have their own sense of meaning and hope challenged (Pearlman & Caringi, 2009). Cultivating mindfulness can enhance concentration, the ability to be present and accepting, and the capacity for compassion toward self and clients (Cashwell, Bentley, & Bigbee, 2007). Having a rich mindfulness practice not only mirrors a grounded, relaxed way of being and bringing forth our best inner resources but also facilitates healing through an internal process of attunement, disruption, and repair with self. Engaging in trauma work from a place of counselor "heartfulness" (keeping our hearts open to the full range of emotional experiencing) and "soulfulness" (awareness of the meaning and purpose of life and a sense of the interconnectedness of all that is) provides even deeper sustenance for counselors (Cashwell et al., p. 67).

Hazards of Practice

Trauma counselors face many challenges to maintaining counselor wellness. These include client factors such as trauma history and interpersonal behaviors, as well as aspects of the counselor's personality, work situation, history of trauma, and current life context (Cummins, Massey, & Jones, 2007; Skovholt,

2001). Counselors with unresolved trauma may avoid discussing clients' trauma history or fail to empathically attune to their emotional sharing (Briere & Scott, 2006). Research found that helpers who avoid traumatic material and those with insecure attachment styles experience greater negative effects from the work (Pearlman & Caringi, 2009). When therapists actively connect to clients' trauma and begin to lose their grounding in self, they need to practice strategies to disengage *skillfully*, rather than reactively, or the tendency will be to use minimization, dissociation, and escape tactics to defensively cope with emotional intensity.

Norman (2004) uses metaphors and somatic terms that illustrate how counselors feel during the empathic experience of connecting with clients:

> The deep struggles within the client register as pings on our radar screen, torpedoes incoming! The range of psychotherapy hits is endless, infinite, and painfully personal to each therapist…. It is a feeling that sits in our stomachs, a heaviness that threatens and awakens us in the night and distracts us in the day. (p. 70)

Counselors need to be aware of the risks associated with trauma work, including vicarious trauma, compassion fatigue, and burnout. It is crucial that they recognize that these are normal reactions to empathic presence with trauma (Baranowsky, Gentry, & Schultz, 2010; Gentry, 2010; Pearlman & Saakvitne, 1995). Vicarious trauma is a process of negative changes in self, experience, and meaning for those whose work involves empathic connection with traumatized people (Pearlman & Saakvitne, 1995). Through their desire and responsibility to help those in pain, counselors themselves may experience increased fear and powerlessness, diminished concentration and self-efficacy, and disruptions in their ability to trust self and others. Vicarious trauma impacts counselors in many of the same ways trauma impacts survivors, with its effects unique to each helper, and its impact modifiable with awareness and intervention. Pearlman and Caringi (2009) recommend the following strategies for ameliorating the effects of vicarious trauma: (1) social support; (2) consultation; (3) spiritual renewal; (4) self-care; (5) managing and respecting boundaries; (6) developing a theoretical framework to guide practice; and (7) engaging in a variety of activities to broaden one's perspective. The Accelerated Recovery Program for Compassion Fatigue includes an emphasis on connection and self-soothing, as well as time for sharing one's story, and empowerment through self-supervision (Gentry, 2010; Gentry & Baranowsky, 1998).

Clinical supervision and peer consultation serve a crucial role in mediating vicarious trauma by broadening one's perspective and creating a safe place to discuss the interplay between self and client (Dubi & Sanabria, 2010; Pearlman and Saakvitne, 1995). Sommer (2008) advocates for "trauma-sensitive supervision" (p. 61) requiring that supervisors (1) have a strong theoretical understanding of trauma, (2) provide information and support to address the process of vicarious traumatization and the need for counselor self-care, (3) attend to changes in counselors' behavior and attitudes that may reflect vicarious trauma, (4) prioritize both verbal and nonverbal dynamics in the therapy relationship and the supervision process, and (5) create a collaborative strength-based relationship with supervisees. We recommend that counselors seek personal therapy to address their unresolved trauma issues. Only when we have navigated the way through our own struggles can we guide others through the process and discern clearly between what is ours and what belongs to the client.

In-Session Practices to Promote Wellness

Interventions practiced within the trauma session itself are vital for preventing vicarious trauma. Courtois et al. (2009) stressed the importance of therapists' self-regulation and attentive monitoring of vicarious trauma and countertransference reactions within the *moment-to-moment interplay* of the session. Counselors need practical strategies to support their capacity for clear thinking, including ways to balance the level of empathic engagement and regulate nervous system arousal (Rothschild, 2006). Mirror neurons may explain the mechanism of empathy and the exchange of traumatic experiencing in therapy (Iacoboni, 2007; Ivey, Ivey, Zalaquett, & Quirk, 2009; Rothschild, 2006). Somatic and mindfulness-based interventions provide effective tools to mediate this impact. In *Help for the Helper,* Rothschild offers concrete strategies for counselors to stay attuned to their own somatic and emotional responses to the work, including making empathy conscious, learning to disconnect from traumatic experiencing while remaining engaged in the therapy, and practicing active self-care throughout sessions. Somatic empathy occurs through a process whereby two or more people experience the same emotions as they "commonly, spontaneously, and unconsciously copy each other's facial expressions and postures" (Rothschild, 2006, p. 41). When somatic empathy is unconscious, counselors may misunderstand their cognitive, emotional, and physical reactions. Counselors can develop greater body awareness and make choices to change postures, facial expressions, and breathing patterns as a way to reconnect with self and disconnect from affectively experiencing clients. Strategies as simple as sitting up straight, crossing or uncrossing legs, deepening one's breath, taking a drink, writing notes, stretching, and moving around between sessions can break the mirroring process, moderate arousal levels, and strengthen counselor resiliency.

Further Reading

Resources that specifically address the impact of trauma on therapists and provide education and tools to transform its effects include *Transforming the Pain: A Workbook on Vicarious Traumaization* (Saakvitne & Pearlman, 1996), *Managing Traumatic Stress Through Art* (Cohen, Barnes, & Rankin, 1995), and *Treatment*

Manual for Accelerated Recovery Program for Compassion Fatigue (Gentry & Baranowsky, 1998). Additionally, *The Therapist's Workbook* (Kottler, 1998), *The Resilient Practitioner* (Skovholt, 2001), and *Leaving It at the Office* (Norcross & Guy, 2007) offer resources and helpful interventions to address general risk factors and concerns of the counseling profession.

Gratitude for Humanistic Connection

Many trauma survivors face the devastating sense of aloneness when they cannot find words to describe their experience or accept the receptivity of caring others to be present with their pain. As counselors, it is critical that we have a strong conceptual framework that can sustain us as we provide hope and empathy. Humanistic philosophy provides a bedrock for that sustenance.

While risks are inherent in counseling work with traumatized persons, so are tremendous rewards. Witnessing the inordinate strength and courage of those who faced horrendous realities—and then emerged from the darkness—provides inspiration, instills hope, and promotes our own resiliency and courage as human beings. It is a life-altering and life-enriching journey to accompany trauma survivors on their path to freedom and one for which we are both immeasurably thankful.

REFERENCES

Axline, V. (1974). *Play therapy.* New York: Random House.

Baggerly, J. (2010). Systematic trauma interventions for children: A 10 step protocol. In J. Webber & J. B. Mascari (Eds.), *Terrorism, trauma, and tragedies: A counselor's guide to preparing and responding* (3rd ed., pp. 130–136). Alexandria, VA: American Counseling Association Foundation.

Baranowsky, A. B., Gentry, J. E., & Schultz, D. F. (2010). *Trauma practice, tools for stabilization and recovery* (2nd ed.). Cambridge, MA: Hogrefe Publishing.

Bohart, A. C. (2007). The actualizing person. In M. Cooper, M. O'Hara, P. F. Schmid, & G. Wyatt (Eds.). *The handbook of person-centred psychotherapy and counselling* (pp. 47–63). New York: Palgrave Macmillan.

Bowman, M. (1997). *Individual differences in posttraumatic response: Problems with the adversity–distress connection.* Mahwah, NJ: Erlbaum.

Bratton, S. C., Ceballos, P. L., & Ferebee, K. W. (2009). Integration of structured expressive activities within a humanistic group play therapy format for preadolescents. *Journal for Specialists in Group Work, 34*(3), 251–275.

Bratton, S., & Ray, D. (2002). Humanistic play therapy. In D. Cain & J. Seeman (Eds.), *Humanistic psychotherapies* (pp. 369–402). Washington, DC: American Psychological Association.

Briere, J., & Scott, C. (2006). *Principles of trauma therapy.* Thousand Oaks, CA: Sage Publications.

Brymer M., Jacobs A., Layne C., Pynoos, R., Ruzek J., Steinberg, A., et al. (2006, July). *Psychological first aid: Field operations guide* (2nd ed.). National Child Traumatic Stress Network and National Center for Posttraumatic Stress Disorder. Retrieved from www.nctsn.org

Calhoun, L. G., & Tedeschi, R. G. (2006). The foundations of posttraumatic growth: An expanded framework. In L. G. Calhoun & R. G. Tedeschi (Eds.), *Handbook of posttraumatic growth: Research and practice* (pp. 3–23). New York: Psychology Press.

Cashwell, C. S., Bentley, D. P., & Bigbee, A. (2007). Spirituality and counselor wellness. *Journal of Humanistic Counseling, Education and Development, 46*, 66–81.

Chu, J. A. (1998). *Rebuilding shattered lives: The responsible treatment of complex posttraumatic and dissociative disorders.* New York: John Wiley & Sons.

Cohen, B. M., Barnes, M. M., & Rankin, A. B. (1995). *Managing traumatic stress through art.* Baltimore, MD: Sidran Press.

Courtois, C. A., & Ford, J. D. (Eds.). (2009). *Treating complex traumatic stress disorders: An evidence-based guide.* New York: Guilford Press.

Courtois, C. A., Ford, J. D., & Cloitre, M. (2009). Best practices in psychotherapy for adults. In C. A. Courtois & J. D. Ford (Eds.), *Treating complex traumatic stress disorders: An evidence-based guide.* (pp. 82–103). New York: Guilford Press.

Cummins, P. N., Massey, L., & Jones, A. (2007). Keeping ourselves well: Strategies for promoting and maintaining counselor wellness. *Journal of Humanistic Counseling, Education and Development, 46*, 35–49.

DeDomenico, G. S. (2002). Sandtray-wordplay: A psychotherapeutic and transformational sandplay technique for individuals, couples, families, and groups. *Sandtray Network Journal, 6*(2). Retrieved from http://visionquest.us/vqisr/publications.htm/#textbook

Dubi, M., & Sanabria, S. (2010). The Clearness Committee: A peer supervision model for trauma and crisis counselors. In J. Webber & J. B. Mascari (Eds.), *Terrorism, trauma, and tragedies: A counselor's guide to preparing and responding* (3rd ed., pp. 169–171). Alexandria, VA: American Counseling Association Foundation.

Echterling, L. G., Presbury, J., & McKee, J. E. (2005). *Crisis intervention: Promoting resilience and resolution in troubled times.* Upper Saddle River, NJ: Pearson.

Echterling, L. G., & Stewart, A. L. (2010). Pathways to resilience at Virginia Tech. In J. Webber & J. B. Mascari (Eds.), *Terrorism, trauma, and tragedies: A counselor's guide to preparing and responding* (3rd ed., pp. 83–88). Alexandria, VA: American Counseling Association Foundation.

Edwards, N. N., & Lambie, G. W. (2009). A person-centered counseling approach as a primary therapeutic support for women with a history of childhood sexual abuse. *Journal of Humanistic Counseling, Education and Development, 48*, 23–35.

Foa, E. B., Keane, T. M., & Friedman, M. J. (Eds.). (2000). *Effective treatments for PTSD: Practice guidelines from the International Society for Traumatic Stress Studies.* New York: Guilford Press.

Fosha, D. (2000). *The transforming power of affect.* New York: Basic Books.

Fosha, D. (2003). Dyadic regulation and experiential work with emotion and relatedness in trauma and disorganized attachment. In M. F. Solomon & D. J. Siegel (Eds.), *Healing trauma: Attachment, mind, body, and brain* (pp. 221–281). New York: W. W. Norton & Company.

Fosha, D., Paivio, S. C., Gleiser, K., & Ford, J. D. (2009). Experiential and emotion-focused therapy. In C. A. Courtois & J. D. Ford. (Eds.), *Treating complex traumatic stress disorders: An evidence-based guide* (pp. 286–311). New York: Guilford Press.

Gentry, E. (2010). Compassion fatigue: Our Achilles heel. In J. Webber & J. B. Mascari (Eds.), *Terrorism, trauma, and tragedies: A counselor's guide to preparing and responding* (3rd ed., pp. 13–17). Alexandria, VA: American Counseling Association Foundation.

Gentry, E., & Baranowsky, A. (1998). *Treatment manual for Accelerated Recovery Program for Compassion Fatigue.* Toronto, Canada: Psych Ink.

Gil, E. (2001). *The healing power of play.* New York: Guilford Press.

Gil, E. (2006). *Helping abused and traumatized children: Integrating directive and nondirective approaches.* New York: Guilford Press.

Goodman, R. F., Morgan, A. V., Juriga, S., & Brown, E. J. (2004). Letting the story unfold: A case study of client-centered therapy for childhood traumatic grief. *Harvard Review of Psychiatry, 12*(4), 199–212.

Green, E. J., Crenshaw, D. A., & Kolos, A. C. (2010). Counseling children with preverbal trauma. *International Journal of Play Therapy, 19*(2), 95–105.

Greenberg, L. S. (2002). *Emotion-focused therapy: Coaching clients to work through their feelings.* Washington, DC: American Psychological Association.

Gurman, A. S., & Messer, S. B. (2003). Contemporary issues in the theory and practice of psychotherapy: A framework for comparative study. In A. S. Gurman & S. B. Messer (Eds.), *Essential psychotherapies: Theory and practice* (2nd ed., pp. 1–23). New York: Guilford Press.

Herman, J. L. (1997). *Trauma and recovery.* New York: Basic Books.

Iacoboni, M. (2007). Face to face: The neural basis of social mirroring and empathy. *Psychiatric Annals, 37,* 236–241.

Ivey, A., Ivey, M. B., Zalaquett, C., & Quirk, K. (2009, November 22). Reader viewpoint: Counseling and neuroscience: The cutting edge of the coming decade. *Counseling Today Online.* Retrieved from http://www.counseling.org/Publications/CounselingTodayArticles.aspx?AGuid=1ddd9bc8-2e8f-45f0-b384-444c6059bf83

Joseph, S. (2004). Client-centred therapy, post-traumatic stress disorder, and post-traumatic growth: Theoretical perspectives and practical implications. *Psychology and Psychotherapy: Theory, Research, and Practice, 77,* 101–119.

Kalff, D. M. (2003). *Sandplay: A psychotherapeutic approach to the psyche.* Cloverdale, CA: Temenos Press.

Kinsler, P. J., Courtois, C. A., & Frankel, A. S. (2009). Therapeutic alliance and risk management. In C. A. Courtois & J. D. Ford. (Eds.), *Treating complex traumatic stress disorders: An evidence-based guide* (pp. 183–201). New York: Guilford Press.

Kirschenbaum, H. (2004). Carl Rogers's life and work: An assessment on the 100th anniversary of his birth. *Journal of Counseling & Development, 82*(1), 116–124. Retrieved from http://draweb.njcu.edu:2048/login?url=http://search.ebscohost.com/login.aspx?direct=true&db=aph&AN=12342946&site=ehost-live

Kottler, J. A. (1998). *The therapist's workbook: Self-assessment, self-care, and self-improvement exercises for mental health professionals.* San Francisco: Jossey-Bass.

Levine, P. A. (1997). *Waking the tiger: Healing trauma.* Berkeley, CA: North Atlantic Books.

Myers, J. E., & Sweeney, T. J. (1999). *The Five Factor Wellness Inventory.* Greensboro, NC: Authors.

Norcross, J. C. (2002). *Psychotherapy relationships that work: Therapist contributions and responsiveness to patients.* New York: Oxford University Press.

Norcross, J. C., & Guy, J. D. (2007). *Leaving it at the office: A guide to psychotherapist self-care.* New York: Guilford Press.

Norman, D. M. (2004). Lessons learned along the therapy path: Implications for students. *Journal of Humanistic Counseling, Education and Development, 43,* 65–71.

Paivio, S. C., & Nieuwenhuis, J. A. (2001). Efficacy of emotion-focused therapy for adult survivors of child abuse: A preliminary study. *Journal of Traumatic Stress, 14*(1), 115–133.

Paivio, S. S., & Pascual-Leone, A. (2010). *Emotion-focused therapy for complex trauma: An integrative approach.* Washington, DC: American Psychological Association.

Payne, A., Liebling-Kalifani, H., & Joseph, S. (2007). Client-centered group therapy for survivors of interpersonal trauma: A pilot investigation. *Counselling and Psychotherapy Research, 7*(2), 100–105.

Pearlman, L. A., & Caringi, J. (2009). Living and working self-reflectively to address vicarious trauma. In C. A. Courtois & J. D. Ford (Eds.), *Treating complex traumatic stress disorders: An evidence-based guide* (pp. 202–224). New York: Guilford Press.

Pearlman, L. A., & Saakvitne, K. W. (1995). *Trauma and the therapist.* New York: W.W. Norton & Company.

Rogers, C. (1951). *Client-centered therapy.* Boston: Houghton Mifflin.

Rogers, C. (1961). *On becoming a person.* New York: Houghton Mifflin.

Rogers, C. (1980). *A way of being.* New York: Houghton Mifflin.

Rothschild, B. (2000). *The body remembers: The psychophysiology of trauma and trauma treatment.* New York: W. W. Norton & Company.

Rothschild, B. (2006). *Help for the helper: Self-care strategies for managing burnout and stress.* New York: W. W. Norton & Company.

Saakvitne, K. W., & Pearlman, L. A. (Eds.). (1996). *Transforming the pain: A workbook on vicarious traumatization.* New York: W. W. Norton & Company.

Serlin, I., & Cannon, J. T. (2004). A humanistic approach to the psychology of trauma. In D. Knafo (Ed.), *Living with terror, working with trauma: A clinician's handbook* (pp. 313–330). Lanham, MD: Rowman & Littlefield.

Shapiro, F. (2001). *Eye movement desensitization and reprocessing: Basic principles, protocols and procedures* (2nd ed.). New York: Guilford Press.

Siegel, D. J. (2003). An interpersonal neurobiology of psychotherapy: The developing mind and the resolution of trauma. In M. F. Solomon & D. J. Siegel (Eds.), *Healing trauma: Attachment, mind, body, and brain* (pp. 1–56). New York: W. W. Norton & Company.

Skovholt, T. M. (2001). *The resilient practitioner: Burnout prevention and self-care strategies for counselors, therapists, teachers, and health professionals.* Boston: Allyn & Bacon.

Solomon, M. F., & Siegel, D. J. (Eds.). (2003). *Healing trauma: Attachment, mind, body, and brain.* New York: W. W. Norton & Company.

Sommer, C. A. (2008). Vicarious traumatization, trauma-sensitive supervision, and counselor preparation. *Counselor Education & Supervision, 48*, 61–71.

Stamm, B. H. (2009). *Professional Quality of Life: Compassion Satisfaction and Fatigue Version 5 (ProQOL).* Retrieved from http://www.proqol.org/uploads/ProQOL_5_English_Selfscore.pdf

Steele, K., & van der Hart, O. (2009). Treating dissociation. In C. A. Courtois & J. D. Ford (Eds.), *Treating complex traumatic stress disorders: An evidence-based guide* (pp. 145–165). New York: Guilford Press.

Tedeschi, R. G., & Calhoun, L. G. (1995). *Trauma and transformation: Growing in the aftermath of suffering.* Thousand Oaks, CA: Sage.

Terr, L. (1990). *Too scared to cry: Psychic trauma in childhood.* New York: Harper & Row.

Thompson, M. (2009, December 14). A mounting suicide rate prompts an Army response. *TIME*, Retrieved from http://www.time.com/time/nation/article/0,8599,1947405,00.html

van der Kolk, B. A. (2003). Posttraumatic stress disorder and the nature of trauma. In M. F. Solomon & D. J. Siegel (Eds.), *Healing trauma: Attachment, mind, body, and brain* (pp. 168–195). New York: W. W. Norton & Company.

van der Kolk, B. A. (2009). Afterword. In C. A. Courtois & J. D. Ford (Eds.), *Treating complex traumatic stress disorders: An evidence-based guide* (pp. 455–466). New York: Guilford Press.

Venart, E., Vassos, S., & Pitcher-Heft, H. (2007). What individual counselors can do to sustain wellness. *Journal of Humanistic Counseling, Education and Development, 46,* 50–65.

Wampold, B. E. (2001). *The great psychotherapy debate: Models, methods, and findings.* Mahwah, NJ: Erlbaum.

Webber, J., & Mascari, J. B. (2008). Sand tray therapy and the healing process in trauma and grief counseling. In G. Walz, J. C. Bleuer, & R. Yep (Eds.), *VISTAS 2008* (pp. 1–6). Alexandria, VA: American Counseling Association. Retrieved from http://www. counselingoutfitters.com

Webber, J., & Mascari, J. B. (2010). Psychological first aid: A new paradigm for disaster mental health. In J. Webber & J. B. Mascari (Eds.), *Terrorism, trauma, and tragedies: A counselor's guide to preparing and responding* (3rd ed., pp. 201–205). Alexandria, VA: American Counseling Association Foundation.

Webber, J., Mascari, J. B., & Runte, J. (2010). Unlocking traumatic memory through sand therapy. In J. Webber & J. B. Mascari (Eds.), *Terrorism, trauma, and tragedies: A counselor's guide to preparing and responding* (3rd ed., pp. 13–17). Alexandria, VA: American Counseling Association Foundation.

III

APPLICATIONS IN EDUCATIONAL SETTINGS

8

Humanistic Perspectives on Addressing School Violence

PAULA HELEN STANLEY, ROBERT SMALL,
STEPHEN S. OWEN, AND TOD W. BURKE

Parents, teachers, and students rightfully expect that school environments must be safe havens, free from violence, giving students a positive environment in which to learn and to grow. Unfortunately, as headlines too often proclaim, violence does frequently occur in school settings. And, as Kevorkian and D'Antona (2008) suggested, conceptions of violence need not be limited to physical attacks:

> Name-calling that makes a child feel anxious, angry, or unworthy may diminish a student's drive for education. Many times this will happen in front of peers. Teasing can have severe and even life-long consequences. Exposed to this type of abuse for a long time, these children may become incapable of reaching their potential. They actually feel like they deserve to be picked on. Kids are left feeling like they are not important and don't belong in school. (p. 21)

The focus of this chapter is on the relationship between humanism—or, rather, lack of humanism—and school violence. The chapter will proceed as follows. First, invitational education will be discussed as a means by which humanism may be introduced into a school setting.

Second, several forms of school violence will be described and analyzed, with a discussion of their prevalence and characteristics. The reader will be challenged to consider the potential for humanism to reduce these acts. Selected "Invitational Counselors in Action" scenarios will provide examples of how counselors may lend their expertise to the development of invitational programming to reduce school violence.

Third, while humanism and invitational education lead to positive outcomes for schools, they are not practiced as fully as they could be and must be. The reasons for this failure lie in the context of contemporary school policies, which will be profiled with a consideration of how they, in some cases, promote the very values that are contrary to humanistic approaches. It is important to be aware of these trends, as they shape the environments that may challenge invitational approaches.

The final portion of the chapter establishes an argument as to *why* humanistic and invitational education may help to mitigate against school violence. The chapter concludes with a series of broad recommendations, in which counselors may take a leadership role, to infuse humanism and invitational practices within educational settings.

HUMANISM AND INVITATIONAL EDUCATION

Humanism is a powerful construct with deep philosophical roots, as described in Chapter 1 of this volume: "Humans can be understood only as whole beings and should never be viewed as by-products of other processes. Individualism, respect for subjectivity, and respect for the dignity of each person are the three primary elements of human irreducibility" (p. 5). Certainly, this is a valuable perspective within educational settings, as person-centered and humanistic approaches have been found to be associated with positive student outcomes (e.g., Cornelius-White, 2007).

The Concept of Invitational Education

The concept of invitational education has gained currency and is consistent with humanistic philosophies. Purkey and Novak (2008) argued that schools should be welcoming places, where students, teachers, staff, and parents may be comfortable and engaged with the school's work. This requires deliberate action by the school, as invitations to learn cannot occur by accident or happenstance.

Inviting schools must demonstrate four characteristics. The first is *optimism*, which recognizes individuals' potential to succeed, to meet challenges, and to contribute positively to the school environment. The second is *trust* between individuals as manifested in interpersonal interactions, which must be genuine, honest, and ethically responsible. The third is *respect* for persons and particularly for the students; in many ways, respect underlies invitational transactions. "If educators believe that each student is able to learn [and] is worthy of respect ... they will find ways for students to succeed in schools" (Purkey and Novak, 2008, p. 15). Fourth, schools must demonstrate *care*, which can refer both to the deliberation with which invitational pedagogies are structured and to a legitimate concern for the well-being (e.g., intellectual, social, emotional) of students.

Schools may be conceptualized as functioning at one of four levels of invitation, categorized by whether they are inviting and by whether efforts have been intentional: (1) intentionally disinviting; (2) unintentionally disinviting; (3) unintentionally inviting; and (4) intentionally inviting (Purkey & Novak, 2008). Schools that are intentionally disinviting require tremendous work, including changes in their guiding philosophy, to adopt an invitational stance. On the other hand, schools that are unintentionally disinviting or unintentionally inviting may, under the leadership of an able counselor and with the support of a building principal, undertake self-study and programming to remedy disinviting practices and to formalize the more inviting aspects of the school.

Counselors play a central role in the development of invitational programs and practices. Indeed, one of the first tasks of counselors working to promote invitational education, whether to enhance school safety or for other positive educational outcomes, is to provide instruction to members of the school community about what invitational practice entails (Stanley, Juhnke, & Purkey, 2004). Then, as Schmidt (1997) noted, counselors may promote and assist in many invitational endeavors:

> In applying invitational principles, school counselors design instructional services for teachers to integrate with the curriculum; create preventive strategies for the welfare of the entire school community; and establish individual and small group processes to focus on particular concerns of students, parents, and teachers. (p. 14)

Invitational education need not be understood as a complex restructuring of the nation's schools. A simple but powerful starting point toward invitational leadership can simply be the promotion of "collaborative acts of kindness" (Purkey & Siegel, 2003, p. 183). It is important for adults to model kindness in interpersonal behaviors, as doing so can subsequently shape children's prosocial behaviors (Kevorkian & D'Antona, 2008).

Benefits of Invitational Education

Both humanism and invitational education share a concern about the value of persons, with the requisite emphasis on respect, dignity, and care for individuals. In this way, invitational education can be conceptualized as an operationalization of humanistic philosophies in an educational setting.

In an era of educational accountability, it is useful to note that invitational leadership as demonstrated by building principals is positively related to the job satisfaction of teachers, teachers' perceptions of a principal's effectiveness and leadership for school improvement, and state rankings of school district performance (Egley, 2003). In addition, invitational education strategies are related to effective classroom management (Riner, 2003).

Adopting an invitational model and humanistic principles (e.g., a focus on the value of persons as individuals; the potential for self-actualization; empathetic and positive relationships between individuals) can further benefit a school community along two dimensions. First, students and staff may benefit from the positive climate at the school itself. As suggested following, there is reason to believe that such an environment may lead to greater norms of civility and the potential to prevent threatening acts, such as bullying and violence. Second, children spend a substantial part of their day at school. Between the 1981–1982 and 2002–2003 school years, the average amount of time per week spent at school increased from 26 hours, 21 minutes to 32 hours, 27 minutes—the largest single block of time per week other than sleeping (Juster, Ono, & Stafford, 2004). At the same time, some schools and districts have considered lengthening the school day or the school year.

Such an increase affords schools a unique opportunity to model humanistic philosophies that students, staff, and parents may observe, experience, and subsequently absorb into their own daily interactions with others. This is certainly consistent with Dewey's (1959) notion "that education is the fundamental method of social progress and reform" (p. 30) and, as such, "is a process of living" (p. 22). On the other hand, longer school days and years can potentially increase student stress, anger, hostility, and pain in schools that are not invitational in their approach.

Invitational Counseling in Action: The School's Physical Environment

Purkey and Novak (2008) observed that the physical environment may "offer the best opportunity for immediate improvement" (p. 22) under an invitational model, in part "because the physical environment is so visible" (p. 21). Creating a welcoming physical environment that fosters a sense of value and care while also promoting "pride of place" may lead to reductions in conduct problems (Duke, 1998, p. 24). This is consistent with theories that have found crime prevention value in promoting a sense of ownership of place (Newman, 1996) and in cleaning up a disorderly physical environment (Wilson & Kelling, 1982).

Counselors are in an excellent position to pose questions to students, faculty, staff, and guests, such as, "What about the school environment makes you comfortable (or uncomfortable)?", in addition to making their own observations on the matter. Unintentionally disinviting physical attributes—such as a barren or darkened hallway, untidy facilities, or even a disagreeable paint scheme—can be readily addressed and transformed into something intentionally inviting. Likewise, the attributes unique to a school that are unintentionally inviting can be routinized into more formal and widespread practice.

At Cooper Elementary School in Westland, Michigan, the principal—working collaboratively with a committee to empower decision making—instituted physical changes to the school. For instance, "Student artwork was prominently displayed where blank, brown brick walls had previously stood … [and] curtains were sewn and hung in the front lobby" (Kalec, 2004, p. 78). Simple changes such as these were received positively by students, parents, and staff, as the building was transformed to reflect "a burst of optimism" (p. 78) manifested by a simple but powerful increase in smiles, which can be invitational in itself.

Therefore, the first steps toward invitational education need not be complex. Counselors should capitalize upon the value of place. Simply looking at the environment, asking a few questions about its level of invitation, and making some modifications can go a long way in having an actual impact on the members of the school community while also serving as a very tangible indicator that the school is serious about its invitational transformation.

VIOLENCE IN SCHOOLS

Lethal School Violence

When thinking about school violence, one of the first images that comes to mind is live news coverage, or front-page headlines, about a tragic school shooting. From 1992–1993 through 2008–2009, there were a total of 462 violent deaths that occurred at elementary and secondary schools, traveling to and from school, or associated with a school-related event, and this does not include incidents at colleges and universities, such as the 2007 Virginia Tech tragedy. The reasons for violent death at school vary (and in some cases are unknown) but include interpersonal disputes, suicides, and incidents of gang violence (National School Safety Center, 2009).

The subject of a feature film (*Bowling for Columbine*), the school shooting most associated with secondary school violence occurred at Columbine High School in Littleton, Colorado (for a well-researched account of this incident, readers are referred to Cullen, 2009). While it is tempting to attempt to profile school shootings or to seek a common explanatory factor underlying them, the reality is that there is not a single explanation for them (for a survey of academic research on potential causes, classifications, and contributors to school shooting incidents, see Muschert, 2007).

Indeed, a study of 37 incidents of targeted violence in schools (approximately three-quarters of which resulted in fatalities), sponsored by the U.S. Secret Service and the U.S. Department of Education, found that "there is no accurate or useful 'profile' of students who engaged in targeted school violence" (Vossekuil, Fein, Reddy, Borum, & Modzeleski, 2002, p. 19). There were, however, some commonalities.

Perpetrators often were themselves bullied, had prior thoughts of suicide or suicide attempts, and had experienced losses in their lives. Although the perpetrators generally had no criminal history and the attacks generally occurred without an *overt* threat, some persons (usually "a friend, schoolmate, or sibling"; see Vossekuil et al., 2002, p. 25) often had an awareness that the perpetrators were planning something. Prior to the attacks, some persons (potentially including classmates or friends, but usually adults) were typically concerned by their observations of the perpetrators' behavior.

Nonlethal School Violence

While tragic, violent deaths in schools are a fairly rare event. However, lesser acts of school crime and violence are more prevalent. According to the most recent *Indicators of School Crime and Safety* (Dinkes, Kemp, Baum, & Snyder, 2009), in 2007 there were 26 acts of violence and 31 thefts per 1,000 elementary and secondary school students.

Of 9th–12th graders, 12% reported being in a fight at school, and 6% reported that they had brought a weapon to school within the past 30 days. Among 12–18-year-old students, 10% reported that hate-related words had been directed toward them at school, and 7% reported avoiding particular school activities or places due to fear. Finally, 6% of schools reported the frequent (i.e., weekly) verbal abuse of teachers by students (Dinkes et al., 2009).

Once again, attempting to explain the etiology of school crime and violence is a complex task. A study of crime in Philadelphia schools concluded, "The thesis that 'bad' kids or 'bad' communities directly import violence into any school is unsupported by our results. Rather, individual student characteristics (e.g., effort, belief in rules, positive peer associations) exert stronger influences on student misconduct" (Welsh, Greene, & Jenkins, 1999, p. 106).

Other research has explored the impact on crime of communal schools, meaning those with "supportive relationships between and among teachers, administrators, and students, a common set of goals and norms, and a sense of collaboration and involvement" (Payne, Gottfredson, & Gottfredson, 2003, p. 751). Schools marked by these characteristics have less victimization of teachers and less delinquency by students; in addition, such schools lead to greater student bonds with the school, which subsequently are also associated with less delinquency by students.

It is worthwhile to pause at this point to consider some potential implications of this. What if school teachers, counselors, and administrators worked in an environment where they were highly valued, respected, and collaborated regularly to discuss the needs of their students? Based on the previous review, there is reason to believe that student needs could better be identified so students could be provided with appropriate services and care, which could have the potential to reduce acts of targeted violence.

What if schools were structured to provide the communal atmosphere that promotes student bonding with the school, which could enhance positive peer associations, self-esteem, problem-solving skills, and so on? Based on the previous review, there is reason to believe that this emphasis may lead to reduced incidence of crime and violence. A caring, supportive, and inviting approach could well be the philosophy that threads through a school's organization and programming, structured to reduce crime and violence.

Invitational Counseling in Action: Promoting Peer Mediation

Invitational education seeks, among other goals, to promote the peaceful and respectful resolution of conflict. As such, programs can be structured to teach students how to productively resolve conflict to the satisfaction of the parties involved—which may prevent conflicts from escalating into something more serious (Stanley et al., 2004). Indeed, the broad concept of peacemaking has been advocated by criminologists as a means by which to resolve conflicts without imposing further harm onto the parties involved (see Pepinsky, 1999, for an example of the application of peacemaking in a middle school setting).

With a knowledge of both conflict resolution and of student development, counselors are the most well-prepared personnel to implement peer mediation programs, to train the student mediators, and to supervise the mediation sessions. Peer mediation may contribute to an intentionally inviting environment by minimizing a reliance on disinviting disciplinary practices, such as the use of out-of-school suspension without the provision of services or attention to the needs of individual students.

Peace Pals is an example of an effective peer mediation program. Implemented in an elementary school setting, the program was motivated in part by "the need to prevent and reduce violence in elementary schools" (Schellenberg, Parks-Savage, & Rehfuss, 2007, p. 476). The program seeks to empower students in the conflict resolution process.

When a student conflict or dispute is referred to the program, student mediators, known as Peace Pals, facilitate a Peace Talk between the involved students. The session draws upon a model of conflict resolution in which student mediators are trained. Upon resolution of the conflict, the parties prepare a written Peace Treaty (Schellenberg et al., 2007).

Research has found that elementary peer mediation programs do yield benefits, and the Peace Pals program is no exception. All incidents referred to the program during a 1-year study were found to be resolved successfully, meaning that "both parties and the mediators agreed that the conflict or dispute was satisfactorily resolved" (Schellenberg et al., 2007, p. 478).

In addition, since the implementation of the program, disciplinary suspensions have declined substantially, as has school violence. For instance, annual suspensions declined from 25 to 4 for physical conflict, from 3 to 1 for verbal conflict, and from 129 to 3 for disruptive behaviors (Schellenberg et al., 2007). These dramatic results suggest that peer mediation programs can permit the peaceful resolution of conflict that attends to the needs of the whole persons of the students, leading to safer school environments while also providing the potential to teach students conflict management skills that can be applied in other settings.

Hazing

In addition to the previously described acts, it is also important to consider two behaviors that, while long in history, have only in recent practice come to be viewed as violent. The first is hazing, which includes acts that are required to gain admission to a group or organization and that cause harm to self or others or involve demeaning or harassing behavior in general. Hazing is often attributed to notions of tradition, beliefs in its efficacy for bonding, or organizational dynamics fostering groupthink; it is also often accelerated by alcohol use (see Owen, Burke, & Vichesky, 2008).

While often associated with colleges and universities, hazing also frequently occurs in high school settings. According to a national survey (Hoover & Pollard), "Forty-eight percent of [high school] students who belong to groups reported being subjected to hazing activities" (p. 1), and 71% of hazed students reported negative impacts from hazing, ranging from illness to delinquency to poor school achievement, and more. Over one-third of the students indicated that there is no one to whom they would feel comfortable reporting hazing incidents.

Student-on-Student Bullying in Schools

The second behavior increasingly recognized as violent is bullying, which is "deliberate hurtful behavior, that is repeated, and it is difficult for the target to defend him or herself (imbalance of power)" (Brown, 2008, p. 101). This can include physical behaviors and verbal taunts as well as exclusions from groups and activities in which others may join. Bullying can cause "schools [to] become a place of survival rather than a place of learning" (Kevorkian & D'Antona, 2008, p. 3).

Finkelhor, Turner, Ormrod, and Hamby (2010) reported a decline in the proportion of students who were physically bullied from 2003 to 2008, from 21.7% to 14.8%. However, the incidence of verbal bullying has remained fairly constant over the same time period, at 24.9% in 2003 and 22% in 2008.

A decline in physical bullying is commendable, but verbal bullying remains as a significant concern due to its detrimental impacts on students. A particularly common form of verbal bullying includes comments referencing sexual orientation (regardless of the actual sexual orientation of their target): "Third graders through high schoolers say 'faggot,' 'you're so gay,' and 'homo,' with little or no regard for the pain they may cause. Such verbal abuse [is] ... often dismissed as kids' jargon" (Kevorkian & D'Antona, 2008, p. 2; see also Pascoe, 2007).

It is important to focus on bullying, beyond the more severe forms of violence previously described, because bullying may lead to further delinquent acts. In addition to its relationship to school shootings, being bullied may lead to disciplinary problems at school (Gastic, 2008) as well as "violent behaviours and carrying a weapon" (Arseneault, Bowes, & Shakoor, 2010, pp. 721–722). For this reason, it is important to understand characteristics both of students who bully and of students who are bullied to better inform the development of prevention programming.

Similar to domestic violence and other forms of assault, bullying is a matter of unequal power and control between the person who is bullied and the person who engages in bullying behaviors. It is important to observe that bullying can occur between students of the same or different ages.

The relationship between students who bully and students who are bullied is not always easily discernable. This is, in part, because students who are bullied may have some characteristics that are similar to those of students who engage in bullying behaviors. For example, both sometimes share poor social skills and negative behaviors (e.g., substance abuse). However, while anyone can be a victim of bullying, certain children may be targeted in greater frequency.

For instance, males portraying personality traits deemed as weak, non-aggressive, or defenseless are often victimized by bullies; females failing to display feminine characteristics are often labeled by the bullies (and their peer associates) as "dykes," forcing many of these female victims into social isolation. Students who bully often possess a sense of entitlement, lack empathy toward the students they bully, believe that bullying is a means to foster respect, and rationalize their behavior as normal. These negative characteristics generate a threat to a safe learning environment (Kevorkian & D'Antona, 2008).

Bullying behavior is learned; for instance, children who are bullied or who witness bullying at home (by siblings or parents) may bring that behavior with them to school. In an attempt to change this negative behavior, Bradshaw, Sawyer and O'Brennan (2007) advocated intervention by adults, including parents, teachers, and school administrators. Kevorkian & D'Antona (2008) agreed:

> We must take positive role modeling seriously in order to be sure that we are not passing on destructive social skills.... [In] an environment where a negative behavior is not monitored or stopped, the behavior will flourish ... [becoming] a part of the continuum of interpersonal violence. (p. 56)

Schools must offer an atmosphere where students do not feel threatened, where the educational experience is not tainted by bullying behaviors, and where interpersonal interaction is valued, not feared. In response to concerns about bullying, many schools have implemented antibullying programs, although the research on these programs is mixed. A 2007 meta-analysis (Ferguson, San Miguel, Kilburn, & Sanchez, 2007) found antibullying programs to be generally ineffective, but a 2008 meta-analysis (Merrell, Gueldner, Ross, & Isava, 2008) found significant positive impacts for approximately one-third of their effect sizes.

Other Forms of Bullying in Schools

Bullying and its detrimental impacts are not limited to encounters only between students. In a study of elementary school teachers, 57% reported that they had been bullied by one or more of their students, encompassing acts that attempt "to control the classroom with disruptive behavior that implies contempt for the teacher" (Twemlow, Fonagy, Sacco, & Brethour, 2006, p. 191).

Teachers can also be bullied by parents and administrators. A Canadian study found that 36% of elementary teachers and 22% of secondary teachers reported being bullied by parents, including the use of threats and the actual disruption of class. The same study found that approximately 25% of teachers had been bullied by an administrator through "trivial fault finding," "pressure on teachers to change schools," and "excessive monitoring of their work" (Ontario Secondary School Teachers' Federation, 2005, p. 10).

Results of teacher bullying, whether by students, parents, or administrators, include anger, absenteeism, "a loss of self-confidence," and "withdrawal from or avoidance of their colleagues at work" (Ontario Secondary School Teachers' Federation, 2005, p. 18). Schools in which staff members lack confidence in their work or in which they avoid interactions with others are hardly invitational. Rather, they can model the very negative attributes that invitational education works to remedy.

More pernicious is teacher bullying of students. Defined as the use of "power to punish, manipulate, or disparage a student beyond what would be a reasonable disciplinary procedure," 40.3% of a sample of elementary school teachers self-reported having done this on one or more occasions (Twemlow et al., 2006, p. 191). Because this is self-report data, the actual incidence may be higher. Research suggests that teacher bullying of students may in fact lead to behavioral problems among students (Twemlow & Fonagy, 2005). As an immediate first step for schools to take to become more invitational, any bullying by teachers or administrators simply must stop, and parent bullying must not be tolerated.

At this point, it is worthwhile to pause once again. What if, rather than tacitly accepting hazing or feeling hopeless to its widespread existence, schools were structured in such a way that all were valued, perhaps decreasing the incidence of hazing and fears of reporting it? Or, what if, rather than an antibullying *program*, there were antibullying *schools* characterized by invitational practices? Humanism and invitational education are perspectives that could meet these laudable goals.

Invitational Counseling in Action: Helping Teachers Address Bullying

Classroom teachers are faced with myriad issues, one of which is the prevention of bullying. But bullying is a complex phenomenon, and many myths must be debunked before meaningful bullying prevention and response may occur. How can this information best be conveyed to classroom teachers?

Here, counselors can play a significant role. Training about bullying is essential, and most counselors are well prepared to provide it. In addition to understanding the dynamics of student interaction, counselors may also contextualize training to correspond to the unique dynamics and issues of a particular school.

One model of training is a program called Bully Busters, in which teachers receive education in eight modules: "Increasing Awareness of Bullying," "Preventing Bullying in Your Classroom," "Building Personal Power," "Recognizing the Bully," "Recognizing the Victim," "Recommendations and Interventions for Bullying Behavior," "Recommendations and Interventions for Helping Victims," and "Relaxation and Coping Skills" (Horne, Orpinas, Newman-Carlson, & Bartolomucci, 2004, p. 307). After training, teacher groups meet periodically to facilitate continued dialog and to provide a support network, recognizing that response to bullying is a school-wide, or perhaps even a community-wide, endeavor.

In many ways, Bully Busters goes beyond being a one-shot exercise, toward being a more comprehensive effort to systematically address the problem of bullying. A substantial focus of Bully Busters is helping teachers to identify and refute myths about bullying (Horne et al., 2004). This has an invitational effect by maintaining an implicit focus on the importance of the invitational assumptions of trust, care, respect, and optimism (Purkey & Novak, 2008).

In addition, the training can help challenge assumptions that may perpetuate an unintentionally disinviting school environment. A lack of awareness of bullying, or of the impact of verbal bullying or shunning behaviors, may lead to the perpetuation or toleration of disinviting behaviors. Therefore, while teachers have primary responsibility for their classrooms, it is important to note the critical role that counselors play in teaching the teachers about practices consistent with invitational education.

HUMANISM AND INVITATIONAL EDUCATION IN CURRENT PRACTICE

In spite of the benefits that invitational education may yield (the "Invitational Counseling in Action" sections profiled only a few potential examples), evidence suggests that many schools are not currently inviting places marked by the principles of humanism. The following trends have the potential to impede the empathy, individuality, dignity, and care that underlie humanistic approaches (see Cain, 2001) and the intentionally optimistic, respectful, trustful, and caring designs of invitational schools (see Purkey & Novak, 2008). It is important for all school personnel, but particularly counselors and principals, to consider how these trends may impact the delivery of invitational policies and programs.

Resource Availability

Resource disparities among school systems sometimes result in *savage inequalities*, as Kozol (1991) described in his book with the same title. Because school funding formulas rely not only on state budget allocations but also on local revenue streams, inequitable funding can result. An affluent suburb may be able to provide state-of-the-art facilities and rich cocurricular programming, while an area with low property tax or sales tax revenues may struggle to meet the most minimal of educational needs.

Although some headway has been made (in part through litigation) to reduce these disparities (Dayton & Dupre, 2004), inequities still remain, which may have several negative impacts. Fiscally stressed schools may have lower outcomes, as school funding is positively associated with educational achievement (Greenwald, Hedges, & Laine, 1996). Schools with diminished resources may also find it difficult either to provide security services or to offer the necessary programming opportunities that promote invitational education and humanistic principles, creating a vulnerable climate.

From a more critical perspective, attending or working in an inadequately funded school may convey an indifference or lack of concern and care for the students and staff, which can pose a cognitive barrier to invitational efforts. Once a school is labeled (see Lemert, 1972 on labeling theory) as "poor" or "inadequate" or "low quality," members of that school community may internalize those labels and see themselves as poor, inadequate, or low quality. This can diminish the sense of empowerment and potential for self-actualization that is so important for safe, welcoming, successful schools.

High-Stakes Testing

The role of high-stakes testing may undermine invitational and humanistic philosophies. This testing is labeled as "high-stakes" because the results are used for purposes beyond measuring a student's progress or comprehension of ideas. Rather, they may be required for passage to the next grade level, for making decisions about teacher and administrator effectiveness, or for assigning ratings to a school or district (Nichols and Berliner, 2007).

High-stakes testing has led to "narrowing curricular content to those subjects included in the test ... and compelling teachers to use more ... teacher-centered pedagogies" (Au, 2007, p. 264). These restrictions may make infusion of invitational and humanistic strategies difficult.

High-stakes testing may also lead to decisions or values that actually run counter to those that would be expected in an invitational setting. Consider the following observations made by Nichols and Berliner (2007) in their study of such testing practices: "A Florida superintendant noted, 'When a low-performing child walks into a classroom, instead of being seen as a challenge, or an opportunity for improvement, for the first time since I've been in education, teachers are seeing [that child] as a liability'" (p. 58).

Nichols and Berliner (2007) continue by noting "that the need to test has replaced the need to care, a corruption of the traditional role of teachers" (p. 73). Children are not liabilities, and schools must not disregard their compassion or humanity in exchange for test scores. Yet, in schools where pressures mount to increase test scores, it is no wonder that schools may appear uninviting and focused only on quantitative outcomes rather than working for their students with a focus on who they are and what they need, all while attending to them as whole persons.

Student Discipline

Disciplinary practices as currently conceptualized and applied may make impossible holistic approaches to staff–student interactions. Much school discipline policy is currently based on notions of retributive, rather than restorative, justice: "Retributive justice essentially refers to the repair of justice through unilateral imposition of punishment, whereas restorative justice means the repair of justice through reaffirming a shared value-consensus in a bilateral process" (Wenzel, Okimoto, Feather, & Platow, 2008, p. 375). In other words, retributive justice focuses primarily on the infliction of punishment, whereas restorative justice seeks to repair harms that were done to all parties involved, including the victim, the community, and even the offender.

Some schools still rely on physical discipline for students (Owen & Wagner, 2006) as a disciplinary alternative, which may actually be positively associated with school violence (see Arcus, 2002). Others schools have adopted zero-tolerance discipline including mandatory punishments (generally suspension or expulsion) for a variety of strictly defined offenses—sometimes leading relatively minor acts to be punished severely. Stories abound, including the suspension for sharing lemon drops with classmates and expulsion when a "five-year-old found a razor blade at his bus stop and brought it to school to show his teacher" (Skiba & Peterson, 1999, p. 375).

One analysis of zero-tolerance policies concluded:

> While some evidence indicates that zero tolerance policies have reduced school violence, the unintended negative effects of these policies outweigh these reductions. Zero tolerance policies result in increased use of out-of-school suspension and expulsion, severe consequences for minor infractions, increased use of punitive sanctions for minority students, and a school-to-prison pipeline [in which zero tolerance policies increasingly refer students to the criminal justice system, with the consequences that entails]. Zero tolerance has been legislated into many state statutes, thereby providing a vehicle for schools to push out low-performing, disruptive students. (MacGillivary, Medal, & Drake, 2008, p. 192)

Kevorkian and D'Antona (2008) suggested, "Teachers, counselors, administrators, and parents who interact with children every day must be certain to model kindness. They need to become familiar with identifying when children are playing, joking, and fighting or when bullying is occurring. We must pay attention to the difference" (p. 21). Other research has concluded that zero-tolerance models provide *authoritarian* discipline rather than the *authoritative* discipline that is both more appropriate for adolescents and more likely to provide support that students need (Gregory & Cornell, 2009).

A zero-tolerance approach often leaves literally no room for humanistic interactions. Of course, one reason for the development of such policies is a legitimate concern about violence in schools and an attempt to prevent its occurrence. However, Suvall (2009) argued for restorative approaches to be incorporated as a disciplinary alternative in school settings, as has been attempted in some locations. While it may not be possible to do away with more punitive disciplinary measures, consider how this description of restorative school discipline might mesh with both invitational education and humanism:

> By taking into account the costs of harm to the broader school community, restorative justice provides an opportunity to address victims' needs and to reinforce strong positive social values. At the same time, restorative justice strengthens the bonds between the offender and the school community, reducing alienation and withdrawal from the school environment. (p. 369)

This may be a positive step toward addressing behavioral problems within schools.

Surveillance

Also in the wake of acts of violence, schools have become instruments of surveillance. Demonstrating what Foucault (1977) called *panopticism*, schools may serve as "a functional mechanism that must improve the exercise of power by making it lighter, more rapid, more effective, a design of subtle coercion for a society to come" (p. 209), accomplished by turning an omnipresent gaze upon its students and staff (see also Simmons, 2010).

Security hardware and cameras join with school rules to provide an environment in which not only behaviors but also whole persons are subject to regularized scrutiny, monitoring, regulation, and control (Casella, 2010). Coupled with zero-tolerance and retributive discipline, this further reinforces the anonymous nature of a modern school, in which individual persons and their unique concerns, hopes, and identities are subsumed by instruments designed to control rather than to facilitate holistic interactions.

When security hardware becomes the sole defining characteristic of a school environment, prospects for welcoming and humanistic schools may fade. Simon (2007) argued that this is precisely what has happened, as "crime has become an axis around which to recast much of the form and substance of schools" (p. 209). When any institution has control and surveillance as its central role, it begins to take on the qualities of the penitentiary that are, to say the least, not welcoming to the tenants and the practice of humanism.

At this point, two observations are noteworthy. First, taken together, many of the prominent trends in contemporary education do not naturally promote learning environments that are welcoming and consistent with the principles of humanism but rather can promote places that students may hate to come to, resent, and fear. If a school wishes to become more welcoming and to promote humanism, it must take deliberate and positive steps to do so.

Second, nothing written here should be taken to imply that schools should not assess their curricula and their students' performances, that schools should not provide discipline and recognize that some students will invariably be suspended or expelled, or that schools do have a security interest that they must acknowledge and address. After all, students and staff must be provided with their basic needs, which (drawing upon Maslow, 1970) include safety needs as second only to those that are purely physiological.

However, there is reason to believe that welcoming schools that use an invitational model can aid in all of these measures, if given a chance to do so. The benefit of an invitational approach is that it is proactive, helping to address the issues that underlie concerns about school safety. A school that is caring and inviting may lead both to improved student performance and to greater school safety. The value that administrators, counselors, teachers, and even students trained in humanism can bring to an institution simply cannot be replaced with high-technology surveillance systems. Surely the two can coexist, aiming to satisfy the needs in Maslow's (1970) hierarchy and yielding the greatest benefit to students and to society.

HUMANISM, INVITATIONAL EDUCATION, AND SCHOOL VIOLENCE

There are several reasons humanistic educational practices, particularly as manifested through invitational education and the examples described previously, have the potential to reduce school violence. First among these is their ability to enhance social capital. As defined by Putnam (2000), "Social capital refers to connections among individuals—social networks and the norms of reciprocity and trustworthiness that arise from them" (p. 19).

The principles of invitational education can promote social capital, as illustrated by the following example of school administration:

> [The administrator] strategically invites everyone to pool knowledge for the benefit of the meeting and the school as a whole. The result is that there is an absence of empire-building and a great emphasis on a form of mutual appreciation that is manifest in the careful, courteous way in which individual reports are listened to and discussed. Such encounters lack rancour and exude goodwill. Consequently, they invite all those present to participate fully, thus adding to the school's stock of social capital. (Halpin, 2003, p. 84)

The significance of the link among humanism, invitational education, and social capital is this: Social capital is associated with lower levels of violence and "pugnacity," generally (Putnam, 2000, p. 310), and with lower levels of violence by adolescents, more particularly (Wright & Fitzpatrick, 2006). In their study of school violence, Laub and Lauritsen (1998) identified social capital as an element that, if strengthened, could promote safe schools.

Second, whereas zero-tolerance models are largely reactive approaches to violence and school disorder, humanistic and inviting schools may be able to foster more positive and proactive approaches. Rather than treating students as inmates in an institutionalized school, models of invitational education can create open dialogues and processes that allow students to work with school staff in the joint production of a safe and healthy learning environment. This positive result may be particularly apparent when invitational education is used in conjunction with other strategies, such as parent education and engaging pedagogies, as a comprehensive strategy aimed at violence reduction (Friedland, 1999).

Stanley et al. (2004) described how surveys and interactive group processes can assess a school's "Five Ps (people, places, policies, programs, and processes)" (p. 305) to appraise how welcoming they are and to identify areas of improvement that will lead to a better and safer environment for all constituents. The authors described the utility of this approach:

> [This concept can] help assess individual children and groups of children to determine factors in the school environment that may be contributing to disruptive, unhealthy, or self-defeating behavior. Counselors can develop programs that provide ideas about how students, parents, and school personnel can be more intentional in their interactions with each other and use more healthy ways of resolving conflict. When everyone in a school behaves in ways that communicate to others that each person in the school is significant, valuable, and responsible and is to be treated that way, schools will be safer and students will be more successful. (pp. 308–309)

This is a powerful statement in support of humanism's emphasis on the whole person and its efforts to focus on individual self-actualization, dignity, and empowerment. Valuing individuals in this way benefits the school, and potentially society as a whole.

RECOMMENDATIONS FOR BUILDING HUMANISTIC AND INVITING SCHOOLS

As suggested already, humanism and invitational education may represent a departure from traditional practice and current policy in many schools. However, their potential for addressing social problems of concern to the public argues in favor of adopting these innovative approaches. In fact, a report on preventing targeted violence in schools recommended that schools should foster "a culture of respect"; recognize emotional intelligence, meaning an understanding and awareness of one's own emotions and an empathy for the emotions of others (see also Goleman, 1995); and recognize that "connection through human relationships is a central component of a culture of safety and respect" (Fein et al., 2002, pp. 11–12).

A study on security technology in schools, after finding that entry control devices (ECDs) and duress alarms (DAs) were not perceived as effective solutions by school safety administrators, recommended the following: "If districts diverted funds from prohibitively expensive technologies such as intricate metal detection programs, complicated ECD systems, or inefficient DA systems, they could funnel resources into any number of programs and policies that would aid in the regeneration of the school community" (Garcia, 2003, p. 50). Accordingly, there is recognition that school violence prevention is about more than hardware, profiling, and control but rather can be strengthened by respectful and trusting communities as well.

What, then, can schools do to promote humanistic and invitational principles with the aim of reducing violent behaviors at school? A natural starting point is for schools to examine their current practices, with a particular focus on the problematic areas already highlighted. Several broad recommendations will be presented in the context of the following scenario. Assume that a school faces a problem with bullying against those whom Greene (1994) calls "America's 'designated victims' … a boy, usually slender, usually thoughtful, who would prefer creating beauty to crushing bones. Because they might enjoy gymnastics, fencing, acting, writing, or band practice rather than football practice, these boys are called 'faggots' and that's just for openers" (para. 3).

As noted earlier, this sort of name-calling and labeling can be devastating to the students against whom it is targeted, regardless of their sexual orientation (Pascoe, 2007). But what can be done to address this problem behavior, particularly if widespread at a school? The following steps—in which counselors can, and must, play a significant role—illustrate how schools can move toward an invitational approach, both generally and in the context of the scenario.

Assess the Current Climate at Each School

Before new policies can be implemented, school administrators and other personnel must have an honest and accurate understanding of the conditions at their school. This requires an assessment of the interactions between students and staff, the school building itself, school rules and policies, curriculum and cocurricular programs, and the broader school culture (Purkey & Novak, 2008). The processes described in Stanley et al. (2004) may serve as a good starting point; only after this initial baseline has been determined can change be meaningfully planned and evaluated.

For this scenario, school personnel must understand when and how often the problem behaviors are occurring. One question this begs is whether the school is inviting enough for students to even feel comfortable reporting their victimization. If not, why not, and what can be done about it? In either case, what do school rules specify about verbal bullying? Who is doing the bullying and who is being bullied? Are there any programs currently in place, and has their effectiveness been measured?

Of course, it is not enough to ask these questions only when a situation arises; rather, schools must engage in continuous assessment for the welfare of their students and staff. Without this information, it is difficult to shape a fully informed response to the problem.

Provide Opportunities for Schools to Share Their Approaches

There is no single way humanism and invitational education can be implemented. Schools may be creative in their approaches, working to meet their own needs, given their resources and their unique set of circumstances. But with this comes an obligation to share news about programs and their impacts (and coincident to that, an obligation to evaluate programs)—and schools and districts should reach out to one another and establish regular opportunities for doing so.

For this scenario, a counselor or school principal might, as a first step, contact neighboring jurisdictions to see if they have experienced similar bullying problems. If they have, what invitational approaches to the problems have proved effective? After implementing a response at the school, the building principal or counselor might then work to share the results, whether through a publication, presentation, or other means.

Fully Staff Counseling Positions and Empower Counselors to Foster Invitational Education Strategies

As mental health professionals, counselors are well prepared to play a primary role in the transformation of schools into invitational institutions. However, to do so, staffing must be sufficient to meet "routine" needs of the school as well as to promote invitational programming, and counselors must be full partners with teaching staff and administrators. While invitational education is a school-wide philosophy, it may also be useful to have a counselor to serve as a "point person" for the provision of invitational programming, for invitational assessment, and for maintaining accountability to the invitational paradigm.

For this scenario, counselors must be prepared to quickly take a leadership role, and they must be supported by the administration and the faculty in doing so. Upon becoming aware of the issue, counselors might coordinate some of the work from the first and second recommendations. Counselors are also well positioned to see the school as a whole unit, as well as appreciating the diversity within it, to instruct students and staff alike on how to best create an invitational environment that prevents bullying.

Train All School Personnel in Invitational Education and Support the Concept of Caring and, as Necessary, Authoritative (but Not Authoritarian) Approaches

Fortunately, there are many resources available to help staff, even reluctant staff, understand the invitational approach. Training in invitational education should be provided to teachers, counselors, school administrators, librarians, secretarial staff, support staff, maintenance personnel—and any other members of the school community. Many resources are available from the International Alliance for Invitational Education. But training by itself is insufficient. To succeed, an understanding of, and commitment to, the philosophy of invitational education is required—again, by all members of the school community. This is not a strategy that can be practiced piecemeal by only a few persons at an institution, nor is it one that can be given "lip service" without true commitment to the ideals and processes that underlie it.

For this scenario, all school staff should come together to take ownership of the issue. Drawing upon the expertise of the counselors, staff may be challenged to implement solutions, to mentor students, to care for students who are victimized and for those who engage in bullying behaviors, to model prosocial behavior, and even to change their own behaviors if they (even unintentionally) contribute to or facilitate the problem. These are difficult challenges, but staff must be willing to look both inward and outward to create safe learning spaces.

Humanism and Invitational Education Begin at Home

It is imperative that parents or guardians understand the importance of humanistic approaches to education. After all, education does not begin or end in the classroom. By enhancing the quality of children's lives at home, the hope is that they will better understand the importance of their actions, perceptions, and behavior, translating respect, trust, and care into a safer school environment.

For this scenario, counselors or other staff must be prepared to provide an outreach role. Because "bullying prevention is a community endeavor" (Kevorkian & D'Antona, 2008, p. 145), it is important for parents (and organizations, such as parent–teacher associations) to become involved in bullying prevention, particularly from an invitational perspective.

Similarly, educators must be aware that students' home lives have the potential to effect the success of invitational education in the classroom; both home and school need to be welcoming environments for learning to take place. This is consistent with Dewey's (1959) notion of education as life, which transcends schoolhouse walls.

Taken together, these recommendations can serve to infuse invitational perspectives into educational practice. Doing so may reap many benefits for a school, not the least of which is promoting a safe learning environment for students.

CONCLUSION

School violence is not a new phenomenon. Rather than a one-size-fits-all approach to preventing violence, the authors provided an alternative approach to minimizing school violence, through invitational education and humanistic perspectives. The goal is to create an inviting learning environment using cooperative learning, trust, and respect from all parties involved as a foundation for a satisfying, enriching, and safe learning environment (Purkey, 1999).

REFERENCES

Arcus, D. (2002). School shooting fatalities and school corporal punishment: A look at the states. *Aggressive Behavior, 28*, 173–183.

Arseneault, L., Bowes, L., & Shakoor, S. (2010). Bullying victimization in youths and mental health problems: 'Much ado about nothing'? *Psychological Medicine, 40*, 717–729.

Au, W. (2007). High-stakes testing and curricular control: A qualitative metasynthesis. *Educational Researcher, 36*, 258–267.

Bradshaw, C., Sawyer, A., & O'Brennan, L. (2007). Bullying and peer victimization at school: Perceptual differences between students and school staff. *School Psychology Review, 36*, 361–382.

Brown, J. R. (2008). What is bullying? *Journal of Adolescent Health*, 43, 101–102.

Cain, D. J. (2001). Defining characteristics, history, and evolution of humanistic psychotherapies. In D. J. Cain & J. Seeman (Eds.), *Humanistic psychotherapies: Handbook of research and practice* (pp. 3–54). Washington, DC: American Psychological Association.

Casella, R. (2010). Safety or social control? The security fortification of schools in a capitalist society. In T. Monahan & R. D. Torres (Eds.), *Schools under surveillance: Cultures of control in public education* (pp. 73–86). New Brunswick, NJ: Rutgers University Press.

Cornelius-White, J. (2007). Learner-centered teacher-student relationships are effective: A meta-analysis. *Review of Educational Research, 77*, 113–143.

Cullen, D. (2009). *Columbine*. New York: Twelve.

Dayton, J., & Dupre, A. (2004). School funding litigation: Who's winning the war? V*anderbilt Law Review, 57*, 2351–2413.

Dewey, J. (1959). My pedagogic creed. In M. S. Dworkin (Ed.), *Dewey on education* (pp. 19–32). New York: Columbia University Teachers College Bureau of Publications. (Original work published 1897.)

Dinkes, R., Kemp, J., Baum, K., & Snyder, T. D. (2009). *Indicators of school crime and safety: 2009*. Washington, DC: U.S. Department of Education and U.S. Department of Justice.

Duke, D. L. (1998). *Does it matter where our children learn?* White paper commissioned by the National Research Council of the National Academy of Sciences and the National Academy of Engineering. Retrieved from http://www.casenex.com/casenex/WhereOurChildrenLearn.pdf

Egley, R. (2003). Invitational leadership: Does it make a difference? *Journal of Invitational Theory and Practice, 9*, 57–70.

Fein, R. A., Vossekuil, B., Pollack, W. S., Borum, R., Modzeleski, W., & Reddy, M. (2002). *Threat assessment in schools: A guide to managing threatening situations and to creating safe school climates.* Washington, DC: U.S. Secret Service and U.S. Department of Education.

Ferguson, C. J., San Miguel, C., Kilburn, J. C., & Sanchez, P. (2007). The effectiveness of school-based anti-bullying programs: A meta-analytic review. *Criminal Justice Review, 32,* 401–414.

Finkelhor, D., Turner, H., Ormrod, R., & Hamby, S. L. (2010). Trends in childhood violence and abuse exposure: Evidence from 2 national surveys. *Archives of Pediatrics and Adolescent Medicine, 164,* 238–242.

Foucault, M. (1977). *Discipline and punish: The birth of the prison.* New York: Vintage Books.

Friedland, S. (1999, June). Violence reduction? Start with school culture. *School Administrator, 56,* 14–16.

Garcia, C. A. (2003). School safety technology in America: Current use and perceived effectiveness. *Criminal Justice Policy Review, 14,* 30–54.

Gastic, B. (2008). School truancy and the disciplinary problems of bullying victims. *Educational Review, 60,* 391–404.

Goleman, D. (1995). *Emotional intelligence* (10th anniversary ed.). New York: Bantam Books.

Greene, B. (1994, Winter). America's designated victims: Our creative young. *Alan Review, 21*(2). Retrieved from http://scholar.lib.vt.edu/ejournals/ALAN/winter94/Greene.html

Greenwald, R., Hedges, L. V., & Laine, R. D. (1996). The effect of school resources on student achievement. *Review of Educational Research, 66,* 361–396.

Gregory, A., & Cornell, D. (2009). "Tolerating" adolescent needs: Moving beyond zero tolerance policies in high school. *Theory Into Practice, 48,* 106–113.

Halpin, D. (2003). *Hope and education: The role of the utopian imagination.* New York: RoutledgeFalmer.

Hoover, N. C., & Pollard, N. J. (2000). *Initiation rites in American high schools: A national survey.* Retrieved from Alfred University, http://www.alfred.edu/hs_hazing/docs/hazing__study.pdf

Horne, A. M., Orpinas, P., Newman-Carlson, D., & Bartolomucci, C. L. (2004). Elementary school Bully Busters program: Understanding why children bully and what to do about it. In D. L. Espelage & S. M. Swearer (Eds.), *Bullying in American schools: A social-ecological perspective on prevention and intervention* (pp. 297–325). Mahwah, NJ: Lawrence Erlbaum Associates.

Juster, F. T., Ono, H., & Stafford, F. P. (2004). *Changing times of American youth: 1981–2003.* Ann Arbor: University of Michigan Institute for Social Research.

Kalec, A. W. (2004). Invitational education at Cooper Elementary. *Journal of Invitational Theory and Practice, 10,* 73–81.

Kevorkian, M., & D'Antona, R. (2008). *101 facts about bullying: What everyone should know.* New York: Rowman and Littlefield Education.

Kozol, J. (1991). *Savage inequalities: Children in America's schools.* New York: HarperPerennial.

Laub, J. H., & Lauritsen, J. L. (1998). The interdependence of school violence with neighborhood and family conditions. In D. S. Elliott, B. A. Hamburg, & K. R. Williams (Eds.), *Violence in American schools* (pp. 127–155). New York: Cambridge University Press.

Lemert, E. M. (1972). *Human deviance, social problems, and social control* (2nd ed.). Englewood Cliffs, NJ: Prentice Hall.

MacGillivary, H., Medal, M., & Drake, C. (2008). Zero tolerance policies: A precarious balance between school safety and educational opportunity for all. In K. G. Welner & W. C. Chi (Eds.), *Current issues in educational policy and the law* (pp. 191–217). Charlotte, NC: IAP – Information Age Publishing.

Maslow, A. H. (1970). *Motivation and personality* (2nd ed.). New York: Harper and Row.

Merrell, K. W., Gueldner, B. A., Ross, S. W., & Isava, D. M. (2008). How effective are school bullying intervention programs? A meta-analysis of intervention research. *School Psychology Quarterly, 23*, 26–42.

Muschert, G. W. (2007). Research in school shootings. *Sociology Compass, 1*, 60–80.

National School Safety Center. (2009, August 21). *The National School Safety Center's report on school associated violent deaths.* Retrieved from National School Safety Center, http://www.schoolsafety.us/School-Associated-Violent-Deaths-p-6.html

Newman, O. (1996). *Creating defensible space.* Washington, DC: U.S. Department of Housing and Urban Development. Retrieved from http://www.huduser.org/publications/pdf/def.pdf

Nichols, S. L., & Berliner, D. C. (2007). *Collateral damage: How high-stakes testing corrupts America's schools.* Cambridge, MA: Harvard Education Press.

Ontario Secondary School Teachers' Federation. (2005). Bullying in the workplace survey, April 2005. Retrieved from http://www.osstf.on.ca/Default.aspx?DN=5af56939-6367-4ab4-a45d-a482373463d5

Owen, S. S., Burke, T. W., & Vichesky, D. (2008). Hazing in student organizations: Prevalence, attitudes, and solutions. *Oracle: The Research Journal of the Association of Fraternity Advisors, 3*, 40–58.

Owen, S. S., & Wagner, K. (2006). Explaining school corporal punishment: Evangelical Protestantism and social capital in a path model. *Social Justice Research, 19*, 471–499.

Pascoe, C. J. (2007). *Dude, you're a fag: Masculinity and sexuality in high school.* Berkeley: University of California Press.

Payne, A. A., Gottfredson, D. C., & Gottfredson, G. D. (2003). Schools as communities: The relationships among communal school organization, student bonding, and school disorder. *Criminology, 41*, 749–777.

Pepinsky, H. (1999). Peacemaking primer. In B. A. Arrigo (Ed.), *Social justice, criminal justice: The maturation of critical theory in law, crime, and deviance* (pp. 52–70). Belmont, CA: West/Wadsworth.

Purkey, W. W. (1999). Creating safe schools through invitational education. *ERIC Digest.* Retrieved from ERIC: http://www.eric.ed.gov/ERICDocs/data/ericdocs2sql/content_storage_01/0000019b/80/15/f3/fa.pdf

Purkey, W. W., & Novak, J. M. (2008). *Fundamentals of invitational education.* Kennesaw, GA: International Alliance for Invitational Education.

Purkey, W. W., & Siegel, B. L. (2003). *Becoming an invitational leader: A new approach to professional and personal success.* Atlanta, GA: Humanics Trade Group.

Putnam, R. D. (2000). *Bowling alone: The collapse and revival of American community.* New York: Simon & Schuster.

Riner, P. S. (2003). The intimate correlation of invitational education and effective classroom management. *Journal of Invitational Theory and Practice, 9*, 41–55.

Schellenberg, R. C., Parks-Savage, A., & Rehfuss, M. (2007). Reducing levels of elementary school violence with peer mediation. *Professional School Counseling, 10*, 475–481.

Schmidt, J. J. (1997). Invitational counselling: An expanded framework for comprehensive school counselling programs. *Canadian Journal of Counselling, 31*, 6–17.

Simmons, L. (2010). The docile body in school space. In T. Monahan & R. D. Torres (Eds.), *Schools under surveillance: Cultures of control in public education* (pp. 55–70). New Brunswick, NJ: Rutgers University Press.

Simon, J. (2007). *Governing through crime: How the war on crime transformed American democracy and created a culture of fear.* New York: Oxford University Press.

Skiba, R., & Peterson, R. (1999, January). The dark side of zero tolerance: Can punishment lead to safe schools? *Phi Delta Kappan, 80*, 372–382.

Stanley, P. H., Juhnke, G. A., & Purkey, W. W. (2004). Using an invitational theory of practice to create safe and successful schools. *Journal of Counseling and Development, 82,* 302–309.

Suvall, C. (2009). Restorative justice in schools: Learning from Jena High School. *Harvard Civil Rights—Civil Liberties Law Review, 44,* 547–569.

Twemlow, S. W., & Fonagy, P. (2005). The prevalence of teachers who bully students in schools with differing levels of behavioral problems. *American Journal of Psychiatry, 162,* 2387–2389.

Twemlow, S. W., Fonagy, P., Sacco, F. C., & Brethour, J. R. (2006). Teachers who bully students: A hidden trauma. *International Journal of Social Psychiatry, 52,* 187–198.

Vossekuil, B., Fein, R. A., Reddy, M., Borum, R., & Modzeleski, W. (2002). *The final report and findings of the safe school initiative: Implications for the prevention of school attacks in the United States.* Washington, DC: U.S. Secret Service and U.S. Department of Education.

Welsh, W. N., Greene, J. R., & Jenkins, P. H. (1999). School disorder: The influence of individual, institutional, and community factors. *Criminology, 37,* 73–115.

Wenzel, M., Okimoto, T. G., Feather, N. T., & Platow, M. J. (2008). Retributive and restorative justice. *Law and Human Behavior, 32,* 375–389.

Wilson, J. Q., & Kelling, G. L. (1982, March). Broken windows: The police and neighborhood safety. *Atlantic Monthly,* 29–38.

Wright, D. R., & Fitzpatrick, K. M. (2006). Social capital and adolescent violent behavior: Correlates of fighting and weapon use among secondary school students. *Social Forces, 84,* 1435–1453.

9

Ecohumanism
Integrating Humanism and Resilience Theory

ROLLA E. LEWIS

In this chapter I will review humanism and the resilience construct and demonstrate ways ecohumanism provides a theoretical and practical integration of these perspectives. Ecohumanism connects the resilience construct to humanistic counseling by linking the systems perspective inherent in the resilience literature with humanistic counseling's concern for individual self-actualization. In this chapter, ecohumanism is defined as a way of viewing human beings as embedded in chronological, social, and biological contexts where they develop in time, as social beings, and as part of the natural world. Each of us is born at a unique historic moment characterized by distinctive cultural connections within any variety of biological and social ecologies.

Broadly speaking, resilience is the human capacity to spring back from risk posed by adversity and ability to take actions to navigate satisfying life trajectories. As a counseling construct, resilience is celebrated because research reveals that many individuals who seem to have the deck stacked against them are able to overcome the odds and build satisfying lives for themselves and their families (Werner, 1996; Werner & Smith, 1977, 1982, 1992, 2001). Although there is widespread acceptance of the resilience construct as useful for informing counseling (Benard & Slade, 2009; Lewis, 2007), there is a perennial nature–nurture debate as to whether resilience results from something innate in individuals, something in the environment, or some combination of both (Benard, 2004; Luthar, 2006; Masten, 2001, 2007; Masten & Coatsworth, 1998; Masten, Cutuli, Herbers, & Reed, 2009; Siegel, 2010). Rather than getting bogged down in those debates, this chapter builds upon the most important insight from the diverse literature concerning resilience—that relationship and the relational environment matter most in the lives of people, especially youth at risk. Consistent with humanism, relationship is the most important protective system for fostering human resilience

(Masten et al., 2009). Put simply and concretely, a relationship with one caring, empathic adult makes all the difference in the world for most people, especially for youth. Put in another way, after getting knocked down or falling down, it is easier to get up if an empathic person is there lending a hand to help pull you up to your feet. That empathic person with the helping hand is fostering resilience. Although a counselor might be the empathic person giving the helping hand, it is important to note that counselors can also point the person on the ground to other people or *things* that also might help them get to their feet and moving on with their lives. The construct of resilience and humanistic counseling are both informed by a deep understanding of the important role relationships and the relational environment play for most people who successfully create satisfying lives for themselves (e.g., Cain, 2001; Hansen, 2010; Rogers, 1957, 1961, 1969, 1980).

Humanistic counselors and resilience advocates have similar foundations in fostering empathic and authentic relationships, and both are in alignment believing in the potential in others, encouraging choice, fostering growth, recognizing the importance of feeling, human creativity, wholeness, and the purposive nature of being a person (Benard, 2004; Maslow, 1962, 1970; Raskin & Rogers, 1989; Raskin, Rogers, & Witty, 2008; Rogers, 1957, 1980; Werner & Smith, 1992, 2001). However, because humanistic discourse is so embedded in the cultural lexicon, the connections between humanistic and resilience constructs are not always made explicit by resilience researchers. Ways of talking about and seeing the world can become so rooted in everyday cultural discourses that we forget the origins of the ideas that gave rise to certain conversational practices (Lakoff & Johnson, 1999; McWhorter, 2001). This chapter makes some of those connections more explicit by integrating humanism and resilience theory into an ecohumanistic perspective by drawing upon the wisdom of Carl Rogers, who viewed all of humanity as part of a cultural world where life flows and life changes. He put his understanding of life's continual change this way: *"Life, at its best, is a flowing, changing process in which nothing is fixed"* (Rogers, 1961, p. 27, italics in original). Even humanistic theory is not fixed; it is evolving (Scholl, 2008). Integrating these two approaches into ecohumanism helps both humanistic counselors and resilience advocates align their moral obligation to take action in fostering more just and caring communities.

Before the ecohumanistic integration of humanistic theory and resilience theory is highlighted in this chapter, the key differences between humanistic theory and resilience theory are briefly recognized and discussed. The key differences between humanistic theory and resilience theory are humanistic counseling theory's emphasis on the individual subjective experiences and resilience theory's stress upon placing the individual within environmental contexts. In stepping beyond these key differences, three points should be made about humanistic theory, resilience theory, and possibilities drawing upon both in practice.

First, as important as individual experiences are, humanistic theorists and practitioners view the individual and define some key humanistic constructs, such as congruence, empathy, and holism from different points of view. Some humanistic theorists call for expanding the notion of the individual by connecting the person to the environment through broadening and redefining key constructs like congruence and empathy. Cornelius-White (2007), for instance, redefines congruence as the "internal, relational and ecological integration of persons" (p. 168), and Hedges (2010) extends empathy to include "understanding the broader contexts" in the clients' lives, including their "communication networks, patterns, relationships" (p. 123). Noe (2009) expands the holistic notion of human irreducibility by saying consciousness or individual awareness is the product of three interdependent factors: mind, body, and the environment. Individuals are not apart from the world and stuck alone in their heads: Their bodies and environment make them who they are. Mind, body, and environment cannot be separated when taking individuals into account. These theorists claim that overemphasis on the interior life of the individual cuts off individuals from experiencing life as interconnected and interdependent beings existing in social and biological communities (Conn, 1998; Kuhn, 2001). Pilisuk (2001) even asserts that overemphasis on the individual promotes isolation and leads to individuals defining themselves by what they consume. Notions of what constitutes being an individual are being transformed.

Second, resilience researchers and humanists differ on matters of subjective feeling but are aligned in terms of the value of personal meaning. Resilience researchers "strongly emphasize overt behavioral success" as assessed by others, such as "teachers, classmates, friends, parents, and others" (Luthar, 2006, p. 753). Subjective feelings are not explored because resilience researchers like Luthar ask teachers, classmates, friends, parents, and others to assess the subjects' behaviors to obtain their data. At the same time, focus groups and other approaches have been used to explore how students feel about their school experience and the degree to which they experience care and support in their environments (Benard & Slade, 2009). Resilience theory's recognition that the transactional environment plays a powerful role in the lives of individuals does not displace the positive impact that individuals' own search for meaning might have on their lives over their life span (Benard, 2004). Thus, although resilience researchers underplay subjective feelings in assessing behavior, they do see a vital need to facilitate individuals' search for meaning.

Third, both resilience and humanistic theory assert that there is an innate capacity and desire for humans to grow and to develop. Resilience is an innate capacity that is bolstered by supportive environmental factors, such as caring and supportive parents (Benard, 2004). Innate capacity is akin to Maslow's (1970) notion of self-actualization. Resilience theory's recognition of the need for supportive environments is the simple affirmation that individuals exist in ecological contexts and relational environments can range from very supportive to not supportive at all.

WEAVING THE RESILIENCE AND HUMANISTIC LITERATURE INTO AN ECOHUMANISM

Consistent with humanism, resilience in youth can be defined as a dynamic developmental process of healthy human development growing out of nurturing relationships that support social, academic, and vocational competence in spite of adversity and environmental challenges. Although there are key differences, resilience and humanistic literature have constructs that are similar and easily woven together. This section discusses relationship, self-actualizing, self-righting, constructing meaning, the dignity of every human being, and humanistic links to resilience traits and protective factors. Other constructs could be explored, but these were selected to spotlight some commonalities between resilience and humanist theory.

Relationship

Both humanistic counselors and resilience researchers view relationships as vital to promoting positive development. Rogers (1980) viewed three elements as crucial to helping relationships: (1) genuineness, realness, or congruence; (2) acceptance and caring; and (3) empathic understanding. Resilience theorists view relationship differently because resilience is understood as existing in trans-actional and interactive contexts that can be challenging for any relationship. Youth may have solid mentoring relationships with caring adults, but those relationships do not take them out of the dysfunctional school they attend or drug-infested neighborhood where they live. As such, relationships are considered in broader socially constructed and ecologically embedded contexts where poverty, racism, and injustice are rooted. Having a relationship with a caring adult can enhance resilience, but such relationships do not eliminate risk (Werner & Smith, 2001). Still, having a supportive and caring relationship in any environment helps immensely, and key research points out that the ability to spring back from adversity emerges when environmental supports, such as positive relationships with parents, teachers, and other adults, are present (Benard, 2004; Deater-Deckard, Ivy, & Smith, 2006; Kaplan, 2006; Luthar, Cicchetti, & Becker, 2000a, 2000b; Masten, 2001, 2007; Masten & Coatsworth, 1998; Masten et al., 2009; Ungar, 2004, 2005; Werner, 1989, 1996, 2006; Werner & Smith, 1982, 1992, 2001; Wright & Masten, 2006). Thus, positive relationships are vital. Werner and Smith (1992) concluded that the life stories of the members in their cohort show helpers that "competence, confidence, and caring can flourish, even under adverse circumstances, if children encounter persons who provide them with the secure basis for the development of trust, autonomy, and initiative" (p. 209). Relationships are foundational in helping others. Resilience theorists and humanists both agree that if we expect competence, confidence, and caring to flourish, relationships must be cultivated. With resilience, however, helpers are challenged to foster positive relationships in systems, such as schools, and other environments, such as family and neighborhoods, wherever possible. Benard (1997) states, "Personality and individual outcomes are the result of a transactional process between self, agency, and environmental influences" (p. 69). To be successful, prevention interventions promoting resilience focus on enhancing and creating positive relationships in families, schools, and communities.

Self-Actualizing and Self-Righting

Resilience theorists recognize the self-righting capacity for individuals to spring back from exposure to adversity and other environmental stressors, especially when caring and support are present (Lewis, 2007; Luthar et al., 2000a, 2000b). This dynamic and self-righting capacity does not occur in a social vacuum, may emerge at different developmental stages, and frequently entails having a caring teacher or an adult mentor available for youth (Benard, 2004; Werner & Smith, 2001). Werner and her colleagues concluded that resilience is the natural human capacity for self-righting (Werner, 1996, 2006; Werner & Smith, 1982, 1992, 2001). People are active, self-righting organisms continuously adapting to their environment (Werner & Smith, 1992). In other words, consistent with humanistic theory, human beings have an imperative for growth and development. Furthermore, most delinquent youth turn their lives around in positive ways at some point in time when they are helped by caring and supportive allies (Werner, 1996, 2006; Werner & Smith, 1992, 2001).

Consistent with Rogers's (1980) humanistic understanding that life is an active process directed toward development and Maslow's (1970) understanding of the human push toward self-actualization, Masten (2001) asserted that "resilience does not come from rare and special qualities, but from the everyday magic of the ordinary, normative human resources in the minds, brains, and bodies of children, in their families and relationships, and in their communities" (p. 235). Resilience is the "power of the ordinary" (p. 235). Individuals who are aware of their own resilience become more resilient (Smith, Tooley, Christopher, & Kay, 2010). Both resilience researchers and humanistic counselors believe that to be human is to continually learn and develop. Benard (2004) asserted the radical, and I would say humanistic, notion that "resilience is a capacity all youth have for healthy development and successful learning" (p. 4). Resilience advocates and humanistic counselors believe that those they are helping can change in positive ways.

Constructing Meaning

Both resilience theorists and humanists assert that people actively and intentionally construct meaning in their lives. Interventions fostering resilience shift to creating healthy systems that invite youth to connect with caring adults and encourage youth to take action by participating in meaningful activities that contribute to their schools and communities (Benard & Slade, 2009). Self-efficacy "is strongly influenced by the degree to which adults encourage or hinder" youth's efforts to have some impact upon their environment (Luthar, 2006, p. 776). Like Rogers (1969, 1980), resilience advocates recognize the vital role youth have in taking action to demonstrate social competence, problem-solving skills, their own autonomy, and developing a sense of purpose and belief in a hopeful future (Benard, 2004). Youth have to be invited into active roles in their families, schools, and communities (Masten & Coatsworth, 1998; Masten et al., 2009; Ungar, 2004; Wright & Masten, 2006). Key longitudinal resilience research has demonstrated that youth become self-righting when they are provided with structures and opportunities that foster positive development for themselves, their peers, and their community (Werner & Smith, 1992, 2001). Thus, opportunities for contribution help youth to find meaning and to enhance their self-righting and self-actualizing tendencies. In the Werner and Smith (1992) study, youth who overcame the odds and became self-righting "began to perceive themselves as movers of their destiny rather than as pawns in a power game played by outsiders" (p. 21).

Dignity of Every Human Being

Both resilience theorists and humanistic counselors believe in the dignity of every human being, even those who have been having a rough time in life. People can and do change. The vast majority of delinquent youth in the Werner and Smith studies did not become adult career criminals (Werner, 1996, 2006; Werner & Smith, 1992, 2001). The majority of chronic criminals from the study cohort consisted of a small group who had averaged four or more arrests before becoming 18 years old. Those who did become persistent offenders needed remedial educational help (usually reading) prior to age 10, were considered troublemakers by their fifth-grade teachers and parents, and had grown up in homes where significant caregivers were absent for extended periods of time during adolescence (Werner & Smith, 1992). Werner and Smith found youth were "not predestined" to criminality, broken homes, or mental illness, and that at "each developmental stage" there are opportunities to tap competencies and to overcome the negative impact of adverse and challenging experiences (p. 171). With adequate support, most youth tap into their self-righting tendencies and move toward normal adult development. Youth and adults who turned their lives around later in life did so after finding partners who had high expectations for them, cared for them, and connected them to a spiritual path or community that helped them appreciate a larger sense of meaning in their lives (Werner & Smith, 2001). Werner and Smith (Werner, 1996, 2006; Werner & Smith, 1992, 2001) and the resilience literature provide humanistic counselors with support for believing in the dignity of every human being and for advocating for youth by creating opportunities for them to develop competence, confidence, ability to care for others, and opportunities to participate in meaningful activities.

Connecting Resilience Traits and Protective Factors to Humanism

Benard (2004) describes social competence, problem solving, autonomy, and sense of purpose as resilience traits. The resilience trait of *social competence* (responsiveness, flexibility, empathy and caring, communication skills, and a sense of humor) aligns with the humanistic counseling emphasis on empathy and the enhancement of each individual's experience. The *problem-solving skills* trait (thinking abstractly and reflectively, planning skills, and flexibility) links to the humanistic concern for people's freedom, rights, and ability to choose. The *autonomy* trait (internal locus of control, sense of power, self-discipline, and adaptive distancing) can be connected to individuals as self-actualizing and the notion that each person has dignity. Benard's (2004) *sense of purpose and future* trait (healthy expectations, goal directedness, success orientation, educational aspirations, persistence, hopefulness, hardiness, belief in bright or compelling future, and a sense of coherence or meaning) links directly to the humanistic concern with a sense of purpose, which is understood as the primary influence on human behavior because individuals actively and intentionally construct meaning in their lives.

Additionally, protective factors, those environmental characteristics that support positive youth development defined by resilience advocates, align with humanistic constructs. Benard (2004) described the three key protective factors as caring relationships, high expectations, and opportunities to participate and contribute in a meaningful manner. The protective factors are connected to humanistic constructs below. The *caring relationships* protective factor (having a connection with at least one caring person) is the single most important factor in fostering resilience in youth. Relationships noted for stable care, affection, attention, intergenerational social networks, and a basic sense of trust foster climates of care and support. Caring relationships are conceptually similar to the humanistic assumption that empathy is necessary for individual development, promoting tolerance, appreciating diversity, and advocating for human rights (Cain, 2001). The *high expectations* protective factor implies that adults see strengths and assets more than problems and deficits and recognize each youth's potential for maturity, responsibility, self-discipline, and common sense. Adults foster resilience for children who are at risk by providing structure, order, clear expectations, and honoring cultural traditions, as well as by promoting social and academic excellence. Competence becomes a form of adaptation for youth at risk (Luthar, 2006). For humanists, individuals are viewed as self-actualizing, which is tied to competence, creativity, and a desire to be engaged fully in living (Maslow, 1970). The *opportunities to participate and contribute* protective factor is understood as growing naturally from relationships based on caring and high expectations (Benard, 2004). Participation connects youth to other people, interests, and their valuing life itself. The essence of meaningful participation emerges when participants have socially and economically useful tasks, responsibility for decision making, planning, and a valued sense that they are helping others. This protective factor links to a number of humanistic constructs, beginning with the view that counseling is based on good relationships, and people have the freedom, right, and ability to choose their goals and how to achieve them. Active participation and contribution also connects to the belief that individuals construct meaning in their lives.

TOWARD AN ECOHUMANISM

Ecohumanism provides a way to connect the systemic and ecological foundation inherent in resilience theory with the expanding notion of the self in humanistic theory. This section develops the ecohumanism construct and draws upon theorists and practitioners who have expanded humanistic counseling's scope to include human and biological environmental concerns (e.g., Cahalan, 1995; Conn, 1998; Cornelius-White, 2007; Kuhn, 2001; Pilisuk, 2001; Swanson, 1995; Tapp, 2002). By expanding the notion of the systems humans participate in, ecohumanism integrates Bronfenbrenner's (1979) nested ecology of human development to include both culture and biological systems. Bronfenbrenner's (1979) social ecology is extended to include Davis's (2007) cultural construct that humans are nested in an ethnosphere and the biological reality that all human culture is nested in an ecosphere (Bender, 2003; Capra, 1996, 2002; see Table 9.1).

Individuals are larger than the thoughts rolling around inside their heads; they are embedded in linguistic communities that give them language and biological and social communities that expose (or insulate them from) the physical and social environments that shape their lives. Humans exist simultaneously in multiple systems (Bronfenbrenner, 1979), making it possible to expand the relational environment between and among people to include the human relationship with the physical environment—how humans are connected to the rocks, soils, water, and air on which all life on Earth depends. We have shared-life relationships with the myriad species of flora and fauna found in the ecosphere.

Ecohumanism links the systems perspective inherent in the resilience literature with humanistic counseling's concern for individual self-actualization. Individuals are placed firmly in the natural life-world humans are part of, and counselors work to develop growth-enhancing pathways for those they are helping. Ecohumanists recognize that they exist in a culture that puts all youth at risk, both in terms of their social relationships and in terms of human survival in the natural, living environment.

Table 9.1   An Ecological Model (School Counselors)

Ecological Level	Program Development Examples
Ecosphere (e.g., life systems, bioregions)	Understanding world as living system; projects related to understanding, for example, global warming
	Recognizing that ecological disasters cause demographic shifts; relief efforts for disaster area (e.g., New Orleans, Haiti, Japan)
Ethnosphere (e.g., diverse cultures; language, values, national boundaries, gender roles)	Understanding diverse human cultures throughout the world; making new immigrants welcome at school
	Understanding how students who are fleeing from conflict may require special culturally sensitive programs and additional support
Macrosystem (e.g., national identity, international agreements, socioeconomic status, national wealth, national resources, war)	Identify, for example, community, culture, gender roles, media, and peers on influences on current program and practices
	Understanding how international agreements, cooperation impact students' lives, especially new immigrants
	Understanding and helping students impacted by parents, family, relatives, and friends serving in the armed forces
Exosystem (e.g., public policy)	Identify ecological influences of education and school policies on, for example, counseling program and counselors' role
	Review school counseling licensing and credentialing rules, state policies, and state rules and laws related to school counseling
	Facilitate stakeholders working together to define comprehensive school counseling program within district
	State funding for edible garden projects
Mesosystem (e.g., relationships among microsystems)	Facilitate school counseling program's connections with community resources and other schools with programs via asset mapping
	Include parents, families, teachers, administrators, and community members in school counseling program advisory
	Identify and consider mesosystemic relationships and influences
	Network of edible garden projects in region
Microsystem (e.g., family, friends, school, church, team, work)	Facilitate students' awareness and identification of ecological factors impacting school success
	Facilitate students in identifying one adult mentor or success coach
	Develop edible garden project at school
Individual (e.g., gender, cognitive factors, biological factors)	Facilitate students' awareness of learn to live, learn to learn, learn to work, and learn to contribute
	Facilitate students' abilities to define school success and set goals to achieve it
	Facilitate students' abilities to identify personal strengths and attributes related to school success
	Learning about cooperation, biology, and cooking by participating in edible garden project at school

Soure: Lewis, R. E., California State University, unpublished manuscript, 2010. Used with permission.

Ecohumanists are characterized as integrating and using constructs, such as the importance of relationship, from ecological theory resilience research and practice, and from humanistic counseling. Thus, ecohumanism is a construct that points to the diversity within and appreciation of the range of human experience in this world. Taking concepts from both resilience advocates and humanistic counselors, ecohumanists assert 10 key points:

1. Humans are holistic and members of social and biological communities (e.g., Capra, 1996, 2002). Holism aligns with humanistic counseling and resilience constructs. Counselors are curious about family, home, community, and how the client cares for their body.
2. Individuals exist in and live up to their greatest potential in social and ecological contexts embedded in languages, cultures, and physical environments that they are born into (e.g., Bowers, 1997, 2000, 2001; Lakoff & Johnson, 1999; McWhorter, 2001). This connects humanism's self-actualizing view of the individual with the promotion of tolerance, diversity, and human rights. This also links to the self-righting nature of people described in the resilience literature. Ecohumanistic counselors use curiosity and mindful wonderment in exploring how clients were able to overcome difficulties (Lewis, Lenski, Mukhopadhyay, & Cartwright, 2010). They use narrative ideas to find new possibilities for living (Winslade & Monk, 2007). What worked to help them to learn, grow, or change? What stories have been told or not told?
3. Individuals and communities depend on mutually empathic relationships, and individuals are responsible for understanding the value of diverse cultures and life communities (e.g., promoting tolerance, appreciating differences, resisting forms of sexisim, ecoracism, and sustaining ecologically complex life systems) (see, e.g., Comstock et al., 2008; Bowers, 2001, 2003; Capra, 1996, 2002; Glave, 2010; Siegel, 2010). This aligns with important resilience research, like Werner and Smith (1992) and Luthar (2006) who highlight relationships with caring mentors. This extends the humanistic notion of relationship to include helpers, individuals, communities, and life communities. Counselors explore ways to expand the contact that helpees have with different groups, as well as if helpees see nature as a force to be fought and overcome or a system that sustains life.
4. Individuals are encouraged to live up to their greatest potential. Individuals and communities also are encouraged to recognize how they are responsible for knowing there are usually limited options or choices within their cultural and physical environment; for example, their local market may carry only apples and oranges (that does not mean bananas and passion fruit do not exist) or their water supply cannot sustain

salmon fisheries and cotton farming (e.g., Bowers, 2001; Davis, 2007; Stone, 2009). This connects humanistic self-actualization and choice to ecological limitations and consequences. It also concerns systems and systems change advocated by resilience practitioners. Counselors in this example develop asset maps to determine how best to collaborate with and to tap into community resources (Griffin & Farris, 2010).

5. Relationship and empathy enhances life between and among people but also between and among things within the ecological community, such as sacred mountains and special pets (e.g., Burns, 1998; Milton, 2002; Naess, 2002; Stone, 2009). Caring relationships deepen empathy and the capacity to look at ways to help others and the more than the human world. Counselors expand their use of empathy and relationship to talk about, for example, helpees' special natural areas, care for animals, and gardening.

6. There is worth in the living creatures and ecosystems that sustain them (e.g., Capra, 1996, 2002; Naess, 2002). This extends the humanistic notion of the promotion of tolerance, diversity, and human rights to include other living creatures and the natural environment. For example, counselors in areas like the Gulf Coast explore the impact the oil spill had upon the lives of fishermen. While after the Japan disaster, counselors might find clients exploring disaster preparation and the impact of building nuclear reactors upon public policy, safety, and their own ecological well-being.

7. To be human is to be learning and to have responsibility for taking action by promoting, for example, intergenerational learning and social or ecojustice (e.g., Atkinson & Claxton, 2000; Bowers, 2001, 2003; Capra, 2002; Dweck, 2006; Glave, 2010; Stone, 2009). This view of learning extends the humanistic notion of growth to include more specific reference to elders and honoring the natural environment. Counselors attempt to link clients with elders from their families or communities.

8. Live life creatively in the here and now by loving it, pouring oneself over it, and passing into a "solar ethics" where living life becomes an expressive art (Cupitt, 1995). This affirms the humanistic embrace of creativity and the lived-moment as vital and powerful forces in the lives of people. We are our own artistic projects. Counselors use interventions that explore personal and group creativity, such as poetry, painting, and drama.

9. Take full account of the biological and social context (environment) in moral decision making where choices are informed by situational and ecological ethics (Bowers, 2001, 2003; Capra, 1996, 2002; Fletcher, 1966; Leopold, 1949; Naess, 2002). This position recognizes the humanistic understanding of the importance of choice and affirms ethical consequences. Counselors help clients wrestle with moral decision making, such as continuing to hunt and fish for species that are in serious decline.

10. Act upon what is known; test and evaluate actions for workability and assess if actions bring about more ecological concordance, sustainability, and human wisdom (Bowers, 2001; Capra, 1996, 2002; Conyne & Cook, 2004; Dewey, 1929; Naess, 2002; Stone, 2009). This affirms the humanistic understanding that the active and intentional construction of meaning is best done by a scientific method tempered by wisdom. Counselors use feedback systems, such as the Session Rating Scale (SRS) and the Outcome Rating Scale (ORS), to ask clients to assess the quality of the counseling relationship (Duncan, Miller, & Sparks, 2004).

From Humanism to Ecohumanism

Toward the end of his life Maslow (1968) asserted a need for a "transpersonal, transhuman [psychology], centered in the cosmos rather than in human needs and interest, going beyond humanness" (p. iv). Although he talked about "transcendent" and "transpersonal," Maslow's (1968) key assertion was, "We need something 'bigger than we are' to be awed by and to commit ourselves to in a new, naturalistic, empirical, non-churchly sense" (p. iv). Sutich (1968) described how a number of other terms, like *transhumanistic* and *transhuman psychology*, were described in the dialogues leading up to the use of transpersonal. Ecohumanism might fulfill Maslow's vision because it is naturalistic, empirical, and very much in this world. As a term, *transpersonal* has Neo-Platonic and other-worldly implications that seem to take people outside of or beyond this world where we live our day-to-day lives. Ecohumanism is offered up as a this-worldly construct that contextualizes the human experience as nested in multiple layers of our ecological being, located as we are in language, cultural, and biotic communities. Ecohumanism is defined as a way of viewing human beings as embedded in chronological, social, and biological ecological contexts where they develop in time, as social beings, and as part of the natural world.

The prefix *eco* (from Greek *oikos*, house) and humanism are joined to express that humans are not isolated monads, socially or ecologically. People are not separate from their physical environment; they are not separate from history, language, or the ecosystem (Bateson, 1979; Bender, 2003). Humans are participants in a social ecology surrounding them and producing them and their culture, traditions, and material products. People are born into cultures and languages; individuals are never separate from their cultural or biological contexts, and their freedom to actively choose is shaped by the time and environment where they find themselves embodied in consciousness and culture (Lakoff & Johnson, 1999; Noe, 2009). Ecohumanists take responsibility for being part of and in this world. They see attempts to move humans to think or pretend that they are not part of this world as keeping humans separate from being fully in the world that sustains them. The term eco extends the notion of "house" to mean the entire planet.

Ecohumanism is an affirmation that there is something special and distinctive about the human animal connected to their creativity, language, culture, and passionate desire to explore the lived-experience inherent in their existence (Tapp, 2002). In terms of fostering resilience and being guided by humanistic counseling constructs, ecohumanists look for ways to tie caring, empathy, creativity, holism, sense of purpose, and subjective experience to more dynamic relationships with the social and natural environment. For instance, asking a group of children to wonder about how a bear thinks and asking them to imitate how a bear walks would be ways to deepen their relationship, understanding, and empathy for the world of bears.

Ecohumanists recognize that the land itself can be said to have a language of its own—a language and story embedded in the earth. Ecosystems express an immanent and connected knowledge, growing, changing, evolving, and dying according to the available resources (Bateson, 1979). Geologists, naturalists, and other scientists set out to read and create comprehensive narratives about the world. These scientists give voice to the rocks, trees, and relationships among animals. Their efforts bring about change in the scientific narrative and human practices as new insights and understandings emerge. This expression has much in common with Native American language systems and cultures where humans and animals were integrated in similar, spiritual-physical worlds, where language, culture, spirituality, and Earth are tightly connected (Bowers, 1997, 2000, 2001, 2003).

Philosophically, humanism is anthropocentric, hence possibly at odds with living harmoniously within the biosphere due to human failure to empathize with biotic communities or develop an ethical understanding that humans are part of the biotic communities that sustain them (Leopold, 1949). Any humanism that asserts people can have no other understanding than human understanding sets up conditions where it is more difficult for humans to try to empathize with other living beings, rivers, and oceans. The 2010 Gulf of Mexico oil disaster, for example, sheds light on a deeper need to be concerned with oil workers and fishermen but also the entire Gulf Coast ecosystem. The 2011 Japanese earthquake, tsunami, and nuclear disaster should humble all humanity, especially those of us who put incredible faith in our technology and risk assessments. Ecohumanism recognizes that we are limited to human understanding, but, rather than being the measure of all things, humans have the capacity to appreciate, empathize with, and learn from the myriad creatures and life forms living in this world. Humans have an ethical obligation to become members and citizens within their biotic communities (Bowers, 1997, 2000, 2001; Leopold, 1949; Naess, 2002). Ecohumanism could be presented as a "moral imperative" (Hansen, 2006a, p. 115). Ecohumanism points toward the more basic notion that humans must find pathways for living with and learning from each other and toward living with and learning from the very ecosystem that gives humans life and sustains the cultures that we are part of. Ecohumanism challenges humans to step away from mindless self, social, and cultural destruction and toward a holistic recognition that our participation in life brings huge responsibilities for integrating the physical and the spiritual and for living in harmony with ourselves, our families, our neighbors, our colleagues, our communities, and our planet.

In a broad sense, ecohumanism provides intellectual landmarks and philosophical bearings for humanistic counselors who embrace larger, more expansive notions of the self, their role in education, in communities, and in helping others to appreciate the beauty and wonder of being alive in this world (Bender, 2003; Bowers, 1997, 2000, 2001, 2003; Stone, 2009). Although advocates of ecohumanism do not pretend to offer a grand narrative, they do see ecohumanism as helping counselors navigate life's flowing and changing process in very practical and concrete ways in which nothing is fixed and no eternal truth is claimed (Hansen, 2006b, 2007).

In a practical sense, ecohumanism provides a framework for integrating humanistic counseling and resilience constructs to help youth appreciate their unique and embodied lives in relation to both the social and natural worlds they are part of, offering youth the opportunity to wrestle with their existential aloneness and possibilities for connecting with the cultural and biological systems where they exist. Counselors guided by ecohumanism work with helpees to transform individual isolation by encouraging them to take actions to connect with the social and natural environment in ways that contribute to individual and community well-being and in ways that are playful, expressive, and life enhancing.

Philosophically, ecohumanist counselors align themselves with humanist and other counselors who question, tinker, and challenge themselves and others in a fluid, playful, genuine, and evolving interchange concerned with taking action and reflecting on consequences, or outcomes. Ecohumanists have a deep appreciation for diverse social, cultural, and natural systems because "a diverse community is a resilient community, capable of adapting to changing situations" (Capra, 1996, p. 303). The ecohumanist perspective frees humanistic counseling philosophically from the drift toward solipsism inherent in too much focus on individualism by offering an approach that advocates for greater ecological and social justice (Lewis, 2002). Given that there is no humanistic counseling doctrine or orthodoxy, ecohumanism offers a pathway for connecting resilience and humanistic constructs to Rogers's (1980) "attitude toward nature ... [where individuals] feel a closeness to, and a caring for, elemental nature" (p. 351). Ecohumanism aligns with Rogers's assertion that people had to become "ecologically minded and ... get their pleasure from an alliance with the forces of nature, rather than in the conquest of nature" (p. 351). The next section provides some applications and implications for practitioners.

APPLICATIONS AND IMPLICATIONS FOR PRACTITIONERS

This section describes an ecohumanist fusion of resilience and humanistic counseling in two vignettes with the same middle school student. Using a systems approach aligned with resilience research, the Edible Schoolyard in Berkeley, California, and Sunnyside Environmental School in Portland, Oregon, integrate middle school classroom learning and competence with relationships developed among students and adults, and processes involved in growing and preparing food that students will eat at school (Capra, 2002; Stone, 2009). The Edible Schoolyard project is guided by a tradition that teaches the head, the heart, and the hands along with the additional spirit of connectedness. If the plants get eaten by pests, students must use their heads to find out what happened, have heart not to be discouraged, and use their hands for replanting and maintaining viable solutions for controlling the pests. The students learn to work together; teachers and counselors foster core humanistic values like good relationships, creativity, empathy, and a belief in the dignity of every human being. Students learn to be more resilient by getting up after pests and other problems knock them down and to find the resources necessary to help themselves and others overcome those real-life problems. Students also learn that work is related to community practices that foster passion and hope. Obviously, when it comes to weeding, there might not be much passion, but when it comes to learning how to grow, prepare, serve, and share food, there is the hope that the food from the garden will taste good and be appreciated by others in the school community. By taking on a number of roles and responsibilities that result from participating in processes that range from mulching the soil to planting seeds to clearing the table, middle school students are taught fundamental skills related to living successfully in communities. Interventions in such a context take many forms and pull from a variety of sources that include ways of working with diverse students (Arman, 2002; Brooks & Goldstein, 2001; Burns, 1998; Buzzell & Chalquist, 2009; Chronister, McWhirter, & Kerewsky, 2004; Dweck, 2006; Galassi & Akos, 2007; Gergen, 2006; Gibbs, 2001; Gladding, 1997; Lewis, 1999; Siegel, 2010; Stone, 2009; Taub & Pearrow, 2006; Ungar, 2004, 2005; West-Olatunji, Shure, Garrett, Conwill, & Rivera, 2008; Winslade & Monk, 2007). Given the limits of space, this section describes highlights from two different sessions taking place at the end of the school year and the beginning of a new school year with the same student.

Two Sisters: Empathy and Promoting Learning Resilience

This case involves two Latino sisters in a middle school. Maria was in seventh grade, and Carmen was in eighth grade getting ready to transition into high school. They live in a neighborhood plagued by crime; both parents did not graduate from high school, and each worked two jobs to sustain their family of eight. The sisters would be considered at risk, except both are high achieving, very involved in school activities, and recognized for their efforts by teachers, administrators, and especially their parents. The school is guided by a resilience philosophy that promotes high expectations, care and support, and opportunities for meaningful participation.

The meeting with the counselor was toward the end of the school year when the eighth-grade awards and special recognition for students transitioning to high school had just taken place. Carmen, the older sister, received numerous awards for a variety of contributions, and the parents spent a lot of time celebrating those events, even taking off work to attend events at school and throwing a lavish party for the entire extended family. Maria, the younger, seventh-grade sister met with the school counselor because she felt confused and, without saying it, jealous about her sister. Here is a brief exchange:

Maria: I feel like I will never live up to what Carmen is doing. She's getting all these awards and spending a lot of time with Mom and Dad. For all my efforts and everything I do they don't give awards to seventh graders. I feel I can't do enough and can't get anything. I even failed my math test on Friday. I'm a loser.

Counselor: Maria, you sound frustrated because you are not getting the recognition for all your hard work, and you are having a tough time in math, like a number of other girls in your class.

Like any humanistic counselor, the counselor empathizes with the student. As a school promoting resilience, the math department teachers sends out a Math Alert to the counselors when groups of students fail any test. The school had in place a Morning Math Program to tutor math to students who were struggling with certain concepts. The Morning Math Program was informed by research that linked success in math to effort rather than students' perception of their ability (Dweck, 2006).

Maria: Math stinks. I can't live up to what Carmen is getting. I feel frustrated and angry and don't know what to do.

Counselor: Math is tough. It takes effort sometimes when you hit the wall, so to speak. I'm certain that you know about the Morning Math Program. What's great about it is that math teachers have found a lot of kids hit the wall and need help. Those who put in the time and effort usually get it rather quickly. You are perceptive and right that Carmen is going to get more attention and awards this year because this is her last year here and next year she'll be in high school.

The counselor continues to empathize, adds the metaphor about hitting a wall and getting over it via effort, and offers Maria a learning resource.

Maria: I don't know. It still bothers me that Carmen gets all the attention, and I still think I'm dumb in math.

Counselor: I see. It will bother you about Carmen, but you will blossom. I hardly think you are dumb in math. You have been pretty successful in the past, and you are at that stage when the most important thing you can do is to keep trying and to get the help you need to learn the materials. Lucky for us, you are pretty resilient, and we have the Morning Math Program. You can get it if you choose.

Maria: [Nods her head] What's *resilient*?

Counselor: Oh, sorry. *Resilient* means you know how to bounce back and face problems rather than run from them. Here's something else that you might want to think about doing. Did you know that we are starting a mentoring project next year where eighth-grade students will help new students get adjusted to the school? We will have meetings once a week and about once a month. Student mentors have lunch with new students and help them get oriented to the Edible Schoolyard Project and cover a Checklist for Success form. I figure you'd make a perfect student mentor, if you want to get involved. We can talk about it some other time but just think about it right now. You know how to bounce back and you have something to offer others to grow.

Drawing upon both structures found in resilience fostering organizations and humanistic counseling constructs, the counselor shows faith in Maria's ability to grow and offers an opportunity for her to participate in structured tutoring and a school-based activity. The counselor also builds up Maria's own awareness of her resilience as well as respects her right to choose.

Maria: Maybe I do.

The first exchange demonstrates counselor empathy, use of metaphor to highlight Maria's role in her learning, her ability to take advantage of resilience-enhancing school support for math, and the resilience-promoting opportunities for meaningful participation in the coming year. Counselor empathy is at the heart of humanism. Creative use of metaphors and thoughtful dialogue about responsibility is humanistic. Being helped in a school by a caring and supportive adult who encourages students to take advantage of environmental supports is aligned with resilience practices, as are providing meaningful participation in school the next year. Encouraging involvement in the Edible Schoolyard is an ecohumanistic intervention that ties together the humanistic and resilience practices in a manner that encourages Maria to connect socially and biologically to the school community and to be keenly aware of her own resilience as a person.

Maria's Contribution and Choice to Learn

Maria comes to the counselor's office with a bouquet of sunflowers.

Counselor: Where'd you get the flowers?

Counselor shows warmth and encouragement, characteristic qualities found in both resilience advocates and humanistic counselors.

Maria: You know. I got them from the school garden. My grandmother helps out, and she's showing us how to grow things. [Maria smiles.] I'm here to sign up to be a student mentor. Now that Carmen is in high school, I'd like to help out in some way. I might be a real klutz, but I do know how to garden.

Counselor: Great, I'm glad you want to help. I'll put you on my list of student mentors. We meet tomorrow during lunch.... Yes, you do have a green thumb. These flowers are beautiful. What's this about you being a klutz?

The counselor affirms Maria's choice to participate in the program and explores her self-perception. The counselor combines a systems-based intervention grounded in resilience with an individual intervention designed to encourage Maria to choose to confront her negative self-perception.

Maria: Oh, I'm just not that coordinated. I drop things. I miss balls when playing. Everybody calls me klutz. I guess I am.

Counselor: I love the flowers. You do have a talent. In looking over the grade you got in math, I can say that you know how to tap your own resilience. You know how to try and to improve. Let me know if you ever want to challenge your klutziness. I teach student mentors and just about any student who is interested to juggle.

The counselor affirms the beauty of the flowers the student cultivated, her talent for gardening, and her effort in learning and achieving in math, and invites her to confront her self-perceived klutziness. The counselor attempts to construct a sense of educational resilience, where the client sees herself as able to confront and overcome learning challenges.

Maria: Juggle?

Counselor: Here's how. [She takes three beanbags from the top of her desk, stands up, backs away from the desk, and drops the bags on the ground.] The first lesson is to realize that we will drop the bags and have to pick them up. After that we learn how to toss one bag, then two, then three. When you're ready and want to choose to learn how to juggle, I'll gladly teach you.

The counselor juggles the three bags to demonstrate what can be learned. The counselor actively and playfully engages the student in a specific, embodied learning activity designed to confront klutziness.

Maria: OK, I'm ready. Let's juggle.

The second exchange affirmed that Maria had learning resilience, which means she got up after she was knocked down. After hitting the wall in math, she took advantage of the tutoring after she was encouraged. The counselor affirmed Maria's learning resilience by pointing out how her efforts were rewarded with a good grade in math. Maria also chose to become engaged in meaningful activities at school, both in the garden and as a student mentor. The counseling conversation revealed Maria's feelings about being uncoordinated and the counselor's invitation to confront those feelings with a playful intervention. Maria was invited to choose to learn how to juggle. During the next couple of weeks, in a series of short lessons and coaching sessions, Maria struggled to learn how to juggle three bags and built an alternative story to being a klutz and being a resilient learner. The session takes an ecohumanistic turn from the beginning when Maria shares the flowers from the school garden. The school system has created a learning context where she can feel connected to something beautiful and develop confidence about what she can do in the garden. The counselor takes a playful, embodied approach, helping her connect to her body, her understanding of herself as a learner, and her capacity to take risks to learn how to juggle. The counselor shows that a sense of appreciating learning comes from engaging her hands in juggling, as well as her head in math, and her heart in the desire to be recognized for being able to grow beautiful flowers. The ecohumanistic counselor integrated humanistic and resilience constructs in a manner that celebrated Maria's connection to the garden, her competence, and her courage to try to learn something new. The good relationship with the counselor and positive view of her as self-actualizing set up the conditions to help her choose goals that tapped her creativity and learning.

CONCLUSION

This chapter has shown how resilience can be woven into humanistic counseling and how both can be integrated into an ecohumanism that ties caring, empathy, creativity, holism, sense of purpose, and subjective experience to more dynamic relationships with the social and natural environment. Both resilience advocates and humanistic counselors promote a positive view of the individual as self-actualizing or self-righting. Both understand that a good relationship with an empathic counselor or a caring adult is the cornerstone for helping others. Both are holistic approaches that affirm human creativity, the importance of feelings, choice, tolerance, diversity, human dignity, and play. Both have much in common in their pathways to helping people live up to their highest potential in ways that are respectful and playful.

WEBSITES

Center for Ecoliteracy, http://www.ecoliteracy.org/
The Cloud Institute for Sustainability Education, www.sustainabilityed.org
Edible Schoolyard, http://www.edibleschoolyard.org/
International Resilience Project, www.resilienceproject.org
Sunnyside Environmental School, http://www.pps.k12.or.us/schools-c/ profiles/?id=191
WestEd, http://www.wested.org/cs/chks/print/docs/hks_resilience.html

REFERENCES

Arman, J. (2002). A brief group counseling model to increase resiliency of students with mild disabilities. *Journal of Humanistic Counseling, Education and Development, 41*(2), 120–128.

Atkinson, T., & Claxton, G. (2000). *The intuitive practitioner: On the value of not always knowing what one is doing.* Philadelphia: Open University Press.

Bateson, G. (1979). *Mind and nature: A necessary unity.* New York: Bantam.

Benard, B. (1997). Changing the condition, place, and view of young people in society: An interview with youth development pioneer Bill Lofquist. *Resiliency in Action, 2*(1), 7–18.

Benard, B. (2004). *Resiliency: What we have learned.* San Francisco: WestEd.

Benard, B., & Marshall, K. (1997). *A framework for practice: Tapping innate resiliency.* Minneapolis: University of Minnesota, Center for Applied Research and Educational Improvement, College of Education and Human Development. Retrieved from http:// www.cehd.umn.edu/CAREI/Reports/Rpractice/Spring97/framework.html

Benard, B., & Slade, S. (2009). Listening to students: Moving resilience research to youth development practice and school connectedness. In R. Gilman, E. S. Huebner, & M. J. Furlong (Eds.), *Handbook of positive psychology in schools* (pp. 353–369). New York: Routledge.

Bender, F. L. (2003). *The culture of extinction: Toward a philosophy of deep ecology.* Amherst, NY: Humanity Books.

Bowers, C. A. (1997). *The culture of denial: Why the environmental movement needs a strategy for reforming universities and public schools.* Albany: State University of New York Press.

Bowers, C. A. (2000). *Let them eat data: How computers affect education, cultural diversity, and the prospects of ecological sustainability.* Athens: University of Georgia Press.

Bowers, C. A. (2001). *Educating for eco-justice and community.* Athens: University of Georgia Press.

Bowers, C. A. (2003). *Mindful conservatism: Rethinking the ideological and educational basis of an ecologically sustainable future.* New York: Rowman and Littlefield Publishers.

Bronfenbrenner, U. (1979). *The ecology of human development: Experiments by nature and design.* Cambridge, MA: Harvard University Press.

Brooks, R. B., & Goldstein, S. (2001). *Raising resilient children.* Lincolnwood, IL: Contemporary Books.

Burns, G. W. (1998). *Nature-guided therapy: Brief integrative strategies for health and well-being*. Philadelphia: Brunner/Mazel.

Buzzell, L., & Chalquist, C. (Eds.). (2009). *Ecotherapy: Healing with nature in mind*. San Francisco: Sierra Club Books.

Cahalan, W. (1995). The earth is our real body: Cultivating ecological groundedness in Gestalt therapy. *Gestalt Journal, 18*(1), 87–113.

Cain, D. J. (2001). Defining characteristics, history, and evolution of humanistic therapies. In D. J. Cain & J. Seeman (Eds.), *Humanistic psychotherapies: Handbook of research and practice* (pp. 3–54). Washington, DC: American Psychological Association.

Capra, F. (1996). *The web of life: A new scientific understanding of living systems*. New York: Anchor Books.

Capra, F. (2002). *The hidden connections: Integrating the biological, cognitive, and social dimensions of life into a science of sustainability*. New York: Doubleday.

Chronister, K. M, Linville, D., & Kaag, K. P. (2008). Domestic violence survivors' access of career counseling services: A qualitative investigation. *Journal of Career Development, 34*, 4, 339–361.

Comstock, D. L., Hammer, T. R., Strentzsch, J., Cannon, K., Parsons, J., & Salazar, G. (2008). Relational-cultural theory: A framework for bridging relational, multicultural, and social justice competencies. *Journal of Counseling and Development, 86*(3), 279–287.

Conn, S. A. (1998). Living in the earth: Ecopsychology, health, and psychotherapy. *Humanistic Psychologist, 26*(1–3), 179–198.

Conyne, R. K., & Cook, E. P. (Eds.). (2004). *Ecological counseling: An innovative approach to conceptualizing person-environment interaction*. Alexandria, VA: American Counseling Association.

Cornelius-White, J. (2007). Congruence. In M. Cooper, M. O'Hara, P. F. Schmid, & G. Wyatt (Eds.), *The handbook of person-centered psychotherapy and counselling* (pp. 168–181). New York: Palgrave Macmillan.

Cupitt, D. (1995). *Solar ethics*. London: SCM Press.

Davis, W. (2007). *Light at the edge of the world: A journey through the realm of vanishing cultures*. Vancouver, BC: Douglas and McIntyre.

Deater-Deckard, K., Ivy, L., & Smith, J. (2006). Resilience in gene-environment transactions. In S. Goldstein & R. Brooks (Eds.), *Handbook of resilience in children* (pp. 49–63). New York: Springer Science+Business Media.

Dewey, J. (1929). *The quest for certainty: A study of the relation of knowledge and action*. New York: G. P. Putman's Sons.

Duncan, B. L., Miller, S. D., & Sparks, J. A. (2004). *The heroic client: A revolutionary way to improve effectiveness through client- directed, outcome-informed therapy* (revised edition). San Francisco: Jossey-Bass.

Dweck, C. S. (2006). *Mindset: The new psychology of success*. New York: Random House.

Fletcher, J. (1966). *Situation ethics: The new morality*. Philadelphia: Westminster Press.

Galassi, J. P., & Akos, P. (2007). *Strengths-based school counseling: Promoting student development and achievement*. Mahwah, NJ: Lawrence Erlbaum.

Gergen, K. J. (2006). *Therapeutic realities: Collaboration, oppression and relational flow*. Chagrin Falls, OH: Taos Institute Publications.

Gibbs, J. (2001). *Tribes: A new way of learning and being together*. Windsor, CA: Center Source.

Gladding, S. T. (1997). Stories and the art of counseling. *Journal of Humanistic Education and Development, 36*, 68–73.

Glave, D. (2010). *Rooted in the earth: Reclaiming the African American environmental heritage*. Chicago: Lawrence Hill Books.

Griffin, D., & Farris, A. (2010). School counselors and collaboration: Finding resources through community asset mapping. *Professional School Counseling, 13*(5), 248–256.

Hansen, J. T. (2006a). Humanism as moral imperative: Comments on the role of knowing in the helping encounter. *Journal of Humanistic Counseling, Education and Development, 45*(2), 115–125.

Hansen, J. T. (2006b). Counseling theories within a postmodernist epistemology: New roles for theories in counseling practice. *Journal of Counseling & Development, 84*(3), 291–297.

Hansen, J. T. (2007). Counseling without truth: Toward a neopragmatic foundation for counseling practice. *Journal of Counseling and Development, 85*, 423–430.

Hansen, J. T. (2010). Consequences of the postmodernist vision: Diversity as the guiding value for the counseling profession. *Journal of Counseling and Development, 88*(1), 101–107.

Hedges, F. (2010). *Reflexivity in therapeutic practice.* London: Palgrave Macmillian.

Kaplan, H. B. (2006). Understanding the concept of resilience. In S. Goldstein & R. Brooks (Eds.), *Handbook of resilience in children* (pp. 39–47). New York: Springer Science+Business Media.

Kuhn, J. L. (2001). Toward an ecological humanistic psychology. *Journal of Humanistic Psychology, 41*(2), 9–24. DOI: 10.1177/00222167801412003.

Lakoff, G., & Johnson, M. (1999). *Philosophy in the flesh: The embodied mind and its challenge to Western thought.* New York: Basic Books.

Leopold, A. (1949). *A Sand County almanac: And sketches here and there.* New York: Oxford University Press.

Lewis, R. E. (1999). A write way: Fostering resiliency during transitions. *Journal of Humanistic Education and Development, 37*, 200–211.

Lewis, R. E. (2002, June). Eco-humanism emerging. *C-AHEAD Infochange, 102*, 4–6.

Lewis, R. E. (2007). Resilience in individuals, families, and communities. In D. Capuzzi & D. R. Gross (Eds.), *Youth at risk* (5th ed., pp. 39–68). Alexandria, VA: American Counseling Association.

Lewis, R. E. (2010). Ecological counseling: Making connections. Unpublished manuscript, Department of Educational Psychology, California State University, East Bay, Hayward, California.

Lewis, R. E., Lenski, S. D., Mukhopadhyay, S., & Cartwright, C. T. (2010). Mindful wonderment: Using focus groups to frame social justice. *Journal for Social Action in Counseling and Psychology, 2*, 82–105.

Luthar, S. S. (2006). Resilience in development: A synthesis of research across five decades. In D. Cicchetti & D. J. Cohen (Eds.), *Developmental psychopathology, Vol. 3: Risk, disorder, and adaptation* (pp. 739–795). Hoboken, NJ: John Wiley & Sons.

Luthar, S. S., Cicchetti, D., & Becker, B. (2000a). The construct of resilience: A critical evaluation and guidelines for future work. *Child Development, 71*, 543–562.

Luthar, S. S., Cicchetti, D., & Becker, B. (2000b). Research on resilience: Response to commentaries. *Child Development, 71*, 573–575.

Maslow, A. H. (1962). *Toward a psychology of being.* Princeton, NJ: D. Van Nostrand Co.

Maslow, A. H. (1968). *Toward a psychology of being* (2nd ed.). Princeton, NJ: D. Van Nostrand Co.

Maslow, A. H. (1970). *Motivation and personality* (2nd ed.). New York: Harper and Row.

Masten, A. S. (2001). Ordinary magic: Resilience processes in development. *American Psychologist, 56*, 227–238.

Masten, A. S. (2007). Resilience in developing systems: Progress and promise as the fourth wave rises. *Development and Psychopathology, 19*(3), 921–930.

Masten, A. S., & Coatsworth, J. D. (1998). The development of competence in favorable and unfavorable environments. *American Psychologist, 53*, 205–220.

Masten, A. S., Cutuli, J. J., Herbers, J. E., & Reed, M. J. (2009). Resilience in development. In S. J. Lopez & C. R. Snyder (Eds.), *Oxford handbook of positive psychology* (pp. 117–131). New York: Oxford University Press.

McWhorter, J. H. (2001). *The power of Babel: A natural history of language.* New York: HarperCollins.

Milton, K. (2002). *Loving nature: Towards an ecology of emotion.* New York: Routledge.

Naess, A. (2002). *Life's philosophy: Reason and feeling in a deeper world.* Athens: University of Georgia Press.

Noe, A. (2009). *Out of our heads: Why you are not your brain, and other lessons from the biology of consciousness.* New York: Hill and Wang.

Norman, R. (2004). *On humanism.* New York: Routledge.

Pilisuk, M. (2001). Ecological psychology, caring, and the boundaries of the person. *Journal of Humanistic Psychology, 41*(2), 25–37. DOI: 10.1177/0022167801412004.

Raskin, N. J., & Rogers, C. R. (1989). Person-centered therapy. In R. J. Corsini & D. Wedding (Eds.), *Current psychotherapies* (4th ed., pp. 155–194). Itasca, IL: F. E. Peacock.

Raskin, N. J., Rogers, C. R., & Witty, M. C. (2008). Client-centered therapy. In R. J. Corsini & D. Wedding (Eds.), *Current psychotherapies* (8th ed., pp. 141–186). Belmont, CA: Thomson Brooks/Cole.

Rogers, C. R. (1957). The necessary and sufficient conditions of therapeutic personality change. *Journal of Consulting Psychology, 21*, 95–103.

Rogers, C. R. (1961). *On becoming a person: A therapist's view of psychotherapy.* Boston: Houghton Mifflin.

Rogers, C. R. (1969). *Freedom to learn.* Columbus, OH: Charles E. Merrill.

Rogers, C. R. (1980). *A way of being.* New York: Houghton Mifflin.

Scholl, M. B. (2008). Preparing manuscripts with central and salient humanistic content. *Journal of Humanistic Counseling, Education, and Development, 47*, 3–8.

Siegel, D. J. (2010). *The mindful therapist: A clinician's guide to mindsight and neural integration.* New York: W.W. Norton.

Smith, B., Tooley, E., Christopher, P., & Kay, V. (2010). Resilience as the ability to bounce back from stress: A neglected personal resource? *Journal of Positive Psychology, 5*(3), 166–176. DOI:10.1080/17439760.2010.482186.

Stone, M. K. (2009). *Smart by nature: Schooling for sustainability.* Healdsburg, CA: Watershed Media.

Sutich, A. J. (1968). Transpersonal psychology: An emerging force. *Journal of Humanistic Psychology, 8*(1), 77–78.

Swanson, J. L. (1995). The call for Gestalt's contribution to ecopsychology: Figuring in the environmental field. *Gestalt Journal, 18*(1), 47–85.

Tapp, R. B. (2002). *Ecohumanism.* Amherst, NY: Prometheus Books.

Taub, J., & Pearrow, M. (2006). Resilience through violence prevention in schools. In S. Goldstein & R. Brooks (Eds.), *Handbook of resilience in children* (pp. 357–371). New York: Springer Science+Business Media.

Ungar, M. (2004). *Nurturing hidden resilience in troubled youth.* Toronto: University of Toronto Press.

Ungar, M. (2005). *Handbook for working with children and youth: Pathways to resilience across cultures and contexts.* Thousand Oaks, CA: Sage Publications.

Werner, E. E. (1989). Children of the garden island. *Scientific American, 260*(4), 106–111.

Werner, E. E. (1996). How children become resilient. Observations and cautions. *Resiliency in Action, 1*(1), 18–28.

Werner, E. E. (2006). What can we learn about resilience from large-scale longitudinal studies? In S. Goldstein & R. Brooks (Eds.), *Handbook of resilience in children* (pp. 91–105). New York: Springer Science+Business Media.

Werner, E. E., & Smith, R. S. (1977). *Kauai's children come of age.* Honolulu: University of Hawaii Press.

Werner, E. E., & Smith, R. S. (1982). *Vulnerable but invincible: A longitudinal study of resilient children and youth.* New York: McGraw Hill.

Werner, E. E., & Smith, R. S. (1992). *Overcoming the odds: High risk children from birth to adulthood.* Ithaca, NY: Cornell University Press.

Werner, E. E., & Smith, R. S. (2001). *Journeys from childhood to midlife: Risk, resilience, and recovery.* Ithaca, NY: Cornell University Press.

West-Olatunji, C., Shure, L., Garrett, M., Conwill, W., & Rivera, E. T. (2008). Rite of passage programs as effective tools for fostering resilience among low-income African American male adolescents. *Journal of Humanistic Counseling, Education, and Development, 47*(2), 131–143.

Winslade, J., & Monk, G. (2007). *Narrative counseling in schools: Powerful and brief* (2nd ed.). Thousand Oaks, CA: Corwin Press.

Wright, M. O., & Masten, A. S. (2006). Resilience processes in development. In S. Goldstein & R. Brooks (Eds.), *Handbook of resilience in children* (pp. 17–37). New York: Springer Science+Business Media.

10

Competitive Sports and the Elementary and Middle School Child

A Developmental and Humanistic Perspective

A. Scott McGowan, Frank Brady, and Joseph A. Despres

Children's participation in highly organized adult-directed competitive sports has become an integral part of American culture. The continuous rise in participation rates affirms the belief that youth sports are inherently beneficial (National Center for Education Statistics, 1988). Involvement in sports is seen as enhancing citizenship as well as moral, personality, and character development. However, paralleling this early introduction to organized sports is the departure of many neophyte athletes long before their fitness and sports skills are developed. The high attrition of young athletes appears to be a direct consequence of the negative experiences these children have had with competition (Brubaker, 2007; Doering, 2008; Todd & Kent, 2003; Wankel & Sefton, 1989). Apparently, the potential positive benefits of sports can be reversed by an excessive emphasis on winning, controlling coaches' styles, and lack of fun (Stephens & Schaben, 2002; Weiss & Chaumeton, 1992).

The purpose of this chapter is to address some of the psychological, sociological, and physiological issues that mediate children's sports experience from a humanistic perspective. Additionally, and in light of recent sports pediatric research, we will present recommendations for the increasing roles of professional school counselors as consultants and collaborators with coaches, parents, teachers, and the students themselves to maximize positive outcomes and to minimize the negative outcomes of competitive youth sports.

MOTIVES FOR PARTICIPATION

Numerous research studies have been conducted to determine the predominant motives for youth participation in sports (Gould, Feltz, & Weiss, 1985; Wankel & Kreisel, 1985; Wankel & Sefton, 1989). Researchers cite three categories of motives that inspire sports participation: (1) intrinsic motives are the primary reasons and include having fun, improving skills, testing one's abilities, excitement, and personal accomplishment; (2) motives such as "being on a team" and "being with friends" are moderating motives; and (3) extrinsic motives such as "getting rewards" and "pleasing others" are ranked least important.

Deci and Ryan (1985) explained the conflicting role of extrinsic motives by noting that rewards may have two functions: an informational one and a controlling one. They maintained that intrinsic motivation will be undermined if the controlling function prevails, while it will be enhanced if the informational function is emphasized. They also held that intrinsic motivation not only entails doing something for its own sake but also induces feelings of self-determination and competence associated with mastering skills resulting in increased self-esteem.

Later, as intrinsic motivation has received increased recognition as an important variable in maintaining children's sports participation, adult motivation for participation as coaches—and as parents—must be congruent with that of their child athletes. An emphasis on winning and achieving rewards and awards is all too frequently of paramount importance to the adults, while they may be of secondary importance to the children. Consequently, winning and rewards should not be the guiding principles of an organized sports program. Adults must maximize opportunities for enjoyment by structuring the practice sessions to capitalize on the fun element and the development of skills that can be used throughout the life span, while deemphasizing excessive competitiveness and the need to win (Brubaker, 2007).

MOTIVES FOR ATTRITION

Paralleling the research on motives for participation are studies concerned with motives for attrition from sports. Gilbert, Gilbert, and Morawski (2007) noted that athletes cite multiple reasons for their withdrawal from sports: lack of skill development, lack of fun, lack of playing time, negative coaching style, negative parental involvement, and competitive stress. The overemphasis on competition is frequently identified as a crucial factor in the attrition of athletes (Weiss, 1993); coaches and parents need to be sensitive to this. As we will propose, school counselors are in a unique position to foster sensitivity among coaches and parents, as they advocate for children and their stable development through sports.

MASTERY MOTIVATIONAL CLIMATE: MASTERY GOAL VERSUS EGO GOAL ORIENTATION

The current major theories of motivation identify the self-perception of competence as a critical personal characteristic driving participation, choice, effort, and persistence in an activity, according to Todd and Kent (2003). They asserted that individuals' perception of competence or incompetence was the critical mediator of performance and persistence. Consequently, people behave in a manner to maximize the demonstration of high ability and to minimize the demonstration of low ability. They also noted that the criteria people use to determine their ability vary as a function of age, situations, and individual differences. Prior to age 10, ability and effort tend to be undifferentiated (i.e., effort equals success), while at about age 12 those qualities become completely differentiated (i.e., effort does not necessarily equal success). This developmental conception of ability has important implications for instruction and participation in sports, as ability can be perceived as a fixed and limiting factor, while effort may be viewed as more modifiable. Construing ability as an inherent aptitude increases vulnerability to the adverse effects of failure. Conceptualizing ability as an acquirable skill enhances one's self-efficacy, self-esteem, and sense of competence. Nicholls (1989) contended that individuals approach achievement situations with either an ego goal orientation, in which ability is judged relative to the performance of others, or a mastery goal orientation, in which ability is judged on the basis of self-improvement or mastery of a particular skill. Social comparison and interpersonal competition are the major criteria for inferring success or competence in an ego goal orientation. In a mastery goal orientation, by contrast, the determinants of success and competence are self-referenced, and the role of interpersonal competition is diminished. Whichever orientation is salient is a function of past experiences and situational factors. Voight (2005) suggested that parents and coaches often convey their own achievement orientation through their interactional patterns and reward systems, and, consequently, children internalize a similar perspective on achievement.

Prior to age 12, children show a clear disposition toward a mastery goal orientation. As they enter adolescence, they move to an ego goal orientation. Furthermore, males have been found continually to be more ego oriented than females (Todd & Kent, 2003; Williams, 1998). This transition to an ego goal orientation may have long-lasting negative consequences for children who have reservations about their ability. Failure in athletics can impact other areas of their lives and directly affect their feelings of self-worth. "Children at this age," wrote Johnson and Kottman (1992), "have their feelings hurt easily and worry a great deal. Being excluded can be very painful" (p. 9). The differentiation between ability and effort becomes complete at this age. Children with a predominant ego orientation, coupled with low ability, may experience frequent failure and thus regard their efforts as futile. Williams (1998) asserted that the culmination of the differentiation process, combined with an increased emphasis on competition, may account for the pervasive attrition from competitive sports after age 12. Children with an ego goal orientation and low ability tend to drop out. These children realize that their abilities and their apparent lack of athletic prowess are exposed; their sense of competence is further diminished as a result of the power of the normative comparison process. However, Ames (1987) stressed that it is not inevitable that children develop an ego goal orientation. He held that cues and feedback given by significant others are critical in determining the goal orientation that children develop. Research has consistently shown that in athletic programs characterized by interpersonal competition, public evaluation, and normative feedback, an ego goal orientation is more likely to result. Conversely, in athletic programs where the emphasis is on the learning process, self-improvement, and participation, a mastery goal orientation is likely to emerge (Roberts and Treasure, 1995).

Andrew—A Case Illustration

When Andrew was 5 and about to start kindergarten, his parents enrolled him in soccer at the local Boys' and Girls' Athletic Club. He was so excited at the first meeting when he was assigned to a team and a coach. The coach was, as every other coach at the club, a volunteer. Unfortunately, Andrew came down with the chicken pox. He missed the first 3 weeks of kindergarten and the first 3 weeks of soccer practice. The parents had been told by the leaders of the club that the emphasis would be on the development of each child's skill level and an enhancement of the love of sports. There were at least four teams at each level, and they played against each other and against other teams in the area. Winning a game was, of course, encouraged, but the primary goal was to teach the basic skills and build up enthusiasm for sports. When Andrew was well enough to play, the parents soon found to their dismay that his coach had a different philosophy from the one expounded by the club: He saw his job as ensuring that "his" team won, even if it meant that he played only his best players. Because Andrew had missed the first few weeks of practice and the coach did little to help him catch up in terms of skill development, he was sent in to play a game only if the team was winning and only for the last few minutes of the game. It was only toward the end of the season that the parents realized what the coach was doing. As a school counselor committed to the development of all children, the father was quite angry with the coach's attitude. He and his wife, who was a college administrator and a former elementary school teacher, then decided that, while it was too late to do much in terms of Andrew, they needed to do an intervention to prevent that coach from damaging other children. They wrote a letter of complaint and were invited to meet with the head of the organization. The coach was let go. Andrew did continue with soccer for several years and had some marvelous coaches but never really blossomed in that sport—the damage had been done. It was only when he discovered basketball that a lifelong love of and participation in sports was engendered. Andrew is now grown and that legacy is being passed down to his own two daughters. Andrew is the son of one of the authors of this chapter— Scott McGowan—and hence Scott's personal as well as professional interest in the nurturing of the child athlete.

Ames (1992) proposed that a mastery goal orientation be promoted in athletic settings to facilitate the optimum development of each participant. Mounting evidence indicated that positive experiences depend on the organizational climate where skill development is emphasized, realistic and challenging goals are established, and success is defined primarily in terms of skill mastery rather than merely winning. Mastery cues are conveyed by many *hows* within the athletic environment: how practice sessions are structured, how children are grouped, how teams are picked for scrimmages, how positions are rotated, how efforts are recognized, and how results are rewarded. Roberts and Treasure (1995) suggested that coaches strive to encourage a mastery climate by focusing on short-term goals, learning, and skill development. As Kirk and Kirk (1993) noted, "The optimal goal is to create an environment in which the student athlete will assimilate experiences and formal education, thereby becoming an asset to his or her profession and to society" (p. xviii).

SOCIAL DEVELOPMENT

Educators and coaches have long exclaimed that children are not miniature adults. However, there is little evidence that practitioners faithfully abide by this maxim. Practices and scrimmages are often conducted as if the children were scaled-down models of the adults. Coakley (1993) cautioned that, before the age of 12, most children have not yet developed the social ability to grasp competitive strategies conceptually. Children of 7 and 8 years old playing soccer seem to resort to "beehive soccer" as both teams swarm after the ball. In youth baseball, similarly, hordes of outfielders descend on the ball if it manages to get by the infield. Such behavior is appropriate to the social developmental level of the child. Yet the inability of children to understand a complex system of social relationships often frustrates and angers coaches and parents. Children are berated for not paying attention or not performing with enough effort. In addition, Coakley stressed that only a "handful of children under twelve will be developmentally ready to fully grasp the idea that a team consists of an interrelated set of positions that shift in response to one another, in response to opponents, and in response to the placement of a ball or some other object" (p. 88). Therefore, as Brubaker (2007) insisted, practices are much more beneficial if coaches focus on skill development rather than the specialized roles that adult sports demand. Organized competitive team sports are generally irrelevant for children about the age of 8 as they are neither socially nor cognitively developed enough to grasp the evolving dynamics of a given sport. That is the developmental age when they should be learning skills and enjoying acquiring skills and learning about the sport within the context of a mastery goal orientation.

IMPLICATIONS FOR PROFESSIONAL SCHOOL COUNSELORS

The American School Counselor Association (ASCA) has provided two major sources of guidance to help school counselors in their work with student athletes. The first is its position brief, "The Role of the Professional School Counselor" (ASCA, 2005a); the second is *The ASCA National Model: A Framework for School Counseling Programs* (ASCA, 2005b). According to the first document, the role of the school counselor consists of three broad processes: counseling, coordination, and consultation. The counseling function is about establishing "trusting and confidential working relationships" with others in the school; coordination is a "leadership process" to organize and manage the school's counseling program; consultation is a "cooperative process in which he/she assists others to think through problems and to develop skills that make them more effective." This latter role is the one that applies most closely to working with student athletes.

The ASCA national model outlines a world-class structure for the delivery of school counseling services. To that end, a school counseling program "facilitates student development in three broad areas: academic development, career development, and personal/social development" (ASCA, 2005b, p. 17). While all three areas certainly impact the life of every student athlete, the area that is of most concern here is that of the student athletes' personal–social development. O'Bryant (1993) stated:

> The school counselor is in the unique position of serving as the preventative mental health specialist, whose goal of promoting positive mental health among student athletes is achieved by educating and collaborating with the people who influence their lives, as well as assisting student athletes themselves to achieve psychologically healthy systems of values that transcend the athletic arena. (p. 21)

One of the most important tasks of the school counselor is to act as consultant to the athletic triangle of coaches, parents, and athletes (Goldberg, 1991). Consultative services can be delivered to these populations in one or more ways, as noted in the following section.

Consultation With Coaches

As we have seen, coaches are powerful figures in the lives of elementary and middle school athletes and can either positively or negatively affect them in terms of athletic and personal development. As Goldberg (1991) noted, in many school districts, coaches are no longer members of the regular school staff and, consequently, may have little or no knowledge of student athletes' in-school performance and little contact with them in any role other than that of athlete. The professional school counselor, therefore, should establish a relationship with coaches to help students be more effective athletes in two important ways. First, provide academic, demographic, and personal information about student athletes to the coach to help better understand them. Second, establish a counselor–coach relationship whereby the counselor can ascertain that the coaching emphasis is on a mastery goal orientation: skills acquisition in a positive learning environment, self-improvement of each athlete, and the participation of all children. Current literature (Brubaker, 2007; Doering, 2008; Todd & Kent, 2003) underscores the benefits of the mastery orientation for elementary and middle school student athletes; school counselors should be knowledgeable about this.

Consultation With Parents

Parents want their children to be accepted, successful, and liked. At the same time, they may have unrealistic expectations about their children's athletic abilities, which may lead them to place undue stress on the children to perform athletically. The stress may, in turn, lead to lowered self-esteem, loss of confidence in their athletic abilities, and negative performance in their academic studies (Gilbert et al., 2007). Of course, competition and winning are realities, and many children seek those opportunities for success through sports. Again, the school counselor can provide helpful consultation with parents in three ways. First, with the cooperation of local coaches, the school counselor can offer to facilitate a group guidance session to inform parents about developmental stages of children's growth and the ways parents can foster healthy development through sports participation. Second, the school counselor can support local coaches by providing information about the differences between the ego goal orientation and the mastery goal orientation approaches to sports participation as well as the advantages of the latter for their student athletes where the emphasis is on skills acquisition and learning rather than just on winning. Third, the school counselor can help reinforce the crucial role parents have in athletic skills development by strongly urging parents to simply spend time with their children in actively practicing the sport. According to Simcox, Nuijens, and Lee (2006) (and also stressed by Bailey, Getich, & Chen-Hayes, 2003; Fagan, 2002), today school counselors are assuming an advocacy role in their work with students and their families.

Consultation With Athletes

The ASCA national model charges the professional school counselor to enhance the academic, career, and personal–social development of all children. The latter category, which this chapter highlights, also incorporates the emotional, psychological, and even physical development of all children. Sports and athletic competition provide valuable avenues for such growth; however, they can also inhibit and even damage children if such participation takes place within an ego goal orientation environment rather than a mastery goal one. As we have reiterated, the school and athletic climate should foster the mastery of athletic skills and the carefree enjoyment of every child rather than overemphasizing competition for the sake of winning and building egos.

As we mentioned already, the school counselor can intervene directly with the coach to ensure that children are trained within a mastery goal orientation climate. In addition, again, with the cooperation of the local coaches, the counselor might consult directly with the students in several ways: through large-group guidance sessions in which the counseling staff informs student athletes about the positive benefit of sports and the ways such participation can help or hinder their healthful growth as persons; small-group counseling sessions with members of particular sports teams to discuss the successes or lack thereof they are experiencing in practices and how to place their sports participation in perspective with other areas of their life, such as school work; and case management or individual counseling to provide particular students with support and encouragement to continue with their athletic endeavors within a healthy developmental perspective.

An Additional Resource: Consultation With Teachers

Teachers are the eyes and ears for the counselor in children's academic and social progress. Counselors must work closely with them (Amatea, Smith-Adcock, & Villares, 2006) to monitor their developmental progress in the areas emphasized by the ASCA model. However, for the purposes of this chapter, the teacher's role in children's academic achievement vis-à-vis their athletic participation and skills acquisition is to be highlighted. As for the potential of fledgling student athletes, periodic evaluation of their academic, athletic, and social progress should take place so that individual or group counseling interventions can occur at the first sign of difficulties. Teachers and counselors should be alerted not to permit student athletes any special breaks, such as coming late to class or neglecting homework assignments. Further, the interaction of athletes during recess should be monitored by both teachers and counselors, especially to observe athletes' relationships with peers. The joint assessment of athletes' abilities to compete both athletically and academically should be shared with the other members of the athletic triangle.

CONCLUSION

Campbell (1992) stressed that to be effective in the area of school consultation the professional school counselor must demonstrate the following:

- Personal traits such as genuineness, caring, and empathy
- Expertise in the areas of child development, human relations, curriculum development, assessment, and counseling theory
- Consultation skills that include but are not limited to process, mental health, behavioral, and advocacy consultation
- Knowledge of the American Counseling Association's and the American School Counselor Association's ethical standards as they pertain to consultation

For the purposes of this chapter, we would also add:

- An appreciation of the value of and at least a cursory knowledge of sports
- Athletics, their place in the developmental stages of children, as well as their impact, directly and indirectly, on their health and welfare

The professional school counselor can, indeed, play a significant role in the development of children as athletes through the consultative process with coaches, parents, students, and teachers. On one hand, the counselor can communicate a healthy view of athletic competition and emphasize the wellness that can result from both participation in, and enjoyment of, athletics that commences in childhood and continues throughout the life span. On the other hand, the counselor can help foster a mastery goal orientation as opposed to an ego goal orientation and thereby provide student athletes the climate within which to take risks and to build their self-esteem requisite to reach their athletic potential. This is a very satisfying space for the school counselor and a very healthy space for elementary and middle school student athletes.

REFERENCES

Amatea, E. S., Smith-Adcock, S., & Villares, E. (2006). From family deficit to family strength: Viewing families' contributions to children's learning from a family resilience perspective. *Professional School Counseling, 9*(3), 177–189.

American School Counselor Association (ASCA). (2005a). *The role of the professional school counselor.* Retrieved April 25, 2008 from http://www.schoolcounselor.org

American School Counselor Association (ASCA). (2005b). *The ASCA national model: A framework for school counseling programs* (2nd. ed.). Alexandria, VA: Author.

Ames, C. (1987). The enhancement of student motivation. In D. A. Kleiber & M. Maehr (Eds.), *Advances in motivation and achievement* (pp. 123–148). Greenwich, CT: JAI Press.

Ames, C. (1992). Achievement goals, motivational climate, and motivation processes. In G. C. Roberts (Ed.), *Motivation in sport and exercise* (pp. 161–176). Champaign, IL: Human Kinetics.

Bailey, D. F., Getich, Y. Q., & Chen-Hayes, S. (2003). Professional school counselors as social and academic advocates. In B. T. Erford (Ed.), *Transforming the school counseling profession* (pp. 411–434). Upper Saddle River, NJ: Merrill Prentice Hall.

Brubaker, K. (2007). Coaching and teaching our athletes. *Coach and Athletic Director, 3*, 30–33.

Campbell, C. A. (1992). The school counselor as consultant: Assessing your aptitude. *Elementary School Guidance & Counseling, 26*, 237–249.

Coakley, J. (1993). Social dimensions of intensive training and participation in youth sports. In B. R. Cahill & A. J. Pearl (Eds.), *Intensive participation in children's sports.* (pp. 77–94). Champaign, IL: Human Kinetics.

Deci, E. L., & Ryan, R. M. (1985). *Intrinsic motivation and self-determination in human behavior.* New York: Plenum.

Doering, L. (2008). Middle school athletics: Make it a beginning, not an ending. *Coach & Athletic Director, 4*, 4.

Fagan, T. K. (2002). Trends in the history of school psychology in the United States. In A. Thomas & J. Grimes (Eds.), *Best practices in school psychology* (14th ed., pp. 209–221). Bethesda, MD: National Association of School Psychologists.

Gilbert, J. N., Gilbert, W., & Morawski, C. (2007). Coaching strategies for helping adolescents cope with stress. *Journal of Physical Education, Recreation & Dance, 78*, 13–24.

Goldberg, A. D. (1991). Counseling the high school student-athlete. *School Counselor, 38*, 332–340.

Gould, D., Feltz, D., & Weiss, M. (1985). Motives for participating in competitive youth swimming. *International Journal of Sport Psychology, 6*, 126–140.

Johnson, W., & Kottman, T. (1992). Developmental needs of middle school students: Implications for counselors. *Elementary School Guidance & Counseling, 27*, 3–14.

Kirk, W. D., & Kirk, S. V. (Eds.). (1993). *Student athletes: Shattering the myths & sharing the realities.* Alexandria, VA: American Counseling Association.

National Center for Education Statistics. (1988). *National Educational Longitudinal Study— 1988 (NELS 88).* Washington, DC: Author.

Nicholls, J. G. (1989). *The competitive ethos and democratic education.* Cambridge, MA: Harvard University Press.

O'Bryant, B. J. (1993). School counseling and the student athlete. In W. D. Kirk & S. V. Kirk (Eds.), *Student athletes: Shattering the myths & sharing the realities* (pp. 13–24). Alexandria, VA: American Counseling Association.

Roberts, G. C., & Treasure, D. C. (1995). Achievement goals, motivational climate, and achievement strategies and behaviors in sport. *International Journal of Sport Psychology, 26*, 64–80.

Simcox, A. G., Nuijens, K. L., & Lee, C. C. (2006). School counselors and school psychologists: Collaborative partners in promoting culturally competent schools. *Professional School Counseling, 9*(4), 272–277.

Stephens, L. J., & Schaben, L. A. (2002). The effect of interscholastic sports participation on academic achievement of middle level school students. *National Association of Secondary School Principals' Bulletin, 86*, 34–41.

Todd, S. Y., & Kent, A. (2003). Student athletes' perceptions of self. *Adolescence, 38*, 659–667.

Voight, M. (2005). Integrating mental-skills training into everyday coaching. *Journal of Physical Education, Recreation & Dance, 76*, 38–47.

Wankel, L. M., & Kreisel, P. S. J. (1985). Factors underlying enjoyment of youth sports: Sport and age group comparisons. *Journal of Sport Psychology, 7,* 51–64.

Wankel, L. M., & Sefton, J. M. (1989). A season-long investigation of fun in youth sports. *Journal of Sport and Exercise Psychology, 11,* 355–366.

Weiss, M. R. (1993). Psychological effects of intensive sport participation on children and youth: Self-esteem and motivation. In B. R. Cahill & A. J. Pearl (Eds.), *Intensive participation in children's sports* (pp. 39–69). Champaign, IL: Human Kinetics.

Weiss, M. R., & Chaumeton, N. (1992). Motivational orientation in sport. In T. S. Horn (Ed.), *Advances in sport psychology* (pp. 61–99). Champaign, IL: Human Kinetics.

Williams, L. (1998). Contextual influences and goal perspectives among female youth sports participants. *Research Quarterly for Exercise and Sport, 69,* 47–57.

11

Humanism in College and University Counseling

ALAN M. "WOODY" SCHWITZER

This chapter explores applications of the humanistic perspective to contemporary college counseling. Although college counseling professionals—including professional counselors, psychologists, clinical social workers, psychiatrists, and others working in counseling centers, mental health centers, health centers and other offices on 2- and 4-year college and university campuses—tend to be more visible during crises such as the April 16, 2007, Virginia Tech shooting tragedy, they serve student mental health needs every day. In fact, an estimated 1.5 million students are served annually by college counseling centers on U.S. campuses (Gallagher, 2009). In turn, staff members of counseling and mental health centers on college campuses have a unique opportunity to positively impact the lives of a wide range of late adolescents, young adults, and nontraditionally aged learners.

College counseling and mental health centers are specialized offices that provide services within a very specific institutional context (May, 1988). Their purpose is to support their institution's academic mission by "helping students work through psychological and emotional issues that may affect their academic success and personal development" (Dungy, 2003, p. 345). In exchange for the resources they receive, counseling centers are expected to produce student outcomes that benefit the college or university's efforts to produce successful learners and graduates (Boyd et al., 2003; Schwitzer, 1997). Likewise, college health centers provide public health services, including psychiatry, in the context of the college or university institutional community (Reifler, Liptzin, & Fox, 2006). On one hand, much of college counseling work takes the form of one-on-one services for individual students, including individual and group counseling, psychological testing and assessment, and emergency services (Boyd et al., 2003). On the other hand, contemporary college counselors' roles have expanded to include prevention, psychoeducation, and developmental intervention—as well as consultation and institutional crisis responses—in which "the entire campus environment" is the client (Archer & Cooper, 1998, p. 8).

Generally speaking, these primary college counseling services can be divided into three categories: prevention, intermediate intervention, and psychotherapeutic intervention (Drum & Lawler, 1988). These three types of services each require different approaches and strategies on the part of the college counselors who provide them. In the sections that follow, this chapter will explore the close fit with, as well as the limitations of, the humanistic perspective when engaging in preventive, intermediate, and psychotherapeutic college counseling work. First, the college counseling context and the tripartite response model are more fully described. Next, humanism and its relationships to preventive, intermediate, and psychotherapeutic interventions each are discussed. An illustration using a common college counseling problem, eating concerns among university women, is included. Finally, concluding comments are provided.

THE PREVALENCE OF SEVERE PSYCHOLOGICAL PROBLEMS AMONG COLLEGE STUDENTS AND THE TRIPARTITE INTERVENTION MODEL

Previous authors have described the challenges faced by today's college and university counseling centers, including a substantial overall demand for clinical services and outreach services, the need to serve an increasingly diverse student population, and pressures to address students who present increasingly complex counseling issues and increasingly severe diagnosable mental disorders (Bishop, 2006; Hodges, 2001; Stone & Archer, 1990). Considering overall demand, large numbers of students continue to seek college counseling for moderate adjustment, developmental, and other personal problems (Gallagher, 2009). Regarding adjustment, they seek counseling assistance with concerns including academic adjustment, institutional adjustment, social adjustment, and personal-emotional adjustment (Baker, McNeil, & Siryk, 1985; Baker & Siryk, 1984; Schwitzer, Ancis, & Brown, 2001). Regarding development, students seek assistance with concerns related to psychosocial development (Chickering & Reisser, 1993; Reisser, 1995), cognitive development, career development, ethical and moral development, gender identity, racial identity, or sexual identity (Evans, Forney, & Guido-DiBrito, 1998). Regarding the personal concerns that bring students to the counseling center, common presenting problems range from managing time to feelings of moderate depression to dealing with periods of suicidal ideation or bizarre thoughts (Bishop, Bauer, & Becker, 1998; Gallagher, 2009).

Alongside these traditional college student counseling needs, the demand for more intensive mental health services on today's campuses is well documented. In fact, according to the annual National Survey of College Counseling Center Directors, about half of the student clients seen at counseling centers in a recent year presented "severe psychological problems," including diagnosable depressive disorders and suicidal ideation, anxiety disorders and panic attacks, and other concerns (Gallagher, 2009; p. 3). Similarly, counseling center directors reported increases in the numbers of students needing crisis counseling, reports of student self-injury, students presenting eating disorders, and students reporting sexual assault. Many of these students would be unlikely to remain in, and succeed in, college without the availability of counseling services, psychiatric services, or both; further, increasingly, for some students, access to psychiatric medication and occasional hospitalization are needed supports (Gallagher, 2009). It should be emphasized that there is some debate in the college counseling field as to whether levels of student psychopathology have progressively increased to the degree perceived by counselors themselves or whether other factors (e.g., increased overall demands on college counselors' time, increased pressures of managed care and session limits, and increased use of psychiatric medication) might also influence clinicians' perceptions of client severity (Jenks Kettman et al., 2007; Meadows, 2000; Schwartz, 2006; Sharkin, 1997); however, there is agreement that the severity of student concerns has been at least steady through the 1990s and 2000s (Schwartz, 2006; Jenks Kettman et al., 2007) and that college clients' needs have clearly become increasingly complex and exhausting of counseling resources (Archer & Cooper, 1998; Davis & Humphrey, 2000; Rudd, 2004).

Tripartite Intervention Model

To respond to the full range of college students' adjustment, developmental, and mental health needs, Drum and Lawler (1988) developed a tripartite intervention model that is applicable to the counseling demands of the college and university setting. This comprehensive response model includes three types of approaches—preventive, intermediate, and psychotherapeutic—which are implemented according to the characteristics of a target population. These characteristics include (1) current level of need, (2) perceived sense of urgency, and (3) motivation for change. Goals and service delivery methods differ according to the type of intervention approach implemented.

According to the model, prevention strategies are intended to prevent or forestall the onset of problems or personal-emotional needs. Although no current need for assistance may exist, susceptibility to a particular problem is possible or probable. Students feel no urgent need for services and have low (or no) motivation for change. Prevention relies most heavily on providing information to increase understanding, enhance attitudes, and promote healthier behavior. Preventive methods include psychoeducational formats such as lectures and outreach programs, media presentations, brochures and web-based resources, and emphasis on self-assessment.

Intermediate intervention is implemented when the need for support is characterized as emerging or clearly present. These interventions facilitate normally expected adjustment or psychosocial development, or mitigate moderate psychoemotional concerns, by helping individuals add new skills or dimensions to their lives or by preventing derailment of adjustment or a developmental process because of underlying conflicts or dysfunction. Intermediate interventions may be implemented when a problem exists, causes some difficulties, and has the potential to grow but currently falls short of severely impairing individuals' daily functioning. The goals of intermediate intervention are to promote planned self-directed inquiry and develop problem-solving strategies while maintaining low levels of client–student resistance. Active service delivery modes such as problem assessment, limited individual counseling, theme- and skill-focused counseling and support groups, and interactive workshops are used.

Finally, according to the model, more intensive or extensive individual and group psychotherapy is used to address recurrent issues and "entrenched dysfunctional life patterns" (Drum & Lawler, 1988, p. 13). At this level of difficulty, a high sense of urgency and moderately high motivation for change are usual. However, in some cases, persons tend to remain defensive and resistant to assistance regardless of their distress. Sometimes, multidisciplinary treatment, psychiatric medication, hospitalization, off-campus referrals, or separation from the institution are required to best serve students' needs at this level of intervention. How does humanism fit into this context?

HUMANISM AND PREVENTIVE INTERVENTION

Humanism emphasizes intervention practices that are designed and implemented in ways that engage individuals in "growth-producing ways" (Bohart, 2003, p. 107) and focuses on individuals' sense of purpose (Raskin, Rogers, & Witty, 2008). Humanistic approaches attempt to capitalize on individuals' own subjective experiences—their own attitudes, values, and beliefs—and their innate abilities to creatively address the life concerns they encounter (Raskin et al., 2008). Humanistic interventions are "people-responsive" (Bohart, 2003, p. 107).

College counseling preventive intervention practices are closely grounded in these humanistic concepts. Preventive interventions target individuals with situations ranging from no current need to possible susceptibility to preliminarily emerging needs (Drum & Lawler, 1988). Some college campus examples pertaining to *adjustment* include first-year residential students who are susceptible to academic problems (Schwitzer, McGovern, & Robbins, 1991) and African American matriculants on predominantly White campuses who are susceptible to social adjustment hurdles (Schwitzer, Griffin, Ancis, & Thomas, 1999). Gay men and lesbians beginning to deal with young adult identity issues (Meyer & Schwitzer, 1999) offer one example pertaining to a *developmental* situation that might be the target of preventive intervention. Among the various *personal concerns* to which specialized college populations may be susceptible, two examples are nontraditional students of color who may potentially experience factors detrimental to their wellness (Myers & Mobley, 2004) and college women experiencing body dissatisfaction who may potentially experience aspects of diagnosable eating disorders (Choate & Schwitzer, 2009)—both of which could be targeted for prevention services.

There is evidence that counseling center efforts aimed at preventing the emergence of adjustment problems (DeStefano, Mellott, & Peterson, 2001; Schwitzer & Thomas, 1998), mitigating the negative influences of developmental issues (Meilman, 2001), or anticipating the emergence of psychological concerns (Gonzalez, Tinsley, & Kreuder, 2002; Kahn, Wood, & Wiesen, 1999) can be beneficial for the students who take advantage of them. However, paradoxically, a difficulty in making these preventive services successful is that although distress or dysfunction may be likely to emerge later on individuals targeted for prevention are those who at present usually have no sense of urgency or perhaps a very modest sense of urgency and low or no motivation for change (Drum & Lawler, 1988). Therefore, to reach these students prevention strategies must attract and engage the targeted population and maintain low levels of resistance or other negative reactions. According to the model, these types of strategies mainly focus on (1) equipping students with new information about the adjustment, developmental, or personal concern that is the prevention topic; (2) equipping students with new and better information about self in relation to the topic; (3) enhancing students' attitudes about the benefits of engaging in the topic; and (4) attempting to promote or motivate healthier behavior or actions.

To accomplish this, prevention intentionally invokes humanistic elements by approaching the targeted students holistically, as whole individuals who are active, self-directed agents in their own well-being, rather than more narrowly defining them according to the problems to which they are susceptible (Davidson, 2000). Prevention is simply aimed at giving those targeted the tools with which they can hopefully make better and more adaptive decisions, choices, and behavior patterns. Likewise, prevention is intended to advance the participants' own beliefs and attitudes so they can become more aware of their situation, possible needs, and role in forestalling or mitigating future potential hurdles and negative situations. To be effective, prevention must lean toward passively providing good information, including topical information and information about self, and must rely on individuals to access their own energies and personal resources to positively act on this information. In other words, following humanistic principles, the focus is on attempting to influence students' subjective experience and then relying on them to transfer these influences into action and respecting their ability to do so (Bohart, 2003; Raskin et al., 2008).

CASE ILLUSTRATION: COLLEGE WOMEN
AND EATING-RELATED CONCERNS

It may be helpful to consider an example applying the tripartite response model to a representative college counseling problem. Previous authors have described application of the model to the issue of college women and eating-related concerns (Choate & Schwitzer, 2009; Schwitzer, Bergholtz, Dore, & Salimi, 1998; Schwitzer, Rodriguez, Thomas, & Salimi, 2001; Schwitzer et al., 2008). In part, this is an important example because college counseling professionals are responding increasingly to culturally specific and gender-related mental health problems on campus (Arnstein, 1995; Guinee & Ness, 2000; Lippincott & Lippincott, 2007). In addition, college women's eating-related concerns present an interesting college counseling issue because although a very high incidence of eating disorders and eating-relating problems among college girls and women is well documented (Gallagher, Golin, & Kelleher, 1992; Koszewski, Newell, & Higgins, 1990; Miller & Rice, 1993; Schwitzer et al., 1998; Schwitzer, Rodriguez, et al., 2001) only a few of these students tend to experience problems that meet the criteria for the most severe, complex eating disorders, namely, bulimia and anorexia. For example, early on, Koszewski et al. (1990) found that although 25% of college women believed their eating was out of control, only 6% reported the type of vomiting or laxative use associated with more severe disorders. Primarily, these students are susceptible to the possible emergence of moderate problems centering on dissatisfaction with body image, weight preoccupation, difficulties with weight control, and problematic aspirations to become thinner (cf. Choate & Schwitzer, 2009; Schwitzer et al., 1998, 2008; Schwitzer, Rodriguez, et al., 2001). Further, Schwitzer and colleagues (1998, 2001, 2008) found that these girls and women also had the potential to develop several predictable associated psychological features, including fragile self-esteem, moderate depression, problematic perfectionism, interpersonal problems, and other adjustment concerns.

Drum and Lawlers's (1988) tripartite response model has been effectively employed to offer a comprehensive program of counseling center eating disorders services on campuses. Using the model, the targeted populations for preventive intervention in the case of women's eating problems are female students who exhibit normally expected eating, exercise, and weight management skills and behaviors but who may be susceptible to the development of problematic behavior. Susceptibility to eating-related problems can be estimated by membership in groups traditionally identified with high incidences of eating disorders (such as women athletes; Skowron & Friedlander, 1994; Sykora et al., 1993); experiences or perceptions of student affairs staff (e.g., student activities advisors, residence hall staff, or coaches), relevant faculty (e.g., health sciences and psychology faculty), or key students (e.g., resident assistants or sorority leaders); trends in the campus's counseling, wellness, and health centers; or other methods of needs assessment.

As described earlier, preventive strategies rely most heavily on providing topical information and information about self to increase understanding, enhance attitudes, and promote more effective behavior. Prevention strategies usually include psychoeducational workshops and lectures and media presentations, brochures and web-based information, and self-assessment. With eating disorders, college counselors can collaborate with health center staff, health educators, dining service and nutritional staff, faculty, and others on campus to develop preventive interventions that operationalize humanistic principles.

One strategy is to offer inviting programs, events, and workshops that aim to heighten women's awareness of social and cultural pressures for female thinness and to assist students to reconsider and, ideally, change their attitudes and self-perceptions pertaining to body image and overvaluation of appearance (Keel, 2005; Levine & Piran, 2004; Stice & Hoffman, 2004). Choate (2008) referred to this as increasing girls' and women's media literacy. Such workshops focus on the influence of media and social environment on women's development of body dissatisfaction and eating problems. In the workshops, counselors facilitate participants' examination of the trend toward a progressively thinner, culturally derived feminine ideal (Andersen & DiDomenico, 1992; Wiseman, Gray, Mosimann, & Ahrens, 1992). Participants learn to deconstruct and resist social and media messages. For example, participants may review women's magazines' advertisements and then confront questions such as, "Do real women look like these models?", "If I look like this, would my life really become like the one portrayed in the ad?", and "What are the effects of these messages on you and your college peers?" (Choate & Schwitzer, 2009). Likewise, participants may confront information such as the documented decrease in the weight of the *Playboy* magazine Playmate of the Month model in recent decades from 91% to 83% of average weight (Silverstein, Perdue, Peterson, Vogel, & Fantini, 1986; Wiseman et al., 1992). Such programs may also introduce uncomfortable topics like the effects of "fat jokes" and other biased behaviors on women's sense of self. These interventions also might encourage participants to broaden their definitions of beauty to include such nonappearance qualities as empathy, compassion, and kindness (Choate & Schwitzer, 2009). The bottom line of such programs is to engage participants holistically, to facilitate a discussion of their own subjective experiences of body and female identity, to encourage their creative and purposeful examination of self and influences on the self, and thereby hopefully to spark a stronger resilience to potential eating-related problems down the road via engaged self-examination and increased understanding. In turn, participants may leave these programs better able to adopt a more active role in transforming the current cultural climate for girls and women and to adopt better ways to cope with and adjust to this climate (Levine & Piran, 2004). As can be seen, these strategies all employ the central tenets of psychological humanism (Hansen, 2006).

A second strategy is to provide health, physical wellness, and nutritional programs. These prevention programs offer psychoeducation about normative physical development and weight changes across the life span, healthy exercise and weight control plans, and nutrition and realistic eating (Choate & Schwitzer, 2009; Schwitzer et al., 1998, 2008; Schwitzer, Rodriguez, et al., 2001). These programs invite women to explore their own eating and weight management behaviors and provide better, more accurate information about food intake and the body's use of energy sources (Stice, Presnell, Gau, & Shaw, 2007). On campus, one prevention tactic is to provide nutritional education in natural settings. Very early on, Daniel (1988) found that when campus dining services provided nutritional information about their menus students made better choices and consumed more low-fat milk, vegetables, and nutrient-dense foods. This includes passively offering information via menu boards, newsletters or websites, and cards right in the dining hall flagging healthier choices. Counselors also take advantage of the natural campus ecology by incorporating eating disorder prevention into existing programs by adding health and nutrition components to wellness center orientations, dining services nutrition programs, and the like. Here again, the goal is to relate to the students targeted for prevention in "growth-producing ways" (Bohart, 2003, p. 107) that rely on the students themselves to access, consider, integrate, and apply in their own lives wellness information, psychoeducational concepts, and self-assessments that will result in greater resilience against the possible onset of eating-related physical and psychological problems.

HUMANISM AND INTERMEDIATE INTERVENTION

Amplifying humanism's emphasis on "people-responsive" interventions (Bohart, 2003, p. 107), counseling strategies from the psychological humanistic perspective are selected and implemented on the basis of a sound understanding and valuing of clients' intrapersonal and interpersonal experiences (Raskin et al., 2008) and are intended to be growth producing (Bohart, 2003). Further, humanistic practices primarily look forward, emphasizing sense of purpose, rather than primarily looking for causal explanations of behavior based on reductionist mechanisms or psychosocial etiologies (Raskins et al., 2008).

There is considerable heuristic overlap between many of these elements of humanistic practice and the intermediate-level intervention approach defined by Drum and Lawler's (1988) model. Intermediate interventions are aimed at individuals for whom the need for assistance is emerging or clearly present. Intermediate interventions are implemented when a student concern or problem exists, causes some difficulties, and has the potential to grow, but currently falls short of severely impairing the student's everyday adjustment and functioning. One college campus example pertaining to *adjustment* is the difficulty some gay and lesbian students experience with peer relationships and other facets of social adjustment to predominantly heterosexual institutions, when these difficulties begin to interrupt daily functioning and mood (Jurgens, Schwitzer, & Middleton, 2004). Financial aid students who encounter personal or family obstacles when attempting to establish young adult autonomy, and therefore fail to develop the self-reliance abilities needed to complete coursework and other educational requirements, leading to college-career-threatening academic problems, offer an example pertaining to a *developmental* concern that might be targeted for inter-mediate intervention (Schwitzer, Grogan, Kaddoura, & Ochoa, 1993). Students experiencing adjustment disorders or acute stress disorders following large-scale traumatic incidents (such as the 9/11 terrorist attacks on US sites or the 2007 Virginia Tech shootings) exemplify *personal concerns* that might be amenable to intermediate counseling responses (Schwitzer, 2003). This is because although adjustment disorder symptoms interfere with mood and everyday effectiveness students experiencing this level of concern typically can continue to function at least modestly well, and although acute stress disorder symptoms interrupt day-to-day well-being they are present for only a short time span.

Although at this level of difficulty a counseling-related problem is pres-ent and may grow, because the problem is not yet experienced to be severely impairing individuals' sense of urgency for assistance may be low to moderate to moderately high, and their motivation for change generally is low to moder-ate. Therefore, the goal of intermediate counseling responses is to assist indi-viduals in planful, self-directed inquiry and in developing effective problem solving while maintaining low levels of resistance. These responses are intended to facilitate normally expected psychosocial development by helping students to add new skills or dimensions to their lives or by preventing derailment of a developmental process or adjustment experience due to emerging and poten-tially growing dysfunction. Active service delivery modes are used, including problem assessment, limited or brief individual counseling, theme- and skill-focused counseling groups and support groups, and interactive workshops.

These types of midlevel counseling practices intentionally emphasize students' self-experience of distress and motivation, use an approach that is forward look-ing with the goal of forestalling future difficulties and facilitating their return to optimal everyday adjustment, and in turn set out to facilitate growth of skills, coping abilities, and enhanced developmental resilience that will be valued skills and dimensions on which they can rely in the future. That is, intermediate inter-vention practices are a natural operationalization of humanism's holistic and person-centered responsiveness and focus on persons' self-experience and for-ward-directed counseling orientation. Clinicians with a background that includes exposure to humanistic elements of counseling have a variety of the needed heu-ristic tools for intermediate intervention in the college and university context.

CASE ILLUSTRATION: COLLEGE WOMEN
AND EATING-RELATED CONCERNS

This section continues the helpful case example of college women and eating-related concerns, this time applied to intermediate-level intervention. The targeted population includes female students who are experiencing emerging cognitive, emotional, and behavioral aspects of eating-related difficulties but who are not experiencing fully developed symptoms of diagnosable anorexia or bulimia. Girls and women most at risk for developing eating disorders include students who perceive strong pressures to be thin, who internalize the thin ideal as their own standard for self-worth, and who are exposed to negative body image modeling and eating disturbances in their families and elsewhere (Stice, 2002). They tend to experience low self-esteem, low mood, and problematic perfectionism (Bearman, Presnell, Martinez, & Stice, 2006; Schwitzer et al., 1998, 2008; Stice, 2002). They tend to engage in problematic weight control behaviors such as extreme dieting, excessive exercise, episodic binge eating, and occasional use of compensatory behaviors such as self-induced vomiting and laxative and diuretic misuse (Fairburn, 1995; Schwitzer et al., 1998, 2008). One example is the student who is concerned about her appearance despite normal weight and compulsively overexercises at certain times, such as prior to spring break, and periodically deals with feelings of depression and inadequacy. As indicated earlier, this student's sense of urgency for assistance and motivation to address her concerns would likely be low.

As described, the primary goals of intermediate intervention strategies are to facilitate normally expected psychosocial development or adjustment to college life by helping individuals add new skills or dimensions to their lives or by preventing derailment of development or adjustment due to the interference of moderate dysfunctions. In the case of eating concerns, intermediate interventions are designed to improve self-perceptions so that self-esteem is less closely tied to body image; ameliorate feelings of low mood or anxiety; encourage a shift to healthier eating and weight management behaviors; and, especially, forestall the development of full-syndrome diagnosable eating disorders (Choate & Schwitzer, 2009). Generally speaking, intermediate interventions rely on group formats and brief or limited individual counseling. With eating disorders, group formats and the use of groups in combination with one-on-one counseling appear to be especially effective because groups can increase girls' and women's sense of universality, offer social support, and provide other benefits from interacting with similar others (Stice, 2002; Stice & Hoffman, 2004).

On campus, one strategy for addressing the themes important to moderate eating disorders is to provide one-shot, stand-alone workshops as well as brief group formats that emphasize (1) education about one's body-related thoughts, feelings, and behaviors and (2) development of healthier eating and weight control skills. For example, Dworkin and Kerr (1987) found improvements in self-esteem and body image perceptions of students in brief developmental groups with an emphasis on thoughts about self. Weiss and Orysh (1994) reported decreases in eating disorder symptoms and improved mood among women in a theme group that provided education about eating disorder symptoms, self-monitoring skills, and coping strategies. Taking advantage of the campus ecology, these intermediate programs and groups are offered in-house at the counseling center, as part of a campus lecture series, at female residence hall floor meetings, or for women's populations such as female athletic teams and sororities. More recently, web- and media-based programs have been developed on some campuses, in which clients engage with self-help materials along with electronic bulletin boards that offer support and discussion forums (Zabinski et al., 2001).

Supportive and problem-focused individual counseling also is used to meet the needs of women presenting moderate eating disorder symptoms. For the most part, the goals of individual sessions are to help clients identify, examine, and change their problematic beliefs and attitudes about shape, weight, and the importance of appearance (Celio & Winzelberg, 2000; Zabinski et al., 2001). Counselors providing intermediate services sometimes use active strategies that encourage girls and women to confront sociocultural pressures and their own self-beliefs (Stice, Chase, Stormer, & Appel, 2001). Examples include (Choate & Schwitzer, 2009) asking a client to "role play what you might say to girl who is engaging in fat talk and who is comparing herself to unrealistic beauty standards" and asking a client to write a persuasive letter that might dissuade a younger girl that she cares about from accepting the thin ideal as her social comparison standard.

Another effective intermediate approach for women's eating concerns is to use peers and other paraprofessionals. For example, Schwitzer and colleagues (1998, 2001) trained dining hall staff, athletic center and wellness center staff, and aerobics instructors to identify and consult with counseling center eating disorder staff about students who potentially might be experiencing intermediate concerns. Others have found that when students were paired with trained peer counselors or health peer educators, they engaged in less binging, purging, and meal skipping and experienced less perfectionism and compulsiveness (Lenihan & Kirk, 1990).

The aim of all of these intermediate approaches—including brief theme-focused counseling, workshops and groups, and use of peer and paraprofessional supports—is to help female students with midlevel eating concerns learn to become more accepting and appreciative of their bodies and their nonphysical qualities and attributes, to develop a greater capacity for withstanding societal pressures, and to adopt healthier weight and shape management skills and habits. They intentionally reached out to girls and women on campus with moderate concerns to hopefully impact their experience of self and thereby improve their

everyday adjustment and reduce their susceptibility to more substantial problems. Overall, these activities were based on creative, holistic, purposeful themes
and were intended to capitalize on clients themselves to enact positive changes
in their lives.

HUMANISM, STUDENT MENTAL HEALTH CONCERNS, AND PSYCHOTHERAPEUTIC INTERVENTION

As has been discussed so far in this chapter, there is natural overlap between the
core tenets of humanistic counseling and the primary methods by which college
counseling professionals go about providing preventive and intermediate interventions to (1) forestall the development of adjustment, developmental, and mental health concerns among susceptible student populations and to (2) address
these types of concerns early in their emergence to mitigate their negative impact
on students' academic success and everyday intrapersonal and interpersonal
functioning. Turning to the final phase of Drum and Lawler's (1988) model,
which calls for the use of psychotherapeutic intervention, there also are potential
limits to the overlap between the practice of college counseling and the humanistic perspective. These potential limits stem from the severity or complexity of
some college clients' concerns—and the wide range of client conceptualization,
treatment planning, and therapeutic approaches used by college counseling professionals when they assess, set goals for, and employ counseling interventions to
address their clients' psychotherapeutic-level needs.

Hansen (2006) characterized psychological humanism as a negation of reductive theoretical counseling orientations. The humanistic model resists reductionist viewpoints that closely associate individuals' functioning with their thoughts
and behaviors (e.g., with cognitive and cognitive–behavioral approaches) or
intrapsychic structures (e.g., with psychoanalytic and contemporary psychodynamic approaches) (Davidson, 2000). The psychological humanistic perspective
deemphasizes the influences of psychological etiology (whereas these influences
are critical to psychosocial developmental, psychodynamic, family systems, and
other contemporary models of clinical case conceptualization) and physiological
etiology (which is closely examined in the dominant assessment approaches of
clinical and counseling psychology and psychiatry) in favor of an emphasis on
individuals' "sense of purpose" and the positives found in their creative approach
to life and their subjective self-experience (Raskin et al., 2008; p. 146). Likewise,
humanism would resist an importance on diagnosis to reductively characterize a
client's difficulties. Correspondingly, resisting approaches driven by reductionist
views of client distress or dysfunction, humanism emphasizes a good therapeutic
relationship as the basis for effective counseling outcomes (Raskin et al., 2008).

Looking at Drum and Lawler's model (1988), psychotherapeutic intervention
is indicated when students are experiencing personal concerns that are more

advanced; are recurrent, long-standing, or chronically entrenched; and are causing clinically significant distress or dysfunction in the person's life. Typically,
the distress comprises substantial problems in thinking, attitudes, or beliefs
(e.g., hopeless or helpless thinking, clear misperceptions of self or others, or
diminished ability to concentrate and learn) along with disruptive changes in
mood (e.g., depressed or low mood, high anxiety, or problematic anger and rage
or shame and guilt). The dysfunction comprises significant disruptions in the
person's abilities to successfully fulfill daily roles, such as the demands of being
a student, employee, parent, family member, romantic partner, or member of
important campus groups. Physiological disruptions (e.g., sleep or appetite problems) often occur as well as worrisome behaviors like social withdrawal, trouble
managing anger or substance use, or reduced impulse control. Predominant clinical models tend to characterize such needs as full-syndrome problems or diagnosable mental disorders. Developmental, adjustment, and student mental health
problems all can evolve into the "entrenched dysfunctional life patterns" that are
the targets of psychotherapeutic intervention (Drum & Lawler, 1988, p. 13).

   As described at the outset of this chapter, according to the model at this level
of need many individuals feel a high sense of urgency for support and are moderately high to highly motivated for change; however, even with psychotherapeutic
intervention some people remain cautiously resistant, self-protectively defensive,
or hesitant about help seeking and follow-through with counseling. Students'
problems at this level are addressed through more intensive face-to-face treatment. Sometimes they require a combination of modalities—such as individual
counseling or psychotherapy, group counseling or psychotherapy, psychiatric
medication, and inpatient hospitalization. On today's campuses, college counseling professionals' common perceptions are that students with psychotherapeutic-level needs take up the bulk of their professional energies, work time, and
caseloads (Jenks Kettman et al, 2007; Schwartz, 2006)—outweighing their prevention and intermediate-level work.

   When implementing psychotherapeutic interventions to address these student needs, counseling professionals are expected to "understand that the
[counseling] relationship has a natural progression that begins with the building of a therapeutic alliance, leads toward the identification of problems, moves
forward toward working on those problems, and has a clear ending based on the
attainment of goals" (Neukrug & Schwitzer, 2006). According to predominant
approaches, competencies and clinical tools needed at this level of intervention
include diagnostic, case conceptualization, treatment planning, and case management skills (Neukrug & Schwitzer, 2006; Seligman, 2004). Assessment and
diagnostic skills are employed to help the clinician evaluate risk and determine
the primary focus of counseling. These skills allow the counselor to describe and
communicate about the clinically significant concerns, distress and impairment
in important areas of functioning, or increased risks a student is experiencing

(APA, 2000). Case conceptualization is employed so the clinician can observe and assess students' critical areas of need; can use these observations and assessments to find patterns and themes in clients' concerns; and, as a function of the counselor's theoretical orientation and on the basis of best practices and available clinical evidence, can use these patterns and themes to understand, explain, or make clinical judgments about the etiological factors (underlying or root causes) and sustaining factors (features keeping the problem going) associated with students' concerns (Neukrug & Schwitzer, 2006; Seligman, 2004). In turn, treatment planning requires "plotting out the counseling process so that both the counselor and client have a road map that delineates how they will proceed from their point of origin (the client's presenting concerns and underlying difficulties) to their destination, alleviation of troubling and dysfunctional symptoms and patterns, and establishment of improved coping mechanisms" (Seligman, 1993, p. 288; 1996, p. 157). The competent use of these clinical tools is seen as a vital aspect of mental healthcare delivery at the level of psychotherapeutic intervention (Neukrug & Schwitzer, 2006; Jongsma & Peterson, 2003; Seligman, 1993, 1996).

Further, college counseling professionals use a wide range of clinical approaches—matching intervention models with students' needs on the basis of their own theoretical orientations, accepted best practices, evidence-based findings, agency-specific counseling center or health center requirements, or professional training. Solution-focused brief counseling, various cognitive-behavioral therapies (CBT), family systems counseling, various psychodynamic and contemporary psychodynamic models such as object relations therapy, gender-based counseling, multicultural and culturally competent approaches, and other methods all are commonly used on campuses to address student needs for which psychotherapeutic-level interventions are indicated (Archer & Cooper, 1998; Davis & Humphrey, 2000; Lippincott & Lippincott, 2007; May, 1988). For example, among real-life case studies recently appearing in the *Journal of College Counseling* were illustrations of: ecological perspectives to address Latino students' college adjustment problems (Cerezo, O'Neil, & McWhirter, 2009); attachment theory to mitigate student self-injury (Aizenman, 2009); object relations theory to assist a student presenting with borderline personality disorder (Draper & Faulkner, 2009); a multidisciplinary mind–body approach integrating cognitive-behavioral counseling, psychiatric medication, and mindfulness interventions to treat students' mood disorder symptoms (Tucker, Sloan, Vance, & Brownson, 2008); a combination of client-centered and cognitive-behavioral counseling to assist a nonhearing student from deaf culture with his depression and suicidal ideation (Whyte & Guiffrida, 2008); and to help another client presenting the affective problem of depression, a combination of Adlerian, cognitive-behavioral, and Gestalt techniques (Mobley, 2008). Of course, some college counselors also use client-centered therapy as a stand-alone treatment. However, the extant literature suggests that Rogerian approaches alone are not uniformly indicated to address all client concerns. For instance, Scholl (2002) reported that advice-giving some-times is required alongside empathic listening to establish a therapeutic alliance with college clients, and Wester (2007) raised the possibility that client-centered approaches might actually increase, rather than decrease, self-harm among self-injuring college clientele.

Can the gap be bridged between, on one hand, humanistic philosophical foundations emphasizing irreducibility of human experiences to their etiologi-cal causes and underlying processes and elements of humanism that essentially view positive counseling outcomes as derived from a good counseling relation-ship and, on the other hand, college counseling competencies as they are most often employed in everyday psychotherapeutic-level practice? Several concepts are useful in clarifying the important contributions of a general humanistic ori-entation as a backdrop to everyday college therapy practice. These concepts help to facilitate a clearer understanding of the intentionally narrow role of diagnosis, the clinically sensitive application of case conceptualization, and the engaging implementation of the interpersonal counseling process—and the contributions of humanism to the use of these clinical competencies.

The first concept relates to clearly understanding the purposes and uses of mental health diagnosis (APA, 2004; Neukrug & Schwitzer, 2006; Seligman, 2004; Schwitzer & Everett, 1997). The *Diagnostic and Statistical Manual of Mental Disorders,* fourth edition, text revision *(DSM-IV-TR)* (APA, 2000) is a straightforward system based on sets of criteria that are made up of observable features. In other words, *DSM-IV-TR* descriptions of client presentations are criterion referenced. This system of describing and categorizing stems from the traditional medical-scientific method of organizing, naming, and communicat-ing information in as objective a fashion as possible. The main purpose of devel-oping a *DSM-IV-TR*-style diagnosis is to allow clinicians to describe what they see and hear regarding their client and to communicate this to other clinicians who also understand the *DSM-IV-TR.* That is, the purpose of the *DSM* system is to help mental health professionals to describe and communicate with other professionals. It is intended to enhance agreement and improve the sharing of information among clinicians about the client picture they are observing. In the college context, a university counselor who receives a report containing diagnos-tic information from a new client's high school therapist quickly learns about the client's earlier experiences via a succinct clinical vocabulary. For example, when a college counselor learns from a prior therapist that her new client's symptoms previously were described by generalized anxiety disorder, she knows that the problem has persisted at least 6 months and was not due to substance use.

This limited purpose is important to understand because it means that a diag-nosis also does *not* do many things: A diagnosis does not provide etiology or tell the clinician the roots of a client's concerns, and it does not prescribe a plan for treatment. It simply provides the counselor with a vocabulary for determining the area of the client's concerns and communicating about this with another counselor. Further, although the system relies on the medical/scientific approach of organizing client information, the *DSM-IV-TR* does not reflect a theoretical orientation, disciplinary viewpoint, or causal inference. Rather, *DSM-IV-TR* diagnoses are intended to be theory-neutral descriptions of behavior, thoughts, mood, functioning, and distress. In the example of the student experiencing generalized anxiety disorder, the *DSM* provides criteria for describing the client picture but does not indicate whether the person's excessive worry is a product of faulty thinking patterns or is rooted in early parental conflicts. Similarly, a course of treatment, such as relaxation training, is not specified.

One additional possible misperception about clinical diagnosis is that a classification system works to classify or describe people; instead, the *DSM* system actually classifies concerns people are experiencing. In support of this, the *DSM-IV-TR* carefully and consistently uses phrases such as "an individual with Schizophrenia" or "an individual with Alcohol Dependence" rather than terms like "a schizophrenic" or "an alcoholic" throughout the text (APA, 2000).

The diagnosis simply describes and enhances communication. "Individual counselors can communicate with [college] mental health colleagues about the person's basic presentation using *DSM-IV-TR* categories and descriptors—and at the same time apply their own philosophy, belief system, theoretical perspective, and treatment plan in their work with the individual" (Schwitzer & Everett, 1997, p. 57).

The second concept addresses compatibility between the use of interpretive or inferential case conceptualization and treatment planning skills and tools and basic humanistic tenets (Neukrug & Schwitzer, 2006; Schwitzer, 2005; Seligman, 2004). College counseling professionals typically rely on case conceptualization to make inferences about the behavior and experiences of their late adolescent, young adult, and adult clients. Case conceptual models attempt to cast a wide net to gather information about persons' experiences and concerns, to make some sense of these experiences and concerns in the context of the person's everyday life, to use this understanding to plot out a potentially effective way to address their concerns in the context of their everyday life, and when needed to look as deeply as possible at their past and present experiences, events, and functioning to accurately assess risk (e.g., risk of self-harm or harm to others) and provide rational counseling responses to improve their adjustment and functioning (Neukrug & Schwitzer, 2006; Schwitzer, 1997).

As with diagnosis, one possible misperception about case conceptualization is that contemporary conceptual approaches work to classify, interpret, explain, or make inferences about people. An extension of this possible misperception is that case conceptualization narrowly equates persons with their counseling concerns, symptoms, and inferred intrapersonal or interpersonal processes. One additional possible misperception is that conceptual inferences and interpretations are value oriented in nature, that is, that they are personal judgments or criticizing evaluative statements about persons. These are some of the very heuristic elements against which humanism is a counterreaction.

On the contrary, case conceptualization is expected to describe persons' *experiences* as fully and accurately as possible: thoughts, feelings, behaviors, and physiology; intrapersonal and interpersonal themes; distress and dysfunction; and strengths, adaptations, and inner resources. Conceptual pictures are formed tentatively and via engagement with clients. Conceptualizations are formed with an eye clearly on the end goals of improvement and return to better life adjustment and functioning. Further, most importantly, rather than demeaning or negatively judging clients via case conceptual inferences the counselor understands that they are approaching life as well as they can at the moment. For example, among today's interpretive models, contemporary psychodynamic approaches attempt to closely look at how individuals' functioning serves as their innovative "adaptive strategy for self-cure" (Kohut, 1977, p. 880). That is, what might be characterized as clients' "symptoms" are readily and respectfully understood to be personally important, useful methods they have found for managing life's (intrapersonal and interpersonal, sometimes past and present) demands and challenges. As follows, the goal of conceptually driven college counseling is to assist students to find better—less problematic, less distressful, more functional, more effective, more satisfying—strategies for managing, compensating for, or defending against life's concerns.

The third concept pertains to psychotherapeutic interventions and the counseling relationship. A principle of humanism is that counseling is essentially based on a good counselor–client relationship. For its part, the college counseling field applies a wide range of psychotherapeutic models ranging from highly client centered to more highly centered on the clinician as expert (Archer & Cooper, 1998; Davis & Humphrey, 2000; Lippincott & Lippincott, 2007; May, 1988). Ideally, the approach used is derived from the counselors' clinical thinking in the form of diagnosis, case conceptualization, and treatment planning. Counselors variously employ the roles of listener, analyzer, problem solver, and challenger when engaging in psychotherapeutic-level intervention (Neukrug & Schwitzer, 2006).

Neukrug and Schwitzer (2006) made distinctions among stages in the counseling relationship. Each stage requires an emphasis on specific areas of knowledge, attitudes, and skills. The humanistic emphasis on the counseling relationship is seen vividly throughout the process. Effective attitudes and skills pertaining to the professional helping relationship—including acceptance, open-mindedness, and maintenance of one's own psychological adjustment—are needed even prior to a first meeting with a client. According to Neukrug and Schwitzer, during the rapport and trust-building stage (stage 1), the focus is on the counseling relationship and needed abilities include: empathy and alliance building, acceptance, relationship building, and collaboration. During the problem identification stage

(stage 2), collaboration with the client and cognitive complexity for fully under-standing the client's situation are needed. While identifying the problem, the counselor must follow and guide the client's story and maintain rapport. Empathic understanding is needed for delving as deeply as needed into the client's experi-ence and gaining a broad view of the client's situation. Collaboration and cogni-tive complexity continue to be needed during goal setting and treatment planning (stage 3) and the working stage (stage 4). During these stages, the ability to affirm, encourage change, engagingly confront, and offer suggestions and alternatives from within the professional relationship context all are needed tools. Finally, hallmark skills needed at closure (stage 5) comprise: listening carefully and being empathic, being accepting and helpful in understanding and affirming the cli-ent's thoughts and feelings about the close of the relationship, and modeling and being genuine while maintaining one's own psychological adjustment. These critical abilities, attitudes, and skills fit closely with humanism's advancement of the counseling relationship. These tools all are necessary for successful coun-seling outcomes (Neukrug & Schwitzer, 2006). In addition, for some clinicians working with some clients presenting some psychotherapeutic-level concerns, these approaches produce sufficient changes and outcomes.

At the same time, according to the current literature, along with the foun-dational relationship skills just described additional skills usually are needed at each stage (Archer & Cooper, 1998; Davis & Humphrey, 2000; Lippincott & Lippincott, 2007; May, 1988; Neukrug & Schwitzer, 2006). As summarized by Neukrug and Schwitzer (2006), some of the additional tools needed at the rapport and trust-building stage (stage 1) and the problem identification stage (stage 2) are information gathering, structured interviewing, and assessment and diagnostic skills. These are needed to begin understanding the extent of the client's situation and to begin the process of developing a diagnosis and forming a treatment plan. At the goal-setting and treatment-planning stage (stage 3), additional required skills can include goal-setting abilities and tools such as giving advice, offering alternatives, and giving accurate information. The additional skills needed for the work stage (stage 4) are theory driven, derived from the clinician's single, integrative, or eclectic theoretical orientation.

Further, at every stage, clinicians must be aware of their own competencies and limitations regarding their potential to assist the client. "Competency" includes being able to make sound judgments about (1) who the service provider will be (from among specific staff members, or between different types of professionals such as counselors, psychologists, and psychiatrists); (2) what treatment formats will be employed (e.g., individual or group or other counseling modes; emer-gency or crisis services; specialized formats such as career or academic counsel-ing; psychological assessment; or psychiatric intervention and medication); and (3) when responses to risk are required (e.g., voluntary or mandated inpatient hospitalization or separation from the college or university).

As can be seen, on one hand, a wide range of skills derived from the humanistic focus on the counseling relationship are necessary to successfully conduct the various stages of the counseling relationship. On the other hand, according to the predominant viewpoint, at the psychotherapeutic intervention level, college counseling professionals also typically need to employ additional abilities from outside the humanistic perspective during the counseling process.

In sum, the humanistic heuristic has a strong influence on the psychotherapeutic work of college counselors. Although the overlap is not a complete one, humanism guides practice at this intervention level (1) when clinicians are careful about how they use their diagnostic skills, applying the *DSM-IV-TR* system narrowly and conscientiously remembering that diagnoses are neutral descriptions of client symptoms rather than characterizations of students themselves; (2) when counselors sensitively use case conceptualization and treatment planning by respecting the notion that clients are functioning as well as they can toward "adaptive self-cure" (Kohut, 1977, p. 880; Schwitzer, 2005) and by keeping the focus on achieving positive change; and (3) when counselors use the many vital humanistically driven, client-centered relational skills as the foundation for engaging with their clients in the professional helping process. Whether students experiencing psychotherapeutic-level intervention ultimately benefit from individual counseling, group therapy, health and wellness modalities, specialized supports such as disability services or academic counseling, crisis and emergency services, psychiatric medication, hospitalization, separation from the college or university, or some combination of these, their mental health-care experience will be a better one when the college counseling professionals involved include elements of humanism among their professional repertoire.

CASE ILLUSTRATION: COLLEGE WOMEN AND EATING-RELATED CONCERNS

This section revisits the helpful case example of college women and eating-related concerns for a snapshot of psychotherapeutic-level intervention. Although, by far, most college and university girls and women with eating-related concerns tend to experience problems with eating behaviors, weight management, self-esteem, and mood, which fall short of diagnosable anorexia or bulimia, some female students do experience these eating disorders. For a client's symptoms to meet the criteria for anorexia, the student must experience refusal to maintain normal body weight, operationalized as maintaining less than 85% of expected body weight or absence of three consecutive menstrual cycles; intense fear of gaining weight or becoming fat and disturbance in body image; and either restricted eating or binging and purging (APA, 2000). For a client's symptoms to meet the criteria for diagnosable bulimia, the student must be experiencing binge eating and compensatory behaviors (e.g., vomiting, laxative use, or overexercise, with these behaviors occurring at least twice weekly for a period of at least 3 months); and self-evaluation that is unduly influenced by body image (APA, 2000). Women whose symptoms meet these criteria are the target population for psychotherapeutic-level intervention on college campuses (Drum & Lawler, 1988; Schwitzer et al., 1998; Schwitzer et al., 2001).

As described earlier, the goal at this level of intervention is to address clearly present mental health concerns that are entrenched or recurrent and causing clinically significant distress or dysfunction or, as in the case of eating disorders, both. According to the model, at this level of difficulty, a high sense of urgency and moderately high motivation for change are usual. However, in the case of eating disorders, the person often remains defensive and resistant to treatment regardless of her distress.

Students dealing with more advanced eating disorders typically require more intensive, face-to-face treatment than offered via prevention programs or intermediate counseling responses. Multidisciplinary eating disorders treatment teams are recommended where possible. These teams typically include counseling or mental health center staff; physicians, psychiatrists, or other designated student health center professionals; and nutritionists who are located in health centers or dining services. Residence hall staff sometimes are involved in community-level intervention. Further, inpatient hospitalization sometimes is needed, particularly in the case of diagnosable anorexia.

Often on college and university campuses, resources are a problem when developing eating disorder responses. Staff time generally is a key resource consideration when deciding among time and effort to be dividing among prevention, intermediate responses, and psychotherapeutic intervention teams. This is especially salient because counseling centers and health centers often must limit their services to activities that directly support their institution's academic mission. Correspondingly, because prevention and intermediate intervention for eating disorders typically are more resource efficient, some campuses primarily focus on these levels of need and refer students experiencing anorexia or bulimia to off-campus clinicians or programs. In these cases, students and their families sometimes must explore treatment options outside the institution when extensive psychotherapeutic help is needed.

When students arrive at the counseling center in response to advanced eating disorders, they sometimes arrive on their own but commonly avoid identifying eating problems as a presenting problem. For example, they might present academic troubles, family conflicts, or romantic relationship concerns as their reason for coming. Clinicians sometimes must use effective assessment and intake skills to begin identifying these students as potential candidates for eating disorder responses. On campuses where the counseling center can develop effective referral systems, nonprofessionals and paraprofessionals such as wellness center staff and aerobics instructors, health center and dining services personnel, residence life and student affairs staff, and selected faculty may identify and refer students with possible eating disorders.

Team treatment usually comprises individual counseling, group therapy, and medical appointments with health center clinicians or physicians. CBT "is considered the gold standard" for individual counseling for eating disorders and has the most evidence of treatment efficacy (Choate & Schwitzer, 2009, p. 173; Wilson, Grilo, & Vitousek, 2007). Group counseling—in the form of supportive, structured groups which bring together women who are at many different points in the treatment process—is an important aspect of treatment. Further, even when campuses provide the resources for full on-campus programs, some women will require more intensive treatment programs, usually including inpatient or residential programs. In these situations, the counselor assists students or their families to make appropriate arrangements to be temporarily separated from the institution—and later assists with reentry and return to the academic and social aspects of college life. Some campuses set medical or counseling-related reentry requirements when students return to school. These might include mandated counseling center contacts (e.g., ongoing individual counseling or support groups), mandated health center appointments (sometimes including weigh-ins with clearly stated minimum weights individuals must maintain), or mandated releases of information.

As can be seen, college counseling for eating disorders presents a good illustration of the issues raised in this chapter's discussion of humanism, student mental health concerns, and psychotherapeutic intervention. At this level of need, college clinicians require effective assessment and diagnostic skills to determine whether students are good candidates for treatment on campus, might be referred off campus, or require emergency responses. Case conceptualization and treatment planning are needed when the counselor follows established best practices based on current evidence, engaging students in intensive individual counseling with a CBT focus, group counseling, and multidisciplinary health center responses. Sometimes the college counselor is in the expert authority role, facilitating off-campus referral, inpatient treatment, and support with reentry. However, all of these roles are enhanced by elements of humanism when the counselor, through any of these professional actions, assesses and views students holistically, applies diagnoses narrowly and to symptoms rather than individuals, and emphasizes sense of purpose toward future gains and achievements. Finally, whether in the role of individual counselor, group leader, emergency responder, campus official, or gatekeeper, the college counselor will provide students with a better mental healthcare experience in response to their eating concerns when the counselor attends to and values their subjective experience and emphasizes a strong counseling relationship.

CONCLUSION

This chapter described the professional fit between the humanistic counseling perspective and the work of counseling professionals on college and university campuses. The chapter presented a three-part model of college counseling, comprising preventive, intermediate, and psychotherapeutic levels of intervention. Student characteristics such as distress, urgency for support, and motivation for change differ at each of the three levels; correspondingly, counselors apply different strategies to reach target populations at these different levels of need. (As a note, Drum and Lawler [2008] used a different term, developmental intervention, for their middle level of intervention. The phrase intermediate intervention was used in this chapter for greater clarity and better logical flow. Other writers have sometimes referred to this construct as secondary intervention.) The contemporary college and university counseling center was characterized as a community clinic within a special institutional context, and it was noted that counseling center services often are directed toward supporting the institution's academic mission. As the chapter described and illustrated with the case example of eating disorders, humanism contributes substantially to college counseling prevention work and intermediate services and provides the basic foundation on which more advanced psychotherapeutic intervention is built.

REFERENCES

Aizenman, M. B. (2009). College counseling for self-injurious behavior: A case study. *Journal of College Counseling, 12,* 182–191.

American Psychiatric Association (APA). (2000). *Diagnostic and statistical manual of mental disorders* (4th ed., text revision). Washington, DC: Author.

Andersen, A. E., & DiDomenico, L. (1992). Diet vs. shape content of popular male and female magazines: A dose-response relationship to the incidence of eating disorders? *International Journal of Eating Disorders, 11,* 283–287.

Archer Jr., J., & Cooper, S. (1998). *Counseling and mental health services on campus: A handbook of contemporary practices and challenges.* San Francisco: Jossey-Bass.

Arnstein, R. L. (1995). Mental health on the campus revisited. *Journal of American College Health, 43,* 248–251.

Baker, R. W., McNeil, O., & Siryk, B. (1985). Expectations and reality in freshman adjustment to college. *Journal of Counseling Psychology, 32,* 94–103.

Baker, R. W., & Siryk, B. (1984). Measuring adjustment to college. *Journal of Counseling Psychology, 31,* 179–189.

Bearman, S. K., Presnell, K., Martinez, E., & Stice, E. (2006). The skinny on body dissatisfaction: A longitudinal study of adolescent girls and boys. *Journal of Youth and Adolescence, 35,* 217–229.

Bishop, J. B. (2006). College and university counseling centers: Questions in search of answers. *Journal of College Counseling, 9,* 6–19.

Bishop, J. B., Bauer, K. W., & Becker, E. T. (1998). A survey of counseling needs of male and female college students. *Journal of College Student Development, 39,* 205–210.

Bohart, A. C. (2003). Person-centered psychotherapy and related experiential approaches. In A. S. Gurman & S. B. Messer (Eds.), *Essential psychotherapies: Theory and practice* (2nd ed., pp. 107–148). New York: Guilford Press.

Boyd, V., Hattauer, E., Brandel, I. W., Buckles, N., Davidshofer, C., Deakin, S., et al. (2003). Accreditation standards for university and college counseling centers. *Journal of Counseling and Development, 81,* 168–177.

Celio, A. A., Winzelberg, A. J., Wilfley, A. J., Eppstein-Herald, D., Springer, E. A., Dev, P., et al. (2000). Reducing risk factors for eating disorders: Comparison of an Internet- and a classroom-delivered psychoeducational program. *Journal of Consulting and Clinical Psychology, 68,* 650–657.

Cerezo, A., O'Neil, M. E., & McWhirter, B. T. (2009). Counseling Latina/o students from an ecological perspective: Working with Peter. *Journal of College Counseling, 12,* 170–181.

Chickering, A. W., & Reisser, L. (1993). *Education and identity* (2nd ed.). San Francisco: Jossey-Bass.

Choate, L. H. (2008). *Girls' and women's wellness: Contemporary counseling issues and interventions.* Alexandria, VA: American Counseling Association.

Choate, L. H., & Schwitzer, A. M. (2009). Mental health counseling responses to eating-related concerns in young adult women: A prevention and treatment continuum. *Journal of Mental Health Counseling, 31,* 164–182.

Daniel, E. L. (1988). Development of a campus food service nutrition education program. *Journal of College Student Development, 29,* 276–278.

Davidson, L. (2000). Philosophical foundations of humanistic psychology. *Humanistic Psychologist, 28,* 7–31.

Davis, D. C., & Humphrey, K. M. (2000). *College counseling: Issues and strategies for a new millennium.* Alexandria, VA: American Counseling Association.

DeStefano, T. J., Mellott, R. N., & Petersen, J. D. (2001). A preliminary assessment of the impact of counseling on student adjustment to college. *Journal of College Counseling, 4,* 113–121.

Draper, M. R., & Faulkner, G. E. (2009). Counseling a student presenting borderline personality disorder in the small college context: Case study and implications. *Journal of College Counseling, 12,* 85–96.

Drum, D. J., & Lawler, A. C. (1988). *Developmental interventions: Theories, principles, and practice.* Columbus, OH: Merrill.

Dungy, G. J. (2003). Organization and functions of student affairs. In S. R. Komives, D. B. Woodard Jr., & Associates (Eds.), *Student services: A handbook for the profession* (4th ed.), (pp. 339–357). San Francisco: Jossey-Bass.

Dworkin, S. H., & Kerr, B. A. (1987). Comparison of interventions for women experiencing body image problems. *Journal of Counseling Psychology, 34,* 136–140.

Evans, N. J., Forney, D. S., & Guido-DiBrito, F. (1998). *Student development in college: Theory, research, and practice.* San Francisco: Jossey-Bass.

Fairburn, C. G. (1995). *Overcoming binge eating.* New York: Guilford Press.

Gallagher, R. P. (2009, Spring). Highlights of the 2008 National Survey of Counseling Center Directors. *Visions,* 3–6. Alexandria, VA: American College Counseling Association.

Gallagher, R. P., Golin, A., & Kelleher, K. (1992). The personal, career, and learning skills needs of college students. *Journal of College Student Development, 33,* 301–309.

Gonzalez, J. M., Tinsley, H. E. A., & Kreuder, K. R. (2002). Effects of psychoeducational interventions on opinions of mental illness, attitudes toward help seeking, and expectations about psychotherapy in college students. *Journal of College Student Development, 43,* 51–63.

Guinee, J. P., & Ness, E. (2000). Counseling centers of the 1990s: Challenges and changes. *Counseling Psychologist, 28,* 267–280.

Hansen, J. T. (2006). Humanism as moral imperative: Comments on the role of knowing in the helping encounter. *Journal of Humanistic Counseling, Education, and Development, 45,* 115–125.

Hodges, S. (2001). University counseling centers at the twenty-first century: Looking forward, looking back. *Journal of College Counseling, 4,* 161–173.

Jenks Kettmann, J. D., Schoen, E. G., Moel, J. E., Cochran, S. V., Greenberg, S. T., & Corkery, J. M. (2007). Increasing severity of psychopathology at counseling centers: A new look. *Professional Psychology: Research and Practice, 38,* 523–529.

Jongsma Jr., A. E., & Peterson, L. M. (2003). *The complete adult psychotherapy treatment planner* (3rd ed.). Hoboken, NJ: Wiley & Sons.

Jurgens, J. C., Schwitzer, A. M,, & Middleton, T. (2004). Examining attitudes toward college students with minority sexual orientations: Findings and suggestions. *Journal of College Student Psychotherapy, 19,* 57–75.

Kahn, J. S., Wood, A., & Wiesen, R. E. (1999). Student perceptions of college counseling center services: Programming and marketing for a seamless learning environment. *Journal of College Student Psychotherapy, 14,* 69–80.

Keel, P. K. (2005). Prevention. In P. K. Keel & P. Levitt (Eds.), *Eating disorders* (pp. 142–153). Upper Saddle, NJ: Pearson Prentice Hall.

Kohut, H. (1977). *The analysis of the self.* New York: International Universities Press.

Koszewski, W. M., Newell, G. K., & Higgins, J. J. (1990). Effect of a nutrition education program on the eating attitudes and behaviors of college women. *Journal of College Student Development, 31,* 203–210.

Lenihan, G., & Kirk, W. G. (1990). Using student paraprofessionals in the treatment of eating disorders. *Journal of Counseling & Development, 68,* 332–335.

Levine, M. P., & Piran, N. (2004). The role of body image in the prevention of eating disorders. *Body Image, 1,* 57–70.

Lippincott, J. A., & Lippincott, R. B. (Eds.). (2007). *Special populations in college counseling: A handbook for mental health professionals.* Alexandria, VA: American Counseling Association.

May, R. (1988). Boundaries and voices in college psychotherapy. In R. May (Ed.), *Psychoanalytic psychotherapy in a college context.* New York: Praeger.

Meadows, M. E. (2000). The evolution of college counseling. In D. C. Davis & K. M. Humphrey (Eds.), *College counseling: Issues and strategies for a new millennium.* Alexandria, VA: American Counseling Association.

Meilman, P. W. (2001). Fostering development: A case of short doses of psychotherapy over the course of a college career. *Journal of College Student Psychotherapy, 16,* 101–117.

Meyer, S., & Schwitzer, A. M. (1999). Stages of identity development among college students with minority sexual orientations. *Journal of College Student Psychotherapy, 13,* 41–66.

Miller, G. A., & Rice, K. G. (1993). A factor analysis of a university counseling center problem checklist. *Journal of College Student Development, 34,* 98–102.

Mobley, A. K. (2008). College student depression: Counseling Billy. *Journal of College Counseling, 11,* 87–96.

Myers, J. E., & Mobley, A. K. (2004). Wellness of undergraduates: Comparisons of traditional and nontraditional students. *Journal of College Counseling, 7,* 40–49.

Neukrug, E. S., & Schwitzer, A. M. (2006). *Skills and tools for today's counselors and psychotherapists: From natural helping to professional counseling.* Belmont, CA: Thomson Brooks/Cole.

Raskin, N. J., Rogers, C. R., & Witty, M. C. (2008). Client-centered therapy. In R. J. Corsini & D. Wedding (Eds.), *Current psychotherapies* (8th ed., pp. 141–186). Belmont, CA: Thomson Brooks/Cole.

Reifler, C. B., Liptzin, M. B., & Fox, J. T. (2006). College psychiatry as public health psychiatry. *Journal of American College Health, 54,* 317–325.

Reisser, L. (1995). Revisiting the seven vectors. *Journal of College Student Development, 36,* 505–511.

Rudd, M. D. (2004). University counseling centers: Looking more and more like community clinics. *Professional Psychology: Research & Practice, 35,* 316–317.

Scholl, M. (2002). Predictors of client preferences for counselor roles. *Journal of College Counseling, 5,* 124–134.

Schwartz, A. J. (2006). Are college students more disturbed today? Stability in the acuity and qualitative character of psychopathology of college counseling center clients: 1992–1993 through 2001–2002. *Journal of American College Health, 54,* 327–337.

Schwitzer, A. M. (1997). Utilization-focused evaluation: Proposing a useful method of program evaluation for college counselors and student development professionals. *Measurement and Evaluation in Counseling and Development, 30,* 50–61.

Schwitzer, A. M. (2003). A framework for college counseling responses to large scale traumatic incidents. *Journal of College Student Psychotherapy, 18,* 49–66.

Schwitzer, A. M. (2005). Self-development, social support, and student help-seeking: Research summary and implications for college psychotherapists. *Journal of College Student Psychotherapy, 20,* 29–52.

Schwitzer, A. M., Ancis, J. R., & Brown, N. (2001). *Promoting student learning and student development at a distance: Student affairs concepts and practices for televised instruction and other forms of distance learning.* Washington, DC: American College Personnel Association.

Schwitzer, A. M., Bergholz, K., Dore, T., & Salimi, L. (1998). Eating disorders among college women: Prevention, education, and treatment responses. *Journal of American College Health, 46,* 199–207.

Schwitzer, A. M., & Everett, A. (1997). Reintroducing the *DSM-IV*: Responses to ten counselor reservations about diagnosis. *Virginia Counselors Journal, 25,* 54–64.

Schwitzer, A. M., Griffin, O. T., Ancis, J. R., & Thomas, C. R. (1999). Social adjustment experiences of African American college students. *Journal of Counseling & Development, 77,* 189–197.

Schwitzer, A. M., Grogan, K., Kaddoura, K., & Ochoa, L. (1993). Effects of brief mandatory counseling on help-seeking and academic success among at-risk college students. *Journal of College Student Development, 34,* 401–405.

Schwitzer, A. M., Hatfield, T., Jones, A. R., Duggan, M. H., Jurgens, J., & Winninger, A. (2008). Confirmation among college women: The eating disorders not otherwise specified diagnostic profile. *Journal of American College Health, 56,* 607–615.

Schwitzer, A. M., McGovern, T. V., & Robbins, S. B. (1991). Adjustment outcomes of a freshman seminar: A utilization-focused approach. *Journal of College Student Development, 32,* 484–489.

Schwitzer, A. M., Rodriguez, L. E., Thomas, C., Salimi, L. (2001). The eating disorders NOS diagnostic profile among college women. *Journal of American College Health, 49,* 157–166.

Schwitzer, A. M., & Thomas, C. (1998). Implementation, utilization, and outcomes of a minority freshman peer mentor program at a predominantly White university. *Journal of the Freshman Year Experience, 10,* 31–50.

Scissons, E. H. (1993). *Counseling for results.* Pacific Grove, CA: Brooks/Cole.

Seligman, L. (1996). *Diagnosis and treatment planning in counseling* (2nd ed.). New York: Plenum Press.

Seligman, L. (2004). *Diagnosis and treatment planning in counseling* (3rd ed.). New York: Plenum Press.

Sharkin, B. S. (1997). Increasing severity of presenting problems in college counseling centers: A closer look. *Journal of Counseling & Development, 75,* 275–281.

Silverstein, B., Perdue, L., Peterson, B., Vogel, L., & Fantini, D. A. (1986). Possible causes of the thin standard of bodily attractiveness for women. *International Journal of Eating Disorders, 5,* 907–916.

Skowron, E. A., & Friedlander, M. L. (1994). Psychological separation, self-control, and weight preoccupation among elite women athletes. *Journal of Counseling & Development, 72,* 310–315.

Stice, E. (2002). Risk and maintenance factors for eating pathology: A meta-analytic review. *Psychological Bulletin, 128,* 825–848.

Stice, E., Chase, .Stormer, S., & Appel, A. (2001). A randomized trial of a dissonance-based eating disorder prevention program. *International Journal of Eating Disorders, 29,* 247–262.

Stice, E., & Hoffman, E. (2004). Eating disorder prevention programs. In J. K. Thompson (Ed.), *Handbook of eating disorders and obesity* (pp. 33–57). Hoboken, NJ: Wiley & Sons.

Stice, E., Presnell, K., Gau, J., & Shaw, H. (2007). Testing mediators of intervention effects in randomized controlled trials: An evaluation of two eating disorder prevention programs. *Journal of Consulting and Clinical Psychology, 75,* 20–32.

Stone, G., L., & Archer Jr., J. (1990). College and university counseling centers in the 1990s: Challenges and limits. *Counseling Psychologist, 18,* 539–607.

Sykora, C., Grilo, C. M., Wilfley, D. E., & Brownell, K. D. (1993). Eating, weight, and dieting disturbances in male and female lightweight and heavyweight rowers. *International Journal of Eating Disorders, 14,* 203–211.

Tucker, C., Sloan, S. K., Vance, M., & Brownson, C. (2008). Integrated care in college health: A case study. *Journal of College Counseling, 11,* 173–183.

Weiss, C. R., & Orysh, L, K. (1994). Group counseling for eating disorders: A two-phase treatment program. *Journal of College Student Development, 35,* 487–488.

Wester, K. (2007, September). *Assessing, diagnosing, and providing alternatives to clients who self-injure.* Licensed Professional Counselors Association of North Carolina, Durham.

Whyte, A. K., & Guiffrida, D. A. (2008). Counseling deaf college students: The case of Shea. *Journal of College Counseling, 11,* 184–192.

Wilson, G. T., Grilo, C. M., & Vitousek, K. M. (2007). Psychological treatment of eating disorders. *American Psychologist, 62,* 199–216.

Wiseman, C. V., Gray, J. J., Mosimann, J. E., & Ahrens, A. H. (1992). Cultural expectations of thinness in women: An update. *International Journal of Eating Disorders, 11,* 85–89.

Zabinski, M. F., Pung, M. A., Wilfley, D. E., Eppstein, D. L., Winzelberg, A. J., Celio, A., et al. (2001). Reducing risk factors for eating disorders: Targeting at-risk women with a computerized psychoeducational program. *International Journal of Eating Disorders, 29,* 401–408.

IV

APPLICATIONS TO COUNSELOR TRAINING

12

Humanistic Education and Technology in Counselor Education
Crossing the Streams

Michael Walsh and Linda Leech

There's something very important I forgot to tell you: Don't cross the streams! ... It would be very bad! Try to imagine all life as you know it stopping instantaneously and every molecule in your body exploding at the speed of light.... Total protonic reversal!... That's bad. [Pause] Important safety tip. Thanks, Egon! *Ghostbusters*, 1984.

INTRODUCTION

The debate about the effectiveness of using technology-based learning (e-learning) to train counselors has an ongoing history going back to the early 1990s when distance learning was beginning to become a growing trend in higher education (Maddux, 2003). Humanistic philosophy has been a long-standing paradigm within the counseling profession. As noted in the introductory chapter to the current text, humanistic counseling approaches emphasize the importance of the quality of the counselor–client relationship (Raskin, Rogers, & Witty, 2008). It should come as no surprise that counselor educators and students expressed concerns that the lack of face-to-face interaction in the classroom presented barriers to acquisition of relationship-building skills and effective communication.

Further, concerns over the impersonalization of counselor education have impacted the willingness of counselor educators to embrace a technology-based approach to teaching in spite of evidence suggesting that overall the performance of noncounseling students in technology-based programs is comparable to that of noncounseling students in more traditional classroom programs (Waschull, 2005). The argument that these findings cannot be generalized to counselor education frequently is accepted as valid in part because of differences in educational formats, teaching styles, and technological platforms. Rapid changes in available educational technology in combination with the rapidly growing popularity of distance education programs have made research into its effectiveness difficult.

Regardless of such concerns, the trend toward training counselors at a distance continues upward. This trend is driven primarily by the needs of adults seeking to acquire an education while juggling demands of a full-time job, raising children, and other life issues. Is there a fit between a humanistic orientation and the use of technology? Do the paradigms currently in use in higher education preclude application of humanistic tenets and methods?

In the end, our *ghostbusting* friends realized that crossing their streams led to a more powerful approach to ghostbusting. This use of seemingly opposing forces of technology and humanism may also have relevance to counselor education. This chapter explores the ways technology and humanistic education may come together to enhance both students' experiences and educational outcomes. Humanistic approaches to distance education will be examined through a review of the literature surrounding adult learning. Trends in the design of distance education technology will be reviewed to identify areas in which tried and true humanistic counselor education techniques can be employed. The effective design and use of technology in and out of the traditional classroom will be discussed as a means of enhancing the personal growth and development of counselors.

HUMANISM AND EDUCATION

Models of education, like theoretical approaches to counseling, are based on a foundational philosophy that describes the motivation of individuals to learn, the manner in which individuals learn, and the way learning is influenced by outside factors such as a teacher or the environment. Roney (2007), in his synopsis of recent philosophies in education, identified five key philosophies that have influenced the development of modern higher educational and adult education strategies: (1) liberal philosophy; (2) behaviorist adult philosophy; (3) radical adult education; (4) progressive philosophy; and (5) a humanistic teaching approach. These strategies can be contrasted through an exploration of the purpose of education, the role of the learner, the role of the instructor, and the related concepts and key words.

A *liberal philosophy* of education places an emphasis on training the mind rather than training the individual for a particular job or career. Liberal arts programs, as an example, focus on developing learners who have a basic knowledge about the world in which they live. They strive to increase learners' ability to analyze a situation and synthesize information and to make justifiable decisions.

Programs developed with a liberal adult education philosophy are the most common programs found in academic settings (Roney, 2007).

Behaviorist adult philosophy has been the foundation for competency-based and mastery models of education (Roney, 2007). Learning objectives are frequently linked to behavioral objectives. Techniques used include personalization of content and competency modeling. This philosophy has been adopted by corporate training programs because it is grounded in psychological principles that produce observable and measurable outcomes. As with behavioral therapy, the behaviorist model of education is inconsistent with humanism as it fails to adequately acknowledge students' inner subjective experience. This philosophy has guided the development of many e-learning designs that require learners to demonstrate mastery of the course concepts through tests and content application-based assignments.

Radical adult education is founded on the belief that social, political, and economic changes can be brought about through education (Roney, 2007). Examples of radical adult education include programs designed to raise consciousness, to teach critical thinking and reflection, and to spur political action or change. Arguably, this model emphasizes influencing the beliefs and values of learners and consequently runs counter to humanism's emphasis on nondirective methods. Since this type of educational model lends itself to clear and measurable outcomes, it has influenced the development of e-learning approaches. Its focus on critical thinking and evaluation has been seen as important in encouraging adult learners at a distance to develop skills for independently reviewing and evaluating research and theory.

A progressive philosophy emphasizes vocational and utilitarian training (Roney, 2007). Educational programs founded on a progressive philosophy could be described as seeking to better the individual, society, and the organization. Similar to the perspective of the client-centered approach (C. R. Rogers, 1961), progressive educators would describe themselves as student centered. That is, the course design emphasizes the success of learners in achieving the goal rather than the transmission of the content to learners (Dubin & Olshtain, 1986, pp. 75–76). Programs are problem focused with courses being designed around very specific tasks and problem solutions. Also, consistent with humanism, learners are self-directed. They are expected to take initiative for learning and responsibility for successfully completing it. However, the progressive philosophy of education differs from humanism in at least one important way. The educator's role is more active than the facilitator role espoused in the humanistic teaching approach. Under the progressive paradigm, the role of the instructor becomes one of planner, instigator, and arranger of the conditions for learning.

A humanistic teaching approach, by contrast, is based on the premise that all individuals have a need to become self-actualized, a term used by Maslow (1954) and again by Rogers (1969). From this perspective, education is seen as one venue in which individuals may acquire skills in self-direction, confidence, maturity, and flexibility (Roney, 2007). Humanistic education allows students to develop realistic goals through an acceptance of self, their feelings, and others around them. In the next section, we will explore the humanistic philosophy of education in greater depth and detail.

A HUMANISTIC PHILOSOPHY OF EDUCATION

Rogers (1969) described the role of humanistic teachers. He saw teaching as a process of facilitation that encouraged students to desire to learn, grow, inquire, master, and create. Humanistic education strategies such as the open classrooms in K–12 education have waned in recent years after an explosion in popularity in the 1970s. Nonetheless, the basic objectives of humanistic education remain evident in the foundational models of higher education (Roney, 2007). Humanistic adult education targets the development of the whole person, with emphasis on the emotional and affective dimensions of the learner. Programs based on humanistic principles target learners who are highly motivated and self-directed. The instructors act as guides, organizers of learning, and helpers relying heavily on communication and collaboration techniques. The basic objectives of adult humanistic education are to encourage self-direction and independence as well as responsibility for one's own learning, creativity, and inquiry.

Choice or Control

The humanistic approach focuses a great deal on student choice and control over the course of their education (Elias & Merriam, 1994; Galbraith, 2004). Learners are encouraged to focus on a specific subject of interest. Consistent with humanism's emphasis on the individual's sense of purpose (Raskin et al., 2008) as well as Ryan and Deci's (2000) self-determination theory, humanistic educators believe it is important for students to be motivated and engaged in the material they are learning. For example, learners may be encouraged to pursue a specialization of interest, choose a topic of interest for a paper rather than writing on a narrow topic selected by the instructor, or be able to gain credit for job shadowing or community service.

Felt Concern

Humanistic education deals with the emotional reactions of learners throughout their educational process (Elias & Merriam, 1994; Rogers, 1980). It is believed that the overall mood and feeling of the students can either hinder or foster the process of learning. Instructors may encourage learners to present personal applications and reactions to subject matter, may interact with learners around personal experiences that are related to their educational pursuits, and may provide referrals for counseling or other services that will allow learners to continue a path of personal growth throughout their educational experience.

The Whole Person

Consistent with the humanistic principle of irreducibility (Davidson, 2000), humanistic educators believe that both feelings and knowledge are important to the learning process (Rogers, 1980). Humanistic educators do not separate the cognitive and affective domains. In addition, the curriculum is designed to appeal to the many domains of learners' functioning rather than rote memorization and unidimensional activity. Educational settings may be in a traditional classroom, online, or in the field (Ancis, 1998).

Self-Evaluation

Consistent with humanism's emphasis on individuals' sense of purpose and belief that people have the capacity to set personally meaningful goals (Cain, 2001), humanistic educators place a high value on learners' perceptions of the educational experience. They provide opportunities for learners to self-critique their mastery of the material and their skill performance. Peer reviews are often incorporated into the evaluation process. In a humanistic approach to education, grades are seen as less important than the intrinsic motivators present in learners. While testing may be one method for evaluation, tests are not seen as an evaluation tool for the instructor but a learning and evaluation exercise for learners. Regular evaluation activities may be diverse and may incorporate novel techniques.

Teacher as a Facilitator

Along the same lines, as the humanistic counselor in client-centered therapy, the humanistic teacher provides facilitative conditions including genuineness, respect, and empathy to facilitate students' growth and learning. As Rogers (1969) indicated, the role of the facilitator is to be genuine, supportive, and understanding as students seek to integrate new knowledge (pp. 164–166). Rogers believed the job of the educator is to foster an engaging environment for students and to ask inquiry-based questions that promote meaningful learning. Inquiry-based questioning encourages students to continue to assimilate and apply material beyond the basic and most obvious implications of the new learning.

HUMANISTIC PRINCIPLES IN COUNSELOR EDUCATION

In recent years, counselor educators have begun to recognize the need for an educational process that accounts for the needs of whole persons within their own context (Henriksen, 2006). Many counselors and counselor educators have made arguments advocating the use of experiential (Gladding, 2005) and meaning-based (Hansen, 2009) interventions in both clinical practice as well as counselor education. In addition, proposals for innovative meaning-based educational interventions such as the use of popular literature and movies in counselor education (Gibson, 2007) provide useful suggestions for honoring the cognitive and emotional context of our students in the educational process.

Carl Rogers (1969) first addressed teaching and learning in the book *Freedom to Learn*. Along the same lines as humanism's positive view of the individual as self-actualizing (Cain, 2001), Rogers pointed out that human beings have a natural potential and proclivity toward learning. As previously mentioned, he noted the importance of student-driven learning as well as the value of emotion and experience within the learning process. His unique view of the role of the educator has influenced the way counselors are trained and educated. Rogers described teachers as facilitators, arguing that teachers are most effective when acting as a guide rather than an arbiter. The instructor assumes a position as a collaborative partner rather than a hierarchical superior.

Effective facilitators, according to Rogers (1969, pp. 164–166), have common habits that enhance students' involvement in the learning process:

1. Setting the initial mood or climate of the group or class experience
2. Eliciting and clarifying individual students' goals and sense of purpose as well as the more general goals and purposes of the group
3. Relying upon students' sense of purpose and personal meaning as the motivational force behind significant learning
4. Organizing and providing access to the widest possible range of resources for learning
5. Regarding themselves as a flexible resource to be used by the group
6. Remaining alert to student expressions indicative of deep or strong feelings
7. Responding to cognitive and affective expressions in the classroom group and accepting and respecting both forms of expression from students
8. Becoming a participant learner, by increasing degrees following the establishment of a safe and accepting classroom client, and expressing their views as those of one individual only
9. Taking the initiative in sharing themselves with the group—including feelings as well as thoughts—in ways that do not demand nor impose but represent simply a personal sharing that students may take or leave
10. Recognizing and accepting their limitations

From a humanistic standpoint, educators should strive to create learning experiences that are personally relevant to each individual. Humanistic educators honor what is unique about each student and assist in the discovery of ways to integrate and make meaning of the new information being discovered. It is also important that facilitators be genuine in sharing personal reactions and discoveries within the material. In this way, educators become not only facilitators but also colearners, moving side by side with their students through the process of discovery and meaning making. Moreover, humanistic educators are responsible for the facilitation of not only a learning experience but also a learning community (Rogers, 1980).

CURRENT TRENDS IN COUNSELOR EDUCATION

In recent years, trends in counselor education have tended toward reductionistic, skills- and technique-based training (Granello, 2002; Hansen, 2009; Nelson & Neufeldt-Allstetter, 1998). A focus on interpersonal and cognitive skills has dominated the curriculum of many training programs (Bennett-Levy, 2006). Similarly, Buser (2008) noted that skills-based training was one of the most salient trends in the current counselor education literature. This trend stands in contrast to earlier approaches to counselor education that used counseling theories as models for teaching and supervising beginning counselors (Bernard & Goodyear, 2004).

Critics of current counselor education pedagogy (Hansen, 2009; Nelson & Neufeldt-Allstetter, 1998) assert that skills-based training falls far short of humanism's emphasis on educating the whole student. Rather, skills-based training ignores critical areas of counselor functioning such as the social and affective domains (Nelson & Neufeldt-Allstetter). Skills based training speaks most directly to learners whose learning styles mirror that of the instructional design. For example, members of the European American macroculture are more likely to have learning styles compatible with pedagogical techniques emphasizing behavioral performance. This approach to training neglects the affective and relational needs of diverse learners, including women as well as racial and ethnic minorities (Fong, 1998).

More consistent with humanism's emphasis on educating the whole student is Gladding's (2005) recommendation that counselor educators employ experiential, meaning-based approaches in their work with counselors-in-training. An excellent example of Gladding's recommendation can be seen in different methods for teaching students how to communicate empathy for clients. A strictly skills-based approach would focus primarily on the accuracy of the words spoken by the student counselor. However, Miller (1989) drew a distinction between experiencing empathy and the behavioral aspect of the skill of empathy that can be taught. He argued that as opposed to words or techniques, real, therapeutic empathy involved the ability to experience feelings, to understand them as well as possible, and to respond to another person based on those feelings. This is very much in concordance with the experiential, meaning-based approach to counselor training called for by Gladding. It is this meaning-based approach to the process of counseling that may have the most appeal to the diverse population of adult learners enrolled in modern-day counselor education programs.

COUNSELOR EDUCATION AND ADULT LEARNING

Higher education has historically defined the *traditional* student as one who has followed an educational timetable that moves from high school to college through graduate school in a straight uninterrupted path (U.S. Department of Education, 2002). Previously, undergraduate students were seen as post–high school, beginning undergraduate work at ages 17 to 24 (Chickering, 1969). Graduate education served students ranging in age from 24 upward. These traditional learners continue to make up a significant portion of the college population. However, there has been a rapid increase over the past 10 to 20 years in the numbers of older students returning to academia (U.S. Department of Education). This population has brought with it a wide range of experiences and needs that differ from those of younger learners. Contemporary adult learners are goal oriented and focused. They know why they are returning for education and what they plan to do with the degree. The majority of older learners have a rich work history and a well-developed context for the application of new information. These learners are customers as well as students with an expectation that education will be personally fulfilling, challenging, and serious (Donaldson, Flannery, & Ross-Gordon, 1993; Gorham, 1999; Landrum, McAdams, & Hood, 2000; Pollio & Beck, 2000).

As mentioned in Chapter 1 of the current text, the primary principle unifying humanistic approaches to counseling and education is the idea that humans are irreducible to other phenomena (Davidson, 2000). Individualism is a primary branch of the ideological tree of human irreducibility. The humanistic educator is committed to honoring the individuality of each student as well as the unique inner subjective factors that help students to acquire and make meaning of new information. Each learner is seen as an individual with a unique set of educational needs and learning styles. In a time in which the "typical learner" is an outdated and changing construct, graduate educators have sought to design programs that better fit the developmental characteristics of learners.

Knowles (1977) first pointed out the fundamental differences in the learning of adults versus the learning of children. Among these differences, Knowles noted that adults (1) tend to place more value on self-directed learning, (2) bring a more vast and varied array of experiences to the learning process, (3) learn by referencing these experiences in light of the new information, and (4) tend to place more value on experiential approaches to learning.

Each adult has a unique set of requirements for the overall success of the learning process. Adult learners are autonomous and self-directed. Knowles (1977, 1980) asserted that because adults come into educational environments with a tremendous experiential base on which they build their learning it is important for educators to reference adult learners' experiences when introducing new material. Adults will learn best when new material is paired with information adult learners have already internalized.

Adults also place real value on seeing the relevance and practical applications of new information, placing less value on new knowledge "for knowledge sake" and more on "hands-on" instruction (Speck, 1996). This lends support to an experiential model of learning. Adult learners, in many cases, place real value on the practical value of education for things such as licensure, credentials, and job advancement. The value in adult education lies in enhancing and reinforcing the engagement of students on the individual level and with specific attention to the individual interests of students while also decreasing the potential barriers to success (Speck, 1996).

In examining the work of Knowles (1980) and Rogers (1969) side by side, marked similarities can be observed (Boyer, 1984). Both viewed learners as holistic entities, bringing an experiential knowledge base into the learning process on which they rely for both cognitive and affective reference. Both also noted that students tend to learn better when the material is personally relevant. Finally, both Rogers and Knowles acknowledged the value of learning opportunities that are experiential as well as self-directed and self-evaluated.

EDUCATING THE ADULT BRAIN

Humanistic counselors have recognized the importance of a consideration of human development in explaining behavior. Erik Erikson's (1950) theories have been held in high regard for understanding the normal physical and psychosocial factors that impact one's interaction with the social, cognitive, and behavioral dimensions of life. Physical development is of particular relevance to the current discussion as it entails changes and growth that take place in the brain. We believe that providing an overview of how the brain functions, including processes that occur during meaning-based and experiential educational processes, will help clarify how effective technology-assisted approaches to teaching are potentially humanistic.

The human brain weighs about 3 pounds and consists of about 100 billion interconnected cells. Many of those cells are also continuously developing, dying off, and regenerating. These interconnected cells are called neurons. We used to think that we were born with all of the neurons we would ever have, but recent neurological evidence suggests that the regeneration of brain cells occurs consistently throughout the life span (Gould, Reeves, Graziano & Gross, 1999). Not only do cells constantly regenerate, but current evidence also shows that the brain will actually respond to new experiences and learning with actual structural changes (Taubert et al., 2010).

According to neuroscientists, memory is linked with biochemical changes (Pert, 1997, p. 143). Information is constantly carried and sorted out by chemical messengers, known as *neurotransmitters,* within the brain. Each time information is transmitted through the brain, the information leaves a trail of neurochemical markers. Those markers help to track down the information later if we ever need it. The more structures of the brain that are involved with learning new information, the more markers will be left in the brain. In essence, the more of the brain that is involved with a learning task, the better the chances for long-term retention (Fishback, 1998/1999).

The human brain employs a sort of "gear-shifter" to help sort through information and to decide where it should be routed within the brain. This structure, called the anterior cingulate gyrus (ACG), is located near the amygdala and the hippocampus, toward the front of the brain. Messages come in, are routed through our amygdala for an emotional response, and then sent to the ACG for further processing. The ACG's job is to monitor the information for errors, to compare the information briefly to what is already known or understood, and then to route the message out to the appropriate part of the brain for further processing.

If some serious thinking about this new information is required, the message is then often sent off to the part of the brain where logical thinking is housed (the prefrontal cortex). On the other hand, if the new information requires movement or contemplation about moving, the ACG sends the information up to the top of our brains and the motor or premotor cortexes.

Visual information comes in through the eyes, through the ACG, and then gets sent to the visual cortex, located in the very back of the skull. That information is then interpreted and sent back up to the ACG for further follow-up—maybe up to the prefrontal cortex to be thought about or maybe off to other areas like the premotor or motor cortex. This trip that visual information takes through the brain is perhaps part of the reason that visual information tends to be retained more readily by human learners. The greater the distance information travels through the brain, the greater the number of brain structures involved. When more brain structures are involved in the learning process, both retention and the quality of learning are enhanced.

Humanistic educational principles lend themselves well to this paradigm. Quite simply, the more meaning based (Hansen, 2009) and experiential (Gladding, 2005) the educational process is, the more brain structures get involved in the processing, which leads to better learning and retention (Epstein, 1994). Effective technology-assisted learning seeks to incorporate as much of the brain as possible into the learning process, thereby enhancing the *human* experience of the material.

USING TECHNOLOGY TO SUPPORT ADULT LEARNING

Humanistic counselor educators seek to develop educational methodologies that allow individuals to experience activities that enable them to process in their own way new information, to actively engage with the material, to critically analyze and make judgments concerning the validity of new information, and to apply newly developed skills to their own areas of interest. The use of technological applications to enhance student learning presents seven specific challenges that are addressed in adult education and distance learning literature (Stella & Gnanam, 2004; Collison, Elbaum, Haavind, & Tinker, 2000):

1. Instilling technology savvy
2. Building a learning community
3. Enhancing learner collaboration
4. Developing critical thinking skills
5. Enhancing learner self-evaluation skills
6. Effectively teaching and monitoring interpersonal skills
7. Meeting educational standards

Instilling Technological Savvy

As mentioned previously, modern graduate students have likely been exposed to online learning platforms in their undergraduate coursework and likely even earlier in their educational background. They have experience using the Internet through their daily work and social lives. However, nontraditional learners may be older and may have primarily participated in face-to-face classroom education prior to graduate school. Many graduate students are self-described auditory learners, stating that they need the reinforcement of a lecture to help them process what they have read, an assertion supported by the literature within counselor education (Yalom & Leszcz, 2005). These learners may begin their online education with some fear of a new way of learning that requires them to learn differently.

According to Maslow (1954) and his hierarchy of needs model, individuals are ready to act upon their higher growth needs (i.e., need to learn and understand, aesthetic needs, and self-actualization needs) only once their deficiency needs (i.e., physiological needs, safety needs, belongingness and love needs, and esteem needs) have been met. Along the same lines, Rogers (1961) stated that individuals need a sense of psychological safety to participate fully in the world, to create, and to be self-actualizing. Rogers, in speaking of the client–counselor relationship, asserted that the three conditions of empathic understanding, unconditional positive regard, and absence of external evaluation all contribute to an environment of psychological safety for the client.

With regard to education, Rogers (1969) also emphasized the importance of a sense of psychological safety when he noted that students will learn better when barriers to learning and threats to self-confidence are eliminated. Clearly, some technological modalities have the potential for producing anxiety within students. It is plausible that students using unfamiliar technology for the first time may be unintentionally placed in circumstances where meeting their psychological safety needs (deficiency needs) takes precedence over meeting their needs for learning and understanding (growth needs). It is up to us as educators to take steps to reinforce the learning process, including the central position of the student in this process, and to help students by reducing or eliminating potential stressors. In doing this educators also potentially communicate empathic understanding regarding the inhibitory effect stressors can have on student learning and also communicate that they care about the students. Recent research conducted in technology-assisted distance education found that student satisfaction was linked most clearly to the level of experience and comfort students had with the medium used (Walsh, 2009).

Norwood (1999) stated that individuals seek different kinds of information related to their developmental level within Maslow's hierarchy. Learners experiencing anxiety regarding their ability to competently use unfamiliar technology are plausibly concerned with their psychological safety needs and as a result are likely to seek helping information. Consistent with Rogers's (1957) recommendation that counselors provide an environment of safety, distance educators have strategies for helping students to feel more comfortable and less anxious when working with less familiar online technology. Distance educators have identified four strategies for accommodating the needs of students who are anxious or unfamiliar with online technology (SACS, 2000).

1. Design the courses within a program so that they are similar in appearance, format, organization, and the kinds of tasks learners are asked to complete.
2. Design the online site so that learners are able to access all of the necessary learning materials through links that are clearly visible on the home page.
3. Do not require students to download new programs, change settings on their computers, or learn to use any software to access their coursework that would not be part of normal home and work Internet use.
4. Ensure that technology support is available 24 hours a day, 7 days a week and is provided via telephone contact by technicians who are familiar with home computers, the needs of students, and requirements of the distance learning environments.

Although this uniform approach to format may initially appear inconsistent with the humanistic principles of individuality and creativity, it might be argued that a student's need for initial safety and comfort with the learning process is an important precursor to their ability to learn. This is consistent with Maslow's (1954) hierarchy of needs. Specifically, Maslow noted that safety precedes the ability to learn and to problem solve. Rogers (1969) also noted the importance of perceived safety in the learning process (p. 114). Because web-based class management platforms (e.g., Blackboard and WebCT) make communication with students possible even before the semester or quarter begins, it is also possible to begin using technology to facilitate learning the technology well before classes begin, thereby enhancing the student-perceived safety of the learning process. Learners can be asked to take a tour of their classroom and to use the various links that will be routinely used during participation in courses. Many programs and courses offer an online tutorial that may include video, audio, and PowerPoint presentations to illustrate the function of links within the course site, methods for posting information directly to the course site, and the processes for taking tests, submitting work, communicating with the instructor, accessing technical support, dialoguing with other students, and a variety of other tasks that may be required.

Two important principles of humanistic education include the importance of fostering good teacher–student relationships and the importance of individualizing instruction to suit the unique needs of individual learners. An advantage of distance education is that usually faculty are able to access the course roster including students' e-mail addresses prior to the beginning of the course (Hall, Nielsen, Nelson, & Buchholz, 2010). This allows faculty to e-mail students before the beginning of the semester to introduce themselves and to find out more about what each student needs and hopes to accomplish as a result of taking the course. As a result, faculty members can be more intentional with regard to both cultivating good relationships and incorporating instructional elements which address the needs, interests, and learning goals of individual students.

Clearly, these strategies have been developed with the needs of adult learners in mind. They build on the concept that adult learners are individuals who require immediacy of application and presentation of new material that builds on a foundation of previous experience and learning. Learners frequently report that while e-learning requires them to learn differently, they learn as well in the new format as in the more familiar formats. These traditional formats, in fact, are often developed with younger as opposed to older students in mind. Technology-based learning that is effective seeks to take into account the unique needs of adult learners and is thereby a more friendly and student-centered learning environment for those adult students (ITC, 2008; Stella & Gnanam, 2004).

Building a Learning Community

As discussed in Chapter 1 of the current text, Ansbacher (as cited in Raskin et al., 2008) noted that good counseling and education is based on a good relationship. Palloff and Pratt (1999) argued that to foster effective learning using technological applications one must first develop an effective learning community. Hall et al. (2010) noted that a difficult challenge faced by distance educators is building group cohesion among learners. However, if educators are intentional with regard to their implementation of methods and class assignments, interpersonal relationships and a cohesive sense of community can be established. Batson and Bass (1996) recognized early on that technological developments in education would require educators to shift methods and roles from those of imparting information to methods and roles associated with the learning process itself. Interventions that build a community of learners that can interact to share, form, and inform each others' understanding are uniquely humanistic in that each student becomes a learning facilitator for another. This is largely consistent with Rogers's (1969) notion of "process oriented learning" (p. 104) and his notion of "gathering the widest possible range of resources to aid the learning process" (p. 164). The online environment requires independent investigation. However, synthesis of the material requires interactions with classmates. Online techniques include group discussions and peer reviews. Learners may be asked to share plans for a project with other learners for critique and feedback. In addition, they are required to offer thoughts on the prepared material in weekly discussion assignments that require learners to analyze a case study, design a program, or critique the comments of other learners. These assignments may require learners to share a personal experience or otherwise make a personal application.

Another important defining characteristic of humanism is a belief in the importance of practices that promote diversity including equal access to counseling and educational services (Cain, 2001). It is worth noting that technology-based applications such as those described herein can also open courses to people who may not otherwise have been able to participate, given concerns of distance from campus, difficulty with travel, or even disability on the part of the student or instructor. Put simply, it may be argued that technology has opened the counselor education classroom to voices that may not otherwise have been heard. From Rogers (1969) to Knowles (1977, 1980) to Henriksen (2009) to Hansen (2009), humanistic educators have extolled the value of a vast experiential base in the making of meaning in learning.

Enhancing Interpersonal Relationships Through Student Collaboration

As mentioned previously, distance learning founded in humanistic principles should promote good student–student and student–faculty relationships. The effective e-learning format requires participants to interact with peers. Additionally, each learner receives consistent individual feedback from the instructor. Projects are completed in concert with the guidelines provided, the feedback of peers, and interaction with faculty. Most assignments require students to actively engage in application projects. Learners are also encouraged to seek outside input from professionals in the community further promoting the development of relationships with these professionals. Learning is seen as an active collaboration among the learner, the educator, and peers. This is consistent with both Rogers's (1969) call for a collaborative learning environment as well as current thinking with regard to effective technology-based instruction (Palloff & Pratt, 1999).

Developing Critical Thinking Skills

Ansbacher (as cited in Raskin et al., 2008) stated that a sense of purpose is the primary influence on human behavior, and Cain (2001) asserted that people have the ability to choose their goals and how to achieve them. These humanistic education principles strongly imply that educators need to support students' sense of self-efficacy and promote skills that support student intentionality. Perhaps chief among those skills supporting student intentionality is that of critical thinking. As mentioned already, instructors in the online format use methods that require learners to evaluate opinions and conclusions against the research and challenges of educators and peers. Traditional brick-and-mortar classrooms offer more vocal students an opportunity to debate the material they are being presented, whereas less extroverted learners take a back seat. The online format encourages learners to be active in expressing thoughts in writing. Instructors require that opinions and ideas have adequate documentation through citations and identified sources of information.

Assignments in the online environment are completed weekly. This format allows for deeper exploration into topics that develop over the course of the semester. Application and discussion assignments that are reviewed by instructors and peers encourage learners to evaluate their personal reactions through the lens of theory. Effective instructors are skilled at challenging ideas and motivating learners to think outside their own frame of reference. As Granello (2000) noted, cognitive flexibility is a skill that can and should be taught. This format allows instructors an opportunity to help students to develop this flexibility.

Enhancing Learner Self-Evaluation Skills

Because humanism emphasizes that students are motivated by an inner sense of purpose, self-evaluation is a key principle in humanistic education. The previously provided examples illustrate the role of peer and instructor involvement in evaluation in online courses. Online education leaves learners alone to process reading material, expand research outside of what may be required in the course, and make personal application. Weekly discussion assignments and larger projects can be designed to encourage students to evaluate their thinking, the quality of their work, and their overall progress in class. Most online course rooms allow learners to regularly monitor their grades through an electronic gradebook. Weekly grades and the grades for all major assignments are posted within a few days of the submission of the work. Many online courses allow learners to rework assignments with feedback from the instructor when they do not meet the standard. This process allows learners to demonstrate their understanding of the material and the instructions for the assignment. Assignments are seen as a tool for learning rather than simply an evaluation strategy.

Online universities have experience in dealing with the unique needs of learners at a distance. They may have a wealth of resources available to learners to assist them with issues of writing, style and formatting, research, and other issues that are common to all learners. These universities employ staff whose primary role is to design and publicize these resources. Instructor feedback may include a referral to one of these resources. The availability of such resources encourages learners to be self-sufficient in improving their performance. Following is a quote from an online learner following the completion of the course:

> I have discovered that I do not write as well as I thought. I have also been surprised to find how many of the "facts" I thought I knew are not backed up by research. This semester has been difficult in ways and I have found myself getting behind more than once. Looking at it from this end, I realize how much I have learned about the topic of the course. However, my greatest learning was about myself and what I need to do to become the kind of professional I want to be.

This quote reflects the ability of the online format, good course design, and effective instruction to promote personal growth. Feedback on assignments from both peers and the instructor, access and use of appropriate resources, and feedback that is critical but motivational in nature are important tools regardless of the format. The student's comments underscore the usefulness of the online format for supporting the student's sense of purpose and need for self-actualization.

Effectively Teaching and Monitoring Interpersonal Skills

Counselor education literature has highlighted the importance of monitoring the development of communication skills and effective interpersonal process as key indicators of effectiveness as a counselor. One criticism of technology-based education of counselors is the apparent lack of opportunity to observe and impact the way a beginning counselor perceives and is perceived by others. Clearly, there are certain classes that benefit from real-time, in-person instruction. Classes such as Counseling Skills and Techniques, Group Counseling, and other interpersonal skill–related classes should have those in-person components. Some technology and distance-based courses, for example, hold mandatory in-person sessions each semester to ensure the viability and direct observation and learning of interpersonal skills. That said, once learned, the skills can be demonstrated at a distance using technology such as digital video and instructor feedback delivered in the same way.

The availability of affordable and reliable communication has exploded over the past 10 to 15 years. The ability to communicate effectively through electronic media is no longer a luxury. It is a necessity. Social networking through electronic media is a common activity for people of all ages via texting, tweeting, and videoconferencing. Skills in interpersonal relationship building in cyberspace are different from face-to-face interactions. Nonetheless, electronic networking has a structure and format that includes a commonly understood language, protocol, and even rules of courtesy. Interpersonal styles are reflected, and community building occurs as mentioned already.

Effective online communication requires an individual to organize ideas and thoughts in a manner that allows readers to understand the nuances of the message as well as the content. Effective online communicators report that clear, concise communications are more effective than lengthy descriptions and colorful language. Messages need to be direct and to the point. Emotional content needs to be carefully considered, and time needs to be spent in finding the most accurate way of communicating feelings that may be presented face to face through more subtle body cues and facial expressions. Teaching counseling skills at a distance requires careful analysis of the outcomes that are desired, clear communication regarding the skills to be mastered, and creative use of the tools available through modern technology. Standards for evaluation of counseling communications have involved videotaped case presentations and peer-reviewed videos. Digitized technology allows these practices to be used in e-learning settings.

The interpersonal skills of beginning counselors are also evident in the way they interact with peers and instructors. Learning at a distance does not mean less contact with peers or instructors. In many cases, learners have more individualized and goal-oriented communications in the electronic classroom. The use of an electronic course delivery software program such as Blackboard allows students to have more efficient and consistent communicate with one another through e-mail and discussion boards. The use of discussion boards allows all class members, even those who might be more reticent to contribute in traditional in-class discussions, to participate equally and receive quality individual feedback from the faculty members and peers. In effect, students may actually have more quality interaction with peers in a distance education format than they experience in a face-to-face format. Additionally, many distance education programs offer a residency requirement that brings learners and instructors together for an intense and condensed learning activity that stretches across several days.

Meeting Educational Standards

Distance education programs, like other academic programs, meet standards that are applicable to all types of higher education programs. In addition, these programs tend to receive greater scrutiny than more traditional courses. Since most material is presented in written form, courses can be regularly monitored according to criteria that are easily measured and tracked. Such criteria may include monitoring of the instructor's presence in the course room and the number of contacts made with individual learners.

Many courses are designed by a committee rather than an individual instructor with considerable attention being given to ensure that the course meets all educational and professional standards. On its face, of course, design by committee does not appear to be a humanistically grounded practice. However, Rogers (1969, p. 164) notes the importance of the learning facilitator's setting the tone for the course as well as establishing the general purposes of the group. Although counselor education courses are standardized, ensuring that each learner has been exposed to a standard curriculum, instructors are often free to design individual assignments and activities, however, tailoring the content to each student individually. This allows the class to proceed according to accepted standards while still allowing individual instructors and students the freedom to adapt to individual teaching style and learner preferences.

Counselor education accreditation standards are specific in regards to the design of distance programs (CACREP, 2009). These standards ensure that there is a minimally acceptable quality of education offered in online programs and that these programs offer a quality of education that is comparable to that of more traditionally designed programs.

CONCLUSION

Using technology to enhance and support counselor education allows instruction to be individualized. It also provides opportunities for students to employ learning processes that are meaning based and experiential, leading to enhanced retention. This student-centered approach, in helping students to build meaning while participating actively in the learning process, also enhances the relationship between student and facilitator. This is a central tenet in the humanistic literature. As Rogers (1969) noted, it is through the enhanced relationship that learning is best facilitated and integrated. It is clear then that effective technology-based education can be not only good teaching but also fundamentally humanistic at its core.

These meaning-based and experiential learning processes also enhance the cognitive mapping potential of the information (Epstein, 1994). Information that is more efficiently mapped is easier for students to retrieve and use when called upon. Effective technology-enhanced education improves students' abilities to respond proactively and creatively in the clinical environment. This uniquely person-based learning model is remarkably consistent with the humanistic principles of learning advanced by Carl Rogers so many years ago. At the end of the day, it seems clear that humanistic learning and technology-based learning are potentially compatible and complimentary "streams" that can be crossed to form a powerful and innovative methodology that learning facilitators can use to foster the development of counselors-in-training.

REFERENCES

Ancis, J. R. (1998). Cultural competency training at a distance: Challenges and strategies. *Journal of Counseling & Development, 76,* 134–143.

Batson, T., & Bass, R. (1996, March–April). Teaching and learning in the computer age. *Change, 28,* 42–47.

Bennett-Levy, J. (2006). Therapist skills: A cognitive model of their acquisition and refinement. *Behavioural and Cognitive Psychotherapy, 34,* 57–78.

Bernard, J. M., & Goodyear, R. K. (2004). *Fundamentals of clinical supervision* (3rd ed.). Boston: Allyn & Bacon.

Boyer, D. L. (1984). Malcolm Knowles and Carl Rogers: A comparison of andragogy and student-centered education. *Lifelong Learning: An Omnibus of Practice and Research, 7*(4), 17–20.

Buser, T. J. (2008). Counselor training: Empirical findings and current approaches. *Counselor Education and Supervision, 48,* 86–100.

Council on Accreditation of Counseling and Related Programs (CACREP). (2009, February). *CACREP policy document: Review of non-traditional programs.* Author, p. 7. Retrieved from http://www.cacrep.org/doc/Final%20POLICY%20DOCUMENT%203.18.09.pdf

Cain, D. J. (2001). Defining characteristics, history, and evolution of humanistic psychotherapies. In D. J. Cain & J. Seeman (Eds.), *Humanistic psychotherapies: Handbook of research and practice* (pp. 3–54). Washington, DC: American Psychological Association.

Chickering, A. W. (1969). *Education and identity.* San Francisco: Jossey Bass.

Collison, G., Elbaum, B., Haavind, S., & Tinker, R. (2000). *Facilitating online learning. Effective strategies for moderators.* Madison, WI: Atwood Publishing.

Davidson, L. (2000). Philosophical foundations of humanistic psychology. *Humanistic Psychologist, 28,* 7–31.

Donaldson, J. F., Flannery, D., & Ross-Gordon, J. (1993). A triangulated study comparing adult college students' perceptions of effective teaching with those of traditional students. *Continuing Higher Education Review, 57,* 147–165.

Dubin, F., & Olshtain, E. (1986). *Course design: Developing programs and materials for language learning.* Cambridge, UK: Cambridge University Press.

Elias, J., & Merriam, S. (1994). *Philosophical foundations of adult education* (2nd ed.). Malabar, FL: Krieger.

Epstein, S. (1994). Integration of the cognitive and psychodynamic unconscious. *American Psychologist, 49*(8), 709–724.

Erikson, E. H. (1950). *Childhood and society.* New York: Norton.

Fishback, S. J. (1998/1999). Learning and the brain. *Adult Learning 10*(2), 18–22.

Fong, M. (1998). Considerations of a counseling pedagogy. *Counselor Education and Supervision, 38*(2), 106–113.

Galbraith, M. W. (Ed.). (2004). *Adult learning methods: A guide for effective instruction.* Malabar, FL: Krieger Publishing Company.

Gibson, D. M. (2007). Empathizing with *Harry Potter:* The use of popular literature in counselor education. *Journal of Humanistic Counseling, Education, and Development, 46,* 197–210.

Gladding, S. T. (2005). On the roads of life: Becoming a competent counselor and person of integrity. In G. R. Walz & R. K. Yep (Eds.), *Vistas: Compelling perspectives on counseling* (pp. 3–7). Alexandria, VA: American Counseling Association.

Gorham, J. (1999). Diversity in classroom dynamics. In A. L. Vangelisti, J. A. Daly, & G. W. Friedrich (Eds.), *Teaching communication: Theory, research, and methods* (2nd ed., pp. 257–268). Mahwah, NJ: Lawrence Erlbaum.

Gould, E., Reeves, A., Graziano, M., & Gross, C. (1999). Neurogenesis in the neocortex of adult primates. *Science, 286,* 548–552.

Granello, D. H. (2000). Encouraging the cognitive development of supervisees: Using Bloom's taxonomy in supervision. *Counselor Education and Supervision, 40,* 31–46.

Hall, B. S., Nielsen, R. C., Nelson, J. R., & Buchholz, C. E. (2010). A humanistic framework for distance education. *Journal of Humanistic Counseling, Education and Development, 49,* 45–57.

Hansen, J. T. (2009). On displaced humanists: Counselor education and the meaning-reduction pendulum. *Journal of Humanistic Counseling, Education and Development, 48,* 65–76.

Henriksen, R. C. (2006). Multicultural counselor preparation: A transformational pedagogy. *Journal of Humanistic Counseling, Education and Development, 45,* 173–185.

Instructional Technology Council (ITC). (2008). Distance education survey: Tracking the impact of e-learning at community colleges. Washington, DC: Author.

Knowles, M. S. (1977). *The modern practice of adult education: Andragogy versus pedagogy* (8th ed.). New York: Association Press.

Knowles, M. S. (1980). *The modern practice of adult education: From pedagogy to andragogy* (9th ed.). New York: Cambridge Books.

Landrum, R. E., McAdams, J. M., & Hood, J. (2000). Motivational differences among traditional and non-traditional students enrolled in metropolitan universities. *Metropolitan Universities, 11,* 87–92.

Maddux, C. D. (2003). Fads, distance education and the importance of theory. *Computers in the Schools, 20*(3), 121–127.

Maslow, A. (1954). *Motivation and personality.* New York: Harper.

Miller, M. J. (1989). A few thoughts on the relationship between counseling techniques and empathy. *Journal of Counseling and Development, 67,* 350–351.

Nelson, M. L., & Neufeldt-Allstetter, S. (1998). The *pedagogy* of counseling: A critical examination. *Counselor Education and Supervision, 38,* 70–88.

Norwood, G. (1999). Maslow's hierarchy of needs. *The Truth Vectors* (Part I). Retrieved May 2002 from http://www.deepermind.com/20maslow.htm

Palloff, P., & Pratt, K. (1999). *Building learning communities in cyberspace.* San Francisco: Jossey-Bass.

Pert, C. (1997). *Molecules of emotion: The science behind mind–body medicine.* New York: Simon & Schuster.

Pollio, H. R., & Beck, H. P. (2000). When the tail wags the dog: Perceptions of learning and grade orientation in, and by, contemporary college students and faculty. *Journal of Higher Education, 71,* 84–102.

Raskin, N. J., Rogers, C. R., & Witty, M. C. (2008). Client-centered therapy. In R. J. Corsini & D. Wedding (Eds.), *Current psychotherapies* (8th ed., pp. 141–186). Belmont, CA: Thomson Brooks/Cole.

Rogers, C. (1957). The necessary and sufficient conditions of therapeutic personality change. *Journal of Consulting Psychology, 21*, 95–103.

Rogers, C. R. (1961). *On becoming a person: A therapist's view of psychotherapy.* Boston: Houghton Mifflin.

Rogers, C. R. (1969). *Freedom to learn: A view of what education might become.* Columbus, OH: Charles Merill.

Rogers, C. R. (1980). *A way of being.* Boston: Houghton Mifflin Company.

Roney, G. (2007). *What are examples of philosophy of adult education.* Retrieved from http://e-articles.info/e/a/title/What-Are-Examples-of-Philosophy-of-Adult-Education

Ryan, R. M., & Deci, E. L. (2000). Self-determination theory and the facilitation of intrinsic motivation, social development, and well-being. *American Psychologist, 55*, 68–78.

Southern Association of Colleges and Schools (SACS). (2000). *Best practices for electronically offered degree and certificate programs.* Decatur, GA: Author.

Speck, M. (1996). Best practice in professional development for sustained educational change. *ERS Spectrum, 14*, 33–41.

Stella, A., & Gnanam, A. (2004). Quality assurance in distance education: The challenges to be addressed. *Higher Education: The International Journal of Higher Education and Educational Planning, 47,*143–160.

Taubert, M., Draganski, B., Anwander, A., Muller, K., Horstmann, A. Villringer, A., et al. (2010). Dynamic properties of human brain structure: Learning-related changes in cortical areas and associated fiber connections. *Journal of Neuroscience, 30*(35), 11670–11677.

U.S. Department of Education. (2002). National Center for Education Statistics. Profile of undergraduates in U.S. postsecondary education institutions: 1999–2000. NCES Publication, No. 2002–168.

Walsh, M. J. (2009). *Towards effective counselor education: Does student learning style predict student satisfaction in a distance education class?* Theses and Dissertations, Paper 105. Retrieved from http://scholarcommons.sc.edu/etd/105

Waschull, S. B. (2005). Predicting success in online psychology courses: Self-discipline and motivation. *Teaching of Psychology, 32*(3), 190–192.

Yalom, I. D., & Leszcz, M. (2005). *The theory and practice of group psychotherapy* (5th ed.). New York: Basic Books.

13

Humanistic Perspectives on Counselor Education and Supervision

Colette T. Dollarhide and
Darcy Haag Granello

I have come to feel that the only learning which significantly influences behavior is self-discovered, self-appropriated learning. Such self-discovered learning, truth that has been personally appropriated and assimilated in experience, cannot be directly communicated to another. As soon as an individual tries to communicate such experience directly, often with a quite natural enthusiasm, it becomes teaching, and its results are inconsequential. Carl Rogers (1961, p. 276)

COUNSELOR EDUCATION AND SUPERVISION: THE FOUNDATION

Counselor education and supervision is the process by which new counselors are trained and inducted into the profession of counseling. The core purpose of counselor education, then, is to foster the professional skills and professional identity development of future counselors. Through andragogical (Brown, Irby, Fisher, & Yang, 2006) strategies to foster adult learning and supervision strategies that cement that learning, counselor educators and supervisors know that the measure of their efforts is found in both the process and product of professional identity.

The process of counselor professional identity formation can be conceptualized as the internalization of professional standards, problem-solving strategies, values, ethics, skills, and attitudes, plus the internalization of feedback about professional skills and behaviors (Auxier, Hughes, & Kline, 2003; Brott & Myers, 1999; O'Byrne & Rosenberg, 1998; Reisetter et al., 2004; Skovholt & Ronnestad, 1995). This internalization process allows new counselors to enter and function within the professional community of counselors. The product of professional identity is evidence of the development of a professional identity, which may be found in the completion of the three transformational tasks of internalizing (1) one's personal definition of counseling, (2) responsibility for continued professional growth, and (3) development of a systemic identity within the professional community of counselors (Gibson, Dollarhide, & Moss, 2010). When this professional identity is crystallized, the counselor-in-training has internalized the cognitive, affective, behavioral, and contextual goals of training.

Recognizing the responsibilities of counselor educators in the development of professional skills and identity, the American Counseling Association Code of Ethics (ACA, 2005) explicitly addresses the issues of supervision, training, and teaching in Section F. The introduction to this section states, "Counselors aspire to foster meaningful and respectful professional relationships and to maintain appropriate boundaries with supervisees and students. Counselors have theoretical and pedagogical foundations for their work and aim to be fair, accurate, and honest in their assessments of counselors-in-training" (p. 13). It is within this ethical framework that counselor educators and supervisors strive to design learning and training experiences that protect clients, preserve the rights and dignity of students, and honor their responsibility to the professional community to provide well-trained and well-supervised new counselors for future clients. From a legalistic perspective, these standards have implications for liability; from a professional perspective, there are implications for program quality or accreditation.

However, while general guidelines for counselor education and counselor supervision are widely articulated and accepted, theories of pedagogical (common term) and andragogical (referring to adult learning; Brown et al., 2006, p. 32) structures in counselor education are actively sought. In articulating their vision for the future of *Counselor Education and Supervision,* coeditors Black and Helm (2009) call for "critical analysis of the content, sequencing, and utility of the counselor education pedagogy" (p. 84). It is in response to this continued examination of counselor education andragogy that this chapter is written.

In essence, counselor education and supervision serves as a bridge from one side of training to the other. Formal classroom education and formal supervision are the roadways on this bridge, the visible process of getting from one side to the other. The understructure of this bridge consists of girders of epistemological, cognitive, attitudinal, skill, and contextual development that are monitored during the crossing. This bridge has a formal beginning (admissions) and end (entry into the profession); nonetheless, the counselor's journey after the bridge consists of lifelong continued professional development that occurs in the context of the professional community.

The importance of the time in training cannot be underestimated. Although counseling students must do much of the difficult work of self-reflection and growth in cognitive complexity, critical thinking, and attitudinal development themselves, the graduate curriculum and specific instructional experiences can help set the tone for a lifetime of development and growth. Recent research in counselor education lends support to this developmental trajectory during graduate training (Fong, Borders, Ethington, & Pitts, 1997; Granello, 2002, 2010; Lyons & Hazler, 2002; Mayfield, Kardash, & Kivlighan, 1999; McAuliffe & Lovell, 2006), and counselor educators are aware of the need to design curricular and cocurricular experiences that intentionally promote counselor development. Designed with a solid theoretical basis, graduate programs in counselor education can be developed and implemented in intentional ways to help enhance counselor professional identity through cognitive complexity, affective internalization, skill development, and contextual development of counseling students.

To cement the learning acquired during the formal training/classroom experience, supervision provides the theory-to-practice capstone. From a practical perspective, it is during supervision that rough clinical and conceptual skills are refined, yet from a professional perspective supervision provides important benefits to the profession, the supervised or new professional, and the public. According to Bernard and Goodyear (2009), supervision is an intervention within which the skills of the junior professional are enhanced, the quality of the professional services provided by the junior professional is monitored, and the profession is assured that only qualified new professionals will enter the field (p. 7). The purpose of supervision is to provide formative and summative feedback about counseling skills, values, attitudes, and behaviors with the goal to foster the supervisee's professional development and to ensure client welfare (Bernard & Goodyear). While there are important distinctions between education and supervision, there are also multiple congruencies. It is from the perspective of those similarities between education and supervision that this merged discussion of humanistic education and supervision will be offered.

HUMANISTIC EDUCATION AND SUPERVISION

Exploring the potential of humanity through the nature and experience of values, meaning, emotions, intentionality, healthy relationships, self-actualization, creativity, holism, intuition, and responsibility (among other topics), humanistic andragogy and supervision attempt to access the phenomenologically constructed world of the student to facilitate learning. Humanistic andragogy and supervision is holistic, wellness oriented, strengths based, phenomenological, and meaning focused. Because of the emphasis on holism, humanistic education taps all four domains of learning: cognitive development, affective development, skill development, and community-contextual awareness.

In general, humanistic education can be captured in several basic tenets: (1) student-centered learning; (2) training in person-centered, empathic listening;

(3) emphasis on affective and experiential listening; (4) collaborative learning through sharing; and (5) reflection assignments that emphasize personal and professional growth and identity (Goldstein & Fernald, 2009; Pierson & Sharp, 2001). According to one graduate student in a humanistic dental school (Morton, 2008), the educational experience in a humanistic learning environment provided dignity and respect, a positive environment that allowed trainees to focus on learning, opportunities to attain personal empowerment as leaders, and space to learn about collaboration with other professionals.

As an overview, Kleiman (2007) asserted that humanistic education establishes a primary relationship between student and teacher that evolves through interpersonal dialogue, in which the teacher assumes an attitude of dialogic openness—a readiness to listen and engage in an honest discussion of ideas. From this professorial stance, the relationship takes on egalitarian tones, allowing teacher and student to engage in a dialectic journey of discovery about the subject through exploration of thoughts, perceptions, and feelings about the subject. Because the goal is to discover and illuminate values and meanings central to each person's life world, the emphasis is on individuals' modes of being in the world with others (Kleiman). Through this open dialogue, a community of learners is created (Palmer, 1998) in which both commonalities and differences of the teachers and learners are equally celebrated as means of mutual support and growth (Kleiman; Palmer).

The celebration of commonalities and differences in the humanistic classroom is a unique contribution of humanistic education. According to the National Research Council (2000), "Humans are viewed as goal-directed agents who actively seek information. They come to formal education with a range of prior knowledge, skills, beliefs, and concepts that significantly influence what they notice about the environment and how they organize and interpret it" (p. 10). Because humanistic education recognizes and values this diversity of perspectives, it reduces anxiety (Bandura, 1977) and addresses the sense of academic, emotional, social, and behavioral safety necessary for risk taking and ultimately learning (Bluestein, 2001). Recognition of the innate diversity of learners brings the social and cultural realities of both learner and teacher into the discussion of effective pedagogy and andragogy, addressing the layers of richness and dialogue found in multicultural classrooms (Suinn, 2006).

These general humanistic education strategies may be extended into humanistic supervision practices, as supervisors often rely on their therapeutic theory as a model for change for the supervisee (Bernard & Goodyear, 2009, p. 80). Rogers (as cited in Bernard & Goodyear) described person-centered supervision as an extension of person-centered counseling, describing ways that the foundation conditions for growth and change applied to the supervision relationship. Likewise, Adlerian supervision is grounded in the same conditions as individual psychology: phenomenology, relationship, holism, and growth orientation (Dollarhide & Nelson, 2000; Lemberger & Dollarhide, 2006). In our discussion of humanistic educational strategies, we will also tap multiple insights into humanistic supervision.

It is from these perspectives on general humanistic education and supervision that more specific application to humanistic counselor education may emerge. The development of the counseling student is conceptualized as holistic, consisting of cognitive development, affective development, skill/behavioral development, and the systemic/contextual development of a sense of the professional counseling community. Humanistic counselor education, then, provides andragogical structure to a more mature and informed discussion of counselor education and supervision.

HUMANISTIC ANDRAGOGICAL STRUCTURES: THE GIRDERS OF THE BRIDGE

Guiding this discussion of humanistic education and supervision are andragogical structures: the models of epistemological, cognitive, affective, performance, and contextual development that provide shape to these humanistic concepts and inform the strategies for education and supervision. These structures for learning are interwoven and interconnected, as development in one domain resonates, and facilitates, development within the others. Each of the andragogical "girders" of this bridge supports the others; for the humanistic counselor educator, without one, the bridge would fail and the structure would collapse.

Cognitive Development: Epistemology, Reflective Judgment, and Cognitive Complexity

Epistemological development, describing the relationship between the knower and what is known (Gilligan, 1993; Goldberger, Clinchy, Belenky, & Tarule, 1987; Kegan, 1982; King & Kitchener, 1994; Perry, 1981) documents the learner's journey toward greater self-authority in the resolution of ill-structured, ambiguous problems. These problems "cannot be described with a high degree of completeness or solved with a high degree of certainty" (King & Kitchener, 1994, p. 11), and possible solutions must be grounded in relevant data and evaluated to determine validity on the basis of coherence, meaningfulness, and usefulness. While each theory of epistemological development is unique, an overview of numerous epistemological theories yields five similar stages.

In the first stage, the learner looks for truth (as an ultimate definitive) from an all-knowing expert or authority, and thinking consists of a dualistic, right/wrong orientation (dualism). In the second stage, the learner experiences dissonance through the discovery of exceptions to the dualistic rules that govern life, bringing the stage of questioning. Eventually, the questions become overwhelming, the defining characteristic of the third stage called multiplicity; in this stage, the learner has lost the prior "anchors" of right and wrong from the all-knowing authority, and the search for ultimate "truth" to guide decision making is thwarted. The fourth stage, contextual relativity, is characterized by the growing awareness of various contexts in which right and wrong are variously defined; inherent in this discovery is the growing awareness that the guiding determiner of appropriateness within each context is the self. In the fifth and final stage, dialecticism, the learner arrives at the awareness that knowledge is always evolving, that knowing is not *either/or* but *also/and* (holding multiple realities simultaneously) and that the authority of reality is the self. Epistemological development models have been applied to counseling and counselor training (Dollarhide & Scully, 1999), used to examine the cognitive growth of counseling students (Granello, 2002), in measuring counseling skill development (McAuliffe & Lovell, 2006), and as a template for facilitating advisee development (Choate & Granello, 2006).

To foster this development, the learning process can be structured so that the learner is intentionally moved from reliance on external authority in the search for truth, toward an informed and self-authoring position relative to knowledge and the critical evaluation of resolution strategies. King and Kitchener (1994) call this development reflective judgment, or the simultaneous development of epistemology and critical thinking. "These are the assumptions that develop as the person becomes able to differentiate and coordinate increasingly complex cognitive skills" (p. 19). King and Kitchener structure their approach to developing reflective judgment as a series of well-designed challenges surrounding ill-defined problems. These challenging experiences foster learners' process of thinking about what is known and helps them develop ways to gather and evaluate data relevant to the problem.

What is important to note is that, when viewing learners' epistemological development through humanistic lenses, dualistic, externally oriented learners are not developmentally ready to benefit from the autonomy characteristic of the humanistic classroom. For these learners, the assumptions of an internal locus of meaning, motivation, and responsibility for learning are premature. To be a humanistic educator for these students would require more active and directive teaching to enable the learner to master concepts and foster understanding of the ill-structured problems inherent in counselor education. The emergence of self-generated, self-motivated learners would need to be nurtured from the earlier epistemological stages of dualism, questioning, and multiplicity. It is when learners reach contextual relativism that they are epistemologically ready for more autonomy and more responsibility and will move toward self-actualization as learners.

Another often-used taxonomy for measuring the cognitive development of counseling students is Bloom's Taxonomy of Educational Objectives (Anderson et al., 2001; Bloom, Engelhart, Furst, Hill, & Krathwohl, 1956). In this taxonomy, development is measured in terms of what learners can do with what is learned, as each skill in the taxonomy progresses toward greater complexity in the use of data. From the most basic cognitive functions, the taxonomy begins with *remember* (long-term recall of information), progresses through *understand* (constructing meaning from information and context), *apply* (application of what is known), and *analyze* (deconstruct what is known into constituent parts to determine the relationships among the parts), then culminates with *evaluate* (make judgments based on standards) and *create* (putting elements together in novel ways to form a new pattern or structure) (Anderson et al., p. 31). In the overall progression of learning, the ultimate goal is the ability to evaluate existing knowledge and create new knowledge—again, leading to mastery and self-actualization. Within research, this taxonomy has been applied widely in counseling to facilitate the counseling development of supervisees (Granello, 2000b) and the writing skills of graduate students (Granello, 2001) and to foster multicultural counseling training (Whitfield, 1994).

For humanistic counselor educators, fostering the development of cognitive complexity, reflective judgment, critical thinking, and epistemological development is consistent with humanism, as these cognitive tools are necessary for mastery—one of the foundations for self-actualization. It is important to note that these goals of cognitive development are not accomplished in a mechanical or detached process. Rather, this process is considered integral to the foundations of counselor education and takes place within the humanistic structures of experiential knowing, respectful community, and dialogue. It is important to note that humanistic education is not outside of standards of intellectual quality; as stated by Pierson and Sharp (2001), "Heeding the call to this vocation requires successful completion of a substantial body of formal coursework and supervised field experience consonant with the prevailing scientist-practitioner or professional school models of graduate training.... The existential and humanistic perspectives challenge the practitioner to creatively weave together the science, philosophy, and art of psychotherapy" (p. 539). It is this weaving together of science and art that is unique to humanistic education; "the subjective realm is trusted, and access to this sensitive resource within is increasingly fluid and reflective" (Bugental, as cited in Pierson & Sharp, 2001, p. 540).

Affective Development

Access to the subjective and intuitive self is through the values, emotions, intuition, meaning, and creativity that give humanistic education its name. Recall that as counselors-in-training progress through the graduate experience, they not only are acquiring the skills of counseling but also are challenged to internalize a personal definition of counseling, responsibility for continued professional growth, and a systemic identity within the professional community of counselors (Gibson et al., 2010). The process of internalizing values, attitudes, and identity are described in Krathwohl's affective taxonomy (Krathwohl, Bloom, & Masia, 1964).

Within humanistic education, trainees' attitudes, values, motivations, and perceptions are legitimate and desirable educational foci (Dollarhide, 2010; Forsyth, 2003). Humanistic counselor educators would use the affective taxonomy to foster inner awareness, reflection, and experiencing as educational tools and would measure trainees' growth on the basis of attainment of affective milestones in the internalization of professionally relevant educational goals. According to Krathwohl et al. (1964), the milestones within the affective taxonomy are as follows:

1. Receiving a value, in which learners progress from passive awareness to willingness to learn about the value, to selectively attending to the learning about the value
2. Responding to the learning, in which learners first comply with expectations, then respond from increasing inner interest and motivation, and then find satisfaction in immersion in learning about the value
3. Valuing, in which learners progress from accepting the value as their own, to holding a preference for the value and seeking out chances to contact the value, to feeling a sense of commitment to the value
4. Organization, in which learners conceptualize the value and desire to understand all they can about it, to organization of a value system in which learners merge the new value with their existing value system
5. Characterization by a value or value complex, in which learners first view all problems in terms of the value and then evidence a consistent philosophy of life based on the new value, usually not attainable until many years after formal training

In terms of professional identity, the taxonomy can provide an important tool as counselor educators conceptualize the internalization of a professional counselor identity. Using the taxonomy allows educators to facilitate students' progress from attending classes and merely completing assigned tasks, to feeling pride in becoming a counselor, to exploring counselor literature in students' free time, to merging the values of counseling with students' personal value systems, and finally, to *becoming* a counselor through demonstrating a consistent philosophy of life based on counseling values (Dollarhide, 2010).

Making explicit use of this taxonomy, and the concurrent discussions with students about the affective journey they embark upon in counseling training, allows the humanistic counselor educator to discuss the implicit curriculum of counselor education: that of the evolution of the "personhood of the counselor." Discussions of meaning, feelings of hope and fear, memories, experiences, expectations, perceptions—all of this material is now accessible as educational tools to facilitate learning (Goleman, 1995). With the affective domain accessible for educators, cognitive, affective, and skill growth are connected, enhanced, and reinforced; concepts now have a scaffold of meaning on which to develop, and cognitive concepts, theories, and abstractions can progress from *remember* to *understand*. With behavioral and skill development, students can now merge cognitive theory and skills to *apply* counseling skills, dealing with the fear, anxiety, expectations, and triumphs of clinical training. Once these feelings are understood and integrated, students can then *analyze* their skill sets, *evaluate* their performance without fear of punishment, and *create* new cognitive structures and new attitudes as they internalize counseling concepts, values, and skills (Anderson et al., 2001; Krathwohl et al., 1964).

Behavioral and Skill Development

Concurrent with cognitive development and affective development, humanistic counselor educators are also facilitating counseling skill development, and the foundation of these skills is humanism. It is important to realize that most counseling skills texts use humanistic/existential/Rogerian structures in the skills taught (e.g., Brems, 2000; Corey, 2009; Ivey, Ivey, & Zalaquett, 2010), and this foundation of honesty, congruence, respect, and positive client regard is also embedded in the ethics of the profession (ACA, 2005). Counseling students are fully immersed in humanism from their first class in counseling.

Humanistic andragogical underpinnings for skill development may be found in teaching that is termed *student centered* (Forsyth, 2003). At the foundation of this andragogical structure is the knowledge that *discovery* will foster greater learning than *lecturing*, and that as students engage with the material and their discoveries are drawn into the classroom, significant development will result. In these classrooms for conceptual or skill development, students are given the respect and responsibility (Forsyth) to learn, to become independent thinkers and practitioners who can merge theory and practice for the benefit of clients. In spite of students' perennial desire for a cookbook for counseling in which they will find the recipe for success with this issue or that client, the humanistic counselor educator knows that the development of conceptual skills and counseling skills comes only with practice, application, and discovery of outcomes. The goals of the humanistic counselor educator in this domain are to help students learn from discoveries that are uncomfortable, to help students manage their performance anxiety during the learning process, and to facilitate students' reflection and internalization of supervisory feedback and therapeutic results during the application of counseling skills.

Systemic and Community Development

When students encounter a counseling classroom in which they do not feel respected, or the counseling professor is disingenuous and incongruent, confusion results: How can a profession that espouses humanistic values and trains others in the skills of humanistic interaction *not* provide such a growth-producing environment for its students? It is a difficult question to answer, especially since such growth-producing conditions are core concepts for the humanistic counselor educator. For humanists, the community, which is built from the valuing of and interconnection with each individual, is an integral part of learning.

Recall that one of the transitional tasks for the internalization of professional identity is the awareness of oneself as a professional embedded in, responsive to, and responsible to a professional community. The building of that sense of community, of the self as a part of a larger reality, begins in the humanistic classroom, where the emphasis is on the respectful, inclusive, responsive relationship among the learner, the educator, and the subject (Palmer, 1998). Much like the process by which a counselor "joins" with a client to facilitate growth, the process in which a humanistic teacher builds classroom community involves a willingness to be vulnerable, a trust in students or clients (partners in the learning or change process), and the desire to allow the growth process to take priority over ego.

Palmer (1998) speaks eloquently about this "community of truth" in which the educator, the student, and the subject become interconnected. This process of interconnection begins with the educator, as Palmer reflects on his personal experiences: "In every class I teach, my ability to connect with my students, and to connect them with the subject, depends less on the methods I use than on the degree to which I know and trust my selfhood—and am willing to make it available and vulnerable in the service of learning" (p. 10). He continues, "Good teachers possess a capacity for connectedness. They are able to weave a complex web of connections among themselves, their subjects, and their students so that students can learn to weave a world for themselves" (p. 11).

Next, the process of forming those connections requires that the educator must learn to trust the student: "I no longer teach to their imputed ignorance, having rejected that assessment as both inaccurate and self-serving. Instead, I try to teach to their fearful hearts, and when I am able to do so, their minds come along as well" (Palmer, 1998, p. 46). The awareness and acknowledgment of the fear that underlies their silence, withdrawal, and cynicism are profound catalysts to learning, and once fear is addressed then teaching to the students' curiosity, hope, empathy, or honesty becomes possible. The ability to connect with students from their affective development allays their fear and opens the discussion about the third element of the community: the subject.

When the subject is addressed in the classroom in which the teacher and students are fully present, collaborative, and valued, the subject no longer is owned by the teacher but rather is a shared construct cocreated by all in the learning community. "As we try to understand the subject in the community of truth, we enter into complex patterns of communication—sharing observations and interpretations, correcting and complementing each other, torn by conflict this moment and joined by consensus in the next. The community of truth, far from being linear and static and hierarchical, is circular, interactive, and dynamic" (Palmer, 1998, p. 103). It is the subject that demands the learner's attention, not "pleasing the professor," and as understanding evolves so does the learner's intimate connection with the subject.

In the humanistic counselor education classroom, then, this community of truth both *creates* and *results from* the cognitive skills of self-authoring and reflective judgment, the affective skills of internalizing values and core beliefs, the counseling skills based on humanistic practice, and the vulnerability of knowing and not knowing. For an aerial view of this bridge, the initial efforts of the humanistic educator would involve (1) preparing the cognitive development of students by providing structure, information, and support; (2) assessing students' affective readiness to learn by introducing affect and values into the conversations about learning; (3) provide skill training, experiences, and introduction of the ambiguity of clinical practice; and (4) structure the learning community so that respectful dialogue could ensue. As the counselor-in-training approaches the end of the bridge, there are more opportunities for self-discovery, reflection, self-authoring, and expansion of professional goals to include those personal goals that engender intrinsically motivated learning. When this training process has finished and the new counselor's professional identity and professional skills are crystallized, the counselor-in-training has internalized the cognitive, affective, contextual, and behavioral tools of the professional counselor and is now able to navigate the professional environment.

HUMANISTIC ANDRAGOGICAL PRACTICES: THE VISIBLE ROADWAY OF THE BRIDGE

In practice, the humanistic counselor educator brings all these humanistic structures into the learning process: curriculum design, process illumination, the relationship, the tone of the classroom, and the learning strategies themselves.

Curriculum Design

To foster holistic development, the overall design of the curriculum must both *support* and *challenge* the students, as various strategies for design can facilitate student development. One such strategy, sequencing of courses, can be used to accommodate developmentally appropriate content and learning strategies and to challenge students to engage in higher levels of cognitive, affective, and skill complexity and integration (Granello & Hazler, 1998). Based on developmental models of cognitive complexity and critical thinking, Granello and Hazler offered the means of matching cognitive level with counselor education content. For example, because new students are usually in dualistic thinking, appropriate coursework would involve counseling foundations, basic counseling techniques, and research. Midprogram students, who may be characterized as operating with multiplistic thinking, would benefit most from courses that tap their openness to various "truths" (e.g., counseling theories and group counseling). Finally, advanced coursework, which requires students to be able to operate with relativistic thinking, might involve diagnosis and ethics. The matching of content complexity of the class with the cognitive complexity of students can yield the appropriate level of challenge without overwhelming the student. As summarized by Granello and Hazler (1998), the developmental goal of this progression of courses and teaching styles would be to:

> Continually push graduate learners to move past their dualistic mentality into the next stages of learning.... Dualistic learners ... must be actively pushed into multiplistic learning by faculty who present contradictory and ambiguous information to students. During the multiplistic stage of learning, students can become overwhelmed and discouraged and may need faculty guidance and reassurance. At the relativistic stage, faculty can begin to pull away and allow students to monitor their own learning, seeking assistance from faculty when needed. (p. 99)

Another humanistic curriculum strategy is cognitive scaffolding, a dynamic process that provides individualized support for learners and facilitates students' ability to build on prior knowledge and internalize new information. Scaffolding also follows humanistic tenets, in that individuals' current phenomenological status and current knowing (strengths) are used as a measure of where to begin building new concepts and new understanding.

A third strategy is controlled floundering, also known as the Yerkes–Dodson Law (Yerkes & Dodson, 1908), which states that persons' performance can be improved if they are aroused. However, if the level of arousal increases too much, performance decreases. In this strategy, self-directed learning and discovery is encouraged through loosely structured learning challenges and tasks, but students' anxiety levels are monitored so that they do not flounder beyond the limits of frustration. This means that humanistic counselor educators are connected and attuned to students' arousal and anxiety levels, constantly monitoring the extent to which students are engaged but not overwhelmed by new tasks. Thus, a curriculum that is intentionally designed and sequential and supports increasing levels of cognitive complexity is the first component of a humanistic developmental curriculum.

Process Illumination

Based on the work of Yalom (1970), process illumination is the andragogical tool of connecting experience with developmental trajectory. While grounded in group process theory, the implications for developing the learning community are profound. This is another example of the parallel process between counseling and educating.

According to Yalom (1970), if the powerful therapeutic factor of interpersonal learning (community) is to be set in motion, then the group must recognize, examine, and understand *process*. In essence, the group must be willing to examine itself and study its own interaction. It is not sufficient to simply live through the experience; the group or community must integrate the learning that comes from fully understanding the experience. In Yalom's view, the group leader is responsible for escorting the group through this understanding of the process as a benevolent guide who helps group members navigate the unfamiliar territory of change. More than just a here-and-now focus, process illumination provides an important second tier of learning that facilitates self-examination and self-understanding. Ultimately, it calls on group (learning community) members to follow the track of their exchanges, reflect upon them, and use them to better understand themselves.

Within counselor education, process illumination can help students better understand their own developmental trajectory. Students can feel uncomfortable in their new learning and want to revert back to the relative safety of their old ways of behaving. Cognitive complexity is not necessarily generalizable across domains (Granello, 2002; Welfare & Borders, 2010), and students who are cognitively advanced in other areas of their lives may feel threatened or embarrassed by their newfound dualism when they enter the field of counseling. Process illumination allows counselor educators to give a name to the students' experiences. When students hear of this typical developmental trajectory, they have a roadmap and an understanding of where they are in their journey (moving from dualism through multiplicity to relativistic thinking and dialectism). Ultimately, this gives students permission to engage in the *process* of the journey rather than focus only on the ultimate destination.

In a humanistic context, process illumination can begin with the first contact between instructor and student: in the syllabus. In this document, instructors can provide information about (1) the process of their learning, by describing meta-cognitive processes as one of the course objectives, and (2) the goals of their learning, to help them understand *why* they are engaging in the activities and experiences of the class, using research that shows that counselors who can engage in cognitive complexity are better counselors. Then, periodically throughout the class, humanistic educators will step back and reflect on where the students are in the process, how they got there, and what the next step is in their journey. This helps students understand the andragogical choices of the instructor and helps them contextualize discussion—which is often different from how they are used to being taught. As stated by Yalom (1970, pp. 176–177, bracketed information offers the context of this discussion inserted into the quote):

> Throughout therapy [learning], we ask our clients [students] to think, to shift internal arrangements, to examine the consequences of their behavior. It is hard work, and it is often unpleasant, frightening work. It is not enough simply to provide

clients [students] with information or explanations; you must also facilitate the assimilation of new information.... Remember, no comments, not even the most brilliant ones, can be of value if their delivery is not accepted, if the client [student] rejects the package unopened and uninspected. The relationship, the style of delivery, and the timing are thus as essential as the contents of the message.... Clients [students] are always more receptive to observations that are framed in a supportive fashion.

The Relationship Between Student and Professor

The multiple supportive relationships of the counselor trainee within the context of graduate education all have an important role to play in teaching and learning. In the cocreation of a community of learners, the relationship between the student and professor is paramount, as old assumptions about learning and teaching are continuously challenged. Whereas undergraduate education has been grounded in the principles of pedagogy that have promoted instructor-directed learning, the principles of andragogy that underlie adult education allow for a greater complexity of roles to facilitate student-directed learning. Instructors, supervisors, and peers are conceptualized more as mentors, facilitators, and collaborators, presenting alternative ways of thinking and acting, drawing attention to contradictions and ambiguities, and prompting scrutiny of unchallenged assumptions (Forsyth, 2003; Palmer, 1998). Faculty advisors can be conceptualized as individuals who help facilitate the overall development of the trainee, across the multiple courses and experiences of graduate school (Choate & Granello, 2006). In these and other ways, counselor education programs can make intentional use of the multiple sources of support and challenge that are available within the students' lives to encourage their overall development as counselors.

Integral to this process is *trust* (1) of self, (2) of other, and (3) of the learning process. Through "guiding, mentoring, facilitating, collaborating, and coordinating" (Forsyth, 2003, p. 88), the educator demonstrates trust in students and asks for their trust in return. By providing options (e.g., as in learning contracts) rather than mandates, the counselor educator is able to place the locus of control and responsibility in the hands of learners. While not often experienced in undergraduate education, such trust provides graduate students in counseling with the opportunities for discovery and self-appropriated learning.

Along with trust comes immense value placed on the diverse perspectives and experiences of the students. Such diversity includes, but is not limited to, ethnicity, gender, age, sexual orientation, national origin, religion or spiritual expression, first language, physical abilities—the infinite range of human uniqueness. Because the whole student is welcomed and valued in the humanistic classroom, each student is safe (Bluestein, 2001). According to Rogers (1961), learners and clients deserve "deep respect and full acceptance" for the student as he/she is, and this deep respect needs to be expressed with "sufficient warmth" and "the most profound type of liking or affection for the core of the person" (pp. 74–75). The core of respect for the personhood of students pervades the classroom and the counselor educator models "I–thou" relationships (Buber, cited by Kirschenbaum & Henderson, 1989) as appropriate interaction around difficult discussions of content, diversity, or learning goals. Affective realities are contextualized in the class content, and articulation of values, attitudes, and feelings are sought and processed.

Because affect becomes an appropriate and fitting part of the classroom experience, empathy with boundaries is an important part of the relationship between counselor educator and student. Balancing the needs of the class with the needs of the individual is a delicate act, as no one student is allowed to hijack the learning of the community, and no group within the community is allowed to silence any individual. Communally derived and authored norms and rules for the learning community will make boundaries and expectations clear for the students.

When researchers examined what the best college professors do in the classroom, certain interpersonal qualities were found to enhance the bond between learner and teacher (Bain, 2004). These teachers exhibited "awe and curiosity about life," which manifested in "a sense of humility about themselves and their own learning" (p. 142). Their "trust and openness produced an interactive atmosphere in which students could ask questions without reproach or embarrassment, and in which a variety of views and ways to understand could be freely discussed" (p. 142). They "found affinity with their students in their own ignorance and curiosity, in their love of life and beauty, and in their mixture of respect and fear, and in that mix they discovered more similarities than differences between themselves and the people who populated their classes" (p. 144). These teachers were able to use their relationship with their students and their "veneration of the unknown" to generate the "quiet conviction … that they and their students could do great things together" (p. 144). In this way, these teachers used their humanity to foster respectful, awe-filled classrooms in which their students could thrive.

Tone of the Classroom

Extrapolated from the relationship, the tone of the classroom is:

- *Creative,* with consideration given for diverse ideas and perspectives (Amabile, 1996; Csikszentmihalyi, 1990, 1996, 1997; May, 1975; Root-Bernstein & Root-Bernstein, 1999)
- *Phenomenologically grounded,* with a focus on the unique realities and meaning each student brings to the conversation
- *Holistic,* which honors the whole student: thoughts, feelings, actions, choices, knowing and not knowing

- *Idealistic and hopeful*, which allows for growth in trust of self, of other, and of the proces
- *Process focused*, while not losing sight of the product of counselor education and supervision; the *journey* of learning is also valued
- *Diversity sensitive and welcoming*, so that there is dialogue about what is known and how to know beyond what we currently see, think, feel, and believe
- *Safe and challenging*, as a place for students to try new thinking and feeling, to try new skills, and to reach for their personal excellence
- *Accountable and responsible,* in that students and instructors are accountable for their actions and are responsible to all the others in the learning community

Parker Palmer (1998) describes five paradoxes found in a classroom environment that qualifies as a community of truth. First, the classroom must be focused on the subject, yet students must be free to speak about the subject in ways that foster their growth. Second, the classroom must be hospitable and calm, inviting students' input and thoughts but also charged with the excitement of learning. Third, the classroom environment must invite the voice of the individual and the group, so that students are able to speak their truths but that the group can "affirm, question, challenge, and correct the voice of the individual" (p. 75). Fourth, the classroom must provide space for the stories of the personal experiences of students and space for the big stories of the discipline or subject. Finally, the classroom must support solitude and time for reflection and contemplation as well as "dialogical exchange in which our ignorance can be aired, our ideas tested, our biases challenged, and our knowledge expanded, an exchange in which we are not simply left alone to think our own thoughts" (p. 76).

Humanistic Learning Strategies

Within courses and cocurricular activities, specific andragogical techniques can be employed to facilitate higher levels of learning and development. Strategies such as contextual teaching and learning, service learning, and problem-based assessment are all teaching methods that have broad application to counselor education and the development of counselors. Employing these strategies within a developmental framework can assist with transfer of learning from the classroom to counseling practice, foster personal and professional development, and energize professional skill and identity development.

Many humanistic learning strategies can be captured under the conceptual umbrella of contextual teaching. According to Granello (2000a), in contextual teaching students' learning and knowledge are rooted to the context in which the knowledge is constructed, and it is up to the teacher to help students coconstruct the meaning for the learning experience. To accomplish this, five conditions must be met: (1) learning should be experienced, or situated, in the same context in which it will later be expressed; (2) the natural peer group of students should be used to facilitate shared construction of meaning; (3) the peer group should be used as a means of tapping the collective knowledge of the learning community; (4) learning should be grounded in realistic work-related problems inherent to the training; and (5) authentic assessment should be used to measure the extent of the learning. In counselor education, these strategies for humanistic counselor education are used in the following ways.

Experiential Focus

To bring the full experience of learners into the classroom, learning experiences are designed to allow for personal, immediate experience with the material being learned. For counselor education, assignments that involve firsthand interaction would be very valuable. An example of an experiential assignment in a multicultural counseling class would be the immersion experience, in which students are asked to immerse themselves into cultures or groups about which they have the most preconceived ideas. This assignment and the processing of the experience would allow students to (1) evaluate their reactions to the immersion group, (2) evaluate their reactions to the immersion experience, (3) consider how the experience has changed their thinking about the immersion group, (4) connect class concepts of cultural encapsulation, privilege, and the experience of isolation within a group to the reality of the student, and (5) facilitate the students' awareness of and sensitivity to diversity in this society. Within this learning strategy are opportunities for students to advance both cognitively (learning about the immersion group), affectively (learning about self in relation to that immersion group), behaviorally (learning about transcultural interaction that can inform the counseling process; Harper & McFadden, 2003), and contextually (learning about cultural communication and messages of inclusion and exclusion).

Experience can be fostered through a variety of venues. For example, Dollarhide, Smith, and Lemberger (2007) found that demonstrating a transparent counseling session in which the clinical thinking of the counselor was articulated for the observing class was instrumental in helping students experience the counseling in a more personal way, which fostered comprehension, retention, and integration. Bringing the profession to life for students will facilitate their experiences and their learning.

Case Study

The ability to connect learning with the depth of insight required of counseling professionals is evident in the use of case studies in humanistic counselor education. Examples of such learning experiences abound in counseling textbooks. Because case studies are designed to allow students to grapple with counseling's ill-structured problems and because there are multiple avenues for treatment within various counseling theories, this andragogical tool allows students to struggle with the multiplicity of perspectives inherent in counseling work. Within these discussions or assignments are cognitive applications in which students learn about ambiguity in counseling, affective applications in which students learn about how to manifest ethical values, behavioral applications in which students learn about complex case conceptualization and intervention planning, and contextual applications in which students experience collegial conversations about professional expectations.

Sources of these case studies abound: counseling textbooks (e.g., Corey, 2009); books about counseling and therapy (e.g., Kottler & Blau, 1989; Yalom, 1989); movies (e.g., Koch & Dollarhide, 2000; Villalba & Redmond, 2008); classic literature, poetry, plays, television stories, current events, modern music—the list is endless. Any story or expression of the human experience can be used as a counseling case study in the humanistic counseling course.

Relevant Work Samples

Anchoring humanistic counselor education to other class assignments would involve relevant work samples. If clinical counselors must be able to write treatment plans and school counselors must be able to design classroom experiences within the developmental curriculum, then making such assignments a part of counselor education are intuitive. From a humanistic perspective, these assignments resonate with the phenomenological meaning of the training experience, where the value of such assignments is both concrete and philosophical. Specific cognitive, conceptual, and behavioral learning takes place as well as affective and contextual learning, as the skills being asked of students and the meaning and relevance behind the assignment are discussed with the students.

Connecting Learning Across the Counseling Curriculum

Students, in general, struggle with transfer of learning from one course to another and from one context to another (Granello, 2000a). Students learn things in silos; they are used to compartmentalized knowledge. As humanistic counselor educators and advisors work with students (Choate & Granello, 2006), this integration of cross-course knowledge and application is essential for holistic knowing. Strategies for this integration could include conversations with faculty advisors (Choate & Granello), cross-course assignments, and multiple-course capstone integrative assignments such as portfolios. For example, a culminating portfolio for graduating counselors could be an opportunity to integrate 10–15 meaningful assignments from across the program, complete with a narrative for each artifact explaining the significance of the artifact, the learning generated from the experience behind the artifact, any self-reflections generated by the creation of the artifact in terms of the learning or counseling process, and finally the application of that learning to the profession. A comprehensive, reflective portfolio can increase students' awareness of the learning *process* (what was meaningful and why in their professional training) as well as a tangible *product* that integrates their learning for the eventual job-search process, especially if students are allowed the freedom to present their learning in individual ways. Once again, humanistic learning strategies focus on phenomenological meaning, individual expression of personal/professional discoveries, and the capacity of each individual to contribute to the learning of the whole.

Process Tracking (Journaling)

To better understand each student's unique learning process, asking students to journal their thoughts, feelings, reactions, questions, challenges, and triumphs can help the humanistic educator to connect *content* with *process*. If such a journal is used to help students access their own learning strengths, this type of assignment can affirm a strengths-based curriculum in counseling. Through sharing their process with the instructor and hearing their instructor's reactions to their journal, a connection can begin to form between learner and educator that can deepen the trust between them. In addition, from an andragogical perspective, reading students' learning journals can help instructors track specific content that triggers confusion or frustration for students, thereby allotting greater time and attention to those content-related affective realities.

Service Learning

According to Learn and Serve America (n.d.), service learning is "a teaching and learning strategy that integrates meaningful community service with instruction and reflection to enrich the learning experience, teach civic responsibility, and strengthen communities." Juxtaposed with practicum or internship experiences, service learning places students in a professionally relevant site to provide preprofessional services that are anchored in classroom learning and service rather than in accumulation of hours toward graduation. In other words, the focus is on *service*, not on students' completion of graduation requirements. Usually such service learning takes place in the context of a single class within the counseling curriculum rather than at the culmination of training. For example, a service learning assignment for a class in counseling through play would entail providing play-oriented counseling services to residents of a children's home in the community. Service learning for a school counseling foundations class could involve mentoring local elementary students; similar service learning for clinical counseling students could entail intake counseling in a homeless shelter.

For the service to be connected to learning, journaling is often required, and there is a focused effort to connect the cognitive and skill content of the class with the affective and contextual realities of the service setting. The tripartite emphasis on (1) community-within-classroom, (2) the professional community's responsibility to give back to society, and (3) the needs of the larger community in which the training program is located all culminate in rich learning for the counseling student.

Contract Learning and Independent Study

As andragogical tools, contract learning and independent study place the locus of control and responsibility for learning in the hands of students. The humanistic aspect of contract learning and independent study is the explicit connection with the meaning making that students bring to the learning environment. If trust is the cornerstone for the learning-oriented relationship, then a profound expression of that trust is conveyed by providing learners with various ways and means to engage, interpret, and then manifest that learning has taken place, honoring the multiple intelligences and diversity of each learner (Bain, 2004; Lazear, 1999).

Discussion and Socratic Dialogue

Posing important questions and facilitating each student's unique answer to those questions is a foundation of any humanistic andragogical strategy. While this is not to say that lecturing is not a useful tool for instruction, the key, as Forsyth (2003) points out, is when to use it—when to talk, when to remain silent, when to probe, when to ask. Through large- and small-group discussions, students engage the material in deeper ways than merely recording what the expert says and, in the process, tap their own reactions, responses, prior knowledge, and questions. They engage the material, not just the instructor (Forsyth, 2003). In addition, they engage *each other*, cementing social and professional connections, creating collaboratives, and engaging each other as consultants to coconstruct meaning.

According to McKeachie and Svinicki (2006) discussions can begin with common experience, a controversy, questions, or a problem or case that represents challenges for the profession. In each of these situations, the discussion would be shaped and guided to remain on topic by the instructor, bounded by the rules of the community of learners.

Are there more humanistic strategies and resources than these listed? Of course there are. As counselor educators, we are bound only by the limits of our own imaginations in the myriad ways that we engage students in cognitive development, affective development, skill development, and community development.

HUMANISTIC COUNSELOR SUPERVISION

The final challenge for counseling students is the field experience, where the rubber hits the road and students are asked to perform as professional counselors. During this final stage of training, counseling students experience supervision, the intense scrutiny of the new professional's comprehension, attitudes, skills, and contextual awareness that signals the transition from trainee to colleague. As previously stated, the goals of supervision are counselor self-actualization, the development of cognitive complexity and conceptual fluidity, professional identity development, professional skill development, and protection of the client.

Humanistic theories of supervision, especially as manifest in Adlerian, person-centered, Gestalt, and existential supervision, inform the foundations of humanistic supervision, with contemporary contributions found in transcultural counseling approaches (Harper & McFadden, 2003) and feminist counseling (Prouty, 2001; Smith, 2007). Resources abound for each of these theoretical perspectives. In all of these approaches, consistent emphasis is placed on the actions and attitudes of the supervisor:

1. Humanistic supervision will focus on the supervisee's phenomenological perspectives, taking such perspectives into the supervision process to foster the supervisee's growth and development.
2. Humanistic supervision will reflect the trust of one professional guiding and mentoring another.
3. Humanistic supervision will foster a developmental focus, in that the innate direction of the supervisee toward wellness, holism, and growth is used as a template for future development.

Humanistic Supervision Strategies

Toward these goals, humanistic supervision applies the same structures for cognitive, affective, skill, and contextual development as humanistic education. Extending these andragogical insights into supervision means that many of the same strategies for education would also apply to the supervision setting. In addition, the following supervision strategies for the humanistic supervisor would be added.

Meeting the Supervisee's Needs With Support and Challenge

Humanistic supervisors know that it is developmentally appropriate for new field placement students (who are usually in dualism) to need some answers. As a result, supervision provided during practicum is very different from the type of supervision provided in internship or in postdegree supervision. Students in practicum want answers, and they need the safety of at least *some* answers, some concrete ideas—and then they need to be pushed, gently, to take more and more risks on their own. If students' needs are not met developmentally, they will indeed seek "answers"—just not necessarily from reliable resources. In this way, humanistic supervisors provide the safety of something to hold onto when supervisees are experiencing something new.

Process illumination of Yerkes–Dodson Law

The balance between arousal and performance, as reflected in the Yerkes–Dodson Law (Yerkes & Dodson, 1908), highlights that students need to have some level of anxiety because it improves performance—but too much anxiety can paralyze. In supervision, process illumination of this foundation concept of education can empower students to talk about their level of performance anxiety and stress. This model can be taught to students so they can start to name their own levels of arousal and notice when their anxiety is causing them to have diminished success in counseling.

Strengths Analysis

Humanistic supervisors focus on the supervisee's counseling strengths as the foundation of supervision, expanding from that foundation to explore the supervisee's "growing edges" of skills, cognitions, affect, and contextual awareness. Taking a "glass is half-full" attitude allows the supervisor to form a solid working alliance (Bernard & Goodyear, 2009) with the supervisee, which reduces supervisee resistance and increases honest supervisee self-evaluation and help seeking.

Supervision Contracting

Similar to contract learning, the supervision contract would provide an opportunity for the supervisee to specify content and practice desired by the supervisee. This would increase the supervisee's perception of meaning of the supervision experience and further improve the working alliance.

Self-Reflection

Similar to journaling, the use of supervisee or supervisor self-reflection allows both parties to make their clinical or supervisory thinking transparent for the other. Sharing these reflection documents would provide more dialogue and open more honest communication between supervisor and supervisee about progress in supervision, concurrently improving trust and enhancing the quality of the working alliance (Bernard & Goodyear, 2009).

Unstructured Supervision

If the hallmark of humanistic supervision is trust in the process of the learner (supervisee), then the supervisor would share control of and responsibility for the direction of supervision with the supervisee. It is true that the boundaries of supervision would be established at the onset of the supervision relationship (Bernard & Goodyear, 2009), but then supervision would reflect more spontaneous movement through the supervision process as both supervisor and supervisee brought issues and topics to the supervision conversation.

Including Supervisee at Professional Events

While this is not an activity that is commonly included in clinical supervision, it is nonetheless an important way that the supervisor fosters the contextual and professional-community awareness of the supervisee. Introducing the supervisee to professional colleagues, encouraging the supervisee to make a professional contribution through service or presentations, and mentoring the supervisee at professional events can expand the supervisee's awareness of the professional community.

CONCLUSIONS

It goes without saying, perhaps, that humanistic counselor education and supervision is not for every counselor educator or supervisor, nor might these learning and supervision strategies be appropriate for every counseling student. But it's not all or nothing—faculty, supervisors, and students might benefit from humanistic approaches at some times and not others and in some situations but not others. For individuals who are highly cognitive, for example, humanistic education and supervision strategies might at first appear soft or without rigor. It is possible that such highly cognitive individuals would find it uncomfortable to be in classrooms or in teaching–learning relationships that are less structured, more fluid, and more meaning oriented. Some students might be confused and frustrated by a professor who does not tell them what to think, what to do, and how to get an A on the test, as dualistic thinkers struggle with the anxiety of multiplicity. Dialogue with students as a primary andragogical strategy (as opposed to lecture) might be interpreted as laziness or lack of preparation and might be reflected in teaching evaluations. Making the rationale for these strategies apparent would help students understand their role in the classroom and responsibilities for learning, as is highlighted in the discussion of process illumination. For some students, this may be the first time in their lives when their natural desire to learn would be allowed expression.

In response to the perception that humanistic andragogy and supervision are without rigor, the observation would be made that not all learning is cognitive. Not all counselor education topics are memorizable, measurable, countable, or quantifiable. For many students, the greater challenge is the affective, attitudinal, or contextual learning that is required in counseling—the learning about self and self-in-community. Students might memorize data for a test, but they cannot memorize rapport, connection, trust, or caring. These things are learned not by the head but by the heart (Palmer, 1998), and for some students these are the hardest lessons of all. Rather than being without rigor, humanistic counselor education is actually more rigorous, more stringent, and more demanding because it is intentional education of the *whole* person-as-counselor.

Likewise, it is important for counselor educators to note the context of their academic environment: Would their humanistic classroom interactions, with concurrent emphasis on self-directed learning and quality relationships with students, be perceived by colleagues as too informal? It is important that humanistic educators and supervisors be aware of the expectations and values of their academic environment so that they can educate their colleagues and adjust their presentation to both fit that community and remain true to their humanistic philosophy of education and supervision.

In spite of these limitations, the humanistic counselor educator or supervisor is given the responsibility and privilege to be fully present and fully whole in interactions with students and supervisees. As stated by Palmer (1998), "...What we teach will never 'take' unless it connects with the inward, living core of our students' lives, with our students' inward teachers.... Deep speaks to deep, and when we have not sounded our own depths, we cannot sound the depths of our students' lives" (p. 31). Humanistic teaching and supervision requires that we face our own fears, find our own truths, and then foster that exploration and vision quest in our students—that is the core of counselor education at its best.

REFERENCES

Amabile, T. M. (1996). *Creativity in context.* Boulder, CO: Westview.

American Counseling Association (ACA). (2005). *ACA code of ethics.* Alexandria, VA: Author. Retrieved February 9, 2010 from http://www.counseling.org/Resources/ CodeOfEthics /TP/Home/CT2.aspx

Anderson, L. W., Krathwohl, D. R., Airasian, P. W., Cruikshank, K. A., Mayer, R. E., Pintrick, P. R., et al. (Eds.). (2001). *A taxonomy for learning, teaching, and assessing: A revision of Bloom's Taxonomy of Educational Objectives* (abridged ed.). New York: Longman.

Auxier, C. R., Hughes, F. R., & Kline, W. B. (2003). Identity development in counselors-in-training. *Counselor Education and Supervision, 43,* 25–38.

Bain, K. (2004). *What the best college teachers do.* Cambridge, MA: Harvard University Press.

Bandura, A. (1977). *Social learning theory.* Upper Saddle River, NJ: Prentice Hall.

Bernard, J. M., & Goodyear, R. K. (2009). *Fundamentals of clinical supervision* (4th ed.). Upper Saddle River, NJ: Merrill.

Black, L. L., & Helm, H. M. (2009). Counselor education and supervision: Our voice, vitality, and vision. *Counselor Education and Supervision, 49,* 82–85.

Bloom, B. S., Engelhart, M. D., Furst, E. J., Hill, W. H., & Krathwohl, D. R. (1956). *Taxonomy of educational objectives: Handbook I: Cognitive domain.* New York: David McKay.

Bluestein, J. (2001). *Creating emotionally safe schools: A guide for educators and parents.* Deerfield Beach, FL: Health Communications.

Brems, C. (2000). *Dealing with challenges in psychotherapy and counseling.* Belmont, CA: Wadsworth.

Brott, P. E., & Myers, J. E. (1999). Development of professional school counselor identity: A grounded theory. *Professional School Counseling, 2,* 339–348.

Brown, G., Irby, B. J., Fisher, A., & Yang, L. (2006, Winter). Using the andragogical model for a graduate course in educational leadership. *Delta Kappa Gamma Bulletin, 72,* 32–36.

Choate, L. H., & Granello, D. H. (2006). Promoting student cognitive development in counselor preparation: A proposed expanded role for faculty advisors. *Counselor Education and Supervision, 46,* 116–130.

Corey, G. (2009). *Theory and practice of counseling and psychotherapy* (8th ed.). Belmont, CA: Thomson.

Csikszentmihalyi, M. (1990). *Flow: The psychology of optimal experience.* New York: Harper.

Csikszentmihalyi, M. (1996). *Creativity: Flow and the psychology of discovery and invention.* New York: Harper.

Csikszentmihalyi, M. (1997). *Finding flow: The psychology of engagement with everyday life.* New York: Harper.

Dollarhide, C. T. (2010). *Learning in the affective domain: A necessary element of professional identity.* Manuscript submitted for publication.

Dollarhide, C. T., & Nelson, M. (2000). Adlerian supervision: A proposed model. *Canadian Journal of Adlerian Psychology, 30*(1), 35–46.

Dollarhide, C. T., & Scully, S. (1999). The counseling/learning model: Using epistemological theory in college counseling. *Journal of the Pennsylvania Counseling Association, 2,* 3–18.

Dollarhide, C. T., Smith, A. T., & Lemberger, M. E. (2007). Counseling made transparent: Pedagogy for a counseling theories course. *Counselor Education and Supervision, 46,* 242–253.

Fong, M. L., Borders, L. D., Ethington, C. A., & Pitts, J. H. (1997). Becoming a counselor: A longitudinal study of student cognitive development. *Counselor Education and Supervision, 37,* 100–114.

Forsyth, D. R. (2003). *The professor's guide to teaching psychological principles and practices.* Washington, DC: American Psychological Association.

Gibson, D. M., Dollarhide, C. T., & Moss, J. (2010). Professional identity development: A grounded theory of transformational tasks of new counselors. *Counselor Education and Supervision, 50,* 21–38.

Gilligan, C. (1993). *In a different voice.* Cambridge, MA: Harvard University Press.

Goldberger, N. R., Clinchy, B. M., Belenky, M. F., & Tarule, J. M. (1987). Women's ways of knowing: On gaining a voice. In P. Shaver & C. Hendrick (Eds.), *Sex and gender* (pp. 201–228). Beverly Hills, CA: Sage.

Goldstein, G., & Fernald, P. (2009). Humanistic education in a capstone course. *College Teaching, 57*(1), 27–36. Retrieved February 9, 2010 from http://wilsontxt.hwwilson.com.proxy.lib.ohio-state.edu/pdffull/03828/p9d7i/gs9.pdf

Goleman, D. (1995). *Emotional intelligence: Why it can matter more than IQ.* New York: Bantam.

Granello, D. H. (2000a). Contextual teaching and learning in counselor education. *Counselor Education and Supervision, 39,* 270–283.

Granello, D. H. (2000b). Encouraging the cognitive development of supervisees: Using Bloom's taxonomy in supervision. *Counselor Education and Supervision, 40,* 31–46.

Granello, D. H. (2001). Promoting cognitive complexity in graduate written work: Using Bloom's taxonomy as a pedagogical tool to improve literature reviews. *Counselor Education and Supervision, 40,* 292–307.

Granello, D. H. (2002). Assessing the cognitive development of counseling students: Changes in epistemological assumptions. *Counselor Education and Supervision, 41,* 279–293.

Granello, D. H. (2010). Cognitive complexity among practicing counselors: How thinking changes with experience. *Journal of Counseling and Development, 88,* 92–100.

Granello, D. H. & Hazler, R. J. (1998). A developmental rationale for curriculum order and teaching styles in counselor education programs. *Counselor Education and Supervision, 38,* 89–105.

Harper, F. D., & McFadden, J. (2003). *Culture and counseling: New approaches.* Boston: Allyn & Bacon.

Ivey, A. E., Ivey, M. B., & Zalaquett, C. P. (2010). *Intentional interviewing and counseling: Facilitating client development in a multicultural society* (7th ed.). Belmont, CA: Brooks/Cole.

Kegan, R. (1982). *The evolving self: Problem and process in human development.* Cambridge, MA: Harvard University Press.

King, P. M., & Kitchener, K. S. (1994). *Developing reflective judgment: Understanding and promoting intellectual growth and critical thinking in adolescents and adults.* San Francisco: Jossey-Bass.

Kirschenbaum, H., & Henderson, V. L. (Eds.). (1989). *Carl Rogers: Dialogues.* Boston: Houghton Mifflin.

Kleiman, S. (2007). Revitalizing the humanistic imperative in nursing education. *Nursing Education Perspectives, 28*(4), 209–213. Retrieved February 9, 2010 from Ebscohost.

Koch, G., & Dollarhide, C. T. (2000). Using a popular film in counselor education: "Good Will Hunting" as a teaching tool. *Counselor Education and Supervision, 39*(3), 203–210.

Kottler, J. A., & Blau, D. S. (1989). *The imperfect therapist: Learning from failure in therapeutic practice.* San Francisco: Jossey-Bass.

Krathwohl, D. R., Bloom, B. S., & Masia, B. B. (1964). *Taxonomy of educational objectives: The classification of educational goals. Handbook II: Affective domain.* New York: Longman.

Lazear, D. (1999). *Eight ways of teaching: The artistry of teaching with multiple intelligences* (3rd ed.). Arlington Heights, IL: SkyLight.

Learn and Serve America, National Service-Learning Clearinghouse. (n.d.) *What is service learning?* Retrieved March 11, 2010 from http://www.servicelearning.org/whatservice-learning

Lemberger, M. E., & Dollarhide, C. T. (2006). Encouraging the supervisee's style of counseling: An Adlerian model for counseling supervision. *Journal of Individual Psychology, 62*(2), 106–125.

Lyons, C., & Hazler, R. (2002). The influence of student development level on improving counselor student empathy. *Counselor Education & Supervision, 42,* 119–130.

May, R. (1975). *The courage to create.* New York: Norton.

Mayfield, W. A., Kardash, C. M., & Kivlighan, D. M. (1999). Differences in experienced and novice counselors' knowledge structures about clients: Implications for case conceptualization. *Journal of Counseling Psychology, 46,* 504–514.

McAuliffe, G., & Lovell, C. (2006). The influence of counselor epistemology on the helping interview: A qualitative study. *Journal of Counseling & Development, 84,* 308–317.

McKeachie, W. J., & Svinicki, M. (2006). *Teaching tips: Strategies, research, and theory for college and university teachers.* Boston: Houghton-Mifflin.

Morton, N. A. (2008). Benefits of a humanistic education: A student perspective. *Journal of Dental Education, 72*(1), 45–47. Retrieved February 9, 2010 from http://www.jdentaled.org.proxy.lib.ohio-state.edu/cgi/content/full/72/1/45??

National Research Council. (2000). *How people learn: Brain, mind, experience, and school.* Washington, DC: National Academic Press.

O'Byrne, K., & Rosenberg, J. I. (1998). The practice of supervision: A sociocultural perspective. *Counselor Education and Supervision, 38,* 34–42.

Palmer, P. J. (1998). *The courage to teach: Exploring the inner landscape of a teacher's life.* San Francisco, CA: Jossey Bass.

Perry Jr., W. G. (1981). Cognitive and ethical growth. In A. Chickering (Ed.), *The modern American college* (pp. 76–92). San Francisco: Jossey Bass.

Pierson, J. F., & Sharp, J. G. (2001). Cultivating psychotherapist artistry: A model existential-humanistic training program. In K. J. Schneider, J. Bugental, & J. F. Pierson (Eds.), *The handbook of humanistic psychology: Leading edges in theory, research, and practice* (pp. 539–554). Thousand Oaks, CA: Sage.

Prouty, A. M. (2001). Experiencing feminist family therapy supervision. *Journal of Feminist Family Therapy, 12,* 171–203.

Reisetter, M., Korcuska, J. S., Yexley, M., Bonds, D., Nickels, H., & McHenry, W. (2004). Counselor educators and qualitative research: Affirming a research identity. *Counselor Education and Supervision, 44,* 2–16.

Rogers, C. R. (1961). *On becoming a person: A therapist's view of psychotherapy.* New York: Houghton/Mifflin.

Root-Bernstein, R., & Root-Bernstein, M. (1999). *Sparks of genius: The thirteen thinking tools of the world's most creative people.* Boston: Houghton-Mifflin.

Skovholt, T. M., & Ronnestad, M. H. (1995). *The evolving professional self: Stages and themes in therapist and counselor development.* Chichester, England: Wiley.

Smith, A. T. (2007). *Feminist supervision: An inquiry into integration.* Unpublished doctoral dissertation, University of South Carolina, Columbia.

Suinn, R. M. (2006). Teaching culturally diverse students. In W. J. McKeachie & M. Svinicki (Eds.), *Teaching tips: Strategies, research, and theory for college and university teachers* (12th ed.). New York: Houghton Mifflin.

Villalba, J. A., & Redmond, R. E. (2008). *Crash*: Using a popular film as an experiential learning activity in a multicultural counseling course. *Counselor Education and Supervision, 47,* 264–276.

Welfare, L. E., & Borders, L. D. (2010). Counselor cognitions: General and domain-specific complexity. *Counselor Education & Supervision, 49,* 162–178.

Whitfield, D. (1994). Toward an integrated approach to improving multicultural counselor education. *Journal of Multicultural Counseling and Development, 22,* 239–252.

Yalom, I. D. (1970). *The theory and practice of group psychotherapy.* New York: Basic.

Yalom, I. D. (1989). *Love's executioner & other tales of psychotherapy.* New York: Harper.

Yerkes, R. M., & Dodson, J. D. (1908). The relation of strength of stimulus to rapidity of habit-formation. *Journal of Comparative Neurology and Psychology, 18,* 459–482.

V

CONCLUSION

14

Epilogue

MARK B. SCHOLL, A. SCOTT MCGOWAN,
AND JAMES T. HANSEN

As we mentioned in Chapter 1 of the current text, the one principle that unifies the many diverse elements of humanism is the idea that humans are irreducible to other phenomena (Davidson, 2000). This means that humans can be understood only as whole beings. From a philosophical standpoint, the organizing principle of irreducibility logically leads to three supporting elements: (1) individualism; (2) a focus on subjective experience; and (3) an emphasis on the dignity of each person. In addition, we believe that it bears repeating that the term *humanism* applies to practices that highlight "relating to human beings in growth-producing ways" (Bohart, 2003, p. 107). Given that philosophical foundation as the basis for a common understanding of the definition of humanism, the current book has two primary purposes. First, it is intended to highlight humanistic principles inherent in current, effective approaches to counseling, education, and counselor training. Second, this book is intended to demonstrate the power of humanistic thinking for uniting diverse elements of practice in these areas.

To more easily recognize the humanistic principles inherent in effective counseling and educational practices, it is helpful to once again refer to Ansbacher's list of humanistic principles, cited in Raskin, Rogers, and Witty (2008, p. 146):

1. Creativity is a powerful force in the lives of people.
2. A holistic approach is more effective than a reductionistic approach.
3. Counseling is essentially based on a good relationship.
4. Sense of purpose, rather than cause, is the primary influence on human behavior.
5. It is necessary for counselors to understand and value individuals' subjective experiences (e.g., feelings, opinions, values).

These abstract principles are closely related to the attitudes, beliefs, and actions of humanistic counselors and educators. As previously mentioned in Chapter 1,

Cain (2001, pp. 6–13) provided the following defining characteristics of humanistic approaches to counseling:

1. A positive view of the individual as self-actualizing
2. An emphasis on the critical role of empathy in enhancing the quality of the individual's experience
3. A belief that individuals have the capacity to actively and intentionally construct meaning in their lives
4. A belief that people have the freedom, right, and ability to choose their goals and how to achieve them
5. A belief in the dignity of every human being

To the five characteristics identified by Cain we add another:

6. A belief in the importance of practices that promote tolerance and diversity and uphold human rights

Based on the themes presented in the 12 content chapters of the current text, we believe that the aforementioned principles and characteristics can be distilled into five primary humanistic themes summarized in the following sections.

IRREDUCIBILITY

Repeatedly the authors of the chapters of the current text mentioned the importance of a holistic approach to counseling and education. The descriptions of effective approaches indicate that a holistic approach is more effective than a reductionistic one. Repeatedly, the chapter authors indicate that the optimal counseling or educational approach is one that incorporates as many aspects of the person or as much of an individual's identity into the process as possible.

INDIVIDUALISM

Another prevalent theme found in a number of chapters in the current text is the humanistic principle that each person is unique. In Chapter 1, the practices of assessing clients' levels of readiness for change and eliciting their ideas for how change might be facilitated in motivational interviewing (MI) were cited as exemplifying this principle. Another example is the fact that a number of current therapies tap into clients' unique inner resources and potential for generating creative solutions to their personal problems. Further, Cain (2001) observed that humanistic therapies are becoming increasingly "individualized" (p. 44) to meet the specific characteristics and needs of specific clients. As discussed in the following sections of this chapter, the principle of individualism is repeatedly supported and illustrated in the effective counseling approaches reviewed in this book.

SUBJECTIVE EXPERIENCE

This humanistic principle has two primary components. First, it entails the belief that it is necessary for counselors to understand and value individuals' inner subjective experiences. These subjective experiences include, but are not limited to, individuals' feelings, opinions, values, goals, sense of purpose, and religious and spiritual beliefs. Second, this principle includes an emphasis on the important role of empathy in enhancing the quality of individuals' experiences.

THE DIGNITY OF EACH PERSON

The next prevalent theme was the principle that effective counselors and educators exhibit respect for the dignity of the individuals they serve. Central to this theme is the importance of having a positive view of human nature including each individual. This positive view entails the belief that people have the capacity to actively and intentionally construct meaning in their lives and the belief that people have the freedom, right, and ability to choose their goals and how to achieve them. Respect for the dignity of each person is predicated upon the belief that each person is endowed with innate self-righting and self-actualizing tendencies. Further, individuals are capable of constructing meaning in their lives and are guided by their own unique sense of purpose. Because these tendencies are inherent within all humans, humanistic practitioners act in the best interests of clients when they facilitate individuals' development as opposed to employing a more active, directive, or controlling approach.

In addition, we believe that having respect for the dignity of each person requires integrity on the part of the practitioner. Chickering and Reisser (1993) defined integrity as a process entailing movement toward "not only increased congruence between behavior and values, but also movement toward responsibility for self and others and the consistent ability to thoughtfully apply ethical principles" (p. 236). Respect for the dignity of the person requires the humanistic counselor to have integrity as well as to understand and respectfully respond to the integrity or evolving integrity of the student or client.

Lastly, respect for each person necessarily entails exhibiting appreciation for diversity and recognizing and supporting human rights (Scholl, 2008). Adopting a strengths-based perspective with regard to individuals from diverse cultures is consistent with possessing a positive view of human nature. Individuals' sense of integrity must be understood in terms of their unique cultural perspectives. It is important to understand clients or students as whole persons and to avoid referring to or viewing them in terms of demographic or diagnostic labels.

A GOOD RELATIONSHIP

Carl Rogers's (1957) client-centered or person-centered therapy includes the central tenet that there are core or facilitative conditions that are necessary and sufficient for facilitating the development of an effective relationship and promoting the growth of the individual. Rogers identified and described three core conditions that he believed should be provided and communicated by the humanistic practitioner: genuineness, respect, and empathy. *Genuineness* refers to the degree to which the humanistic practitioner is authentic. Rogers described *respect* as an unconditional regard for, or prizing of, the student or client as a person. *Empathy* refers to a professional who both accurately understands and clearly communicates understanding of individuals' subjective experiences. Repeatedly, the contributors to this book described effective approaches as entailing the provision of good relationships by practitioners, and these relationships clearly reflect the core conditions described by Rogers.

CONCLUSION

One recurring observation with regard to the application of humanistic principles to educational and counseling practices is that there appear to be limitations with regard to the extent to which some of the principles can be applied. In some instances, two or more humanistic principles may be in conflict. In general, appropriate resolutions seem to honor the principle of *individualism* and require attitudes and actions that promote well-being and avoid causing harm. For example, in Chapter 13 Dollarhide and Granello assert that when working with beginning counseling supervisees it is not advisable to encourage them to be autonomous or self-directed. To accommodate dualistic thinking in supervisees, they recommend that supervisors adopt a more authoritarian stance than might be expected from a strictly humanistic standpoint. This is an individualized approach that accommodates the supervisee's developmental status.

Another example in which humanistic principles may be in conflict is the case of individuals who suffer from a severe mental illness. For example, in cases where individuals have an eating disorder that is life-threatening or a serious substance abuse problem that threatens their health or the safety of others, mandated treatment may be required. Mandating therapy might be interpreted as violating the principle regarding the importance of respecting the *dignity* of each person. Again, in keeping with the principle of *individualism,* it is arguably more important to intentionally respond to and accommodate the needs and abilities of individual clients and to adhere to ethical principles. Thus, it is more humanistic to mandate treatment for the safety and welfare of clients with a potentially life-threatening mental health problem than to treat them as if they are high functioning. Although mandated treatment may appear to violate the humanistic principle of *dignity*, it is consistent with the principle of *individualism*.

At the same time, in Chapter 5, Scholl, Kendrick, Wilkes, and Hagedorn noted that motivational interviewing, which is largely based upon Rogerian counseling principles, shows promise as a means of enhancing intrinsic motivation and reducing drinking in clients with a substance abuse disorder and a coexisting severe mental illness (DiClemente, Nidecker, & Bellack, 2008; Graeber, Moyers, Griffith, Guajardo, & Tonigan, 2003; Martino, Carroll, Kostas, Perkins, & Rounsaville, 2002). Further, Martino et al. developed an approach known as dual diagnosis motivational interviewing (DDMI) to accommodate the impairments of clients with a coexisting severe mental disorder. As one example of a modification, in DDMI the counselor employs only simple open questions to accommodate clients' difficulty organizing responses to complex questions. There is recognition that the clients are less high functioning, and the standard MI procedure is modified honoring the principle of individualism. DDMI procedure upholds the dignity of clients by employing a modified form of open-ended questioning rather than abandoning the client-centered approach altogether.

The same principle is reflected in Alan Schwitzer's (Chapter 11) description of the humanistic approach to working with college students who suffer from severe mental disorders. Clients are viewed holistically as a human being whose behaviors, thoughts, or emotions are consistent with a diagnostic category. Importantly, the approach described by Schwitzer is holistic and respectful of clients' dignity. We believe these examples attest to an important principle. Namely, educators and counselors should aspire to uphold humanistic principles regardless of the degree of severity of the problems of the individual. We believe that Martino et al.'s (2002) DDMI should serve as an example for researchers and practitioners to follow in terms of developing refinements and extensions of effective humanistic approaches to accommodate the needs of individuals suffering from severe mental health problems.

The current text was written to fulfill two primary purposes. First, this book was written to highlight humanistic principles inherent in current effective approaches in counseling and education. Second, this book was written to show the power of humanistic thinking to unite diverse counseling practices. Moreover, we wanted to demonstrate that humanism has the potential for serving as a general theory of counseling for the helping professions. We believe that through the cumulative talents and expertise of the contributing authors, the aforementioned purposes have been fulfilled. The descriptions of approaches to counseling and education clearly indicate that humanistic principles are essential and integral to their success. Also, the finding that fundamental humanistic principles are integral to diverse cutting-edge approaches affirms our initial belief that humanism has the power to unite diverse counseling approaches and serve as a perspective unifying the counseling professions.

Further, a third important finding was that the historical development of counseling approaches frequently follows an increasingly humanistic trajectory. Although the medicalization of modern mental health culture has had a suppressive impact on humanism, all of the diverse theories and practice modalities represented by the chapters in this book have been part of this humanistic trajectory. This suggests that there is a strong humanistic groundswell that is rising up to challenge the dominant forces in mental health culture.

As an example of this humanistic trend, in the past scholars and practitioners in the field of marital counseling previously believed that focusing on the clients' subjective emotions was too touchy-feely. However, more recently the role of emotions has become recognized as a central component of marital counseling (Peluso & Vensel, Chapter 6). In addition, approaches to substance abuse counseling are becoming more respectful of the dignity of clients and more individualized. It is evident from the chapters of this book that effective therapies are becoming increasingly individualized, holistic, respectful, and based on a good relationship rather than less so. Approaches as diverse as Donna Henderson's descriptions of incorporating creativity and the arts into counseling and Colette Dollarhide and Darcy Granello's descriptions of humanistic counseling supervision practices reflect the principle that effective approaches encourage individuals (clients and students) to access as much of themselves as possible. Outmoded approaches such as an ego-oriented approach to coaching youth sports, nonemotional models of marital counseling, and a "tear 'em down to build 'em up" philosophy of substance abuse counseling are becoming less prevalent in favor of a mastery approach to coaching youth sports, emotion-focused couples counseling, and relatively nonconfrontational motivational interviewing. Models and approaches that ignore or neglect the humanistic principles are falling by the wayside.

Humanism, as we argued in our introductory chapter, has, indeed, been suppressed by modern mental health culture. The diverse contributions to this book, however, make it clear that there are active theoretical currents in multiple areas of counseling that have been inspired by humanistic ideology. The reason humanism appears suppressed, then, is because these currents have not been theoretically grouped together as a humanistic tidal wave. The fact that the many diverse contributions of this book all had humanism in common demonstrates that there is, indeed, a humanistic tidal wave that will hopefully hit the shores of mental health culture soon. Therefore, one of the main contributions of this book has been to theoretically group seemingly diverse theories under a humanistic banner so that the Goliath of the reductive, medicalized mental health approaches to counseling can be challenged by a unified force instead of by the individual

Davids of separate systems of thought. In modern times, approaches that are consistent with humanistic values and principles are required to effectively address the problems and challenges faced by contemporary clients, counselors, and educators.

REFERENCES

Bohart, A. C. (2003). Person-centered psychotherapy and related experiential approaches. In A. S. Gurman & S. B. Messer (Eds.), *Essential psychotherapies: Theory and practice* (2nd ed., pp. 107–148). New York: Guilford Press.

Cain, D. J. (2001). Defining characteristics, history, and evolution of humanistic psychotherapies. In D. J. Cain & J. Seeman (Eds.), *Humanistic psychotherapies: Handbook of research and practice* (pp. 3–54). Washington, DC: American Psychological Association.

Chickering, A. W., & Reisser, L. (1993). *Education and identity* (3rd ed., p. 236). San Francisco: Jossey-Bass Publishers.

Davidson, L. (2000). Philosophical foundations of humanistic psychology, *Humanistic Psychologist, 28,* 7–31.

DiClemente, C. C., Nidecker, M., & Bellack, A. S. (2008). Motivation and the stages of change among individuals with severe mental illness and substance abuse disorders. *Journal of Substance Abuse Treatment, 34*(1), 25–35.

Graeber, D. A., Moyers, T. B., Griffith, G., Guajardo, E., & Tonigan, S. (2003). A pilot study comparing motivational interviewing and an educational intervention in patients with schizophrenia and alcohol use disorders. *Community Mental Health Journal, 39*(3), 189–202.

Martino, S., Carroll, K., Kostas, D., Perkins, J., & Rounsaville, B. (2002). Dual diagnosis motivational interviewing: A modification of motivational interviewing for substance-abusing patients with psychotic disorders. *Journal of Substance Abuse Treatment, 23*(4), 297–308.

Raskin, N. J., Rogers, C. R., & Witty, M. C. (2008). Client-centered therapy. In R. J. Corsini & D. Wedding (Eds.), *Current psychotherapies* (8th ed., pp. 141–186). Belmont, CA: Thomson Brooks/Cole.

Rogers, C. R. (1957). The necessary and sufficient conditions of therapeutic personality change. *Journal of Consulting Psychology, 21,* 95–103.

Scholl, M. B. (2008). Preparing manuscripts with central and salient humanistic content. *Journal of Humanistic Counseling, Education and Development, 47,* 3–8.

Index